Presidential Rhetoric: 1961 to the Present

Third Edition
Edited by

Theodore Windt
University of Pittsburgh

KENDALL/HUNT
PUBLISHING COMPANY
Dubuque, Iowa

Copyright © 1978, 1980, 1983 by Kendall/Hunt Publishing Company

Library of Congress Catalog Card Number: 83–81606

ISBN 0–8403–3084–7

Printed in the United States of America

B   403084   01

Contents

Preface

At the urging of members of the Department of Speech and Theatre Arts of the University of Pittsburgh, I began offering a new course in "Presidential Rhetoric" for upperclassmen in 1970. Twenty students enrolled initially. Now, five hundred to six hundred students enroll each term.

When we began the course we concentrated on understanding the role rhetoric played in the administrations of John F. Kennedy and Lyndon B. Johnson. We also tried to devise methods to analyze and place the speeches that were being given by President Nixon and Vice President Agnew in proper critical perspective. At that time, there were several editions of Kennedy's and Johnson's speeches in print. We had only to read *The New York Times* or watch television to study Nixon's speeches. Since then, all these books have gone out of print. That was one of the major reasons for the first edition of *Presidential Rhetoric:* to return some of the original transcripts to students and others interested in the Presidency in a single volume.

The transcripts of the speeches of the Presidents are reprinted from the appropriate volumes of the *Public Papers of the Presidents* or from the appropriate issues of the *Weekly Compilation of Presidential Documents.*

In 1980, the second edition of *Presidential Rhetoric* was expanded to include speeches by Presidents Gerald Ford and Jimmy Carter. Though I saw no reason by virtue of new evidence or different thinking to alter the judgments I made in the "Introduction" about the Presidencies of Kennedy, Johnson, or Nixon, I believed certain observations were needed about changes in the Presidency under Ford and Carter.

The first edition concluded with an Epilogue that quoted from President Ford's first official speech as President: "our long national nightmare is over." In concluding the book on that note, I had high hopes this country would be moved away from the imperial policies that had brought our nation to disgrace. I thought I had good reasons to believe that. President Ford served honorably in a most difficult period, moving us from the turmoil of Watergate to a more stable, albeit prosaic, Presidency. President Carter appeared to chart a new course in foreign policy with his speeches at the United Nations and at Notre Dame University and with his early insistence on a comprehensive energy policy. His active participation in the tangled situation in the Middle East culminated in the Camp David Summit in late 1978. In sum, I had hopes that the old nightmares of the past would be replaced by the new dreams for tomorrow.

But they were not. From the mood of anger and disillusionment during the years of Vietnam and Watergate, a new mood—not of hope, but of "quiet desperation"—descended upon us. And we began to drift in the debris of history. Mastery of our fate, we were told, was beyond our leaders or ourselves. We drifted in this direction and that in uncharted waters. And we seemed to master little more than our desperation. There were, I believed, three reasons for this new mood.

First, power had shifted from the President to Congress, just as our major problems became domestic rather than foreign. It was a significant change. In the past a President could order a blockage of Cuba, send troops into the Dominican Republic, or order an invasion of Cambodia without formal approval of Congress. Whether one agreed or not, one saw the President acting. One could draw the line, as it were, about where one stood on national affairs. But times changed, and the President seemed unable to act so dramatically in domestic affairs. He could propose legislation to Congress to engage the energy problem or inflation, but he could not act without the consent of Congress and its authorization of funds. In other words, the President proposes; Congress disposes . . . usually at its leisure.

We entered then a new period in American history, a period comparable to that of the late nineteenth century, a period Woodrow Wilson described as one of Congressional government. Perhaps, this re-emergence of Congressional government was necessitated by the legacy of Vietnam and Watergate, perhaps required by the switch from concern about foreign affairs to domestic affairs. But many reared on the drama of the nineteen-sixties and early seventies (especially as brought to us by television) were ill-prepared psychologically to cope with the slow, tedious process by which Congress responds to pressing national needs.

Second, Congress—then in ascendency of power—is itself greatly changed and indeed in search of a new collective identity. Party discipline, once the clarion call for Congressional action, hardly exists anymore. In the past, the party of ten served as the buffer between the politician and special interest groups. Politicians then were judged by how they rose above party considerations to act in the public interest. Now, politicians do not serve party interests as much as special interests, especially those influential among their constituencies. The question is whether these groups are worthy or perfidious. The question is whether members of Congress can rise above special interests to act in the public interest. Thus far, few have been able to do so, and the result has been further disarray in the body politic. The problem this poses for the President is that he must appeal to those interest groups that influence the most influential Congressmen and Senators rather than develop a coherent political platform and agenda that the party can rally behind in an election or on issues.

Finally, both Ford and Carter were rhetorical failures. Lacking party support in Congress, a President must go over its head to rally the public behind his programs. Neither President Ford nor Carter was rhetorically effective enough to do this. On specific issues, Ford and Carter were specific. But on the greater issue of the direction and hope of America they were sadly inarticulate. They were unable to present forceably to the American people a consistent vision of what this country might be and should be after the traumas of Vietnam and Watergate and in the midst of oil embargoes, hostages in Iran, and the Soviet invasion of Afghanistan. Whatever judgment one may render about Kennedy, Johnson, or Nixon, one is forced to admit (even grudgingly) that each had a vision for America, a vision on occasion articulated forceably as well as clearly. That Ford and Carter had such a vision I do not doubt. That neither was able to articulate it is a matter of public record. Looking back over their administrations, can one remember one memorable speech given by Ford or Carter? Can one even remember one memorable phrase? These two post-imperial Presidents attracted attention because they were Presidents, but their words did not hold nor secure the public mind in ways that inspired people to act beyond their own self-interest. Thus, with Congress in disarray and the Presidency inarticulate, the public was left to shift for itself without clear direction or vision. And thus too, as the public looked to the 1980 election and to the last two decades of this century, it did so with apprehension and "quiet desperation."

The third edition of *Presidential Rhetoric* is expanded to include major speeches by President Ronald Reagan from his Inaugural well into the third year of his administration. These speeches represent the "New Beginning" candidate Reagan promised the American people during the 1980 campaign. President Reagan seized upon the opportunities of the "rhetorical Presidency" to control the national political agenda and to present a consistent and coherent program to the public. Though seldom speaking in a style that could be called eloquent, Reagan clearly is a master of the spoken word and one of the most effective communicators as President since Franklin Roosevelt.

* * * * * * * * *

I wish to express appreciation to those graduate and undergraduate students over the years who have helped in a variety of ways that they themselves may not even know to get this volume underway and later expanded.

For the unlimited encouragement they have given me, I want to thank Professor Robert P. Newman and Professor Jack Matthews of the University of Pittsburgh. A special thanks is extended to Dr. Lynn Hinds of WTAE-TV in Pittsburgh and Carolyn Smith, now of ABC-TV in New York, for their early studies of President Nixon and for their intellectual companionship.

My deep appreciation goes to Everett Lee Hunt, Dean (Emeritus) of Swarthmore College for his friendship and correspondence during the past twenty years; and to Harold F. Harding, H. Y. Benedict Professor of Rhetoric (Emeritus) at the University of Texas at El Paso. Professor Harding first interested me in the Presidency as a subject of scholarly research, directed my doctoral dissertation, and has remained a prolific letter writer and questioner of Presidential politics.

I am grateful to Mr. Gary Caruse, Special Assistant to U.S. Representative Austin Murphy, for his help in securing Presidential speeches and assorted other materials.

Five years ago the National Endowment for the Humanities issued a grant for Restructuring the Humanities at the University of Pittsburgh. Part of that grant allowed me to do additional research on Presidents Nixon, Ford, and Carter and to expand my course in "Presidential Rhetoric" into two courses. I wish to express my appreciation to the National Endowment and to Professor Benjamin Bart, Director of Interdisciplinary Humanities Courses, and to the University Council on the Humanities for this financial aid.

Ms. Margie Schramm and Ms. Jill Birnie, my two industrious assistants several years ago, were most helpful in doing part of the xeroxing for me. I am deeply appreciative to Ms. Birnie, especially, for her invaluable research into the Panama Canal Treaties and President Carter's energy proposals.

For the third edition, I am grateful to Ms. Judy Canelos for her proofreading of sections of the manuscript.

Finally, I want to thank publicly Ms. Beth Ingold—my co-editor of *Essays in Presidential Rhetoric,* the companion volume to this one—for her thoughtful suggestions and for her insightful research and writings about the first two years of the Reagan administration.

Although I am appreciative to the people named here for reasons mentioned, I alone bear responsibility for this edition and for the judgments expressed in it.

Pittsburgh, Pennsylvania

June, 1983

Introduction

I.

Politics is about power. In elections one group strives mightily to wrest power from another group. Indeed, our elections are our institutionalized equivalents of civil war in other countries.

Once in office politicians must wrestle with one another as well as with members of other branches of government for the enactment of policies. At the same time, they must tend to their constituencies so as not to dissipate their power base. It is within the context of political power that policies, politicians, and speeches can be viewed.

Sweeping assertions? Yes. Exhaustive analysis? No. Certainly, there are legal boundaries to the exercise of power. So too, there are moral limits, though these are not as distinct as we sometimes believe. But at the core of politics is power that "may corrupt—or ennoble or frighten or inspire or distract. . . ."[1]

The Presidency is at the center of American political life.[2] Citizens view a President as "moral leader of the country" who will use his "bully pulpit" to represent, as only he can, "all the people." In this sense he becomes symbolic of our national aspirations, our national mood, our national prestige. Above all, a President is seen as the most powerful man in the country, if not the world. But on what does his power rest?

"Presidential *power*," Richard Neustadt aptly observed, "is the power to persuade."[3] But who is he to persuade and by what authority?

Every President recognizes that he has three general areas or resources of power available to him. First, he has Constitutional authority, generally called his power to command. Sections 2 and 3 of Article II of the Constitution outline the President's responsibilities as Commander-in-Chief in wartime, as chief administrator and executive of the United States. But to have his commands obeyed, a President must persuade the appropriate members of executive agencies to do his will.

Second, a President has power with Congress through his role as nominal leader of his party. However, he cannot command Congress to enact his policies, for they have constituencies of their own whose interests may be in opposition to the President's interests. Or the President's party may be the minority party in which case he must fashion an ideological majority. Regardless, his ability to get Congress to act rests on his ability, in part, to persuade Congressmen and Senators to do what he wants them to do.

1

But these powers, I believe, depend on a greater, more fundamental power: public opinion. Marshalling public support is a distinctively *rhetorical* power available to the President. Since he is viewed as "President of all the people," he must maintain a strong image of that support if he is to make ample use of his other powers.

Take a dramatic example. Prior to October, 1973, several impeachment resolutions had been introduced into the House of Representatives about the Watergate scandals. But the House refused to act directly. Then, President Nixon fired Archibald Cox, the Special Prosecutor, and closed his office. The public was outraged and expressed it immediately. Within days, impeachment became a possibility as the House Judiciary Committee prepared for the serious proceedings that eventually led to the resignation of Nixon. Indeed, the loud voice of the people on that occasion gave backbone to Congress to move ahead when previously it had been reluctant to act at all.

Presidential rhetoric is a study of how Presidents gain, maintain, or lose support of the public. It is not a study in literary or rhetorical style. It is not an academic study of rhetorical techniques intended to refine rhetorical theory. It is a study of power, of the fundamental power in a democracy: public opinion and public support.

A President speaks on topics ranging from Thanksgiving Day to war. In so doing, he reveals the intellectual and political cast of his mind. He must speak so often and on such varied topics that he will invariably come to depend upon certain predictable techniques that begin to establish a pattern or style for him. In a different context James David Barber wrote:

> For all the complexities of personality, there are always regularities, habitual ways of handling similar situations, just as the demands and opportunities of the Presidency are complex, but patterned. Thus, the President-as-person interacts with the set of recurrent problems and opportunities presented by the Presidency; the pattern of this interaction is his political style. He copes, adapts, leads, and responds not as some shapeless organism in a flood of novelties, but as a man with a memory in a system with a history.[4]

Thus, it did not take Doris Kearns in her book, *Lyndon Johnson and the American Dream,* to tell us that Johnson made a distinct separation between thought and action, though her work is valuable in other respects. One need only read Johnson's speeches to know that they are problem-solving speeches geared primarily to action. And one's understanding of Richard Nixon can be enhanced once one discovers the pattern in his rhetoric. It is a negative rhetoric in which Nixon persistently defines himself and his constituency by what they are opposed to, rather than by what they are for.

But if a President's speeches are a reflection of his mind, they are also a reflection on the public. Voters must choose whom they will vote for, and citizens must choose up sides when controversial subjects are presented. Presidential speeches provide major pieces of information and argument that influence us in making those choices. A citizen cannot wait 10 or 20 years, as an historian might, to determine what happened or what the best course of action might be. He must decide in the heat of actual events based on whatever scanty evidence comes to him.

In this age of television the President enjoys an enormous advantage over others in getting that information to the public. Practically at whim, he can appear on television to speak to the American public on issues he believes warrant its consideration. In so doing, he can define an issue in ways most favorable to him and thus set the terms for argument to which others must react. There is power in that advantage because the man who can define issues usually can win arguments.

The national forum available to a President allows him to establish the context in which our national debates proceed. In one sense, his political vocabulary becomes our national political vocabulary. Supporters adopt it even as opponents try to develop another vocabulary to thwart his policies or his ambitions. On a simple level, supporters may use political short-hand to identify themselves as members of "The New Frontier" or "The Great Society" or "The Silent Majority." Adversaries may have to fight off allegations that they are "Nervous Nellies" or only a part of a "Vocal Minority." More important, the effectiveness of a President to impress his language, his way of thinking about issues upon a majority of the public directly affects his ability to maintain public support and thus directly affects his flexibility in the exercise of his other powers. Public thought does not exist without a public language. The President of the United States has the greatest opportunity not only to influence but frequently to set the political language of our country and thus direct the thinking of our citizens. Presidential rhetoric is a study of how Presidents have used or abused that power.

II.

Presidential speeches represent the public record of a President. The speeches contained in this volume represent the contemporary Imperial Age of the Presidency from 1961 to 1974. I have borrowed and enlarged the word, "imperial" from Arthur Schlesinger, Jr.[5] Each sought, in different ways and in different degrees, powers that undermined democratic civility or democratic institutions. And I think it appropriate to label some of their actions as imperial. It was, after all, these three Presidents who dominated our political lives during a tumultuous period in American history: from the reckless adventure with nuclear war under Kennedy, through the tragedies of the American-Vietnamese war under Johnson, to Nixon's Watergate. Each sought to make his mark in history as each no doubt will, but for reasons other than each supposed. Each was an activist President in a Presidential age, and each abused his power and the trust of the American people.

The central development of American politics in the twentieth-century has been the flow of power from Congress to the Presidency. With the notable exceptions of Andrew Jackson and Abraham Lincoln, Congress dominated American politics in the nineteenth-century.

Theodore Roosevelt began to turn the tide toward the Presidency as he exercised a vigorous executive leadership, establishing thereby a model for contemporary Presidents. Woodrow Wilson conceived of the Executive Branch in ways similar to Roosevelt and asserted "his constitutional right and duty as executive to guide the legislative process."[6] But it required a Franklin Roosevelt to consolidate power in the Executive, a man who:

> beyond all twentieth-century Presidents put the stamp both of personality and crisis on the presidency. In the solution of the problems of an economic crisis . . . he claimed for the national government in general and for the President in particular powers hitherto exercised only on the justification of war. Then when the greatest crisis in the history of our international relations arose he imparted to the President's diplomatic powers new extension now without consulting Congress, now with Congress's approval; and when at last we entered the Second World War he endowed the precedents of both the Civil War and the First World War with unprecedented scope.[7]

So pervasive was Roosevelt's influence that Americans came to believe the President was American government; so pervasive also was his influence that upon his death Congress acted through a Constitutional amendment to limit future Presidents to only two terms.

President Eisenhower began to reverse the flow of power. He took a less active, more benign approach. For many, the eight years of his Administration appeared to be years of drift rather than direction, years of apathy rather than leadership.

Many chafed at Eisenhower's style of leadership. They longed for the dynamic and dramatic Presidents of other years. Few were more vocal than Richard Neustadt. In his immensely influential book, *Presidential Power: The Politics of Leadership* published in 1960, Neustadt called for a President who would exercise his power to the fullest and offered an analysis of how that might be achieved.[8]

Senator John F. Kennedy agreed. In an Address before the National Press Club on January 18, 1960 (only shortly after he announced his candidacy for the Democratic Presidential nomination), Kennedy stated:

> Whatever the political affiliation of our next President, whatever his views may be on all the issues and problems that rush in upon us, he must above all be the Chief Executive in every sense of the word. He must be prepared to exercise the fullest powers of his Office—all that are specified and *some that are not.*[9]

Truly in 1960, America stood at the threshold of a period of activist Presidents, a period in which we would have to bear burdens and pay prices we could hardly have imagined at the time.

The activist President requires three things to be activist: a strong personality, crisis, and drama. Kennedy, Johnson and Nixon each had personalities suitable to the imperial age. Crises either erupted or were provoked. And television in its coverage from the terror of the Cuban missile crisis through the American-Vietnamese war to the Senate Watergate Hearings provided the drama. It was an era of illegal wiretapping, unauthorized surveillance, misused Federal agencies, riots, polarization, violence. And it culminated in the greatest political scandal our country has seen as well as one of the worst Presidencies in our history.

III.

For the most part the speeches, news conferences and statements contained in this volume represent public utterances given at critical moments involving a President's power as he sought to exercise that power to move the United States ahead or to protect America's interests as he saw them, or to protect his own power as President. I have also included an inaugural address, a state of the union address, and nomination acceptance speech as examples of other distinct forms of Presidential rhetoric. And I have included two speeches by Kennedy and Johnson on reporting by news media. Vice President Agnew presented the Nixon Administration's views on this subject on November 13, 1969 in Des Moines, Iowa to which those interested are directed. Finally, these speeches were chosen as the basic materials for my students in "Presidential Rhetoric," my undergraduate class at the University of Pittsburgh. Some may quarrel with my selections. I hope they will, and that from such disagreements will come other collections of Presidential addresses.

To assist the reader I have provided very brief over-views of each Administration and brief introductions before each speech. In some introductions I have gone beyond merely giving the background against which the speech was given to insert judgments of my own.

Not every speech nor every piece of writing by a President merits careful reading by the public. But I believe these do, for they form a basic part of the public record of our recent Imperial Age.

Notes

1. James David Barber, *The Presidential Character* (Englewood Cliffs, N.J.: Prentice-Hall, 1972), p. 17.
2. Cf. Barber, pp. 4-7.
3. Richard E. Neustadt, *Presidential Power* (New York: John Wiley & Sons, 1960), p. 10.
4. James D. Barber, "Adult Identity and Presidential Style: The Rhetorical Emphasis," *Daedalus* vol. 97 (Summer, 1968), pp. 938-939.
5. Cf. Arthur M. Schlesinger, Jr., *The Imperial Presidency* (New York: Houghton Mifflin, 1974).
6. Edward S. Corwin, *The President: Office and Powers 1787-1957* (New York: New York University Press, 1964), p. 268.
7. *Ibid.*, p. 311.
8. Cf. Neustadt.
9. *John Fitzgerald Kennedy. A Compendium of Speeches, Statements, and Remarks Delivered During His Service in the Congress of the United States* (Washington, D.C.: U.S. Government Printing Office, 1964), p. 1107. *Emphasis added.*

John Fitzgerald Kennedy
(1961–1963)

John F. Kennedy entered the Presidency amid a hail of praise for his stirring Inaugural Address. But his political prospects at that time hardly were as bright. Kennedy has been elected by only .1% of the total votes cast or approximately 112,000 votes over Nixon. He also was indebted to the South that perhaps out of pride in Lyndon Johnson had not broken from the Democratic party in the election. Thus, he had no mandate to urge the passage of the progressive legislation he had proposed during the campaign, and he owed Southern conservatives in Congress who would undoubtedly oppose such legislation.

In April, 1961 Kennedy compounded his problems through his handling of the Bay of Pigs invasion. When it was learned that some 1,400 Cuban exiles had landed in Zapata Swamp, the Kennedy Administration lied by denying American participation in the invasion. However, it was quickly ascertained that Americans had trained the Cubans, Americans had transported them to Cuba, and American frogmen had been in the waters at the landing. Kennedy reversed field and accepted responsibility for the disaster. Furthermore, the mishandling of the Cuban enterprize seemed to lend credence to Nixon's charges during the campaign that Kennedy was too inexperienced in foreign affairs to be an effective President. At this point, Kennedy appeared as a weakened and vulnerable President.

From a rhetorical standpoint, Kennedy's Administration can be divided into two periods. First, the conservative years from January 1961 to November 1962 when Kennedy sought to stabilize his fragile constituency and hopefully to expand it into a majority of the American people. The second period extended from November 1962 to November 22, 1963 in which he was able to make a turn to the left and take more progressive positions than he had before.

During the first period Kennedy sacrificed much of his domestic legislation to Southern Congressmen so as to get some movement on his civil rights legislation.[1] And his speeches on civil rights became muted. In his first year in office he hardly brought up the topic at all unless forced to do so. When rioting broke out at the University of Mississippi over the admission of James Meredith, Kennedy spoke over television about the need for the great state of Mississippi to obey the court-ordered integration, thus treating the issue as just another legal issue he had to deal with. He acted against the steel companies in 1962 because they double-crossed him and threatened to reduce his support from labor unions. In foreign affairs, he took a hard-line, conservative approach toward the Soviet Union and Vietnam and Berlin. During the Berlin "crisis" of 1961 he employed an apocalyptic rhetoric that caused many to believe we were on the verge of nuclear war with the Soviet Union.[2] He increased our "advisors" in Vietnam and created a special unit, the Green Berets, who were to be trained in the tactics of guerrilla warfare. In October, 1962 he announced over national television he was willing to run the ultimate risk of nuclear war to have the Soviet offensive missile sites removed from Cuba. The rhetoric of this period is cautious and conservative, especially conservative in foreign affairs.

Kennedy changed direction dramatically after the Congressional elections in November, 1962. Traditionally, the President's party loses 15-25 seats in these elections. Should his party lose more than 25 seats, the President is considered to be losing popularity with the public in direct proportion to how many more were lost. Conversely, should he lose less than 15, he is believed to be gaining in popularity. Though seats in Congress were exchanged in 1962, the Democratic party over-all did not lose any, the number of Democrats and Republicans remaining in Congress stayed the same. This was viewed symbolically as a smashing victory for Kennedy and his growing popularity with the American public.

Kennedy realized the opportunity, seized it, and moved away from the conservative positions he had taken during the first two years. On November 20 he announced he had signed Executive Order 11063 that directed Federal departments and agencies to take legal action to end discrimination in the rental or sale of housing facility owned or operated by the Federal government as well as prevent discrimination in other areas of Federally supported housing. The timing of this announcement was symbolic and significant. During the 1960 campaign Kennedy had often chided President Eisenhower for not signing the Order and implied that he would do so as soon as he gained the office. But he waited, much to the consternation of Black leaders, for two years. Now, no longer needing to cater to the South, Kennedy moved ahead on civil rights. On June 11, 1963 he switched from a moderate "law and order" speech he had used when the University of Mississippi was integrated to a stronger moral rhetoric when George Wallace tried to block the entrance of several Blacks into the University of Alabama. And later in August President Kennedy endorsed the historic March on Washington.

On foreign affairs Kennedy did an about-face also from the hard-line confrontation policies he pursued over Berlin and Cuba. On June 10, 1963 he proposed a policy of accommodation or *detente* with the Soviet Union so as to seek peace rather than risk war. His initiatives led that summer to the signing of the limited nuclear test ban treaty, the first positive agreement between the United States and the Soviet Union since the advent of the cold war and Kennedy's chief progressive accomplishment in his Presidency. If we can believe the memoirs of his advisors, he intended after being safely re-elected to disengage from our venture in Vietnam, to replace Dean Rusk as Secretary of State, to move perhaps toward a more reasonable policy toward the People's Republic of China. But it all ended in Dallas on November 22, 1963.

John Kennedy's rhetoric is a mixture of stylistic eloquence and hard-nosed politics. The techniques he used are the most varied and flexible of any of the three Presidents represented in this collection. He employed whatever methods he thought appropriate to protect his power and to maintain his constituency. The tragic conclusion to his Presidency, however, leaves us with more promise than performance, a triumph of style over substance.

Notes

1. For a detailed discussion of Kennedy's difficulties with Congress over his domestic legislation, see Tom Wicker, *JFK and LBJ. The Influence of Personality upon Politics* (New York, William Morrow, 1968), pp. 25-148.
2. The best examination of the politics of the Berlin "crisis" can be found in Richard J. Walton, *Cold War and Counterrevolution. The Foreign Policy of John F. Kennedy* (Baltimore, Pelican, 1973), pp. 75-93.

"Let Us Begin"
Washington, D.C.
January 20, 1961

Kennedy's Inaugural Address became his most memorable and most quoted speech. It set forth a mixed tone of vigor, pessimism, and daring that would soon characterize the "New Frontier." Indeed, even as it was praised for its stylistic eloquence, the Inaugural Address set a mood for the nineteen-sixties.

unifying: close election

We observe today not a victory of party but a celebration of freedom—symbolizing an end as well as a beginning—signifying renewal as well as change. For I have sworn before you and Almighty God the same solemn oath our forebears prescribed nearly a century and three quarters ago.

The world is very different now. For man holds in his mortal hands the power to abolish all forms of human poverty and all forms of human life. And yet the same revolutionary beliefs for which our forebears fought are still at issue around the globe—the belief that the rights of man come not from the generosity of the state but from the hand of God.

We dare not forget today that we are the heirs of that first revolution. Let the word go forth from this time and place, to friend and foe alike, that the torch has been passed to a new *unity* generation of Americans—born in this century, tempered by war, disciplined by a hard and bitter peace, proud of our ancient heritage—and unwilling to witness or permit the slow undoing of those human rights to which this nation has always been committed, and to which we are committed today at home and around the world.

Let every nation know, whether it wishes us well or ill, that we shall pay any price, bear any burden, meet any hardship, support any friend, oppose any foe to assure the survival and the success of liberty.

This much we pledge—and more.

To those old allies whose cultural and spiritual origins we share, we pledge the loyalty of faithful friends. United, there is little we cannot do in a host of cooperative ventures. Divided, there is little we can do—for we dare not meet a powerful challenge at odds and split asunder.

To those new states whom we welcome to the ranks of the free, we pledge our word that one form of colonial control shall not have passed away merely to be replaced by a far more iron tyranny. We shall not always expect to find them supporting our view. But we shall always hope to find them strongly supporting their own freedom—and to remember that, in the past, those who foolishly sought power by riding the back of the tiger ended up inside.

To those peoples in the huts and villages of half the globe struggling to break the bonds of mass misery, we pledge our best efforts to help them help themselves, for whatever period is required—not because the communists may be doing it, not because we seek their votes, but because it is right. If a free society cannot help the many who are poor, it cannot save the few who are rich.

To our sister republics south of our border, we offer a special pledge—to convert our good words into good deeds—in a new alliance for progress—to assist free men and free governments in casting off the chains of poverty. But this peaceful revolution of hope cannot become the prey of hostile powers. Let all our neighbors know that we shall join with them to oppose aggression or subversion anywhere in the Americas. And let every other power know that this Hemisphere intends to remain the master of its own house.

To that world assembly of sovereign states, the United Nations, our last best hope in an age where the instruments of war have far outpaced the instruments of peace, we renew our pledge of support—to prevent it from becoming merely a forum for invective—to strengthen its shield of the new and the weak—and to enlarge the area in which its writ may run.

Finally, to those nations who would make themselves our adversary, we offer not a pledge but a request: that both sides begin anew the quest for peace, before the dark powers of destruction unleashed by science engulf all humanity in planned or accidental self-destruction.

We dare not tempt them with weakness. For only when our arms are sufficient beyond doubt can we be certain beyond doubt that they will never be employed.

But neither can two great and powerful groups of nations take comfort from our present course—both sides overburdened by the cost of modern weapons, both rightly alarmed by the steady spread of the deadly atom, yet both racing to alter that uncertain balance of terror that stays the hand of mankind's final war.

So let us begin anew—remembering on both sides that civility is not a sign of weakness, and sincerity is always subject to proof. Let us never negotiate out of fear. But let us never fear to negotiate.

Let both sides explore what problems unite us instead of belaboring those problems which divide us.

Let both sides, for the first time, formulate serious and precise proposals for the inspection and control of arms—and bring the absolute power to destroy other nations under the absolute control of all nations.

Let both sides seek to invoke the wonders of science instead of its terrors. Together let us explore the stars, conquer the deserts, eradicate disease, tap the ocean depths and encourage the arts and commerce.

Let both sides unite to heed in all corners of the earth the command of Isaiah—to "undo the heavy burdens . . . (and) let the oppressed go free."

And if a beach-head of cooperation may push back the jungle of suspicion, let both sides join in creating a new endeavor, not a new balance of power, but a new world of law, where the strong are just and the weak secure and the peace preserved.

All this will not be finished in the first one hundred days. Nor will it be finished in the first one thousand days, nor in the life of this Administration, nor even perhaps in our lifetime on this planet. But let us begin.

In your hands, my fellow citizens, more than mine, will rest the final success or failure of our course. Since this country was founded, each generation of Americans has been summoned to give testimony to its national loyalty. The graves of young Americans who answered the call to service surround the globe.

Now the trumpet summons us again—not as a call to bear arms, though arms we need—not as a call to battle, though embattled we are—but a call to bear the burden of a long twilight struggle, year in and year out, "rejoicing in hope, patient in tribulation"—a struggle against the common enemies of man: tyranny, poverty, disease and war itself.

Can we forge against these enemies a grand and global alliance, North and South, East and West, that can assure a more fruitful life for all mankind? Will you join in that historic effort?

In the long history of the world, only a few generations have been granted the role of defending freedom in its hour of maximum danger. I do not shrink from this responsibility—I welcome it. I do not believe that any of us would exchange places with any other people or any other generation. The energy, the faith, the devotion which we bring to this endeavor will light our country and all who serve it—and the glow from that fire can truly light the world.

And so, my fellow Americans: ask not what your country can do for you—ask what you can do for your country.

My fellow citizens of the world: ask not what America will do for you, but what together we can do for the freedom of man.

Finally, whether you are citizens of America or citizens of the world, ask of us here the same high standards of strength and sacrifice which we ask of you. With a good conscience our only sure reward, with history the final judge of our deeds, let us go forth to lead the land we love, asking His blessing and His help, but knowing that here on earth God's work must truly be our own.

Lessons to Be Learned from the Bay of Pigs Invasion

Address before the American Society of Newspaper Editors
Washington, D.C.
April 20, 1961

On April 17 some 1400 Cuban exiles landed in Zapata Swamp in the Bay of Pigs intent either on overthrowing the Castro regime or joining with anti-Castro rebels in the interior. The mission ended quickly in failure as the Cuban military rallied behind Castro and killed or captured most of the invaders. This failed policy turned into a disaster when the Administration, at first, denied involvement and then admitted complicity in the invasion fiasco. Protests against the American participation in the invasion came from friends and foes abroad, from conservatives and liberals alike in the United States. Kennedy realized that he was in deep political trouble. Therefore, he decided to use his forum before the Newspaper Editors, a speech that had been scheduled long before the invasion, to attempt to shore up his political defenses in the face of failure.

The President of a great democracy such as ours, and the editors of great newspapers such as yours, owe a common obligation to the people: an obligation to present the facts, to present them with candor, and to present them in perspective. It is with that obligation in mind that I have decided in the last 24 hours to discuss briefly at this time the recent events in Cuba.

On that unhappy island, as in so many other arenas of the contest for freedom, the news has grown worse instead of better. I have emphasized before that this was a struggle of Cuban patriots against a Cuban dictator. While we could not be expected to hide our sympathies, we made it repeatedly clear that the armed forces of this country would not intervene in any way.

Any unilateral American intervention, in the absence of an external attack upon ourselves or an ally, would have been contrary to our traditions and to our international obligations. But let the record show that our restraint is not inexhaustible. Should it ever appear that the inter-American doctrine of noninterference merely conceals or excuses a policy of nonaction—if the nations of this Hemisphere should fail to meet their commitments against outside Communist penetration—then I want it clearly understood that this Government will not hesitate in meeting its primary obligations which are to the security of our Nation!

Should that time ever come, we do not intend to be lectured on "intervention" by those whose character was stamped for all time on the bloody streets of Budapest! Nor would we expect or accept the same outcome which this small band of gallant Cuban refugees must have known that they were chancing, determined as they were against heavy odds to pursue their courageous attempts to regain their Island's freedom.

But Cuba is not an island unto itself; and our concern is not ended by mere expressions of nonintervention or regret. This is not the first time in either ancient or recent history that a small band of freedom fighters has engaged the armor of totalitarianism.

It is not the first time that Communist tanks have rolled over gallant men and women fighting to redeem the independence of their homeland. Nor is it by any means the final episode in the eternal struggle of liberty against tyranny, anywhere on the face of the globe, including Cuba itself.

Mr. Castro has said that these were mercenaries. According to press reports, the final message to be relayed from the refugee forces on the beach came from the rebel commander when asked if he wished to be evacuated. His answer was: "I will never leave this country." That is not the reply of a mercenary. He has gone now to join in the mountains countless other guerrilla fighters, who are equally determined that the dedication of those who gave their lives shall not be forgotten, and that Cuba must not be abandoned to the Communists. And we do not intend to abandon it either!

The Cuban people have not yet spoken their final piece. And I have no doubt that they and their Revolutionary Council, led by Dr. Cardona—and members of the families of the Revolutionary Council, I am informed by the Doctor yesterday, and involved themselves in the Islands—will continue to speak up for a free and independent Cuba.

Meanwhile we will not accept Mr. Castro's attempts to blame this nation for the hatred which his onetime supporters now regard his repression. But there are from this sobering episode useful lessons for us all to learn. Some may be still obscure, and await further information. Some are clear today.

First, it is clear that the forces of communism are not to be underestimated, in Cuba or anywhere else in the world. The advantages of a police state—its use of mass terror and arrests to prevent the spread of free dissent—cannot be overlooked by those who expect the fall of every fanatic tyrant. If the self-discipline of the free cannot match the iron discipline of the nailed fist—in economic, political, scientific and all the other kinds of struggles as well as the military—then the peril to freedom will continue to rise.

Secondly, it is clear that this Nation, in concert with all the free nations of this hemisphere, must take an ever closer and more realistic look at the menace of external Communist intervention and domination in Cuba. The American people are not complacent about Iron Curtain tanks and planes less than 90 miles from their shore. But a nation of Cuba's size is less a threat to our survival than it is a base for subverting the survival of other free nations throughout the hemisphere. It is not primarily our interest or our security but theirs which is now, today, in the greater peril. It is for their sake as well as our own that we must show our will.

The evidence is clear—and the hour is late. We and our Latin friends will have to face the fact that we cannot postpone any longer the real issue of survival of freedom in this hemisphere itself. On that issue, unlike perhaps some others, there can be no middle ground. Together we must build a hemisphere where freedom can flourish; and where any free nation under outside attack of any kind can be assured that all of our resources stand ready to respond to any request for assistance.

Third, and finally, it is clearer than ever that we face a relentless struggle in every corner of the globe that goes far beyond the clash or armies or even nuclear armaments. The armies are there, and in large number. The nuclear armaments are there. But they serve primarily as the shield behind which subversion, infiltration, and a host of other tactics steadily advance, picking off vulnerable areas one by one in situations which do not permit our own armed intervention.

Power is the hallmark of this offensive—power and discipline and deceit. The legitimate discontent of yearning people is exploited. The legitimate trappings of self-determination are employed. But once in power, all talk of discontent is repressed, all self-determination disappears, and the promise of a revolution of hope is betrayed, as in Cuba, into a reign of terror. Those who on instruction staged automatic "riots" in the streets of free nations over the efforts of a small group of young Cubans to regain their freedom should recall the long roll call of refugees who cannot now go back—to Hungary, to North Korea, to North Viet-Nam, to East Germany, or to Poland, or to any of the other lands from which a steady stream of refugees pours forth, in eloquent testimony to the cruel oppression now holding sway in their homeland.

We dare not fail to see the insidious nature of this new and deeper struggle. We dare not fail to grasp the new concepts, the new tools, the new sense of urgency we will need to combat it—whether in Cuba or South Viet-Nam. And we dare not fail to realize that this struggle is taking place every day, without fanfare, in thousands of villages and markets—day and night—and in classrooms all over the globe.

The message of Cuba, of Laos, of the rising din of Communist voices in Asia and Latin America—these messages are all the same. The complacent, the self-indulgent, the soft societies are about to be swept away with the debris of history. Only the strong, only the industrious, only the determined, only the courageous, only the visionary who determine the real nature of our struggle can possibly survive.

No greater task faces this country or this administration. No other challenge is more deserving of our every effort and energy. Too long we have fixed our eyes on traditional military needs, on armies prepared to cross borders, on missiles poised for flight. Now it should be clear that this is no longer enough—that our security may be lost piece by piece, country by country, without the firing of a single missile or the crossing of a single border.

We intend to profit from this lesson. We intend to reexamine and reorient our forces of all kinds—our tactics and our institutions here in this community. We intend to intensify our efforts for a struggle in many ways more difficult, than war, where disappointment will often accompany us.

For I am convinced that we in this country and in the free world possess the necessary resource, and the skill, and the added strength that comes from a belief in the freedom of man. And I am equally convinced that history will record the fact that this bitter struggle reached its climax in the late 1950's and the early 1960's. Let me then make clear as the President of the United States that I am determined upon our system's survival and success, regardless of the cost and regardless of the peril!

The President and the Press
Address Before the American Newspaper Publishers Association
New York City
April 27, 1961

This speech, in which Kennedy implicitly called for newsmen to impose self-censorship upon their stories in the name of "national security," raised a furor. A group of editors and publishers who later met with the President about this subject rejected his analysis of the world situation. They saw no special peril to the United States that would require such a drastic step as the President had implied. With the exception of his cancellation of his subscription to the New York Herald Tribune, Kennedy seldom voiced public complaints about reporting of his Administration any more, but relied instead on private messages to publishers and editors. Several close aides of Kennedy considered this speech a mistake.

I appreciate very much your generous invitation to be here tonight.

You bear heavy responsibilities these days and an article I read some time ago reminded me of how particularly heavily the burdens of present day events bear upon your profession.

You may remember that in 1851 the New York Herald Tribune, under the sponsorship and publishing of Horace Greeley, employed as its London correspondent an obscure journalist by the name of Karl Marx.

We are told that foreign correspondent Marx, stone broke, and with a family ill and undernourished, constantly appealed to Greeley and Managing Editor Charles Dana for an increase in his munificent salary of $5 per installment, a salary which he and Engels ungratefully labeled as the "lousiest petty bourgeois cheating."

But when all his financial appeals were refused, Marx looked around for other means of livelihood and fame, eventually terminating his relationship with the Tribune and devoting his talents full time to the cause that would bequeath to the world the seeds of Leninism, Stalinism, revolution and the cold war.

If only this capitalistic New York newspaper had treated him more kindly; if only Marx had remained a foreign correspondent, history might have been different. And I hope all publishers will bear this lesson in mind the next time they receive a poverty-stricken appeal for a small increase in the expense account from an obscure newspaper man.

I have selected as the title of my remarks tonight "The President and the Press." Some may suggest that this would be more naturally worded "The President Versus the Press." But those are not my sentiments tonight.

It is true, however, that when a well-known diplomat from another country demanded recently that our State Department repudiate certain newspaper attacks on his colleague it was unnecessary for us to reply that this Administration was not responsible for the press, for the press had already made it clear that it was not responsible for this Administration.

Nevertheless, my purpose here tonight is not to deliver the usual assault on the so-called one-party press. On the contrary, in recent months I have rarely heard any complaints about political bias in the press except from a few Republicans. Nor is it my purpose tonight to discuss or defend the televising of Presidential press conferences. I think it is highly beneficial to have some 20,000,000 Americans regularly sit in on these conferences to observe, if I may say so, the incisive, the intelligent and the courteous qualities displayed by your Washington correspondents.

Nor, finally, are these remarks intended to examine the proper degree of privacy which the press should allow to any President and his family.

If in the last few months your White House reporters and photographers have been attending church services with regularity, that has surely done them no harm.

On the other hand, I realize that your staff and wire service photographers may be complaining that they do not enjoy the same green privileges at the local golf courses which they once did.

It is true that my predecessor did not object as I do to pictures of one's golfing skill in action. But neither on the other hand did he ever bean a Secret Service man.

My topic tonight is a more sober one of concern to publishers as well as editors. I want to talk about our common responsibilities in the face of a common danger. The events of recent weeks may have helped to illuminate that challenge for some; but the dimensions of its threat have loomed large on the horizon for many years. Whatever our hopes may be for the future—for reducing this threat or living with it—there is no escaping either the gravity or the totality of its challenge to our survival and to our security—a challenge that confronts us in unaccustomed ways in every sphere of human activity.

This deadly challenge imposes upon our society two requirements of direct concern both to the press and to the President—two requirements that may seem almost contradictory in tone, but which must be reconciled and fulfilled if we are to meet this national peril. I refer, first, to the need for far greater public information; and, second, to the need for far greater official secrecy.

I.

The very word "secrecy" is repugnant in a free and open society; and we are as a people inherently and historically opposed to secret societies, to secret oaths and to secret proceedings. We decided long ago that the dangers of successive and unwarranted concealment of pertinent facts far outweighs the dangers which are cited to justify it. Even today, there is little value in opposing the threat of a closed society by imitating its arbitrary restrictions. Even today, there is little value in insuring the survival of our nation if our traditions do not survive with it. And there is very grave danger that an announced need for increased security will be seized upon by those anxious to expand its meaning to the very limits of official censorship and concealment. That I do not intend to permit to the extent that it is in my control. And no official of my Administration, whether his rank is high or low, civilian or military, should interpret my words here tonight as an excuse to censor the news, to stifle dissent, to cover up our mistakes or to withhold from the press and the public the facts they deserve to know.

But I do ask every publisher, every editor, and every newsman in the nation to reexamine his own standards, and to recognize the nature of our country's peril. In time of war, the government and the press have customarily joined in an effort, based largely on self-discipline, to prevent unauthorized disclosures to the enemy. In time of "clear and present danger," the courts have held that even the privileged rights of the First Amendment must yield to the public's need for national security.

Today no war had been declared—and however fierce the struggle may be, it may never be declared in the traditional fashion. Our way of life is under attack. Those who make themselves our enemy are advancing around the globe. The survival of our friends is in danger. And yet no war has been declared, no borders have been crossed by marching troops, no missiles have been fired.

If the press is awaiting a declaration of war before it imposes the self-discipline of combat conditions, then I can only say that no war ever posed a greater threat to our security. If you are awaiting a finding of "clear and present danger," then I can only say that the danger has never been more clear and its presence has never been more imminent.

It requires a change in outlook, a change in tactics, a change in missions—by the government, by the poeple, by every businessman or labor leader, and by every newspaper. For we are opposed around the world by a monolithic and ruthless conspiracy that relies primarily on covert means for expanding its sphere of influence—on infiltration instead of invasion, on subversion instead of elections, on intimidation instead of free choice, on guerrillas by night instead of armies by day. It is a system which has conscripted vast human and material resources into the building of a tightly knit, highly efficient machine that combines military, diplomatic, intelligence, economic, scientific and political operations.

Its preparations are concealed, not published. Its mistakes are buried, not headlined. Its dissenters are silenced, not praised. No expenditure is questioned, no rumor is printed, no secret is revealed. It conducts the Cold War, in short, with a war-time discipline no democracy would ever hope or wish to match.

Nevertheless, every democracy recognizes the necessary restraints of national security—and the question remains whether those restraints need to be more strictly observed if we are to oppose this kind of attack as well as outright invasion.

For the facts of the matter are that this nation's foes have openly boasted of acquiring through our newspapers information they would otherwise hire agents to acquire through theft, bribery or espionage; that details of this nation's covert preparations to counter the enemy's covert operations have been available to every newspaper reader, friend and foe alike; that the size, the strength, the location and the nature of our forces and weapons, and our plans and strategy for their use, have all been pinpointed in the press and other news media to a degree sufficient to satisfy any foreign power; and that, in at least one case, the publication of details concerning a secret mechanism whereby satellites were followed required its alteration at the expense of considerable time and money.

The newspapers which printed these stories were loyal, patriotic, responsible and well-meaning. Had we been engaged in open warfare, they undoubtedly would not have published such items. But in the absence of open warfare, they recognized only tests of journalism and not the tests of national security. And my question tonight is whether additional tests should not now be adopted.

That question is for you alone to answer. No public official should answer it for you. No governmental plan should impose its restraints against your will. But I would be failing in my duty to the Nation, in considering all of the responsibilities that we now bear and all of the means at hand to meet those responsibilities, if I did not commend this problem to your attention, and urge its thoughtful consideration.

On many earlier occasions, I have said—and your newspapers have constantly said—that these are times that appeal to every citizen's sense of sacrifice and self-discipline. They call out to every citizen to weigh his rights and comforts against his obligations to the common good. I cannot now believe that those citizens who serve in the newspaper business consider themselves exempt from that appeal.

I have no intention of establishing a new Office of War Information to govern the flow of news. I am not suggesting any new forms of censorship or new types of security classifications. I have no easy answer to the dilemma that I have posed, and would not seek to impose it if I had one. But I am asking the members of the newspaper profession and the industry in this country to reexamine their own responsibilities, to consider the degree and the nature of the present danger, and to heed the duty of self-restraint which that danger imposes upon us all.

Every newspaper now asks itself, with respect to every story: "Is it news?" All I suggest is that you add the question: "Is it in the interest of the national security?" And I hope that every group in America—unions and businessmen and public officials at every level—will ask the same question of their endeavors, and subject their actions to this same exacting test.

And should the press of America consider and recommend the voluntary assumption of specific new steps or machinery, I can assure you that we will cooperate whole-heartedly with those recommendations.

Perhaps there will be no recommendations. Perhaps there is no answer to the dilemma faced by a free and open society in a cold and secret war. In times of peace, any discussion of this subject, and any action that results, are both painful and without precedent. But this is a time of peace and peril which knows no precedent in history.

II.

It is the unprecedented nature of this challenge that also gives rise to your second obligation—an obligation which I share. And that is our obligation to inform and alert the American people—to make certain that they possess all the facts that they need, and understand them as well—the perils, the prospects, the purposes of our program and the choices that we face.

No President should fear public scrutiny of his program. For from that scrutiny comes understanding; and from that understanding comes support or oppositions. And both are necessary. I am not asking your newspapers to support the Administration, but I am asking your help in the tremendous task of informing and alerting the American people. For I have complete confidence in the response and dedication of our citizens whenever they are fully informed.

I not only could not stifle controversy among your readers—I welcome it. This Administration intends to be candid about its errors; for, as a wise man once said: "An error doesn't become a mistake until you refuse to correct it." We intend to accept full responsibility for our errors; and we expect you to point them out when we miss them.

Without debate, without criticism, no Administration and no country can succeed—and no republic can survive. That is why the Athenian law-maker Solon decreed it a crime for any citizen to shrink from controversy. And that is why our press was protected by the First Amendment—the only business in America specifically protected by the Constitution—not primarily to amuse and entertain, not to emphasize the trivial and the sentimental, not to simply "give the public what it wants"—but to inform, to arouse, to reflect, to state our dangers and our opportunities, to indicate our crises and our choices, to lead, mold, educate and sometimes even anger public opinion.

This means greater coverage and analysis of international news—for it is no longer far away and foreign but close at hand and local. It means greater attention to improved understanding of the news as well as improved transmissions. And it means finally, that government at all levels, must meet its obligation to provide you with the fullest possible information outside the narrowest limits of national security—and we intend to do it.

III.

It was early in the Seventeenth Century that Francis Bacon remarked on three recent inventions already transforming the world: the compass, gunpowder and the printing press. Now the links between the nations first forged by the compass have made us all citizens of the world, the hopes and threats of one becoming the hopes and threats of us all. In that one world's efforts to live together, the evolution of gunpowder to its ultimate limit has warned mankind of the terrible consequences of failure.

And so it is to the printing press—to the recorder of man's deeds, the keeper of his conscience, the courier of his news—that we look for strength and assistance, confident that with your help man will be what he was born to be: free and independent.

Meetings with Khrushchev and de Gaulle

Radio and Television Speech to the American People
Washington, D.C.
June 6, 1961

In late May President Kennedy journeyed to Europe. He met with General de Gaulle in Paris and Prime Minister Macmillan in London. But his most important meetings were with Chairman Nikita Khrushchev on June 3 and 4 in Vienna. Newsmen had reported that those meetings were somber, and in this report to the nation, Kennedy reenforced that assessment. He hinted that we were entering a new phase in Soviet-American relations, especially in reference to Berlin.

I returned this morning from a weeklong trip to Europe and I want to report to you on that trip in full. It was in every sense an unforgettable experience. The people of Paris, of Vienna, of London, were generous in their greeting. They were heartwarming in their hospitality, and their graciousness to my wife in particularly appreciated.

We knew of course that the crowds and the shouts were meant in large measure for the country that we represented, which is regarded as the chief defender of freedom. Equally memorable was the pageantry of European history and their culture that is very much a part of any ceremonial reception, to lay a wreath at the Arc de Triomphe, to dine at Versailles, and Schönbrunn Palace, and with the Queen of England. These are the colorful memories that will remain with us for many years to come. Each of the three cities that we visited—Paris, Vienna, and London—have existed for many centuries, and each serves as a reminder that the Western civilization that we seek to preserve has flowered over many years, and has defended itself over many centuries. But this was not a ceremonial trip. Two aims of American foreign policy, above all others, were the reason for the trip: the unity of the free world, whose strength is the security of us all, and the eventual achievement of a lasting peace. My trip was devoted to the advancement of these two aims.

To strengthen the unity of the West, our journey opened in Paris and closed in London. My talks with General de Gaulle were profoundly encouraging to me. Certain differences in our attitudes on one or another problem became insignificant in view of our common commitment to defend freedom. Our alliance, I believe, became more secure; the friendship of our nation, I hope—with theirs—became firmer; and the relations between the two of us who bear responsibility became closer, and I hope were marked by confidence. I found General de Gaulle far more interested in our frankly stating our position, whether or not it was his own, than in appearing to agree with him when we do not. But he knows full well the true meaning of an alliance. He is after all the only major leader of World War II who still occupies a position of great responsibility. His life has been one of unusual dedication; he is a man of extraordinary personal character, symbolizing the new strength and the historic grandeur of France. Throughout our discussions he took the long view of France and the world at large. I found him a wise counselor for the future, and an informative guide to the history that he has helped to make. Thus we had a valuable meeting.

I believe that certain doubts and suspicions that might have come up in a long time—I believe were removed on both sides. Problems which proved to be not of substance but of wording or procedure were cleared away. No questions, however sensitive, was avoided. No area of interest was ignored, and the conclusions that we reached will be important for the future—in our agreement on defending Berlin, on working to improve the defenses of Europe, on aiding the economic and political independence of the underdeveloped world, including Latin America, on spurring European economic unity, on concluding successfully the conference on Laos, and on closer consultations and solidarity in the Western alliance.

General de Gaulle could not have been more cordial, and I could not have more confidence in any man. In addition to his individual strength of character, the French people as a whole showed vitality and energy which were both impressive and gratifying. Their recovery from the postwar period is dramatic, their productivity is increasing, and they are steadily building their stature in both Europe and Africa, and thus, I left Paris for Vienna with increased confidence in Western unity and strength.

The people of Vienna know what it is to live under occupation, and they know what it is to live in freedom. Their welcome to me as President of this country should be heartwarming to us all. I went to Vienna to meet the leader of the Soviet Union, Mr. Khrushchev. For 2 days we met in sober, intensive conversation, and I believe it is my obligation to the people, to the Congress, and to our allies to report on those conversations candidly and publicly.

Mr. Khrushchev and I had a very full and frank exchange of views on the major issues that now divide our two countries. I will tell you now that it was a very sober 2 days. There was no discourtesy, no loss of tempers, no threats or ultimatums by either side; no advantage or concession was either gained or given; no major decision was either planned or taken; no spectacular progress was either achieved or pretended.

This kind of informal exchange may not be as exciting as a full-fledged summit meeting with a fixed agenda and a large corps of advisers, where negotiations are attempted and new agreements sought, but this was not intended to be and was not such a meeting, nor did we plan any future summit meetings at Vienna.

But I found this meeting with Chairman Khrushchev, as somber as it was, to be immensely useful. I had read his speeches and of his policies. I had been advised on his views. I had been told by other leaders of the West, General de Gaulle, Chancellor Adenauer, Prime Minster Macmillan, what manner of man he was.

But I bear the responsibility of the Presidency of the United States, and it is my duty to make decisions that no adviser and no ally can make for me. It is my obligation and responsibility to see that these decisions are as informed as possible, that they are based on as much direct, firsthand knowledge as possible.

I therefore thought it was of immense importance that I know Mr. Khrushchev, that I gain as much insight and understanding as I could on his present and future policies. At the same time, I wanted to make certain Mr. Khrushchev knew this country and its policies, that he understood our strength and our determination, and that he knew that we desired peace with all nations of every kind.

I wanted to present our views to him directly, precisely, realistically, and with an opportunity for discussion and clarification. This was done. No new aims were stated in private that have not been stated in public on either side. The gap between us was not, in such a short period, materially reduced, but at least the channels of communications were opened more fully, at least the chances of a dangerous misjudgment on either side should now be less, and at least the men on whose decisions the peace in part depends have agreed to remain in contact.

This is important, for neither of us tried to merely please the other, to agree merely to be agreeable, to say what the other wanted to hear. And just as our judicial system relies on witnesses appearing in court and on cross-examination, instead of hearsay testimony or affidavits on paper, so, too, was this direct give-and-take of immeasurable value in making clear and precise what we considered to be vital, for the facts of the matter are that the Soviets and ourselves give wholly different meanings to the same words—war, peace, democracy, and popular will.

We have wholly different views of right and wrong, of what is an internal affair and what is aggression, and, above all, we have wholly different concepts of where the world is and where it is going.

Only by such a discussion was it possible for me to be sure that Mr. Khrushchev knew how differently we view the present and the future. Our views contrasted sharply but at least we knew better at the end where we both stood. Neither of us was there to dictate a settlement or to convert the other to a cause or to concede our basic interests. But both of us were there, I think, because we realized that each nation has the power to inflict enormous damage upon the other, that such a war could and should be avoided if at all possible, since it would settle no dispute and prove no doctrine, and that care should thus be taken to prevent our conflicting interests from so directly confronting each other that war necessarily ensued. We believe in a system of national freedom and independence. He believes in an expanding and dynamic concept of world communism, and the question was whether these two systems can ever hope to live in peace without permitting any loss of security or any denial of the freedom of our friends. However difficult it may seem to answer this question in the affirmative as we approach so many harsh tests, I think we owe it to all mankind to make every possible effort. That is why I considered the Vienna talks to be useful. The somber mood that they conveyed was not cause for elation or relaxation, now was it cause for undue pessimism or fear. It simply demonstrated how much work we in the free world have to do and how long and hard a struggle must be our fate as Americans in this generation as the chief defenders of the cause of liberty. The one area which afforded some immediate prospect of accord was Laos. Both sides recognized the need to reduce the dangers in that situation. Both sides endorsed the concept of a neutral and independent Laos, much in the manner of Burma or Cambodia.

Of critical importance to the current conference on Laos in Geneva, both sides recognized the importance of an effective cease-fire. It is urgent that this be translated into new attitudes at Geneva, enabling the International Control Commission to do its duty, to make certain that a cease-fire is enforced and maintained. I am hopeful that progress can be made on this matter in the coming days at Geneva for that would greatly improve international atmosphere.

No such hope emerged, however, with respect to the other deadlocked Geneva conference, seeking a treaty to ban nuclear tests. Mr. Khrushchev made it clear that there could not be a neutral administrator—in his opinion because no one was truly neutral; that a Soviet veto would have to apply to acts of enforcement; that inspection was only a subterfuge for espionage, in the absence of total disarmament; and that the present test ban negotiations appeared futile. In short, our hopes for an end to nuclear tests, for an end to the spread of nuclear weapons, and for some slowing down of the arms race have been struck a serious blow. Nevertheless, the stakes are too important for us to abandon the draft treaty we have offered at Geneva.

But our most somber talks were on the subject of Germany and Berlin. I made it clear to Mr. Khrushchev that the security of Western Europe and therefore our own security are deeply involved in our presence and our access rights to West Berlin, that those rights are based on law and not on sufferance, and that we are determined to maintain those rights at any risk, and thus meet our obligation to the poeple of West Berlin, and their right to choose their own future.

Mr. Khrushchev, in turn, presented his views in detail, and his presentation will be the subject of further communications. But we are not seeking to change the present situation. A binding German peace treaty is a matter for all who were at war with Germany, and we and our allies cannot abandon our obligations to the people of West Berlin.

Generally, Mr. Khrushchev did not talk in terms of war. He believes the world will move his way without resort to force. He spoke of his nation's achievements in space. He stressed his intention to outdo us in industrial production, to outtrade us, to prove to the world the superiority of his system over ours. Most of all, he predicted the triumph of communism in the new and less developed countries.

He was certain that the tide there was moving his way, that the revolution of rising peoples would eventually be a Communist revolution, and that the so-called wars of liberation, supported by the Kremlin, would replace the old methods of direct aggression and invasion.

In the 1940's and early fifties, the great danger was from Communist armies marching across free borders, which we saw in Korea. Our nuclear monopoly helped to prevent this in other areas. Now we face a new and different threat. We no longer have a nuclear monopoly. Their missiles, they believe, will hold off our missiles, and their troops can match our troops should we intervene in these so-called wars of liberation. Thus, the local conflict they support can turn in their favor through guerrillas or insurgents or subversion. A small group of disciplined Communists could exploit discontent and misery in a country where the average income may be $60 or $70 a year, and seize control, therefore, of an entire country without Communist troops ever crossing any international frontier. This is the Communist theory.

But I believe just as strongly that time will prove it wrong, that liberty and independence and self-determination—not communism—is the future of man, and that free men have the will and the resources to win the struggle for freedom. But it is clear that this struggle in this area of the new and poorer nations will be a continuing crisis of this decade.

Mr. Khrushchev made one point which I wish to pass on. He said there are many disorders throughout the world, and he should not be blamed for them all. He is quite right. It is easy to dismiss as Communist-inspired every anti-government or anti-American riot, every overthrow of a corrupt regime, or every mass protest against misery and despair. These are not all Communist-inspired. The Communists move in to exploit them, to infiltrate their leadership, to ride their crest to victory. But the Communists did not create the conditions which caused them.

In short, the hopes for freedom in these areas which see so much poverty and illiteracy, so many children who are sick, so many children who die in the first year, so many families without homes, so many families without hope—the future for freedom in these areas rests with the local peoples and their governments.

If they have the will to determine their own future, if their governments have the support of their own people, if their honest and progressive measures—helping their people—have inspired confidence and zeal, then no guerrilla of insurgent action can succeed. But where those conditions do not exist, a military guarantee against external attack from across a border offers little protection against internal decay.

Yet all this does not mean that our Nation and the West and the free world can only sit by. On the contrary, we have an historic opportunity to help these countries build their societies until they are so strong and broadly based that only an outside invasion could topple them, and that threat, we know, can be stopped.

We can train and equip their forces to resist Communist-supplied insurrections. We can help develop the industrial and agricultural base on which new living standards can be built. We can encourage better administration and better education and better tax and land distribution and a better life for the people.

All this and more we can do because we have the talent and the resources to do it, if we will only use and share them. I know that there is a great deal of feeling in the United States that we have carried the burden of economic assistance long enough, but these countries that we are now supporting—stretching all the way along from the top of Europe through the Middle East, down through Saigon—are now subject to great efforts internally, in many of them, to seize control.

If we're not prepared to assist them in making a better life for their people, then I believe that the prospects for freedom in those areas are uncertain. We must, I believe, assist them if we are determined to meet with commitments of assistance our words against the Communist advance. The burden is heavy; we have carried it for many years. But I believe that this fight is not over. This battle goes on, and we have to play our part in it. And therefore I hope again that we will assist these people so that they can remain free.

It was fitting that Congress opened its hearings on our new foreign military and economic aid programs in Washington at the very time that Mr. Khrushchev's words in Vienna were demonstrating as nothing else could the need for that very program. It should be well run, effectively administered, but I believe we must do it, and I hope that you, the American people, will support it again, because I think it's vitally important to the security of these areas. There is no use talking against the Communist advance unless we're willing to meet our responsibilities, however burdensome they may be.

I do not justify this aid merely on the grounds of anti-Communism. It is a recognition of our opportunity and obligation to help these people be free, and we are not alone.

I found that the people of France, for example, were doing far more in Africa in the way of aiding independent nations than our own country was. But I know that foreign aid is a burden that is keenly felt and I can only say that we have no more crucial obligation now.

My stay in England was short but the visit gave me a chance to confer privately again with Prime Minister Macmillan, just as others of our party in Vienna were conferring yesterday with General de Gaulle and Chancellor Adenauer. We all agreed that there is work to be done in the West and from our conversations have come agreed steps to get on with that work. Our day in London, capped by a meeting with Queen Elizabeth and Prince Philip was a strong reminder at the end of a long journey that the West remains united in its determination to hold to its standards.

May I conclude by saying simply that I am glad to be home. We have on this trip admired splendid places and seen stirring sights, but we are glad to be home. No demonstration of support abroad could mean so much as the support which you, the American people, have so generously given to our country. With that support I am not fearful of the future. We must be patient. We must be determined. We must be courageous. We must accept both risks and burdens, but with the will and the work freedom will prevail.

The Berlin "Crisis"
Washington, D.C.
July 25, 1961

On his report to the nation on his visit with Khrushchev in June, Kennedy focused American attention on Berlin as the next probable trouble spot in American-Soviet relations. In this speech over radio and television Kennedy raised the issue of Berlin to crisis and urged measures that appeared to be preparation for war. One immediate effect of the speech was the building of private fall-out shelters and the attendant debate over the morality of how to use one's fall-out shelter. Though certain symbolic actions were taken when the East Germans built the Wall separating East and West Germany, the Administration finally capitulated and agreed in September to negotiate the status of Berlin.

Seven weeks ago tonight I returned from Europe to report on my meeting with Premier Khrushchev and the others. His grim warnings about the future of the world, his aide memoire on Berlin, his subsequent speeches and threats which he and his agents have launched, and the increase in the Soviet military budget that he has announced, have all prompted a series of decisions by the Administration and a series of consultations with the members of the NATO organization. In Berlin, as you recall, he intends to bring to an end, through a stroke of the pen, *first* our legal rights to be in West Berlin—and *secondly* our ability to make good on our commitment to the two million free people of that city. That we cannot permit.

We are clear about what must be done—and we intend to do it. I want to talk frankly with you tonight about the first steps that we shall take. These actions will require sacrifice on the part of many of our citizens. More will be required in the future. They will require, from all of us, courage and perseverance in the years to come. But if we and our allies act out of strength and unity of purpose—with calm determination and steady nerves—using restraint in our words as well as our weapons—I am hopeful that both peace and freedom will be sustained.

The immediate threat to free men is in West Berlin. But that isolated outpost is not an isolated problem. The threat is worldwide. Our effort must be equally wide and strong, and not be obsessed by any single manufactured crisis. We face a challenge in Berlin, but there is also a challenge in Southeast Asia, where the borders are less guarded, the enemy harder to find, and the dangers of communism less apparent to those who have so little. We face a challenge in our own hemisphere, and indeed wherever else the freedom of human beings is at stake.

Let me remind you that the fortunes of war and diplomacy left the free people of West Berlin, in 1945, 110 miles behind the Iron Curtain.

This map makes very clear the problem that we face. The white is West Germany—the East is the area controlled by the Soviet Union, and as you can see from the chart, West Berlin is 110 miles within the area which the Soviets now dominate—which is immediately controlled by the so-called East German regime.

We are there as a result of our victory over Nazi Germany—and our basic rights to be there, deriving from that victory, include both our presence in West Berlin and the enjoyment of access across East Germany. These rights have been repeatedly confirmed and recognized in special agreements with the Soviet Union. Berlin is not a part of East Germany, but a separate territory under the control of the allied powers. To our rights there are clear and deep-rooted. But in addition to those rights is our commitment to sustain—and defend, if need be—the opportunity for more than two million people to determine their own future and choose their own way of life.

Thus, our presence in West Berlin, and our access thereto, cannot be ended by any act of the Soviet government. The NATO shield was long ago extended to cover West Berlin—and we have given our word that an attack upon that city will be regarded as an attack upon us all.

For West Berlin—lying exposed 110 miles inside East Germany, surrounded by Soviet troops and close to Soviet supply lines, has many roles. It is more than a showcase of liberty, a symbol, an island of freedom in a Communist sea. It is even more than a link with the Free World, a beacon of hope behind the Iron Curtain, an escape hatch for refugees.

West Berlin is all of that. But above all it has now become—as never before—the great testing place of Western courage and will, a focal point where our solemn commitments stretching back over the years since 1945, and Soviet ambitions now meet in basic confrontation.

It would be a mistake for others to look upon Berlin, because of its location, as a tempting target. The United States is there; the United Kingdom and France are there; the pledge of NATO is there—and the people of Berlin are there. It is as secure, in that sense, as the rest of us—for we cannot separate its safety from our own.

I hear it said that West Berlin is militarily untenable. And so was Bastogne. And so, in fact, was Stalingrad. Any dangerous spot is tenable if men—brave men—will make it so.

We do not want to fight—but we have fought before. And others in earlier times have made the same dangerous mistake of assuming that the West was too selfish and too soft and too divided to resist invasions of freedom in other lands. Those who threaten to unleash the forces of war on a dispute over West Berlin should recall the words of the ancient philosopher: "A man who causes fear cannot be free from fear."

We cannot and will not permit the Communists to drive us out of Berlin, either gradually or by force. For the fulfillment of our pledge to that city is essential to the morale and security of Western Germany, to the unity of Western Europe, and to the faith of the entire Free World. Soviet strategy has long been aimed, not merely at Berlin, but at dividing and neutralizing all of Europe, forcing us back on our own shores. We must meet our oft-stated pledge to the free peoples of West Berlin—and maintain our rights and their safety, even in the face of force—in order to maintain the confidence of other free peoples in our word and our resolve. The strength of the alliance on which our security depends is dependent in turn on our willingness to meet our commitments to them.

So long as the Communists insist that they are preparing to end by themselves unilaterally our rights in West Berlin and our commitments to its people, we must be prepared to defend those rights and those commitments. We will at all times be ready to talk, if talk will help. But we must also be ready to resist with force, if force is used upon us. Either alone would fail. Together, they can serve the cause of freedom and peace.

The new preparations that we shall make to defend the peace are part of the long-term build-up in our strength which has been underway since January. They are based on our needs to meet a world-wide threat, on a basis which stretches far beyond the present Berlin crisis. Our primary purpose is neither propaganda nor provocation—but preparation.

A first need is to hasten progress toward the military goals which the North Atlantic allies have set for themselves. In Europe today nothing less will suffice. We will put even greater resources into fulfilling those goals, and we look to our allies to do the same.

The supplementary defense build-ups that I asked from the Congress in March and May have already started moving us toward these and our other defense goals. They included an increase in the size of the Marine Corps, improved readiness of our reserves, expansion of our air and sea lift, and stepped-up procurement of needed weapons, ammunition, and other items. To insure a continuing invulnerable capacity to deter or destroy any aggressor, they provided for the strengthening of our missile power and for putting 50% of our B-52 and B-47 bombers on a ground alert which would send them on their way with 15 minutes' warning.

These measures must be speeded up, and still others must now be taken. We must have sea and air lift capable of moving our forces quickly and in large numbers to any part of the world.

But even more importantly, we need the capability of placing in any critical area at the appropriate time a force which, combined with those of our allies, is large enough to make clear our determination and our ability to defend our rights at all costs—and to meet all levels of aggressor pressure with whatever levels of force are required. We intend to have a wider choice than humiliation or all-out nuclear action.

While it is unwise at this time either to call up or send abroad excessive numbers of these troops before they are needed, let me make it clear that I intend to take, as time goes on, whatever steps are necessary to make certain that such forces can be deployed at the appropriate time without lessening our ability to meet our commitments elsewhere.

Thus, in the days and months ahead, I shall not hesitate to ask the Congress for additional measures, or exercise any of the executive powers that I possess to meet this threat to peace. Everything essential to the security of freedom must be done; and if that should require more men, or more taxes, or more controls, or other new powers, I shall not hesitate to ask them. The measures proposed today will be constantly studied, and altered as necessary. But while we will not let panic shape our policy, neither will we permit timidity to direct our program.

Accordingly, I am now taking the following steps:

(1) I am tomorrow requesting the Congress for the current fiscal year an additional $3,247,000,000 of appropriations for the Armed Forces.

(2) To fill out our present Army Divisions, and to make more men available for prompt deployment, I am requesting an increase in the Army's total authorized strength from 875,000 to approximately 1 million men.

(3) I am requesting an increase of 29,000 and 63,000 men respectively in the active duty strength of the Navy and the Air Force.

(4) To fulfill these manpower needs, I am ordering that our draft calls be doubled and tripled in the coming months; I am asking the Congress for authority to order to active duty certain ready reserve units and individual reservists, and to extend tours of duty; and, under the authority, I am planning to order to active duty a number of air transport squadrons and Air National Guard tactical air squadrons, to give us the airlift capacity and protection that we need. Other reserve forces will be called up when needed.

(5) Many ships and planes once headed for retirement are to be retained or reactivated, increasing our airpower tactically and our sealift, airlift, and anti-submarine warfare capability. In addition, our strategic air power will be increased by delaying the deactivation of B-47 bombers.

(6) Finally, some $1.8 billion—about half of the total sum—is needed for the procurement of non-nuclear weapons, ammunition and equipment.

The details on all these requests will be presented to the Congress tomorrow. Subsequent steps will be taken to suit subsequent needs. Comparable efforts for the common defense are being discussed with our NATO allies. For their commitment and interest are as precise as our own.

And let me add that I am well aware of the fact that many American families will bear the burden of these requests. Studies or careers will be interrupted; husbands and sons will be called away; incomes in some cases will be reduced. But these are burdens which must be borne if freedom is to be defended—Americans have willingly borne them before—and they will not flinch from the task now.

We have another sober responsibility. To recognize the possibilities of nuclear war in the missile age, without our citizens knowing what they should do and where they should go if bombs begin to fall, would be a failure of responsibility. In May, I pledged a new start on Civil Defense. Last week, I assigned, on the recommendation of the Civil Defense Director, basic responsibility for this program to the Secretary of Defense, to make certain it is administered and coordinated with our continental defense efforts at the highest civilian level. Tomorrow, I am requesting of the Congress new funds for the following immediate objectives: to identify and mark space in existing structures—public and private—that could be used for fall-out shelters in case of attack; to stock those shelters with food, water, first-aid kits and other minimum essentials for survival; to increase their capacity; to improve our air-raid warning and fall-out detection systems, including a new household warning system which is now under development; and to take other measures that will be effective at an early date to save millions of lives if needed.

In the event of an attack, the lives of those families which are not hit in a nuclear blast and fire can still be saved—*if* they can be warned to take shelter and *if* that shelter is available. We owe that kind of insurance to our families—and to our country. In contrast to our friends in Europe, the need for this kind of protection is new to our shores. But the time to start is now. In the coming months, I hope to let every citizen know what steps he can take without delay to protect his family in case of attack. I know that you will want to do no less.

The addition of $207 million in Civil Defense appropriations brings our total new defense budget requests to $3.454 billion, and a total of $47.5 billion for the year. This is an increase in the defense budget of $6 billion since January, and has resulted in official estimates of a budget deficit of over $5 billion. The Secretary of the Treasury and other economic advisers assure me, however, that our economy has the capacity to bear this new request.

We are recovering strongly from this year's recession. The increase in this last quarter of our year of our total national output was greater than that for any postwar period of initial recovery. And yet, wholesale prices are actually lower than they were during the recession, and consumer prices are only 1/4 of 1% higher than they were last October. In fact, this last quarter was the first in eight years in which our production has increased without an increase in the overall-price index. And for the first time since the fall of 1959, our gold position has improved and the dollar is more respected abroad. These gains, it should be stressed, are being accomplished with Budget deficits far smaller than those of the 1958 recession.

This improved business outlook means improved revenues; and I intend to submit to the Congress in January a budget for the next fiscal year which will be strictly in balance. Nevertheless, should an increase in taxes be needed—because of events in the next few months—to achieve that balance, or because of subsequent defense rises, those increased taxes will be requested in January.

Meanwhile, to help make certain that the current deficit is held to a safe level, we must keep down all expenditures not thoroughly justified in budget requests. The luxury of our current post-office deficit must be ended. Costs in military procurement will be closely scrutinized—and in this effort I welcome the cooperation of the Congress. The tax loopholes I have specified—on expense accounts, overseas income, dividends, interest, cooperatives and others—must be closed.

I realize that no public revenue measure is welcomed by everyone. But I am certain that every American wants to pay his fair share, and not leave the burden of defending freedom entirely to those who bear arms. For we have mortgaged our very future on this defense—and we cannot fail to meet our responsibilities.

But I must emphasize again that the choice is not merely between resistance and retreat, between atomic holocaust and surrender. Our peace-time military posture is traditionally defensive; but our diplomatic posture need not be. Our response to the Berlin crisis will not be merely military or negative. It will be more than merely standing firm. For we do not intend to leave it to others to choose and monopolize the forum and the framework of discussion. We do not intend to abandon our duty to mankind to seek a peaceful solution.

As signers of the UN Charter, we shall always be prepared to discuss international problems with any and all nations that are willing to talk—and listen—with reason. If they have proposals—not demands—we shall hear them. If they seek genuine understanding—not concessions of our rights—we shall meet with them. We have previously indicated our readiness to remove any actual irritants in West Berlin, but the freedom of that city is not negotiable. We cannot negotiate with those who say "What's mine is mine and what's yours is negotiable." But we are willing to consider any arrangement or treaty in Germany consistent with the maintenance of peace and freedom, and with the legitimate security interests of all nations.

We recognize the Soviet Union's historical concern about their security in Central and Eastern Europe, after a series of ravaging invasions, and we believe arrangements can be worked out which will help to meet those concerns, and make it possible for both security and freedom to exist in this troubled area.

For it is not the freedom of West Berlin which is "abnormal" in Germany today, but the situation in that entire divided country. If anyone doubts the legality of our rights in Berlin, we are ready to have it submitted to international adjudication. If anyone doubts the extent to which our presence is desired by the people of West Berlin, compared to East German feelings about their regime, we are ready to have that question submitted to a free vote in Berlin and, if possible, among all the German people. And let us hear at that time from the two and one-half million refugees who have fled the Communist regime in East Germany—voting for Western-type freedom with their feet.

The world is not deceived by the Communist attempt to label Berlin as a hot-bed of war. There is peace in Berlin today. The source of world trouble and tension is Moscow, not Berlin. And if war begins, it will have begun in Moscow and not Berlin.

For the choice of peace or war is largely theirs, not ours. It is the Soviets who have stirred up this crisis. It is they who are trying to force a change. It is they who have opposed free elections. It is they who have rejected an all-German peace treaty, and the rulings of international law. And as Americans know from our history on our own old frontier, gun battles are caused by outlaws, and not by officers of the peace.

In short, while we are ready to defend our interests, we shall also be ready to search for peace—in quiet exploratory talks—in formal or informal meetings. We do not want military considerations to dominate the thinking of either East or West. And Mr. Khrushchev may find that his invitation to other nations to join in a meaningless treaty may lead to *their* inviting *him* to join in the community of peaceful men, in abandoning the use of force, and in respecting the sanctity of agreements.

While all of these efforts go on, we must not be diverted from our total responsibilities, from other dangers, from other tasks. If new threats in Berlin or elsewhere should cause us to weaken our program of assistance to the developing nations who are also under heavy pressure from the same source, or to halt our efforts for realistic disarmament, or to disrupt or slow down our economy, or to neglect the education of our children, then those threats will surely be the most successful and least costly maneuver in Communist history. For we can afford all these efforts, and more—but we cannot afford *not* to meet this challenge.

And the challenge is not to us alone. It is a challenge to every nation which asserts its sovereignty under a system of liberty. It is a challenge to all those who want a world of free choice. It is a special challenge to the Atlantic Community—the heartland of human freedom.

We in the West must move together in building military strength. We must consult one another more closely than ever before. We must together design our proposals for peace, and labor together as they are pressed at the conference table. And together we must share the burdens and the risks of this effort.

The Atlantic Community, as we know it, has been built in response to challenge: the challenge of European chaos in 1947, of the Berlin blockade in 1948, the challenge of Communist aggression in Korea in 1950. Now, standing strong and prosperous, after an unprecedented decade of progress, the Atlantic Community will not forget either its history or the principles which gave it meaning.

The solemn vow each of us gave to West Berlin in time of peace will not be broken in time of danger. If we do not meet our commitments to Berlin, where will we later stand? If we are not true to our word there, all that we have achieved in collective security, which relies on these words, will mean nothing. And if there is one path above all others to war, it is the path of weakness and disunity.

Today, the endangered frontier of freedom runs through divided Berlin. We want it to remain a frontier of peace. This is the hope of every citizen of the Atlantic Community; every citizen of Eastern Europe; and, I am confident, every citizen of the Soviet Union. For I cannot believe that the Russian people—who bravely suffered enormous losses in the Second World War—would now wish to see the peace upset once more in Germany. The Soviet government alone can convert Berlin's frontier of peace into a pretext for war.

The steps I have indicated tonight are aimed at avoiding that war. To sum it all up: we seek peace—but we shall not surrender. That is the central meaning of this crisis, and the meaning of your government's policy.

With your help, and the help of other free men, this crisis can be surmounted. Freedom can prevail—and peace can endure.

I would like to close with a personal word. When I ran for the Presidency of the United States, I knew that this country faced serious challenges, but I could not realize—nor could any man realize who does not bear the burdens of this office—how heavy and constant would be those burdens.

Three times in my life-time our country and Europe have been involved in major wars. In each case serious misjudgments were made on both sides of the intentions of others, which brought about great devastation.

Now, in the thermonuclear age, any misjudgment on either side about the intentions of the other could rain more devastation in several hours than has been wrought in all the wars of human history.

Therefore I, as President and Commander-in-Chief, and all of us as Americans, are moving through serious days. I shall bear this responsibility under our Constitution for the next three and one-half years, but I am sure that we all, regardless of our occupations, will do our very best for our country, and for our cause. For all of us want to see our children grow up in a country at peace, and in a world where freedom endures.

I know that sometimes we get impatient, we wish for some immediate action that would end our perils. But I must tell you that there is no quick and easy solution. The Communists control over a billion people, and they recognize that if we should falter, their success would be imminent.

We must look to long days ahead, which if we are courageous and persevering can bring us what we all desire.

In these days and weeks I ask for your help, and your advice. I ask for your suggestions, when you think we could do better.

All of us, I know, love our country, and we shall all do our best to serve it.

In meeting my responsibilities in these coming months as President, I need your good will, and your support—and above all, your prayers.

Thank you, and good night.

The Steel Crisis

Televised News Conference
Washington, D.C.
April 11, 1962

On April 10 Roger M. Blough, chairman of the board of United States Steel, announced that his corporation was increasing its prices by $6 a ton, roughly a 3.5% increase. A number of other steel companies followed suit and raised their prices accordingly. These actions constituted a political crisis for the Administration. Kennedy believed such price increases inflationary and therefore a threat to his economic policies of stimulating growth without inflation. But more was on the line. Through "jawboning," Kennedy had persuaded the United Steel Workers to accept a new two-year contract that kept wages at the same level and increased fringe benefits by only 2.5%. The contract had been signed only a few days before Blough's announcement. Apparently, the Administration had been able to convince the union to accept this contract, which represented one of the least costly in years, by assuring it that the companies would not raise their prices. Not only did the President feel betrayed by the steel companies, the unions felt a Democratic President whom they had supported had betrayed them. If the President could not get the prices rolled back, he could not convincingly ask other unions to hold back inflationary wage demands in the future. More important, Kennedy could not afford to lose even a small part of labor from his fragile constituency if he were to continue as an effective leader and hope for re-election in 1964. Acting quickly, Kennedy decided to marshall public opinion to his side. His press conference was only part of that effort. He also directed Secretary of Defense McNamara to announce the government would henceforth give preferential treatment in alloting government contracts to companies that had not raised their prices. The most notorious incident in this campaign involved a visit from FBI agents to a newsman's home in early morning hours merely to learn whether or not the reporter would stand by a story he had published. This FBI visit, which in no way involved a criminal investigation, raised charges of "Gestapo tactics" against Kennedy. But within 5 days the companies capitulated and the price increase was rescinded.

I have several announcements to make.

[1.] Simultaneous and identical actions of United States Steel and other leading steel corporation increasing steel prices by some $6 a ton constitute a wholly unjustifiable and irresponsible defiance of the public interest. In this serious hour in our Nation's history, when we are confronted with grave crises in Berlin and Southeast Asia, when we are devoting our energies to economic recovery and stability, when we are asking reservists to leave their homes and families for months on end and servicemen to risk their lives—and four were killed in the last 2 days in Viet-Nam—and asking union members to hold down their wage requests at a time when restraint and sacrifice are being asked of every citizen, the American people will find it hard, as I do, to accept a situation in which a tiny handful of steel executives whose pursuit of private power and profit exceeds their sense of public responsibility can show such utter contempt for the interests of 185 million Americans.

If this rise in the cost of steel is imitated by the rest of the industry, instead of rescinded, it would increase the cost of homes, autos, appliances, and most other items for every American family. It would increase the cost of machinery and tools to every American businessman and farmer. It would seriously handicap our efforts to prevent an inflationary spiral from eating up the pensions of our older citizens, and our new gains in purchasing power.

It would add, Secretary McNamara informed me this morning, an estimated $1 billion to the cost of our defenses, at a time when every dollar is needed for national security and other purposes. It would make it more difficult for American goods to compete in foreign markets, more difficult to withstand competition from foreign imports, and thus more difficult to improve our balance of payments position, and stem the flow of gold. And it is necessary to stem it for our national security, if we're going to pay for our security commitments abroad. And it would surely handicap our efforts to induce other industries and unions to adopt responsible price and wage policies.

The facts of the matter are that there is no justification for an increase in steel prices. The recent settlement between the industry and the union, which does not even take place until July 1st, was widely acknowledged to be noninflationary, and the whole purpose and effect of this administration's role, which both parties understood, was to achieve an agreement which would make unnecessary any increase in prices. Steel output per man in rising so fast that labor costs per ton of steel can actually be expected to decline in the next 12 months. And in fact, the Acting Commissioner of the Bureau of Labor Statistics informed me this morning that, and I quote, "employment costs per unit of steel output in 1961 were essentially the same as they were in 1958."

The cost of the major raw materials, steel scrap and coal, has also been declining, and for an industry which has been generally operating at less than two-thirds of capacity, its profit rate has been normal and can be expected to rise sharply this year in view of the reduction in idle capacity. Their lot has been easier than that of one hundred thousand steel workers thrown out of work in the last 3 years. The industry's cash dividends have exceeded $600 million in each of the last 5 years, and earnings in the first quarter of this year were estimated in the February 28th Wall Street Journal to be among the highest in history.

In short, at a time when they could be exploring how more efficiency and better prices could be obtained, reducing prices in this industry in recognition of lower costs, their unusually good labor contract, their foreign competition and their increase in production and profits which are coming this year, a few gigantic corporations have decided to increase prices in ruthless disregard of their public responsibilities.

The Steelworkers Union can be proud that it abided by its responsibilities in this agreement, and this Government also has responsibilities which we intend to meet. The Department of Justice and the Federal Trade Commission are examining the significance of this action in a free, competitive economy. The Department of Defense and other agencies are reviewing its impact on their policies of procurement. And I am informed that steps are under way by those members of the Congress who plan appropriate inquiries into how these price decisions are so quickly made and reached and what legislative safeguards may be needed to protect the public interest.

Price and wage decisions in this country, except for a very limited restriction in the case of monopolies and national emergency strikes, are and ought to be freely and privately made. But the American people have a right to expect, in return for that freedom, a higher sense of business responsibility for the welfare of their country than has been shown in the last 2 days.

Some time ago I asked each American to consider what he would do for his country and I asked the steel companies. In the last 24 hours we had their answer. . . .

Desegregation at the University Of Mississippi: A Legal Issue

Televised Report to the Nation
Washington, D.C.
September 30, 1962

James Meredith, who met all the academic requirements, applied for admission to the University of Mississippi in 1961 and was refused. He sought redress through the courts, and in September, 1962 the courts ordered the University to admit him as a student. On September 30, he was admitted. At the same time, rioting broke out on the Oxford campus and continued into the next day. Two people died. The President called upon federal troops and National Guardsmen, sworn into federal service, to take control of the unruly situation. In the midst of the rioting over Meredith's admission, President Kennedy spoke over national television and radio about the significance of the events in Oxford, Mississippi in a "law and order" speech.

The orders of the court in the case of Meredith versus Fair are beginning to be carried out. Mr. James Meredith is now in residence on the campus of the University of Mississippi.

This has been accomplished thus far without the use of National Guard or other troops. And it is to be hoped that the law enforcement officers of the State of Mississippi and the Federal marshals will continue to be sufficient in the future.

All students, members of the faculty, and public officials in both Mississippi and the Nation will be able, it is hoped, to return to their normal activities with full confidence in the integrity of American law.

This is as it should be, for our Nation is founded on the principle that observance of the law is the eternal safeguard of liberty and defiance of the law is the surest road to tyranny. The law which we obey includes the final rulings of the courts, as well as the enactments of our legislative bodies. Even among law-abiding men few laws are universally loved, but they are uniformly respected and not resisted.

Americans are free, in short, to disagree with the law but not to disobey it. For in a government of laws and not of men, no man, however prominent or powerful, and no mob, however unruly or boisterous, is entitled to defy a court of law. If this country should ever reach the point where any man or group of men by force or threat of force could long defy the commands of our court and our Constitution, then no law would stand free from doubt, no judge would be sure of his writ, and no citizen would be safe from his neighbors.

In this case in which the United States Government was not until recently involved, Mr. Meredith brought a private suit in Federal court against those who were excluding him from the University. A series of Federal courts all the way to the Supreme Court repeatedly ordered Mr. Meredith's admission to the University. When those orders were defied, and those who sought to implement them threatened with arrest and violence, the United States Court of Appeals consisting of Chief Judge Tuttle of Georgia, Judge Hutcheson of Texas, Judge Rives of Alabama, Judge Jones of Florida, Judge Brown of Texas, Judge Wisdom of Louisiana, Judge Gewin of Alabama, and Judge Bell of Georgia, made clear the fact that the enforcement of its order had become an obligation of the United States Government. Even though this Government had not originally been a party to the case, my responsibility as President was therefore inescapable. I accept it. My obligation under the Constitution and the statutes of the United States was and is to implement the orders of the court with whatever means are necessary, and with as little force and civil disorder as the circumstances permit.

It was for this reason that I federalized the Mississippi National Guard as the most appropriate instrument, should any be needed, to preserve law and order while United States marshals carried out the orders of the court and prepared to back them up with whatever other civil or military enforcement might have been required.

I deeply regret the fact that any action by the executive branch was necessary in this case, but all other avenues and alternatives, including persuasion and conciliation, had been tried and exhausted. Had the police powers of Mississippi been used to support the orders of the court, instead of deliberately and unlawfully blocking them, had the University of Mississippi fulfilled its standard of excellence by quietly admitting this applicant in conformity with what so many other southern State universities have done for so many years, a peaceable and sensible solution would have been possible without any Federal intervention.

This Nation is proud of the many instances in which Governors, educators, and everyday citizens from the South have shown to the world the gains that can be made by persuasion and good will in a society ruled by law. Specifically, I would like to take this occasion to express the thanks of this Nation to those southerners who have contributed to the progress of our democratic development in the entrance of students regardless of race to such great institutions as the State-supported universities of Virginia, North Carolina, Georgia, Florida, Texas, Louisiana, Tennessee, Arkansas, and Kentucky.

I recognize that the present period of transition and adjustment in our Nation's Southland is a hard one for many people. Neither Mississippi nor any other southern State deserves to be charged with all the accumulated wrongs of the last 100 years of race relations. To the extent that there has been failure, the responsibility for that failure must be shared by us all, by every State, by every citizen.

Mississippi and her University, moreover, are noted for their courage, for their contribution of talent and thought to the affairs of this Nation. This is the State of Lucius Lamar and many others who have placed the national good ahead of sectional interest. This is the State which had four Medal of Honor winners in the Korean war alone. In fact, the Guard unit federalized this morning, early, is part of the 155th Infantry, one of the 10 oldest regiments in the Union and one of the most decorated for sacrifices and bravery in 6 wars.

In 1945 a Mississippi sergeant, Jake Lindsey, was honored by an unusual joint session of the Congress. I close therefore with this appeal to the students of the University, the people who are most concerned.

You have a great tradition to uphold, a tradition of honor and courage won on the field of battle and on the gridiron as well as the University campus. You have a new opportunity to show that you are men of patriotism and integrity. For the most effective means of upholding the law is not the State policeman or the marshals or the National Guard. It is you. It lies in your courage to accept those laws with which you disagree as well as those with which you agree. The eyes of the Nation and of all the world are upon you and upon all of us, and the honor of your University and State are in the balance. I am certain that the great majority of the students will uphold that honor.

There is in short no reason why the books on this case cannot now be quickly and quietly closed in the manner directed by the court. Let us preserve both the law and the peace and then healing those wounds that are within we can turn to the greater crises that are without and stand united as one people in our pledge to man's freedom.

The Cuban Missile Crisis
Televised Report to the Nation
Washington, D.C.
October 22, 1962

In October, 1962 American intelligence sources learned that offensive missile sites were being erected in Cuba. Upon receiving this information, the President established an Executive Committee (Ex Comm) to advise him on the proper response. But the final decision was Kennedy's. On October 22 in the early evening, the American public learned about the crisis and Kennedy's response to it. His speech is a classic form of Presidential "Crisis Rhetoric," modelled after Roosevelt's December 8, 1941 speech and copied by President Nixon when he announced the invasion of Cambodia in 1970. In the speech Kennedy announced actions that brought the United States to a nuclear confrontation with the Soviet Union, a confrontation other Presidents since 1945 had tried to avoid. He demanded that the missiles be removed from Cuba. After a week of intense activity, private communications, diplomatic maneuvering, threats and counter-threats, Khrushchev agreed to remove the missiles. Although considered by many to be Kennedy's "finest hour," the speech is significant because it brought the world face-to-face for the first time to the possibility of nuclear war and its consequence: human extermination.

This Government, as promised, has maintained the closest surveillance of the Soviet military buildup on the island of Cuba. Within the past week, unmistakable evidence has established the fact that a series of offensive missile sites is now in preparation on that imprisoned island. The purpose of these bases can be none other than to provide a nuclear strike capability against the Western Hemisphere.

Upon receiving the first preliminary hard information of this nature last Tuesday morning at 9 A.M., I directed that our surveillance be stepped up. And having now confirmed and completed our evaluation of the evidence and our decision on a course of action, this Government feels obliged to report this new crisis to you in fullest detail.

The characteristics of these new missile sites indicate two distinct types of installations. Several of them include medium range ballistic missiles, capable of carrying a nuclear warhead for a distance of more than 1,000 nautical miles. Each of these missiles, in short, is capable of striking Washington, D.C., the Panama Canal, Cape Canaveral, Mexico City, or any other city in the southeastern part of the United States, in Central America, or in the Caribbean area.

Additional sites not yet completed appear to be designed for intermediate range ballistic missiles—capable of traveling more than twice as far—and thus capable of striking most of the major cities in the Western Hemisphere, ranging as far north as Hudson Bay, Canada, and as far south as Lima, Peru. In addition, jet bombers, capable of carrying nuclear weapons, are now being uncrated and assembled in Cuba, while the necessary air bases are being prepared.

This urgent transformation of Cuba into an important strategic base—by the presence of these large, long-range, and clearly offensive weapons of sudden mass destruction—constitutes an explicit threat to the peace and security of all the Americas, in flagrant and deliberate defiance of the Rio Pact of 1947, the traditions of this Nation and hemisphere, the joint resolution of the 87th Congress, the Charter of the United Nations, and my own public warnings to the Soviets on September 4 and 13. This action also contradicts the repeated assurances of Soviet spokesmen, both publicly and privately delivered, that the arms buildup in Cuba would retain its original defensive character, and that the Soviet Union had no need or desire to station strategic missiles on the territory of any other nation.

The size of this undertaking makes clear that it has been planned for some months. Yet only last month, after I had made clear the distinction between any introduction of ground-to-ground missiles and the existence of defensive antiaircraft missiles, the Soviet Government publicly stated on September 11 that, and I quote, "the armaments and military equipment sent to Cuba are designed exclusively for defensive purposes," that, and I quote the Soviet Government, "there is no need for the Soviet Government to shift its weapons . . . for a retaliatory blow to any other country, for instance Cuba," and that, and I quote their government, "the Soviet Union has so powerful rockets to carry these nuclear warheads that there is no need to search for sites for them beyond the boundaries of the Soviet Union." That statement was false.

Only last Thursday, as evidence of this rapid offensive buildup was already in my hand, Soviet Foreign Minister Gromyko told me in my office that he was instructed to make it clear once again, as he said his government had already done, that Soviet assistance to Cuba, and I quote, "pursued solely the purpose of contributing to the defense capabilities of Cuba," that, and I quote him "training by Soviet specialists of Cuban nationals in handling defensive armaments was by no means offensive, and if it were otherwise," Mr. Gromyko went on, "the Soviet Government would never become involved in rendering such assistance." That statement also was false.

Neither the United States of America nor the world community of nations can tolerate deliberate deception and offensive threats on the part of any nation, large or small. We no longer live in a world where only the actual firing of weapons represents a sufficient challenge to a nation's security to constitute maximum peril. Nuclear weapons are so destructive and ballistic missiles are so swift, that any substantially increased possibility of their use or any sudden change in their deployment may well be regarded as a definite threat to peace.

For many years, both the Soviet Union and the United States, recognizing this fact, have deployed strategic nuclear weapons with great care, never upsetting the precarious status quo which insured that these weapons would not be used in the absence of some vital challenge. Our own strategic missiles have never been transferred to the territory of any other nation under a cloak of secrecy and deception; and our history—unlike that of the Soviets since the end of World War II—demonstrates that we have no desire to dominate or conquer any other nation or impose our system upon its people. Nevertheless, American citizens have become adjusted to living daily on the bull's-eye of Soviet missiles located inside the U.S.S.R. or in submarines.

In that sense, missiles in Cuba add to an already clear and present danger—although it should be noted the nations of Latin America have never previously been subjected to a potential nuclear threat.

But this secret, swift, and extraordinary buildup of Communist missiles—in an area well known to have a special and historical relationship to the United States and the nations of the Western Hemisphere, in violation of Soviet assurances, and in defiance of American and hemispheric policy—this sudden, clandestine decision to station strategic weapons for the first time outside of Soviet soil—is a deliberately provocative and unjustified change in the status quo which cannot be accepted by this country, if our courage and our commitments are ever to be trusted again by either friend or foe.

The 1930's taught us a clear lesson: aggressive conduct, if allowed to go unchecked and unchallenged, ultimately leads to war. This nation is opposed to war. We are also true to our word. Our unswerving objective, therefore, must be to prevent the use of these missiles against this or any other country, and to secure their withdrawal or elimination from the Western Hemisphere.

Our policy has been one of patience and restraint, as befits a peaceful and powerful nation, which leads to worldwide alliance. We have been determined not to be diverted from our central concerns by mere irritants and fanatics. But now further action is required—and it is under way; and these actions may only be the beginning. We will not prematurely or unnecessarily risk the costs of worldwide nuclear war in which even the fruits of victory would be ashes in our mouth—but neither will we shrink from that risk at any time it must be faced.

Acting, therefore, in the defense of our own security and of the entire Western Hemisphere, and under the authority entrusted to me by the Constitution as endorsed by the resolution of the Congress, I have directed that the following *initial* steps be taken immediately:

First: To halt this offensive buildup, a strict quarantine on all offensive military equipment under shipment to Cuba is being initiated. All ships of any kind bound for Cuba from whatever nation or port will, if found to contain cargoes of offensive weapons, be turned back. This quarantine will be extended, if needed, to other types of cargo and carriers. We are not at this time, however, denying the necessities of life as the Soviets attempted to do in their Berlin blockade of 1948.

Second: I have directed the continued and increased close surveillance of Cuba and its military buildup. The foreign ministers of the OAS, in their communique of October 6, rejected secrecy on such matters in this hemisphere. Should these offensive military preparations continue, thus increasing the threat to the hemisphere, further action will be justified. I have directed the Armed Forces to prepare for any eventualities; and I trust that in the interest of both Cuban people and the Soviet technicians at the sites, the hazards to all concerned of continuing this threat will be recognized.

Third: It shall be the policy of this Nation to regard any nuclear missile launched from Cuba against any nation in the Western Hemisphere as an attack by the Soviet Union on the United States, requiring a full retaliatory response upon the Soviet Union.

Fourth: As a necessary military precaution, I have reinforced our base at Guantanamo, evacuated today the dependents of our personnel there, and ordered additional military units to be on a standby alert basis.

Fifth: We are calling tonight for an immediate meeting of the Organ of Consultation under the Organization of American States, to consider this threat to hemispheric security and to invoke articles 6 and 8 of the Rio Treaty in support of all necessary action. The United Nations Charter allows for regional security arrangements—and the nations of this hemisphere decided long ago against the military presence of outside powers. Our other allies around the world have also been alerted.

Sixth: Under the Charter of the United Nations, we are asking tonight that an emergency meeting of the Security Council be convoked without delay to take action against this latest Soviet threat to world peace. Our resolution will call for the prompt dismantling and withdrawal of all offensive weapons in Cuba, under the supervision of U.N. observers, before the quarantine can be lifted.   *Personalizes issue*

Seventh and finally: I call upon Chairman Khrushchev to halt and eliminate this clandestine, reckless, and provocative threat to world peace and to stable relations between our two nations. I call upon him further to abandon this course of world domination, and to join in an historic effort to end the perilous arms race and to transform the history of man. He has an opportunity now to move the world back from the abyss of destruction—by returning to his government's own words that it had no need to station missiles outside its own territory, and withdrawing these weapons from Cuba—by refraining from any action which will widen or deepen the present crisis—and then by participating in a search for peaceful and permanent solutions.

This Nation is prepared to present its case against the Soviet threat to peace, and our own proposals for a peaceful world, at any time and in any forum—in the OAS, in the United Nations, or in any other meeting that could be useful—without limiting our freedom of action. We have in the past made strenuous efforts to limit the spread of nuclear weapons. We have proposed the elimination of all arms and military bases in a fair and effective disarmament treaty. We are prepared to discuss new proposals for the removal of tensions on both sides—including the possibilities of a genuinely independent Cuba, free to determine its own destiny. We have no wish to war with the Soviet Union—for we are a peaceful people who desire to live in peace with all other peoples.

But it is difficult to settle or even discuss these problems in an atmosphere of intimidation. That is why this latest Soviet threat—or any other threat which is made either independently or in response to our actions this week—must and will be met with determination. Any hostile move anywhere in the world against the safety and freedom of peoples to whom we are committed—including in particular the brave people of West Berlin—will be met by whatever action is needed.

Finally, I want to say a few words to the captive people of Cuba, to whom this speech is being directly carried by special radio facilities. I speak to you as a friend, as one who knows of your deep attachment to your fatherland, as one who shares your aspirations for liberty and justice for all. And I have watched and the American people have watched with deep sorrow how your nationalist revolution was betrayed—and how your fatherland fell under foreign domination. Now your leaders are no longer Cuban leaders inspired by Cuban ideals. They are puppets and agents of an international conspiracy which has turned Cuba against your friends and neighbors in the Americas—and turned it into the first Latin American country to become a target for nuclear war—the first Latin American country to have these weapons on its soil.

B/c we will attack you — .These new weapons are not in your interest. They contribute nothing to your peace and well-being. They can only undermine it. But this country has no wish to cause you to suffer or to impose any system upon you. We know that your lives and land are being used as pawns by those who deny your freedom.

Many times in the past, the Cuban people have risen to throw out tyrants who destroyed their liberty. And I have no doubt that most Cubans today look forward to the time when they will be truly free—free from foreign domination, free to choose their own leaders, free to select their own system, free to own their own land, free to speak and write and worship without fear or degradation. And then shall Cuba be welcomed back to the society of free nations and to the associations of this hemisphere.

My fellow citizens: let no one doubt that this is a difficult and dangerous effort on which we have set out. No one can foresee precisely what course it will take or what costs or casualties will be incurred. Many months of sacrifice and self-discipline lie ahead—months in which both our patience and our will will be tested—months in which many threats and denunciations will keep us aware of our dangers. But the greatest danger of all would be to do nothing.

The path we have chosen for the present is full of hazards, as all paths are—but it is the one most consistent with our character and courage as a nation and our commitments around the world. The cost of freedom is always high—but Americans have always paid it. And one path we shall never choose, and that is the path of surrender or submission.

Our goal is not the victory of might, but the vindication of right—not peace at the expense of freedom, but both peace *and* freedom, here in this hemisphere, and, we hope, around the world. God willing, that goal will be achieved.

Peace

Commencement Address at American University
Washington, D.C.
June 10, 1963

In this speech Kennedy finally and boldly announced a major change in American policy toward the Soviet Union. Sobered by the nuclear confrontation over Cuba in 1962 and bolstered by the failure of the Republicans to pick up seats in the off-term Congressional election, Kennedy apparently felt strong enough politically to advocate a policy of rapprochement with the Soviet Union. Khrushchev called the speech the best by an American President since Roosevelt. This speech set the scene for the successful negotiations that produced the limited nuclear test ban treaty and eventually became the cornerstone of contemporary American-Soviet relations.

It is with great pride that I participate in this ceremony of the American University, sponsored by the Methodist Church, founded by Bishop John Fletcher Hurst, and first opened by

President Woodrow Wilson in 1914. This is a young and growing university, but it has already fulfilled Bishop Hurst's enlightened hope for the study of history and public affairs in a city devoted to the making of history and to the conduct of the public's business. By sponsoring this institution of higher learning for all who wish to learn, whatever their color or their creed, the Methodists of this area and the Nation deserve the Nation's thanks, and I commend all those who are today graduating.

Professor Woodrow Wilson once said that every man sent out from a university should be a man of his nation as well as a man of his time, and I am confident that the men and women who carry the honor of graduating from this institution will continue to give from their lives, from their talents, a high measure of public service and public support.

"There are few earthly things more beautiful than a university," wrote John Masefield, in his tribute to English universities—and his words are equally true today. He did not refer to spires and towers, to campus greens and ivied walls. He admired the splendid beauty of the university, he said, because it was "a place where those who hate ignorance may strive to know, where those who perceive truth may strive to make others see."

I have, therefore, chosen this time and this place to discuss a topic on which ignorance too often abounds and the truth is too rarely perceived—yet it is the most important topic on earth: world peace.

What kind of peace do I mean? What kind of peace do we seek? Not a Pax Americana enforced on the world by Amercian weapons of war. Not the peace of the grave or the security of the slave. I am talking about genuine peace, the kind of peace that makes life on earth worth living, the kind that enables men and nations to grow and to hope and to build a better life for their children—not merely peace for Americans but peace for all men and women—not merely peace in our time but peace for all time.

I speak of peace because of the new face of war. Total war makes no sense in an age when great powers can maintain large and relatively invulnerable nuclear forces and refuse to surrender without resort to those forces. It makes no sense in an age when a single nuclear weapon contains almost ten times the explosive force delivered by all of the allied air forces in the Second World War. It makes no sense in an age when the deadly poisons produced by a nuclear exchange would be carried by wind and water and soil and seed to the far corners of the globe and to generations yet unborn.

Today the expenditure of billions of dollars every year on weapons acquired for the purpose of making sure we never need to use them is essential to keeping the peace. But surely the acquisition of such idle stockpiles—which can only destroy and never create—is not the only, much less the most efficient, means of assuring peace.

I speak of peace, therefore, as the necessary rational end of rational men. I realize that the pursuit of peace is not as dramatic as the pursuit of war—and frequently the words of the pursuer fall on deaf ears. But we have no more urgent task.

Some say that it is useless to speak of world peace or world law or world disarmament— and that it will be useless until the leaders of the Soviet Union adopt a more enlightened attitude. I hope they do. I believe we can help them do it. But I also believe that we must reexamine our own attitude—as individuals and as a Nation—for our attitude is as essential as theirs. And every graduate of this school, every thoughtful citizen who despairs of war and wishes to bring peace, should begin by looking inward—by examining his own attitude toward the possibilities of peace, toward the Soviet Union, toward the course of the cold war and toward freedom and peace here at home.

First: Let us examine our attitude toward peace itself. Too many of us think it is impossible. Too many think it unreal. But that is a dangerous, defeatist belief. It leads to the conclusion that war is inevitable—that mankind is doomed—that we are gripped by forces we cannot control.

We need not accept that view. Our problems are manmade—therefore, they can be solved by man. And man can be as big as he wants. No problem of human destiny is beyond human beings. Man's reason and spirit have often solved the seemingly unsolvable—and we believe they can do it again.

I am not referring to the absolute, infinite concept of universal peace and good will of which some fantasist and fanatics dream. I do not deny the value of hopes and dreams but we merely invite discouragement and incredulity by making that our only and immediate goal.

Let us focus instead on a more practical, more attainable peace—based not on a sudden revolution in human nature but on a gradual evolution in human institutions—on a series of concrete actions and effective agreements which are in the interest of all concerned. There is no single, simple key to this peace—no grand or magic formula to be adopted by one or two powers. Genuine peace must be the product of many nations, the sum of many acts. It must be dynamic, not static, changing to meet the challenge of each new generation. For peace is a process—a way of solving problems.

With such a peace, there will still be quarrels and conflicting interests, as there are within families and nations. World peace, like community peace, does not require that each man love his neighbor—it requires only that they live together in mutual tolerance, submitting their disputes to a just and peaceful settlement. And history teaches us that enmities between nations, as between individuals, do not last forever. However fixed our likes and dislikes may seem, the tide of time and events will often bring surprising changes in the relations between nations and neighbors.

So let us persevere. Peace need not be impracticable, and war need not be inevitable. By defining our goal more clearly, by making it seem more manageable and less remote, we can help all peoples to see it, to draw hope from it, and to move irresistibly toward it.

Second: Let us reexamine our attitude toward the Soviet Union. It is discouraging to think that their leaders may actually believe what their propagandists write. It is discouraging to read a recent authoritative Soviet text on *Military Strategy* and find, on page after page, wholly baseless and incredible claims—such as the allegation that "American imperialist circles are preparing to unleash different types of wars . . . that there is a very real threat of a preventive war being unleashed by American imperialists against the Soviet Union . . . [and that] the political aims of the American imperialists are to enslave economically and politically the European and other capitalist countries . . . [and] to achieve world domination . . . by means of aggressive wars."

Truly, as it was written long ago: "The wicked flee when no man pursueth." Yet it is sad to read these Soviet statements—to realize the extent of the gulf between us. But it is also a warning—a warning to the American people not to fall into the same trap as the Soviets, not to see only a distorted and desperate view of the other side, not to see conflict as inevitable, accommodation as impossible, and communication as nothing more than an exchange of threats.

No government or social system is so evil that its people must be considered as lacking in virtue. As Americans, we find communism profoundly repugnant as a negation of personal freedom and dignity. But we can still hail the Russian people for their many achievements—in science and space, in economic and industrial growth, in culture and in acts of courage.

Among the many traits the peoples of our two countries have in common, none is stronger than our mutual abhorrence of war. Almost unique, among the major world powers, we have never been at war with each other. And no nation in the history of battle ever suffered more than the Soviet Union suffered in the course of the Second World War. At least 20 million lost their lives. Countless millions of homes and farms were burned or sacked. A third of the nation's territory, including nearly two-thirds of its industrial base, was turned into a wasteland—a loss equivalent to the devastation of this country east of Chicago.

Today, should total war ever break out again—no matter how—our two countries would become the primary targets. It is an ironic but accurate fact that the two strongest powers are the two in the most danger of devastation. All we have built, all we have worked for, would be destroyed in the first 24 hours. And even in the cold war, which brings burdens and dangers to so many countries, including this Nation's closest allies—our two countries bear the heaviest burdens. For we are both devoting massive sums of money to weapons that could be better devoted to combating ignorance, poverty, and disease. We are both caught up in vicious and dangerous cycle in which suspicion on one side breeds suspicion on the other, and new weapons beget counterweapons.

In short, both the United States and its allies, and the Soviet Union and its allies, have a mutually deep interest in a just and genuine peace and in halting the arms race. Agreements to this end are in the interests of the Soviet Union as well as ours—and even the most hostile nations can be relied upon to accept and keep those treaty obligations, and only those treaty obligations, which are in their own interest.

So, let us not be blind to our differences—but let us also direct attention to our common interests and to the means by which those differences can be resolved. And if we cannot end now our differences, at least we can help make the world safe for diversity. For, in the final analysis, our most basic common link is that we all inhabit this small planet. We all breathe the same air. We all cherish our children's future. And we are all mortal.

Third: Let us reexamine our attitude toward the cold war, remembering that we are not engaged in a debate, seeking to pile up debating points. We are not here distributing blame or pointing the finger of judgment. We must deal with the world as it is, and not as it might have been had the history of the last 18 years been different.

We must, therefore, persevere in the search for peace in the hope that constructive changes within the Communist bloc might bring within reach solutions which now seem beyond us. We must conduct our affairs in such a way that it becomes in the Communists' interest to agree on a genuine peace. Above all, while defending our own vital interests, nuclear powers must avert those confrontations which bring an adversary to a choice of either a humiliating retreat or a nuclear war. To adopt that kind of course in the nuclear age would be evidence only of the bankruptcy of our policy—or of a collective death-wish for the world.

To secure these ends, America's weapons are nonprovocative, carefully controlled, designed to deter, and capable of selective use. Our military forces are committed to peace and disciplined in self-restraint. Our diplomats are instructed to avoid unnecessary irritants and purely rhetorical hostility.

For we can seek a relaxation of tensions without relaxing our guard. And, for our part, we do not need to use threats to prove that we are resolute. We do not need to jam foreign broadcasts out of fear our faith will be eroded. We are unwilling to impose our system on any unwilling people—but we are willing and able to engage in peaceful competition with any people on earth.

Meanwhile, we seek to strengthen the United Nations, to help solve its financial problems, to make it a more effective instrument for peace, to develop it into a genuine world security system—a system capable of resolving disputes on the basis of law, of insuring the security of the large and the small, and of creating conditions under which arms can finally be abolished.

At the same time we seek to keep peace inside the non-Communist world, where many nations, all of them our friends, are divided over issues which weaken Western unity, which invite Communist intervention of which threaten to erupt into war. Our efforts in West New Guinea, in the Congo, in the Middle East, and in the Indian subcontinent, have been persistent and patient despite criticism from both sides. We have also tried to set an example for others—by seeking to adjust small but significant differences with our own closest neighbors in Mexico and in Canada.

Speaking of other nations, I wish to make one point clear. We are bound to many nations by alliances. Those alliances exist because our concern and theirs substantially overlap. Our commitment to defend Western Europe and West Berlin, for example, stands undiminished because of the identity of our vital interest. The United States will make no deal with the Soviet Union at the expense of other nations and other peoples, not merely because they are our partners, but also because their interests and ours converge.

Our interests converge, however, not only in defending the frontiers of freedom, but in pursuing the paths of peace. It is our hope—and the purpose of allied policies—to convince the Soviet Union that she, too, should let each nation choose its own future, so long as that choice does not interfere with the choices of others. The Communist drive to impose their political and economic system on others is the primary cause of world tension today. For there can be no doubt that, if all nations could refrain from interfering in the self-determination of others, the peace would be much more assured.

This will require a new effort to achieve world law—a new context for world discussions. It will require increased understanding between the Soviets and ourselves. And increased understanding will require increased contact and communication. One step in this direction is the proposed arrangement for a direct line between Moscow and Washington, to avoid on each side the dangerous delays, misunderstandings, and misreadings of the other's actions which might occur at a time of crisis.

We have also been talking in Geneva about other first-step measures of arms control, designed to limit the intensity of the arms race and to reduce the risks of accidental war. Our primary long-range interest in Geneva, however, is general and complete disarmament—designed to take place by stages, permitting parallel political developments to build the new institutions of peace which would take the place of arms. The pursuit of disarmament has been an effort of this Government since the 1920's. It has been urgently sought by the past three administrations. And however dim the prospects may be today, we intend to continue this effort—to continue it in order that all countries, including our own, can better grasp what the problems and possibilities of disarmament are.

The one major area of these negotiations where the end is in sight, yet where a fresh start is badly needed, is in a treaty to outlaw nuclear tests. The conclusion of such a treaty, so near and yet so far, would check the spiraling arms race in one of its most dangerous areas. It would place the nuclear powers in a position to deal more effectively with one of the greatest hazards which man faces in 1963, the further spread of nuclear arms. It would increase our security—it would decrease the prospects of war. Surely this goal is sufficiently important to require our steady pursuit, yielding neither to the temptation to give up the whole effort nor the temptation to give up our insistence on vital and responsible safeguards.

I am taking this opportunity, therefore, to announce two important decisions in this regard.

First: Chairman Khrushchev, Prime Minister Macmillan, and I have agreed that high-level discussions will shortly begin in Moscow looking toward early agreement on a comprehensive test ban treaty. Our hopes must be tempered with the caution of history—but with our hopes go the hopes of all mankind.

Second: To make clear our good faith and solemn convictions on the matter, I now declare that the United States does not propose to conduct nuclear tests in the atmosphere so long as other states do not do so. We will not be the first to resume. Such a declaration is no substitute for a formal binding treaty, but I hope it will help us achieve one. Nor would such a treaty be a substitute for disarmament, but I hope it will help us achieve it.

Finally, my fellow Americans, let us examine our attitude toward peace and freedom here at home. The quality and spirit of our own society must justify and support our efforts abroad. We must show it in the dedication of our own lives—as many of you who are graduating today will have a unique opportunity to do, by serving without pay in the Peace Corps abroad or in the proposed National Service Corps here at home.

But wherever we are, we must all, in our daily lives, live up to the age-old faith that peace and freedom walk together. In too many of our cities today, the peace is not secure because freedom is incomplete.

It is the responsibility of the executive branch at all levels of government—local, State, and National—to provide and protect that freedom for all of our citizens by all means within their authority. It is the responsibility of the legislative branch at all levels, wherever that authority is not now adequate, to make it adequate. And it is the responsibility of all citizens in all sections of this country to respect the rights of all others and to respect the law of the land.

All this is not unrelated to world peace. "When a man's ways please the Lord," the Scriptures tell us, "he maketh even his enemies to be at peace with him." And is not peace, in the last analysis, basically a matter of human rights—the right to live out our lives without fear of devastation—the right to breathe air as nature provided it—the right of future generations to a healthy existence?

While we proceed to safeguard our national interests, let us also safeguard human interests. And the elimination of war and arms is clearly in the interest of both. No treaty, however much it may be to the advantage of all, however tightly it may be worded, can provide absolute security against the risks of deception and evasion. But it can—if it is sufficiently effective in its enforcement and if it is sufficiently in the interests of its signers—offer far more security and far fewer risks than an unabated, uncontrolled, unpredictable arms race.

The United States, as the world knows, will never start a war. We do not want a war. We do not now expect a war. This generation of Americans has already had enough—more than enough—of war and hate and oppression. We shall be prepared if others wish it. We shall be alert to try to stop it. But we shall also do our part to build a world of peace where the weak are safe and the strong are just. We are not helpless before that task or hopeless of its success. Confident and unafraid, we labor on—not toward a strategy of annihilation but toward a strategy of peace.

Civil Rights: A Moral Issue
Washington, D.C.
June 11, 1963

On this date Governor George Wallace of Alabama kept a campaign pledge and stood at the entrace to the administration building of the University of Alabama to bar the admittance of several blacks. Kennedy federalized part of the Alabama National Guard and sent in Federal Marshalls to insure that the University would be integrated. Then, he spoke to the nation to justify his decision. This speech sharply contrasts with the more moderate approach he had taken the previous year in the Meredith case. Most importantly, this civil rights battle pushed Kennedy's speech on American-Soviet relations of the day before at American University off the front pages of the newspapers and thus interrupted his campaign for understanding the vital changes he was advocating in foreign affairs.

This afternoon, following a series of threats and defiant statements, the presence of Alabama National Guardsmen was required on the University of Alabama to carry out the final and unequivocal order of the United States District Court of the Northern District of Alabama. That order called for the admission of two clearly qualified young Alabama residents who happened to have been born Negro.

That they were admitted peacefully on the campus is due in good measure to the conduct of the students of the University of Alabama, who met their responsibilities in a constructive way.

I hope that every American, regardless of where he lives, will stop and examine his conscience about this and other related incidents. This Nation was founded by men of many nations and backgrounds. It was founded on the principle that all men are created equal, and that the rights of every man are diminished when the rights of one man are threatened.

Today we are committed to a worldwide struggle to promote and protect the rights of all who wish to be free. And when Americans are sent to Viet-Nam or West Berlin, we do not ask for whites only. It ought to be possible, therefore, for American students of any color to attend any public institution they select without having to be backed up by troops.

It ought to be possible for American consumers of any color to receive equal service in places of public accommodation, such as hotels and restaurants and theaters and retail stores, without being forced to resort to demonstrations in the street, and it ought to be possible for American citizens of any color to register and to vote in a free election without interference or fear of reprisal.

It ought to be possible, in short, for every American to enjoy the privileges of being American without regard to his race or his color. In short, every American ought to have the right to be treated as he would wish to be treated, as one would wish his children to be treated. But this is not the case.

The Negro baby born in America today, regardless of the section of the Nation in which he is born, has about one-half as much chance of completing a high school as a white baby born in the same place on the same day, one-third as much chance of completing college, one-third as much chance of becoming a professional man, twice as much chance of becoming unemployed, about one-seventh as much chance of earning $10,000 a year, a life expectancy which is 7 years shorter, and the prospects of earning only half as much.

This is not a sectional issue. Difficulties over segregation and discrimination exist in every city, in every State of the Union, producing in many cities a rising tide of discontent that threatens the public safety. Nor is this a partisan issue. In a time of domestic crisis men of good will and generosity should be able to unite regardless of party or politics. This is not even a legal or legislative issue alone. It is better to settle these matters in the courts than on the streets, and new laws are needed at every level, but law alone cannot make men see right.

We are confronted primarily with a moral issue. It is as old as the scriptures and is as clear as the American Constitution.

The heart of the question is whether all Americans are to be afforded equal rights and equal opportunities, whether we are going to treat our fellow Americans as we want to be treated. If an American, because his skin is dark, cannot eat lunch in a restaurant open to the public, if he cannot send his children to the best public school available, if he cannot vote for the public officials who represent him, if, in short, he cannot enjoy the full and free life which all of us want, then who among us would be content to have the color of his skin changed and stand in his place? Who among us would then be content with the counsels of patience and delay?

One hundred years of delay have passed since President Lincoln freed the slaves, yet their heirs, their grandsons, are not fully free. They are not yet freed from the bonds of injustice. They are not yet freed from social and economic oppression. And this Nation, for all its hopes and all its boasts, will not be fully free until all its citizens are free.

We preach freedom around the world, and we mean it, and we cherish our freedom here at home, but are we to say to the world, and much more importantly, to each other that this is a land of the free except for the Negroes; that we have no second-class citizens except Negroes; that we have no class or cast system, no ghettoes, no master race except with respect to Negroes?

Now the time has come for this Nation to fulfill its promise. The events in Birmingham and elsewhere have so increased the cries for equality that no city or State or legislative body can prudently choose to ignore them.

The fires of frustration and discord are burning in every city, North and South, where legal remedies are not at hand. Redress is sought in the streets, in demonstrations, parades, and protests which create tensions and threaten violence and threaten lives.

We face, therefore, a moral crisis as a country and as a people. It cannot be met by repressive police action. It cannot be left to increased demonstrations in the streets. It cannot be quieted by token moves or talk. It is a time to act in the Congress, in your State and local legislative body and, above all, in all of our daily lives.

It is not enough to pin the blame on others, to say this is a problem of one section of the country or another, or deplore the fact that we face. A great change is at hand, and our task, our obligation, is to make that revolution, that change, peaceful and constructive for all.

Those who do nothing are inviting shame as well as violence. Those who act boldly are recognizing right as well as reality.

Next week I shall ask the Congress of the United States to act, to make a commitment it has not fully made in this century to the proposition that race has no place in American life or law. The Federal judiciary has upheld that proposition in a series of forthright cases. The executive branch has adopted that proposition in the conduct of its affairs, including the employment of Federal personnel, the use of Federal facilities, and the sale of federally financed housing.

But there are other necessary measures which only the Congress can provide, and they must be provided at this session. The old code of equity law under which we live commands for every wrong a remedy, but in too many communities, in too many parts of the country, wrongs are inflicted on Negro citizens and there are no remedies at law. Unless the Congress acts, their only remedy is in the street.

I am, therefore, asking the Congress to enact legislation giving all Americans the right to be served in facilities which are open to the public—hotels, restaurants, theaters, retail stores, and similar establishments.

This seems to me to be an elementary right. Its denial is an arbitrary indignity that no American in 1963 should have to endure, but many do.

I have recently met with scores of business leaders urging them to take voluntary action to end this discrimination and I have been encouraged by their response, and in the last 2 weeks over 75 cities have seen progress made in desegregating these kinds of facilities. But many are unwilling to act alone, and for this reason, nationwide legislation is needed if we are to move this problem from the streets to the courts.

I am also asking Congress to authorize the Federal Government to participate more fully in lawsuits designed to end segregation in public education. We have succeeded in persuading many districts to desegregate voluntarily. Dozens have admitted Negroes without violence. Today a Negro is attending a State-supported institution in every one of our 50 States, but the pace is very slow.

Too many Negro children entering segregated grade schools at the time of the Supreme Court's decision 9 years ago will enter segregated high schools this fall, having suffered a loss which can never be restored. The lack of an adequate education denies the Negro a chance to get a decent job.

The orderly implementation of the Supreme Court decision, therefore, cannot be left solely to those who may not have the economic resources to carry the legal action or who may be subject to harassment.

Other features will be also requested, including greater protection for the right to vote. But legislation, I repeat, cannot solve this problem alone. It must be solved in the homes of every American in every community across our country.

In this respect, I want to pay tribute to those citizens North and South who have been working in their communities to make life better for all. They are acting not out of a sense of legal duty but out of a sense of human decency.

Like our soldiers and sailors in all parts of the world they are meeting freedom's challenge on the firing line, and I salute them for their honor and their courage.

My fellow Americans, this is a problem which faces us all—in every city of the North as well as the South. Today there are Negroes unemployed, two or three times as many compared to whites, inadequate in education, moving into the large cities, unable to find work, young people particularly out of work without hope, denied equal rights, denied the opportunity to eat at a restaurant or lunch counter or go to a movie theater, denied the right to a decent education, denied almost today the right to attend a State university even though qualified. It seems to me that these are matters which concern us all, not merely Presidents or Congressmen or Governors, but every citizen of the United States.

This is one country. It has become one country because all of us and all the people who came here had an equal chance to develop their talents.

We cannot say to 10 percent of the population that you can't have that right; that your children can't have the chance to develop whatever talents they have; that the only way that they are going to get their rights is to go into the streets and demonstrate. I think we owe them and we owe ourselves a better country than that.

Therefore, I am asking for your help in making it easier for us to move ahead and to provide the kind of equality of treatment which we would want ourselves; to give a chance for every child to be educated to the limit of his talents.

As I have said before, not every child has an equal talent or an equal ability or an equal motivation, but they should have the equal right to develop their talent and their ability and their motivation, to make something of themselves.

We have a right to expect that the Negro community will be responsible, will uphold the law, but they have a right to expect that the law will be fair, that the Constitution will be color blind, as Justice Harlan said at the turn of the century.

This is what we are talking about and this is a matter which concerns this country and what it stands for, and in meeting it I ask the support of all our citizens.

"Ich Bin Ein Berliner"

Rudolph Wilde Platz
West Berlin
June 26, 1963

This speech represented one of Kennedy's major rhetorical successes. Kennedy stopped in Berlin during his tour of Europe and delivered this brief, harsh address to more than three-fifths of the population of West Berlin who gathered in the Platz to cheer him. The content of the speech directly contradicts his remarks at American University only 16 days before, but the wild reception accorded Kennedy diminished the importance of that contradiction.

I am proud to come to this city as the guest of your distinguished Mayor, who has symbolized throughout the world the fighting spirit of West Berlin. And I am proud to visit the Federal Republic with your distinguished Chancellor who for so many years has committed Germany to democracy and freedom and progress, and to come here in the company of my fellow American, General Clay, who has been in this city during its great moments of crisis and will come again if ever needed.

Two thousand years ago the proudest boast was *"civis Romanus sum."* Today, in the world of freedom, the proudest boast is *"Ich bin ein Berliner."*

There are many people in the world who really don't understand, or say they don't, what is the great issue between the free world and the Communist world. Let them come to Berlin. There are some who say that communism is the wave of the future. Let them come to Berlin. And there are some who say in Europe and elsewhere we can work with the Communists. Let them come to Berlin. And there are even a few who say that it is true that communism is an evil system, but it permits us to make economic progress. *Lass' sie nach Berlin kommen.* Let them come to Berlin.

Freedom has many difficulties and democracy is not perfect, but we have never had to put a wall up to keep our people in, to prevent them from leaving us. I want to say, on behalf of my countrymen, who live many miles away on the other side of the Atlantic, who are far distant from you, that they take the greatest pride that they have been able to share with you, even from a distance, the story of the last 18 years. I know of no town, no city, that has been besieged for 18 years that still lives with the vitality and the force, and the hope and the determination of the city of West Berlin. While the wall is the most obvious and vivid demonstration of the failures of the Communist system, for all the world to see, we take no satisfaction in it, for it is, as your Mayor has said, an offense not only against history but an offense against humanity, separating families, dividing husbands and wives and brothers and sisters, and dividing a people who wish to be joined together.

What is true of this city is true of Germany—real, lasting peace in Europe can never be assured as long as one German out of four is denied the elementary right of free men, and that is to make a free choice. In 18 years of peace and good faith, this generation of Germans has earned the right to be free, including the right to unite their families and their nation in lasting peace, with good will to all people. You live in a defended island of freedom, but your life is part of the main. So let me ask you, as I close, to lift your eyes beyond the dangers of today, to the hopes of tomorrow, beyond the freedom merely of this city of Berlin, or your country of Germany, to the advance of freedom everywhere, beyond the wall to the day of peace with justice, beyond yourselves and ourselves to all mankind.

Freedom is indivisible, and when one man is enslaved, all are not free. When all are free, then we can look forward to that day when this city will be joined as one and this country and this great Continent of Europe in a peaceful and hopeful globe. When that day finally comes, as it will, the people of West Berlin can take sober satisfaction in the fact that they were in the front lines for almost two decades.

All free men, wherever they may live, are citizens of Berlin, and, therefore, as a free man, I take pride in the words *"Ich bin ein Berliner."*

Lyndon Baines Johnson (1963–1969)

Lyndon B. Johnson assumed the Presidency through tragic circumstances. Yet, from a political viewpoint he was in a stronger position than Kennedy had been. The nation, wracked by grief, rallied to the new President's side, and Johnson was not about to ignore the political value of the national unity tragedy had bred. Indeed, in his first speech before Congress on November 27, 1963 he drew upon the grief for the martyred President to press for early passage of the Civil Rights Bill and the tax cut that had been lingering in Congress. And they were passed the next year.

Johnson's Presidential rhetoric may be divided into two periods. The first extends from 1963 to 1966 and may fairly be called a rhetoric of announcements or a rhetoric of justification. Though it over-laps somewhat, the second period runs from 1966 to 1968 and may be described as a rhetoric of defense against his conduct of the American-Vietnamese war.

During the first 3 years of his Administration Johnson encountered little opposition to his programs. He was not in the position of Kennedy before him, nor Nixon after him of having to build a majority constituency. Part of the reason for this lay, as already mentioned, in the mood of unity that accompanied the assassination of Kennedy. A second reason lay in Johnson's mastery of Congress.[1] He knew how to manipulate and persuade and soothe members of Congress as well, if not better, than any man who has ever occupied the Presidency. But most important, his crushing defeat of Senator Barry Goldwater in the 1964 election gave him a "mandate" to act with apparent overwhelming support from the public on the domestic issues that he deemed imperative. Furthermore, that victory left his opposition in disarray. Republicans were divided by the bitter primaries and the defeat of the 1964 election. Conservatives, who opposed Johnson's domestic legislation, muted their criticism in light of the liberal freshmen legislators who had been elected in the wake of the President's victory. Johnson, thus, acted as if he had a "consensus" mandated by the election and began announcing legislation that needed to be passed and limited himself to justifying the reasons for that legislation. He did not need to persuade people to join him, but rather needed to motivate them to act upon the programs he already had announced. With the appearance of great public support and with his influence over Congress, Johnson ruled the country for 3 years as no one has since the days of Franklin Roosevelt.

However, his handling of the Dominican Republic intervention raised questions about both his liberalism in foreign affairs and his veracity in reasoning with the American people.

His transformation of the Vietnam civil war into an American-Vietnamese war beginning in 1965 deeply offended those who had voted against Goldwater because they believed he might do the very things Johnson now was doing in Vietnam.

The turning point came with the Congressional elections of 1966. The Democrats lost 47 House seats and 3 Senate seats. Republicans picked up 8 governorships and 540 state legislative seats. The tide had turned against Johnson. The reasons were varied ranging from distrust of the President to a feeling among the middle-class of white America that Blacks were getting too much from government.

But for Johnson the consuming issue became Vietnam. During the last year and a half of his Presidency he devoted the majority of his attention to that problem. He found himself besieged on the left by those opposed to the war who, on occasion, chanted: "Hey, hey, LBJ! How many kids did you kill today?" The critics on the right castigated him for limiting the war and urged an all-out effort to win. Thus, Johnson was attacked from every quarter and found himself neglecting his Great Society of domestic programs to defend his policies in Vietnam. The result was polarization of the American public, demonstrations that turned into violence, and a period of civil turmoil unmatched since the days of the Depression.

After the Tet Offensive of February, 1968 in which the Viet Cong and North Vietnamese demonstrated that they could not only invade major South Vietnamese cities, but hold them for a time as well, Johnson ordered a review of American policy in Vietnam. On March 31, 1968 he announced his conclusions. He would end the bombing, for the most part, of North Vietnam. He would seek a negotiated withdrawal of American forces. And he would not seek nor would he accept the Democratic nomination for re-election.

Johnson's rhetoric is the least varied of the 3 Presidents of the imperial age. It is a problem-solving rhetoric. A man of action, Johnson saw problems and sought to solve them usually immediately and sometimes without thinking them through clearly.[2] But such a sparse description hardly does justice to him. For all his vanity, his bull-headedness, his self-pity, Johnson possessed a social compassion for those who did not share America's opportunities or riches. His speeches on these matters, especially his concern for Blacks in the United States, are genuinely moving. Undoubtedly, he has already achieved his place in American history as the greatest civil rights President we have yet seen.

But his personal weaknesses— "the credibility gap" as it became known—and his decision to make a small war in Southeast Asia into an American-Vietnamese War doomed his hopes for true greatness as a President. Lyndon Johnson came to the Presidency amid the tragedy of John Kennedy's assassination, and he left the Presidency amid the national tragedy of Vietnam.

Notes

1. Rowland Evans and Robert Novak, *Lyndon B. Johnson: The Exercise of Power* (New York: The New American Library, 1966), pp. 360-382.
2. Cf. Marvin E. Gettleman and David Mermelstein (eds.), *The Great Society Reader: The Failure of American Liberalism* (New York: Vintage Books, 1967), pp. 213-239.

"Let Us Continue"

Address Before a Joint Session of Congress
Washington, D.C.
November 27, 1963

Five days after the assassination of President Kennedy the new President, Lyndon B. Johnson, spoke to Congress and the nation in this televised address. For the American people as well as others around the world, this speech gave them their first glimpse of the man who was now President and the major policies he intended to pursue. The speech has three major sections: (1) a eulogy of Kennedy; (2) a reaffirmation of U.S. commitments at home and abroad; and (3) Johnson's own immediate legislative priorities—the early passage of the civil rights bill and a tax cut. The speech was frequently interrupted by applause which could have been taken by others (especially foreign nations) as symbolic of the support for the President in this uncertain and tragic time.

All I have I would have given gladly not to be standing here today.

The greatest leader of our time has been struck down by the foulest deed of our time. Today John Fitzgerald Kennedy lives on in the immortal words and works that he left behind. He lives on in the mind and memories of mankind. He lives on in the hearts of his countrymen.

No words are sad enough to express our sense of loss. No words are strong enough to express our determination to continue the forward thrust of America that he began.

The dream of conquering the vastness of space—the dream of partnership across the Atlantic—and across the Pacific as well—the dream of a Peace Corps in less developed nations—the dream of education for all of our children—the dream of jobs for all who seek them and need them—the dream of care for our elderly—the dream of an allout attack on mental illness—and above all, the dream of equal rights for all Americans, whatever their race or color—these and other American dreams have been vitalized by his drive and by his dedication.

And now the ideas and the ideals which he so nobly represented must and will be translated into effective action.

Under John Kennedy's leadership, this Nation has demonstrated that it has the courage to seek peace, and it has the fortitude to risk war. We have proved that we are a good and reliable friend to those who seek peace and freedom. We have shown that we can also be a formidable foe to those who reject the path of peace and those who seek to impose upon us or our allies the yoke of tyranny.

This Nation will keep its commitments from South Viet-Nam to West Berlin. We will be unceasing in the search for peace; resourceful in our pursuit of areas of aggreement even with those with whom we differ; and generous and loyal to those who join with us in common cause.

In this age when there can be no losers in peace and no victors in war, we must recognize the obligation to match national strength with national restraint. We must be prepared at one and the same time for both the confrontation of power and the limitation of power. We must be ready to defend the national interest and to negotiate the common interest. This is the path that we shall continue to pursue. Those who test our courage will find it strong, and those who seek our friendship will find it honorable. We will demonstrate anew that the strong can be just in the use of strength; and the just can be strong in the defense of justice.

And let all know we will extend no special privilege and impose no persecution. We will carry on the fight against poverty and misery, and disease and ignorance, in other lands and in our own.

We will serve all the Nation, not one section or one sector, or one group, but all Americans. These are the United States—a united people with a united purpose.

Our American unity does not depend upon unanimity. We have differences; but now, as in the past, we can derive from those differences strength, not weakness, wisdom, not despair. Both as a people and a government, we can unite upon a program, a program which is wise and just, enlightened and constructive.

For 32 years Capitol Hill has been my home. I have shared many moments of pride with you, pride in the ability of the Congress of the United States to act, to meet any crisis, to distill from our differences strong programs of national action.

An assassin's bullet has thrust upon me the awesome burden of the Presidency. I am here today to say I need your help; I cannot bear this burden alone. I need the help of all Americans, and all America. This Nation has experienced a profound shock, and in this critical moment, it is our duty, yours and mine, as the Government of the United States, to do away with uncertainty and doubt and delay, and to show that we are capable of decisive action; that from the brutal loss of our leader we will derive not weakness, but strength; that we can and will act and act now.

From this chamber of representative government, let all the world know and none misunderstand that I rededicate this Government to the unswerving support of the United Nations, to the honorable and determined execution of our commitments to our allies, to the maintenance of military strength second to none, to the defense of the strength and the stability of the dollar, to the expansion of our foreign trade, to the reinforcement of our programs of mutual assistance and cooperation in Asia and Africa, and to our Alliance for Progress in this hemisphere.

On the 20th day of January, in 1961, John F. Kennedy told his countrymen that our national work would not be finished "in the first thousand days, nor in the life of this administration, nor even perhaps in our lifetime on this planet. But," he said, "let us begin."

Today, in this moment of new resolve, I would say to all my fellow Americans, let us continue.

This is our challenge—not to hesitate, not to pause, not to turn about and linger over this evil moment, but to continue on our course so that we may fulfill the destiny that history has set for us. Our most immediate tasks are here on this Hill.

First, no memorial oration or eulogy could more eloquently honor President Kennedy's memory than the earliest possible passage of the civil rights bill for which he fought so long. We have talked long enough in this country about equal rights. We have talked for one hundred years or more. It is time now to write the next chapter, and to write it in the books of law.

I urge you again, as I did in 1957 and again in 1960, to enact a civil rights law so that we can move forward to eliminate from this Nation every trace of discrimination and oppression that is based upon race or color. There could be no greater source of strength to this Nation both at home and abroad.

And second, no act of ours could more fittingly continue the work of President Kennedy than the early passage of the tax bill for which he fought all this long year. This is a bill designed to increase our national income and Federal revenues, and to provide insurance against recession. That bill, if passed without delay, means more security for those now working, more jobs for those now without them, and more incentive for our economy.

In short, this is no time for delay. It is a time for action—strong, forward-looking action on the pending education bills to help bring the light of learning to every home and hamlet in America—strong, forward-looking action on youth employment opportunities; strong, forward-looking action on the pending foreign aid bill, making clear that we are not forfeiting our responsibilities to this hemisphere or to the world, nor erasing Executive flexibility in the conduct of our foreign affairs—and strong, prompt, and forward-looking action on the remaining appropriation bills.

In this new spirit of action, the Congress can expect the full cooperation and support of the executive branch. And in particular, I pledge that the expenditures of your Government will be administered with the utmost thrift and frugality. I will insist that the Government get a dollar's value for a dollar spent. The Government will set an example of prudence and economy. This does not mean that we will not meet our unfilled needs or that we will not honor our commitments. We will do both.

As one who has long served in both Houses of the Congress, I firmly believe in the independence and the integrity of the legislative branch. And I promise you that I shall always respect this. It is deep in the marrow of my bones. With equal firmness, I believe in the capacity and I believe in the ability of the Congress, despite the divisions of opinions which characterize our Nation, to act—to act wisely, to act vigorously, to act speedily when the need arises.

The need is here. The need is now. I ask your help.

We meet in grief, but let us also meet in renewed dedication and renewed vigor. Let us meet in action, in tolerance, and in mutual understanding. John Kennedy's death commands what his life conveyed—that America must move forward. The time has come for Americans of all races and creeds and political beliefs to understand and to respect one another. So let us put an end to the teaching and the preaching of hate and evil and violence. Let us turn away from the fanatics of the far left and the far right, from the apostles of bitterness and bigotry, from those defiant of law, and those who pour venom into our Nation's bloodstream.

I profoundly hope that the tragedy and the torment of these terrible days will bind us together in new fellowship, making us one people in our hour of sorrow. So let us here highly resolve that John Fitzgerald Kennedy did not live—or die—in vain. And on this Thanksgiving eve, as we gather together to ask the Lord's blessing, and give Him our thanks, let us unite in those familiar and cherished words:

America, America,
God shed His grace on thee,
And crown thy good
With brotherhood
From sea to shining sea.

War on Poverty

State of the Union Address
Washington, D.C.
January 8, 1964

In his first State of the Union Address Johnson declared "war on poverty" in America. Typically, his address was oriented to action, not thought. And typically, he promised more than he could possibly deliver.

I will be brief, for our time is necessarily short and our agenda is already long.

Last year's congressional session was the longest in peacetime history. With that foundation, let us work together to make this year's session the best in the Nation's history.

Let this session of Congress be known as the session which did more for civil rights than the last hundred sessions combined; as the session which enacted the most far-reaching tax cut of our time; as the session which declared all-out war on human poverty and unemployment in these United States; as the session which finally recognized the health needs of all our older citizens; as the session which reformed our tangled transportation and transit policies; as the session which achieved the most effective, efficient foreign aid program ever; and as the session which helped to build more homes, more schools, more libraries, and more hospitals than any single session of Congress in the history of our Republic.

All this and more can and must be done. It can be done by this summer, and it can be done without any increase in spending. In fact, under the budget that I shall shortly submit, it can be done with an actual reduction in Federal expenditures and Federal employment.

We have in 1964 a unique opportunity and obligation—to prove the success of our system; to disprove those cynics and critics at home and abroad who question our purpose and our competence.

If we fail, if we fritter and fumble away our opportunity in needless, senseless quarrels between Democrats and Republicans, or between the House and the Senate, or between the South and North, or between the Congress and the administration, then history will rightfully judge us harshly. But if we succeed, if we can achieve these goals by forging in this country a greater sense of union, then, and only then, can we take full satisfaction in the State of the Union.

Here in the Congress you can demonstrate effective legislative leadership by discharging the public business with clarity and dispatch, voting each important proposal up, or voting it down, but at least bringing it to a fair and a final vote.

Let us carry forward the plans and programs of John Fitzgerald Kennedy—not because of our sorrow or sympathy, but because they are right.

In his memory today, I especially ask all members of my own political faith, in this election year, to put your country ahead of your party, and to always debate principles; never debate personalities.

For my part, I pledge a progressive administration which is efficient, and honest and frugal. The budget to be submitted to the Congress shortly is in full accord with this pledge.

It will cut our deficit in half—from $10 billion to $4,900 million. It will be, in proportion to our national output, the smallest budget since 1951.

It will call for a substantial reduction in Federal employment, a feat accomplished only once before in the last 10 years. While maintaining the full strength of our combat defenses, it will call for the lowest number of civilian personnel in the Department of Defense since 1950.

It will call for total expenditures of $97,900 million—compared to $98,400 million for the current year, a reduction of more than $500 million. It will call for new obligational authority of $103,800 million—a reduction of more than $4 billion below last year's request of $107,900 million.

But it is not a standstill budget, for America cannot afford to stand still. Our population is growing. Our economy is more complex. Our people's needs are expanding.

But by closing down obsolete installations, by curtailing less urgent programs, by cutting back where cutting back seems to be wise, by insisting on a dollar's worth for a dollar spent, I am able to recommend in this reduced budget the most Federal support in history for education, for health, for retraining the unemployed, and for helping the economically and the physically handicapped.

This budget, and this year's legislative program, are designed to help each and every American citizen fulfill his basic hopes—his hopes for a fair chance to make good; his hopes for fair play from the law; his hopes for a full-time job on full-time pay; his hopes for a decent home for his family in a decent community; his hopes for a good school for his children with good teachers; and his hopes for security when faced with sickness or unemployment or old age.

Unfortunately, many Americans live on the outskirts of hope—some because of their poverty, and some because of their color, and all too many because of both. Our task is to help replace their despair with opportunity.

This administration today, here and now, declares unconditional war on poverty in America. I urge this Congress and all Americans to join with me in that effort.

It will not be a short or easy struggle, no single weapon or strategy will suffice, but we shall not rest until that war is won. The richest Nation on earth can afford to win it. We cannot afford to lose it. One thousand dollars invested in salvaging an unemployable youth today can return $40,000 or more in his lifetime.

Poverty is a national problem, requiring improved national organization and support. But this attack, to be effective, must also be organized at the State and the local level and must be supported and directed by State and local efforts.

For the war against poverty will not be won here in Washington. It must be won in the field, in every private home, in every public office, from the courthouse to the White House.

The program I shall propose will emphasize this cooperative approach to help that one-fifth of all American families with incomes too small to even meet their basic needs.

Our chief weapons in a more pinpointed attack will be better schools, and better health, and better homes, and better training, and better job opportunities to help more Americans, especially young Americans, escape from squalor and misery and unemployment rolls where other citizens help to carry them.

Very often a lack of jobs and money is not the cause of poverty, but the symptom. The cause may lie deeper—in our failure to give our fellow citizens a fair chance to develop their *beginning to A.A.*

own capacities, in a lack of education and training, in a lack of medical care and housing, in a lack of decent communities in which to live and bring up their children.

not just a Negro problem

But whatever the cause, our joint Federal-local effort must pursue poverty, pursue it wherever it exists—in city slums and small towns, in sharecropper shacks or in migrant worker camps, on Indian Reservations, among whites as well as Negroes, among the young as well as the aged, in the boom towns and in the depressed areas.

Our aim is not only to relieve the symptom of poverty, but to cure it and, above all, to prevent it. No single piece of legislation, however, is going to suffice.

→ We will launch a special effort in the chronically distressed areas of Appalachia.

→ We must expand our small but our successful area redevelopment program.

→ We must enact youth employment legislation to put jobless, aimless, hopeless youngsters to work on useful projects.

→ We must distribute more food to the needy through a broader food stamp program.

→ We must create a National Service Corps to help the economically handicapped of our own country as the Peace Corps now helps those abroad.

Hard to Absorb

→ We must modernize our unemployment insurance and establish a high-level commission on automation. If we have the brain power to invent these machines, we have the brain power to make certain that they are a boon and not a bane to humanity.

→ We must extend the coverage of our minimum wage laws to more than 2 million workers now lacking this basic protection of purchasing power.

→ We must, by including special school aid funds as part of our education program, improve the quality of teaching, training, and counseling in our hardest hit areas.

→ We must build more libraries in every area and more hospitals and nursing homes under the Hill-Burton Act, and train more nurses to staff them.

→ We must provide hospital insurance for our older citizens financed by every worker and his employer under Social Security, contributing no more than $1 a month during the employee's working career to protect him in his old age in a dignified manner without cost to the Treasury, against the devastating hardship of prolonged or repeated illness.

→ We must, as a part of a revised housing and urban renewal program, give more help to those displaced by slum clearance, provide more housing for our poor and our elderly, and seek as our ultimate goal in our free enterprise system a decent home for every American family.

→ We must help obtain more modern mass transit within our communities as well as low-cost transportation between them.

Above all, we must release $11 billion of tax reduction into the private spending stream to create new jobs and new markets in every area of this land.

All will benefit

These programs are obviously not for the poor or the underprivileged alone. Every American will benefit by the extension of social security to cover the hospital costs of their aged parents. Every American community will benefit from the construction or modernization of schools, libraries, hospitals, and nursing homes, from the training of more nurses and from the improvement of urban renewal in public transit. And every individual American taxpayer and every corporate taxpayer will benefit from the earliest possible passage of the pending tax bill from both the new investment it will bring and the new jobs that it will create.

That tax bill has been thoroughly discussed for a year. Now we need action. The new budget clearly allows it. Our taxpayers surely deserve it. Our economy strongly demands it.

And every month of delay dilutes its benefits in 1964 for consumption, for investment, and for employment.

For until the bill is signed, its investment incentives cannot be deemed certain, and the withholding rate cannot be reduced—and the most damaging and devastating thing you can do to any businessman in America is to keep him in doubt and to keep him guessing on what our tax policy is. And I say that we should now reduce to 14 percent instead of 15 percent our withholding rate.

I therefore urge the Congress to take final action on this bill by the first of February, if at all possible. For however proud we may be of the unprecedented progress of our free enterprise economy over the last 3 years, we should not and we cannot permit it to pause.

In 1963, for the first time in history, we crossed the 70 million job mark, but we will soon need more than 75 million jobs. In 1963 our gross national product reached the $600 billion level—$100 billion higher than when we took office. But it easily could and it should be still $30 billion higher today than it is.

Wages and profits and family income are also at their highest levels in history—but I would remind you that 4 million workers and 13 percent of our industrial capacity are still idle today.

We need a tax cut now to keep this country moving.

For our goal is not merely to spread the work. Our goal is to create more jobs. I believe the enactment of a 35-hour week would sharply increase costs, would invite inflation, would impair our ability to compete, and merely share instead of creating employment. But I am equally opposed to the 45- or 50-hour week in those industries where consistently excessive use of overtime causes increased unemployment.

So, therefore, I recommend legislation authorizing the creation of a tripartite industry committee to determine on an industry-by-industry basis as to where a higher penalty rate for overtime would increase job openings without unduly increasing costs, and authorizing the establishment of such higher rates.

Let me make one principle of this administration abundantly clear: All of these increased opportunities—in employment, in education, in housing, and in every field—must be open to Americans of every color. As far as the writ of Federal law will run, we must abolish not some, but all racial discrimination. For this is not merely an economic issue, or a social, political, or international issue. It is a moral issue, and it must be met by the passage this session of the bill now pending in the House.

All members of the public should have equal access to facilities open to the public. All members of the public should be equally eligible for Federal benefits that are financed by the public. All members of the public should have an equal chance to vote for public officials and to send their children to good public schools and to contribute their talents to the public good.

Today, Americans of all races stand side by side in Berlin and in Viet Nam. They died side by side in Korea. Surely they can work and eat and travel side by side in their own country.

We must also lift by legislation the bars of discrimination against those who seek entry into our country, particularly those who have much needed skills and those joining their families.

In establishing preferences, a nation that was built by the immigrants of all lands can ask those who now seek admission: "What can you do for our country?" But we should not be asking: "In what country were you born?"

For our ultimate goal is a world without war, a world made safe for diversity, in all men, goods, and ideas can freely move across every border and every boundary.

We must advance toward this goal in 1964 in at least 10 different ways, not as partisans, but as patriots.

First, we must maintain—and our reduced defense budget will maintain—that margin of military safety and superiority obtained through 3 years of steadily increasing both the quality and the quantity of our strategic, our conventional, and our antiguerrilla forces. In 1964 we will be better prepared than ever before to defend the cause of freedom, whether it is threatened by outright aggression or by the infiltration practiced by those in Hanoi and Havana, who ship arms and men across international borders to foment insurrection. And we must continue to use that strength as John Kennedy used it in the Cuban crisis and for the test ban treaty—to demonstrate both the futility of nuclear war and the possibilities of lasting peace.

Second, we must take new steps—and we shall make new proposals at Geneva—toward the control and the eventual abolition of arms. Even in the absence of agreement, we must not stockpile arms beyond our needs or seek an excess of military power that could be provocative as well as wasteful.

It is in this spirit that in this fiscal year we are cutting back our production of enriched uranium by 25 percent. We are shutting down four plutonium piles. We are closing many nonessential military installations. And it is in this spirit that we today call on our adversaries to do the same.

Third, we must make increased use of our food as an instrument of peace—making it available by sale or trade or loan or donation—to hungry people in all nations which tell us of their needs and accept proper conditions of distribution.

Fourth, we must assure our pre-eminence in the peaceful exploration of outer space, focusing on an expedition to the moon in this decade—in cooperation with other powers if possible, alone if necessary.

Fifth, we must expand world trade. Having recognized in the Act of 1962 that we must *buy* as well as *sell,* we now expect our trading partners to recognize that we must *sell* as well as *buy.* We are willing to give them competitive access to our market, asking only that they do the same for us.

Sixth, we must continue, through such measures as the interest equalization tax, as well as the cooperation of other nations, our recent progress toward balancing our international accounts.

This administration must and will preserve the present gold value of the dollar.

Seventh, we must become better neighbors with the free states of the Americas, working with the councils of the OAS, with a stronger Alliance for Progress, and with all the men and women of this hemisphere who really believe in liberty and justice for all.

Eighth, we must strenghten the ability of free nations everywhere to develop their independence and raise their standard of living, and thereby frustrate those who prey on poverty and chaos. To do this, the rich must help the poor—and we must do our part. We must achieve a more rigorous administration of our development assistance, with larger roles for private investors, for other industrialized nations, and for international agencies and for the recipient nations themselves.

Ninth, we must strengthen our Atlantic and Pacific partnerships, maintain our alliances and make the United Nations a more effective instrument for national independence and international order.

Tenth, and finally, we must develop with our allies new means of bridging the gap between the East and the West, facing danger boldly wherever danger exists, but being equally bold in our search for new agreements which can enlarge the hopes of all, while violating the interests of none.

In short, I would say to the Congress that we must be constantly prepared for the worst, and constantly acting for the best. We must be strong enough to win any war, and we must be wise enough to prevent one.

We shall neither act as aggressors nor tolerate acts of aggression. We intend to bury no one, and we do not intend to be buried.

We can fight, if we must, as we have fought before, but we pray that we will never have to fight again.

My good friends and my fellow Americans: In these last 7 sorrowful weeks, we have learned anew that nothing is so enduring as faith, and nothing is so degrading as hate.

John Kennedy was a victim of hate, but he was also a great builder of faith—faith in our fellow Americans, whatever their creed or their color or their station in life; faith in the future of man, whatever his divisions and differences.

This faith was echoed in all parts of the world. On every continent and in every land to which Mrs. Johnson and I traveled, we found faith and hope and love toward this land of America and toward our people.

So I ask you now in the Congress and in the country to join with me in expressing and fulfilling that faith in working for a nation, a nation that is free from want and a world that is free from hate—a world of peace and justice, and freedom and abundance, for our time and for all time to come.

The Great Society

Commencement Address at the University of Michigan
Ann Arbor, Michigan
May 22, 1964

After assuming the Presidency Johnson cast around for a slogan that would not only distinguish his administration from Kennedy's, but would also bear his particular mark, his personal style. In the "Great Society" he found it. But beyond slogans, this speech—simply written and spoken—pinpointed the major domestic problems facing Americans in 1964. Furthermore, it established the campaign agenda Johnson was prepared to wage against a Republican opponent in the fall Presidential election.

It is a great pleasure to be here today. This university has been coeducational since 1870, but I do not believe it was on the basis of your accomplishments that a Detroit high school girl said, "In choosing a college, you first have to decide whether you want a coeducational school or an educational school."

Well, we can find both here at Michigan, although perhaps at different hours.

I came out here today very anxious to meet the Michigan student whose father told a friend of mine that his son's education had been a real value. It stopped his mother from bragging about him.

I have come today from the turmoil of your Capital to the tranquility of your campus to speak about the future of your country.

The purpose of protecting the life of our Nation and preserving the liberty of our citizens is to pursue the happiness of our people. Our success in that pursuit is the test of our success as a Nation.

For a century we labored to settle and to subdue a continent. For half a century we called upon unbounded invention and untiring industry to create an order of plenty for all of our people.

The challenge of the next half century is whether we have the wisdom to use that wealth to enrich and elevate our national life, and to advance the quality of our American civilization.

Your imagination, your initiative, and your indignation will determine whether we build a society where progress is the servant of our needs, or a society where old values and new visions are buried and under unbridled growth. For in your time we have the opportunity to move not only toward the rich society and the powerful society, but upward to the Great Society.

The Great Society rests on abundance and liberty for all. It demands an end to poverty and racial injustice, to which we are totally committed in our time. But that is just the beginning.

The Great Society is a place where every child can find knowledge to enrich his mind and to enlarge his talents. It is a place where leisure is a welcome chance to build and reflect, not a feared cause of boredom and restlessness. It is a place where the city of man serves not only the needs of the body and the demands of commerce but the desire for beauty and the hunger for community.

It is a place where man can renew contact with nature. It is a place which honors creation for its own sake and for what it adds to the understanding of the race. It is a place where men are more concerned with the quality of their goals than the quantity of their goods.

But most of all, the Great Society is not a safe harbor, a resting place, a final objective, a finished work. It is a challenge constantly renewed, beckoning us toward a destiny where the meaning of our lives matches the marvelous products of our labor.

So I want to talk to you today about three places where we begin to build the Great Society—in our cities, in our countryside, and in our classrooms.

Many of you will live to see the day, perhaps 50 years from now, when there will be 400 million Americans—four-fifths of them in urban areas. In the remainder of this century urban population will double, city land will double, and we will have to build homes, highways, and facilities equal to all those built since this country was first settled. So in the next 40 years we must rebuild the entire urban United States.

Aristotle said: "Men come together in cities in order to live, but they remain together in order to live the good life." It is harder and harder to live the good life in American cities today.

The catalog of ills is long: there is the decay of the centers and the despoiling of the suburbs. There is not enough housing for our people or transportation for our traffic. Open land is vanishing and old landmarks are violated.

Worst of all expansion is eroding the precious and time honored values of community with neighbors and communion with nature. The loss of these values breeds loneliness and boredom and indifference.

Our society will never be great until our cities are great. Today the frontier of imagination and innovation is inside those cities and not beyond their borders.

New experiments are already going on. It will be the task of your generation to make the American city a place where future generations will come, not only to live but to live the good life.

I understand that if I stayed here tonight I would see that Michigan students are really doing their best to live the good life.

This is the place where the Peace Corps was started. It is inspiring to see how all of you, while you are in this country, are trying so hard to live at the level of the people.

A second place where we begin to build the Great Society is in our countryside. We have always prided ourselves on being not only America the strong and America the free, but America the beautiful. Today that beauty is in danger. The water we drink, the food we eat, the very air that we breathe, are threatened with pollution. Our parks are overcrowded, our seashores overburdened. Green fields and dense forests are disappearing.

A few years ago we were greatly concerned about the "Ugly American." Today we must act to prevent an ugly America.

For once the battle is lost, once our natural splendor is destroyed, it can never be recaptured. And once man can no longer walk with beauty or wonder at nature his spirit will wither and his sustenance be wasted.

A third place to build the Great Society is in the classrooms of America. There your children's lives will be shaped. Our society will not be great until every young mind is set free to scan the farthest reaches of thought and imagination. We are still far from that goal.

Today, 8 million adult Americans, more than the entire population of Michigan, have not finished 5 years of school. Nearly 20 million have not finished 8 years of school. Nearly 54 million—more than one-quarter of all America—have not even finished high school.

Each year more than 100,000 high school graduates, with proved ability, do not enter college because they cannot afford it. And if we cannot educate today's youth, what will we do in 1970 when elementary school enrollment will be 5 million greater than 1960? And high school enrollment will rise by 5 million. College enrollment will increase by more than 3 million.

In many places, classrooms are overcrowded and curricula are outdated. Most of our qualified teachers are underpaid, and many of our paid teachers are unqualified. So we must give every child a place to sit and a teacher to learn from. Poverty must not be a bar to learning, and learning must offer an escape from poverty.

But more classrooms and more teachers are not enough. We must seek an educational system which grows in excellence as it grows in size. This means better training for our teachers. It means preparing youth to enjoy their hours of leisure as well as their hours of labor. It means exploring new techniques of teaching, to find new ways to stimulate the love of learning and the capacity for creation.

These are three of the central issues of the Great Society. While our Government has many programs directed at those issues, I do not pretend that we have the full answer to those problems.

But I do promise this: We are going to assemble the best thought and the broadest knowledge from all over the world to find those answers for America. I intend to establish working groups to prepare a series of White House conferences and meetings—on the cities, on natural beauty, on the quality of education, and on other emerging challenges. And from these meetings and from this inspiration and from these studies we will begin to set our course toward the Great Society.

The solution to these problems does not rest on a massive program in Washington, nor can it rely solely on the strained resources of local authority. They require us to create new concepts of cooperation, a creative federalism, between the National Capital and the leaders of local communities.

Woodrow Wilson once wrote: "Every man sent out from his university should be a man of his Nation as well as a man of his time."

Within your lifetime powerful forces, already loosed, will take us toward a way of life beyond the realm of our experience, almost beyond the bounds of our imagination.

For better or for worse, your generation has been appointed by history to deal with those problems and to lead America toward a new age. You have the chance never before afforded to any people in any age. You can help build a society where the demands of morality, and the needs of the spirit, can be realized in the life of the Nation.

So, will you join in the battle to give every citizen the full equality which God enjoins and the law requires, whatever his belief, or race, or the color of his skin?

Will you join in the battle to give every citizen an escape from the crushing weight of poverty?

Will you join in the battle to make it possible for all nations to live in enduring peace—as neighbors and not as mortal enemies?

Will you join in the battle to build the Great Society, to prove that our material progress is only the foundation on which we will build a richer life of mind and spirit?

There are those timid souls who say this battle cannot be won; that we are condemned to a soulless wealth. I do not agree. We have the power to shape the civilization that we want. But we need your will, your labor, your hearts, if we are to build that kind of society.

Those who came to this land sought to build more than just a new country. They sought a new world. So I have come here today to your campus to say that you can make their vision our reality. So let us from this moment begin our work so that in the future men will look back and say: It was then, after a long and weary way, that man turned the exploits of his genius to the full enrichment of his life.

War: The Gulf of Tonkin
Radio and Television Report to the People
Washington, D.C.
August 4, 1964

On August 2 the U.S. destroyer "Maddox" was apparently attacked by 3 PT boats from North Viet Nam. Two days later, the "Maddox" and its companion ship, "Turner Joy," reported that they had been attacked in the Gulf of Tonkin. It is questionable as to whether the second attack occurred. Nonetheless, the President appeared on television a little after 11:30 P.M. to announce retaliatory air strikes against North Viet Nam and to ask for a Congressional Resolution giving him power to act as he saw fit to protect American lives in Viet Nam. The Resolution passed Congress quickly and became Johnson's justification for the American-Vietnamese War.

As President and Commander in Chief, it is my duty to the American people to report that renewed hostile actions against United States ships on the high seas in the Gulf of Tonkin have today required me to order the military forces of the United States to take action in reply.

The initial attack on the destroyer *Maddox,* on August 2, was repeated today by a number of hostile vessels attacking two U.S. destroyers with torpedoes. The destroyers and supporting aircraft acted at once on the orders I gave after the initial act of aggression. We believe at least two of the attacking boats were sunk. There were no U.S. losses.

The performance of commanders and crews in this engagement is in the highest tradition of the United States Navy. But repeated acts of violence against the Armed Forces of the United States must be met not only with alert defense, but with positive reply. That reply is being given as I speak to you tonight. Air action is now in execution against gunboats and certain supporting facilities in North Viet-Nam which have been used in these hostile operations.

In the larger sense this new act of aggression, aimed directly at our own forces, again brings home to all of us in the United States the importance of the struggle for peace and security in southeast Asia. Aggression by terror against the peaceful villagers of South Viet-Nam has now been joined by open aggression on the high seas against the United States of America.

The determination of all Americans to carry out our full commitment to the people and to the government of South Viet-Nam will be redoubled by this outrage. Yet our response, for the present, will be limited and fitting. We Americans know, although others appear to forget, the risks of spreading conflict. We still seek no wider war.

I have instructed the Secretary of State to make this position totally clear to friends and to adversaries and, indeed, to all. I have instructed Ambassador Stevenson to raise this matter immediately and urgently before the Security Council of the United Nations. Finally, I have today met with the leaders of both parties in the Congress of the United States and I have informed them that I shall immediately request the Congress to pass a resolution making it clear that our Government is united in its determination to take all necessary measures in support of freedom and in defense of peace in southeast Asia.

I have been given encouraging assurance by these leaders of both parties that such a resolution will be promptly introduced, freely and expeditiously debated, and passed with overwhelming support. And just a few minutes ago I was able to reach Senator Goldwater and I am glad to say that he has expressed his support of the statement that I am making to you tonight.

It is a solemn responsibility to have to order even limited military action by forces whose overall strength is as vast and as awesome as those of the United States of America, but it is my considered conviction, shared throughout your Government, that firmness in the right is indispensable today for peace; that firmness will always be measured. Its mission is peace.

"We Shall Overcome"
Address to a Joint Session of Congress
Washington, D.C.
March 15, 1965

In early 1965 Dr. Martin Luther King, Jr. decided to concentrate his civil rights activities on Selma, Alabama. The drive he initiated sought to register voters—particularly black voters—in this small, sleepy town. The result was violence and death. The public was repelled. And Lyndon Johnson seized the moment to press for legislation to end discrimination against black voters in the South. This moving address in which Lyndon Johnson placed himself in the forefront of the civil rights movement by adopting the slogan, "we shall overcome," led to the enactment of the Voter Rights Bill of 1965, one of the most important pieces of legislation in twentieth-century American politics. It marked Lyndon Johnson as the greatest President in American history in civil rights.

puts pres. credibility on the line

I speak tonight for the dignity of man and the destiny of democracy.

I urge every member of both parties, Americans of all religions and of all colors, from every section of this country, to join me in that cause.

At times history and fate meet at a single time in a single place to shape a turning point in man's unending search for freedom. So it was at Lexington and Concord. So it was a century ago at Appomattox. So it was last week in Selma, Alabama.

There, long-suffering men and women peacefully protested the denial of their rights as Americans. Many were brutally assaulted. One good man, a man of God, was killed.

There is no cause for pride in what has happened in Selma. There is no cause for self-satisfaction in the long denial of equal rights of millions of Americans. But there is cause for hope and for faith in our democracy in what is happening here tonight.

For the cries of pain and the hymns and protests of oppressed people have summoned into convocation all the majesty of this great Government—the Government of the greatest Nation on earth.

Our mission is at once the oldest and the most basic of this country: to right wrong, to do justice, to serve man.

In our time we have come to live with moments of great crisis. Our lives have been marked with debate about great issues; issues of war and peace, issues of prosperity and depression. But rarely in any time does an issue lay bare the secret heart of America itself. Rarely are we met with a challenge, not to our growth or abundance, our welfare or our security, but rather to the values and the purposes and the meaning of our beloved Nation.

The issue of equal rights for American Negroes is such an issue. And should we defeat every enemy, should we double our wealth and conquer the stars, and still be unequal to this issue, then we will have failed as a people and as a nation.

Bible For with a country as with a person, "What is a man profited, if he shall gain the whole world, and lose his own soul?"

There is no Negro problem. There is no Southern problem. There is no Northern problem. There is only an American problem. And we are met here tonight as Americans—not as Democrats or Republicans—we are met here as Americans to solve that problem.

This was the first nation in the history of the world to be founded with a purpose. The great phrases of that purpose still sound in every American heart, North and South: "All men are created equal"—"government by consent of the governed"—"give me liberty or give me death." Well, those are not just clever words, or those are not just empty theories. In their name Americans have fought and died for two centuries, and tonight around the world they stand there as guardians of our liberty, risking their lives.

Those words are a promise to every citizen that he shall share in the dignity of man. This dignity cannot be found in a man's possessions; it cannot be found in his power, or in his position. It really rests on his right to be treated as a man equal in opportunity to all others. It says that he shall share in freedom, he shall choose his leaders, educate his children, and provide for his family according to his ability and his merits as a human being.

To apply any other test—to deny a man his hopes because of his color or race, his religion or the place of his birth—is not only to do injustice, it is to deny America and to dishonor the dead who gave their lives for American freedom.

Our fathers believed that if this noble view of the rights of man was to flourish, it must be rooted in democracy. The most basic right of all was the right to choose your own leaders. The history of this country, in large measure, is the history of the expansion of that right to all of our people.

Many of the issues of civil rights are very complex and most difficult. But about this there can and should be no argument. Every American citizen must have an equal right to vote. There is no reason which can excuse the denial of that right. There is no duty which weighs more heavily on us than the duty we have to ensure that right.

Yet the harsh fact is that in many places in this country men and women are kept from voting simply because they are Negroes.

Every device of which human ingenuity is capable has been used to deny this right. The Negro citizen may go to register only to be told that the day is wrong, or the hour is late, or the official in charge is absent. And if he persists, and if he manages to present himself to the registrar, he may be disqualified because he did not spell out his middle name or because he abbreviated a word on the application. *Enumeration of problem*

And if he manages to fill out an application he is given a test. The registrar is the sole judge of whether he passes this test. He may be asked to recite the entire Constitution, or explain the most complex provisions of State law. And even a college degree cannot be used to prove that he can read and write.

For the fact is that the only way to pass these barriers is to show a white skin.

Experience has clearly shown that the existing process of law cannot overcome systematic and ingenious discrimination. No law that we now have on the books—and I have helped to put three of them there—can ensure the right to vote when local officials are determined to deny it.

In such a case our duty must be clear to all of us. The Constitution says that no person shall be kept from voting because of his race or his color. We have all sworn an oath before God to support and to defend that Constitution. We must now act in obedience to that oath.

Wednesday I will send to Congress a law designed to eliminate illegal barriers to the right to vote.

The broad principles of that bill will be in the hands of the Democratic and Republican leaders tomorrow. After they have reviewed it, it will come here formally as a bill. I am grateful for this opportunity to come here tonight at the invitation of the leadership to reason with my friends, to give them my views, and to visit with my former colleagues.

I have had prepared a more comprehensive analysis of the legislation which I had intended to transmit to the clerk tomorrow but which I will submit to the clerks tonight. But I want to really discuss with you now briefly the main proposals of this legislation.

This bill will strike down restrictions to voting in all elections—Federal, State, and local—which have been used to deny Negroes the right to vote.

This bill will establish a simple, uniform standard which cannot be used, however ingenious the effort, to flout our Constitution.

It will provide for citizens to be registered by officials of the United States Government if the State officials refuse to register them.

It will eliminate tedious, unnecessary lawsuits which delay the right to vote.

Finally, this legislation will ensure that properly registered individuals are not prohibited from voting.

I will welcome the suggestions from all of the Members of Congress—I have no doubt that I will get some—on ways and means to strengthen this law and to make it effective. But experience has plainly shown that this is the only path to carry out the command of the Constitution.

To those who seek to avoid action by their National Government in their own communities; who want to and who seek to maintain purely local control over elections, the answer is simple:

Open your polling places to all your people.

Allow men and women to register and vote whatever the color of their skin.

Extend the rights of citizenship to every citizen of this land.

There is no constitutional issue here. The command of the Constitution is plain.

There is no moral issue. It is wrong—deadly wrong—to deny any of your fellow Americans the right to vote in this country.

There is no issue of States rights or national rights. There is only the struggle for human rights.

I have not the slightest doubt what will be your answer.

The last time a President sent a civil rights bill to the Congress it contained a provision to protect voting rights in Federal elections. That civil rights bill was passed after 8 long months of debate. And when that bill came to my desk from the Congress for my signature, the heart of the voting provision had been eliminated.

This time, on this issue, there must be no delay, no hesitation and no compromise with our purpose.

We cannot, we must not, refuse to protect the right of every American to vote in every election that he may desire to participate in. And we ought not and we cannot and we must not wait another 8 months before we get a bill. We have already waited a hundred years and more, and the time for waiting is gone.

So I ask you to join me in working long hours—nights and weekends, if necessary—to pass this bill. And I don't make that request lightly. For from the window where I sit with the problems of our country I recognize that outside this chamber is the outraged conscience of a nation, the grave concern of many nations, and the harsh judgment of history on our acts.

But even if we pass this bill, the battle will not be over. What happened in Selma is part of a far larger movement which reaches into every section and State of America. It is the effort of American Negroes to secure for themselves the full blessings of American life.

Their cause must be our cause too. Because it is not just Negroes, but really it is all of us, who must overcome the crippling legacy of bigotry and injustice.

And we shall overcome.

As a man whose roots go deeply into Southern soil I know how agonizing racial feelings are. I know how difficult it is to reshape the attitudes and the structure of our society.

But a century has passed, more than a hundred years, since the Negro was freed. And he is not fully free tonight.

It was more than a hundred years ago that Abraham Lincoln, a great President of another party, signed the Emancipation Proclamation, but emancipation is a proclamation and not a fact.

A century has passed, more than a hundred years, since equality was promised. And yet the Negro is not equal.

A century has passed since the day of promise. And the promise is unkept.

The time of justice has now come. I tell you that I believe sincerely that no force can hold it back. It is right in the eyes of man and God that it should come. And when it does, I think that day will brighten the lives of every American.

For Negroes are not the only victims. How many white children have gone uneducated, how many white families have lived in stark poverty, how many white lives have been scarred by fear, because we have wasted our energy and our substance to maintain the barriers of hatred and terror?

So I say to all of you here, and to all in the Nation tonight, that those who appeal to you to hold on to the past do so at the cost of denying you your future. *Sums up the widening of issue*

This great, rich, restless country can offer opportunity and education and hope to all: black and white, North and South, sharecropper and city dweller. These are the enemies: poverty, ignorance, disease. They are the enemies and not our fellow man, not our neighbor. And these enemies too, poverty, disease and ignorance, we shall overcome. *~ Anthem of C.R. mvmts.*

Now let none of us in any sections look with prideful righteousness on the troubles in

+ maded enormous distance from C.R. as communist

another section, or on the problems of our neighbors. There is really no part of America where the promise of equality has been fully kept. In Buffalo as well as in Birmingham, in Philadelphia as well as in Selma, Americans are struggling for the fruits of freedom.

This is one Nation. What happens in Selma or in Cincinnati is a matter of legitimate concern to every American. But let each of us look within our own hearts and our own communities, and let each of us put our shoulder to the wheel to root out injustice wherever it exists.

As we meet here in this peaceful, historic chamber tonight, men from the South, some of whom were at Iwo Jima, men from the North who have carried Old Glory to far corners of the world and brought it back without a stain on it, men from the East and foom the West, are all fighting together without regard to religion, or color, or region, in Viet-Nam. Men from every region fought for us across the world 20 years ago.

And in these common dangers and these common sacrifices the South made its contribution of honor and gallantry no less than any other region of the great Republic—and in some instances, a great many of them, more.

And I have not the slightest doubt that good men from everywhere in this country, from the Great Lakes to the Gulf of Mexico, from the Golden Gate to the harbors along the Atlantic, will rally together now in this cause to vindicate the freedom of all Americans. For all of us owe this duty; and I believe that all of us will respond to it.

Your President makes that request of every American.

The real hero of this struggle is the American Negro. His actions and protests, his courage to risk safety and even to risk his life, have awakened the conscience of this Nation. His demonstrations have been designed to call attention to injustice, designed to provoke change, designed to stir reform.

He has called upon us to make good the promise of America. And who among us can say that we would have made the same progress were it not for his persistent bravery, and his faith in American democracy.

For at the real heart of battle for equality is a deep-seated belief in the democratic process. Equality depends not on the force of arms or tear gas but upon the force of moral right; not on recourse to violence but on respect for law and order.

There have been many pressures upon your President and there will be others as the days come and go. But I pledge you tonight that we intend to fight this battle where it should be fought: in the courts, and in the Congress, and in the hearts of men.

We must preserve the right of free speech and the right of free assembly. But the right of free speech does not carry with it, as has been said, the right to holler fire in a crowded theater. We must preserve the right to free assembly, but free assembly does not carry with it the right to block public thoroughfares to traffic.

We do have a right to protest, and a right to march under conditions that do not infringe the constitutional rights of our neighbors. And I intend to protect all those rights as long as I am permitted to serve in this office.

We will guard against violence, knowing it strikes from our hands the very weapons which we seek—progress, obedience to law, and belief in American values.

In Selma as elsewhere we seek and pray for peace. We seek order. We seek unity. But we will not accept the peace of stifled rights, or the order imposed by fear, or the unity that stifles protest. For peace cannot be purchased at the cost of liberty.

In Selma tonight, as in every—and we had a good day there—as in every city, we are working for just and peaceful settlement. We must all remember that after this speech I am making tonight, after the police and the FBI and the Marshals have all gone, and after you have promptly passed this bill, the people of Selma and the other cities of the Nation must still live and work together. And when the attention of the Nation has gone elsewhere they must try to heal the wounds and to build a new community.

This cannot be easily done on a battleground of violence, as the history of the South itself shows. It is in recognition of this that men of both races have shown such an outstandingly impressive responsibility in recent days—last Tuesday, again today.

The bill that I am presenting to you will be known as a civil rights bill. But, in a larger sense, most of the program I am recommending is a civil rights program. Its object is to open the city of hope to all people of all races.

Because all Americans just must have the right to vote. And we are going to give them that right.

All Americans must have the privileges of citizenship regardless of race. And they are going to have those privileges of citizenship regardless of race.

But I would like to caution you and remind you that to exercise these privileges takes much more than just legal right. It requires a trained mind and a healthy body. It requires a decent home, and the chance to find a job, and the opportunity to escape from the clutches of poverty.

Of course, people cannot contribute to the Nation if they are never taught to read or write, if their bodies are stunted from hunger, if their sickness goes untended, if their life is spent in hopeless poverty just drawing a welfare check.

So we want to open the gates to opportunity. But we are also going to give all our people, black and white, the help that they need to walk through those gates.

My first job after college was a teacher in Cotulla, Tex., in a small Mexican-American school. Few of them could speak English, and I couldn't speak much Spanish. My students were poor and they often came to class without breakfast, hungry. They knew even in their youth the pain of prejudice. They never seemed to know why people disliked them. But they knew it was so, because I saw it in their eyes. I often walked home late in the afternoon, after the classes were finished, wishing there was more that I could do. But all I knew was to teach them the little that I knew, hoping that it might help them against the hardships that lay ahead.

Somehow you never forget what poverty and hatred can do when you see its scars on the hopeful face of a young child.

I never thought then, in 1928, that I would be standing here in 1965. It never even occurred to me in my fondest dreams that I might have the chance to help the sons and daughters of those students and to help people like them all over this country.

But now I do have that chance—and I'll let you in on a secret—I mean to use it. And I hope that you will use it with me.

This is the richest and most powerful country which ever occupied the globe. The might of past empires is little compared to ours. But I do not want to be the President who built empires, or sought grandeur, or extended dominion.

I want to be the President who educated young children to the wonders of their world. I want to be the President who helped to feed the hungry and to prepare them to be taxpayers instead of taxeaters.

I want to be the President who helped the poor to find their own way and who protected the right of every citizen to vote in every election.

I want to be the President who helped to end hatred among his fellow men and who promoted love among the people of all races and all regions and all parties.

I want to be the President who helped to end war among the brothers of this earth.

Was invited

And so at the request of your beloved Speaker and the Senator from Montana; the majority leader, the Senator from Illionis; the minority leader, Mr. McCulloch, and other members of both parties, I came here tonight—not as President Roosevelt came down one time in person to veto a bonus bill, not as President Truman came down one time to urge the passage of a railroad bill—but I came down here to ask you to share this task with me and to share it with the people that we both work for. I want this to be the Congress, Republicans and Democrats alike, which did all these things for all these people. *Height of uniting Appeals*

Beyond this great chamber, out yonder in 50 States, are the people that we serve. Who can tell what deep and unspoken hopes are in their hearts tonight as they sit there and listen. We all can guess, from our own lives, how difficult they often find their own pursuit of happiness, how many problems each little family has. They look most of all to themselves for their futures. But I think that they also look to each of us.

Salvation & God under God w/ a Vengeance

Above the pyramid on the great seal of the United States it says—in Latin— "God has favored our undertaking."

God will not favor everything that we do. It is rather our duty to divine His will. But I cannot help believing that He truly understands and that He really favors the undertaking that we begin here tonight.

A strong hidden political Appeal.

The Dominican Intervention I: "American Lives Are in Danger"

Televised Address to the Nation
Washington, D.C.
April 28, 1965

On April 24 a bloody civil war burst out in the Dominican Republic. Four days later at 5:14 P.M. President Johnson received a cable from our Ambassador, W. Tapley Bennett, telling him that the lives of Americans were endangered by the fighting. Johnson quickly dispatched some 1,400 Marines to Santo Domingo, the first official American military intervention in the internal affairs of a Latin American country since President Coolidge sent the Marines into Nicaragua in 1925. Then, Johnson went to the Theatre at the White House to announce his decision on television by breaking into regular television programming at 8:40 P.M. and his reading his brief statement.

I have just concluded a meeting with the leaders of the Congress. I reported to them on the serious situation in the Dominican Republic. I reported the decisions that this Government considers necessary in this situation in order to protect American lives.

The members of the leadership expressed their support of these decisions. The United States Government has been informed by military authorities in the Dominican Republic that American lives are in danger. These authorities are no longer able to guarantee their safety and they have reported that the assistance of military personnel is now needed for that purpose.

I have ordered the Secretary of Defense to put the necessary American troops ashore in order to give protection to hundreds of Americans who are still in the Dominican Republic and to escort them safely back to this country. This same assistance will be available to the nationals of other countries, some of whom have already asked for our help.

Pursuant to my instructions 400 Marines have already landed. General Wheeler, the Chairman of the Joint Chiefs of Staff, has just reported to me that there have been no incidents.

We have appealed repeatedly in recent days for a cease-fire between the contending forces of the Dominican Republic in the interests of all Dominicans and foreigners alike.

I repeat this urgent appeal again tonight. The Council of the OAS has been advised of the situation by the Dominican Ambassador and the Council will be kept fully informed.

The Dominican Intervention II: Outsiders Are Seeking to Gain Control

Televised Statement
Washington, D.C.
April 30, 1965

After Johnson's first announcement of American intervention, criticism of his actions began to mount. Therefore, Johnson went on television again. But he repeated the mistake of two days earlier—he broke into regularly scheduled programming unannounced at 7:07 P.M. Thus, even more attention focused on the Dominican Republic. And Johnson began to change his reasons for American intervention, hinting that the Rebel camp was infiltrated by "outsiders."

For 2 days American forces have been in Santo Domingo in an effort to protect the lives of Americans and the nationals of other countries in the face of increasing violence and disorder. With the assistance of these American forces, over 200 Americans and other nationals have been evacuated from the Dominican Republic. We took this step when and only when, we were officially notified by police and military officials of the Dominican Republic that they were no longer in a position to guarantee the safety of American and foreign nationals and to preserve law and order.

In the last 24 hours violence and disorder have increased. There is great danger to the life of foreign nationals and of thousands of Dominican citizens, our fellow citizens of this hemisphere. By an outstanding effort of mediation the Papal Nuncio has achieved an agreement on a cease-fire which I have urged all those concerned to take. But this agreement is not now, as I speak, being fully respected. The maintenance of the cease-fire is essential to the hopes of all for peace and freedom in the Dominican Republic.

Meanwhile there are signs that people trained outside the Dominican Republic are seeking to gain control. Thus, the legitimate aspirations of the Dominican people and most of their leaders for progress, democracy, and social justice are threatened and so are the principles of the inter-American system.

The inter-American system, and its principal organ, the Organization of American States, have a grave and an immediate responsibility. It is important that prompt action be taken. I am informed that a representative of the OAS is leaving Washington very shortly for the Dominican Republic. It is very important that representatives of the OAS be sent to the Dominican Republic, just as soon as they can be sent there, in order to strengthen the cease-fire and in order to help clear a road to the return of constitutional process and free elections. Loss of time may mean that it is too late to preserve the freedom, which alone can lead to the establishment of true democracy. This, I am sure, is what the people of the Dominican Republic want. Late action, or delay, in such a case could mean a failure to accomplish the agreed objectives of the American states.

The eyes of the hemisphere are now on the OAS, both in its meeting today and on the meeting of its foreign ministers contemplated tomorrow. The wisdom, the statesmanship, and the ability to act decisively of the OAS are critical to the hopes of peoples in every land of this continent.

The United States will give its full support to the work of the OAS and will never depart from its commitment to the preservation of the right of all of the free people of this hemisphere to choose their own course without falling prey to international conspiracy from any quarter.

The Dominican Intervention III: "The Revolutionary Movement Took a Tragic Turn"
Televised Address to the Nation
Washington, D.C.
May 2, 1965

Ever since Johnson dispatched Marines to the Dominican Republic, he had brooded over the criticism of his action. It threatened to shatter his precious "consensus." And it came from a part of his constituency that he felt most ill-at-ease with: the liberal press and academics. Thus, he appeared on television yet again, the third time in five days, to speak about the Dominican Republic. This time, however, he did not interrupt a regular program, but instead spoke at 10 P.M. Yet, the result was not good. A mistake with the teleprompter caused him to repeat two paragraphs. Moreover, he made claims he could not substantiate. He claimed the revolution had been taken over by Communists. But when pressed later, the administration could come up only with a lame list of suspected Communists, and the list was quickly discredited. He said he had been in touch with Romulo Betancourt, when, in fact, no major advisor had consulted with him. This long, rambling address exposed a different Lyndon Johnson from the one the public had become accustomed to: a Lyndon Johnson running scared. Two days later Johnson in a mood of self-pity described himself as "the most denounced man in the world." Johnson made 3 major mistakes in his public handling of the Dominican intervention. First, he focused national attention on his actions by going on national television unannounced and by breaking into broadcasts. Second, he changed his reasons for intervention. And third, he dissolved into self-pity when he got criticism rather than the absolute support he sought. Johnson's rhetorical mistakes unveiled the first cracks in his consensus and previewed the "credibility gap" that was soon to plague him.

I have just come from a meeting with the leaders of both parties in the Congress which was held in the Cabinet Room in the White House. I briefed them on the facts of the situation in the Dominican Republic. I want to make those same facts known to all the American people and to all the world.

There are times in the affairs of nations when great principles are tested in an ordeal of conflict and danger. This is such a time for the American nations.

At stake are the lives of thousands, the liberty of a nation, and the principles and the values of all the American Republics. That is why the hopes and the concern of this entire hemisphere are, on this Sabbath—Sunday, focused on the Dominican Republic.

In the dark mist of conflict and violence, revolution and confusion, it is not easy to find clear and unclouded truths.

But certain things are clear. And they require equally clear action. To understand, I think it is necessary to begin with the events of 8 or 9 days ago.

Last week our observers warned of an approaching political storm in the Dominican Republic. I immediately asked our Ambassador to return to Washington at once so that we might discuss the situation and might plan a course of conduct. But events soon outran our hopes for peace.

Saturday, April 24th—8 days ago—while Ambassador Bennett was conferring with the highest officials of your Government, revolution erupted in the Dominican Republic. Elements of the military forces of that country overthrew their government. However, the rebels themselves were divided. Some wanted to restore former President Juan Bosch. Others opposed his restoration. President Bosch, elected after the fall of Trujillo and his assassination, had been driven from office by an earlier revolution in the Dominican Republic.

Those who opposed Mr. Bosch's return formed a military committee in an effort to control that country. The others took to the street and they began to lead a revolt on behalf of President Bosch. Control and effective government dissolved in conflict and confusion.

Meanwhile the United States was making a constant effort to restore peace. From Saturday afternoon onward, our embassy urged a cease-fire, and I and all the officials of the American Government worked with every weapon at our command to achieve it.

On Tuesday the situation of turmoil was presented to the peace committee of the Organization of American States.

On Wednesday the entire Council of the Organization of American States received a full report from the Dominican Ambassador.

Meanwhile, all this time, from Saturday to Wednesday, the danger was mounting. Even though we were deeply saddened by bloodshed and violence in a close and friendly neighbor, we had no desire to interfere in the affairs of a sister republic.

On Wednesday afternoon, there was no longer any choice for the man who is your President. I was sitting in my little office reviewing the world situation with Secretary Rusk, Secretary McNamara, and Mr. McGeorge Bundy. Shortly after 3 o'clock I received a cable from our Ambassador and he said that things were in danger, he had been informed that the chief of police and the governmental authorities could no longer protect us. We immediately started the necessary conference calls to be prepared.

At 5:14, almost 2 hours later, we received a cable that was labeled "critic," a word that is reserved for only the most urgent and immediate matters of national security.

The cable reported that Dominican law enforcement and military officials had informed our embassy that the situation was completely out of control and that the police and the Government could no longer give any guarantee concerning the safety of Americans or of any foreign nationals.

Ambassador Bennett, who is one of our most experienced Foreign Service officers, went on in that cable to say that only an immediate landing of American forces could safeguard and protect the lives of thousands of Americans and thousands of other citizens of some 30 other countries. Ambassador Bennett urged your President to order an immediate landing.

In this situation hesitation and vacillation could mean death for many of our people, as well as many of the citizens of other lands.

I thought that we could not and we did not hesitate. Our forces, American forces, were ordered in immediately to protect American lives. They have done that. They have attacked no one, and although some of our servicemen gave their lives, not a single American civilian and the civilian of any other nation, as a result of this protection, lost their lives.

There may be those in our own country who say that such action was good but we should have waited, or we should have delayed, or we should have consulted further, or we should have called a meeting. But from the very beginning, the United States, at my instructions, had worked for a cease-fire beginning the Saturday the revolution took place. The matter was before the OAS peace committee on Tuesday, at our suggestion. It was before the full Council on Wednesday and when I made my announcement to the American people that evening, I announced then that I was notifying the Council.

When that cable arrived, when our entire country team in the Dominican Republic, made up of nine men—one from the Army, Navy, and Air Force, our Ambassador, our AID man and others—said to your President unanimously: "Mr. President, if you do not send forces immediately, men and women—Americans and those of other lands—will die in the streets"— well, I knew there was no time to talk, to consult, or to delay. For in this situation delay itself would be decision—the decision to risk and to lose the lives of thousands of Americans and thousands of innocent people from all lands.

I want you to know that it is not a light or an easy matter to send our American boys to another country, but I do not think that the American people expect their President to hesitate or to vacillate in the face of danger just because the decision is hard when life is in peril.

Meanwhile, the revolutionary movement took a tragic turn. Communist leaders, many of them trained in Cuba, seeing a chance to increase disorder, to gain a foothold, joined the revolution. They took increasing control. And what began as a popular democratic revolution, committed to democracy and social justice, very shortly moved and was taken over and really seized and placed into the hands of a band of Communist conspirators.

Many of the original leaders of the rebellion, the followers of President Bosch, took refuge in foreign embassies because they had been superseded by other evil forces, and the Secretary General of the rebel government, Martinez Francisco, appealed for a cease-fire. But he was ignored. The revolution was now in other and dangerous hands.

When these new and ominous developments emerged, the OAS met again and it met at the request of the United States. I am glad to say that they responded wisely and decisively. A five-nation OAS team is now in the Dominican Republic acting to achieve a cease-fire to ensure the safety of innocent people, to restore normal conditions, and to open a path to democratic process.

That is the situation now.

I plead, therefore, with every person and every country in this hemisphere that would choose to do so, to contact their ambassador and the Dominican Republic directly and to get firsthand evidence of the horrors and the hardship, the violence and the terror, and the international conspiracy from which U.S. servicemen have rescued the people of more than 30 nations from that war-torn island.

Earlier today I ordered two additional battalions—2,000 extra men— to proceed immediately to the Dominican Republic. In the meeting that I just concluded with the congressional leaders— following that meeting I directed the Secretary of Defense and the Chairman of the Joint Chiefs of Staff to issue instructions to land an additional 4,500 men at the earliest possible moment. The distribution of food to people who have not eaten for days, the need of medical supplies and attention for the sick and wounded, the health requirements to avoid an epidemic because there are hundreds that have been dead for days that are now in the streets, and that further protection of the security of each individual that is caught on that island require the attention of the additional forces which I have ordered to proceed to the Dominican Republic.

In addition, our servicemen have already, since they landed on Wednesday night, evacuated 3,000 persons from 30 countries in the world from this little island. But more than 5,000 people, 1,500 of whom are Americans—the others are foreign nationals—are tonight awaiting evacuation as I speak. We just must get on with that job immediately.

The American nations cannot, must not, and will not permit the establishment of another Communist government in the Western Hemisphere. This was the unanimous view of all the American nations when, in January 1962, they declared, and I quote: "The principles of communism are incompatible with the principles of the inter-American system."

This is what our beloved President John F. Kennedy meant when, less than a week before his death, he told us: "We in this hemisphere must also use every resource at our command to prevent the establishment of another Cuba in this hemisphere."

This is and this will be the common action and the common purpose of the democratic forces of the hemisphere. For the danger is also a common danger, and the principles are common principles.

So we have acted to summon the resources of this entire hemisphere to this task. We have sent, on my instructions night before last, special emissaries such as Ambassador Moscoso of Puerto Rico, our very able Ambassador Averell Harriman, and others to Latin America to explain the situation, to tell them the truth, and to warn them that joint action is necessary. We are in contact with such distinguished Latin American statesmen as Romulo Betancourt and Jose Figueres. We are seeking their wisdom and their counsel and their advice. We have also maintained communication with President Bosch, who has chosen to remain in Puerto Rico.

We have been consulting with the Organization of American States, and our distinguished Ambassador, than whom there is no better—Ambassador Bunker—has been reporting to them at great length all the actions of this Government and we have been acting in conformity with their decisions.

We know that many who are now in revolt do not seek a Communist tyranny. We think it is tragic indeed that their high motives have been misused by a small band of conspirators who receive their directions from abroad.

To those who fight only for liberty and justice and progress I want to join with the Organization of American States in saying, in appealing to you tonight, to lay down your arms, and to assure you there is nothing to fear. The road is open for you to share in building a Dominican democracy and we in America are ready and anxious and willing to help you. Your courage and your dedication are qualities which your country and all the hemisphere need for the future. You are needed to help shape that future. And neither we nor any other nation in this hemisphere can or should take it upon itself to ever interfere with the affairs of your country or any other country.

We believe that change comes and we are glad it does, and it should come through peaceful process. But revolution in any country is a matter for that country to deal with. It becomes a matter calling for hemispheric action only—repeat—*only* when the object is the establishment of a communistic dictatorship.

Let me also make clear tonight that we support no single man or any single group of men in the Dominican Republic. Our goal is a simple one. We are there to save the lives of our citizens and to save the lives of all people. Our goal, in keeping with the great principles of the inter-American system, is to help prevent another Communist state in this hemisphere. And we would like to do this without bloodshed or without large-scale fighting.

The form and the nature of a free Dominican government, I assure you, is solely a matter for the Dominican people, but we do know what kind of government we hope to see in the Dominican Republic. For that is carefully spelled out in the treaties and the agreements which make up the fabric of the entire inter-American system. It is expressed, time and time again, in the words of our statesmen and in the values and hopes which bind us all together.

We hope to see a government freely chosen by the will of all the people.

We hope to see a government dedicated to social justice for every single citizen.

We hope to see a government working, every hour of every day, to feeding the hungry, to educating the ignorant, to healing the sick—a government whose only concern is the progress and the elevation and the welfare of all the people.

For more than 3 decades the people of that tragic little island suffered under the weight of one of the most brutal and despotic dictatorships in the history of the Americas. We enthusiastically supported condemnation of that government by the Organization of American States. We joined in applying sanctions and when Trujillo was assassinated by his fellow citizens we immediately acted to protect freedom and to prevent a new tyranny. And since that time we have taken the resources from all of our people, at some sacrifice to many, and we have helped them with food and with other resources, with the Peace Corps volunteers, with the AID technicians. We have helped them in the effort to build a new order of progress.

How sad it is tonight that a people so long oppressed should once again be the targets of the forces of tyranny. Their long misery must weigh heavily on the heart of every citizen of this hemisphere. So I think it is our mutual responsibility to help the people of the Dominican Republic toward the day when they can freely choose the path of liberty and justice and progress. This is required of us by the agreements that we are party to and that we have signed. This is required of us by the values which bind us together.

Simón Bolívar once wrote from exile: "The veil has been torn asunder. We have already seen the light and it is not our desire to be thrust back into the darkness."

Well, after decades of night the Dominican people have seen a more hopeful light and I know that the nations of this hemisphere will not let them be thrust back into the darkness.

And before I leave you, my fellow Americans, I want to say this personal word: I know that no American serviceman wants to kill anyone. I know that no American President wants to give an order which brings shooting and casualities and death. I want you to know and I want the world to know that as long as I am President of this country, we are going to defend ourselves. We will defend our soldiers against attackers. We will honor our treaties. We will keep our commitments. We will defend our Nation against all those who seek to destroy not only the United States but every free country of this hemisphere. We do not want to bury anyone as I have said so many times before. But we do not intend to be buried.

The Vietnam War Becomes the American-Vietnamese War

Televised News Conference
Washington, D.C.
July 28, 1965

By July the military and political situation in South Viet Nam had become so unstable that the President convoked a major review of American policy during the week of July 21. Johnson had basically five options open to him: (1) keep American support at the same level; (2) go in with full military troops and equipment; (3) pull our of Viet Nam; (4) call up the reserves and thus shock the American people into recognizing the crisis that he believed existed; or (5) increase the number of troops through increasing the draft and thus not alarming or alerting the American people to this change in American policy. The debate finally came down to the last two options, and Johnson chose to minimize the public impact of his decision by increasing the draft rather than calling up the reserves. To deflect attention away from his announcement, the President chose a noon press conference as the platform to state his decisions. Furthermore, he gave newsmen alternative headlines by announcing his appointments John Chancellor to the Voice of America and Abe Fortas to the Supreme Court. All of this was done in a subdued style accompanied by assurances that no substantive change in policy had occurred so as not to provoke a public discussion or to inflame his relations with Congress as it prepared to pass domestic legislation he deemed important. But with this press conference he publicly committed the United States to the defense of South Viet Nam. The candidate who in October 1964 declared we should not send American boys "to do the fighting for Asian boys" now was sending 50,000 additional American boys to do just that.

The President. My fellow Americans:

[I.] Not long ago I received a letter from a woman in the Midwest. She wrote:

"Dear Mr. President:

"In my humble way I am writing to you about the crisis in Viet-Nam. I have a son who is now in Viet-Nam. My husband served in World War II. Our country was at war, but now, this time, it is just something that I don't understand. Why?"

Well, I have tried to answer that question dozens of times and more in practically every State in this Union. I have discussed it fully in Baltimore in April, in Washington in May, in San Francisco in June. Let me again, now, discuss it here in the East Room of the White House.

Why must young Americans, born into a land exultant with hope and with golden promise, toil and suffer and sometimes die in such a remote and distant place?

The answer, like the war itself, is not an easy one, but it echoes clearly from the painful lessons of half a century. Three times in my lifetime, in two World Wars and in Korea, Americans have gone to far lands to fight for freedom. We have learned at a terrible and a brutal cost that retreat does not bring safety and weakness does not bring peace.

It is this lesson that has brought us to Viet-Nam. This is a different kind of war. There are no marching armies or solemn declarations. Some citizens of South Viet-Nam at times, with understandable grievances, have joined in the attack on their own government.

But we must not let this mask the central fact that this is really war. It is guided by North Viet-Nam and it is spurred by Communist China. Its goal is to conquer the South, to defeat American power, and to extend the Asiatic dominion of communism.

There are great stakes in the balance.

Most of the non-Communist nations of Asia cannot, by themselves and alone, resist the growing might and the grasping ambition of Asian communism.

Our power, therefore, is a very vital shield. If we are driven from the field in Viet-Nam, then no nation can ever again have the same confidence in American promise, or in American protection.

In each land the forces of independence would be considerably weakened, and an Asia so threatened by Communist domination would certainly imperil the security of the United States itself.

We did not choose to be the guardians at the gate, but there is no one else.

Nor would surrender in Viet-Nam bring peace, because we learned from Hitler at Munich that success only feeds the appetite of aggression. The battle would be renewed in one country and then another country, bringing with it perhaps even larger and crueler conflict, as we have learned from the lessons of history.

Moreover, we are in Viet-Nam to fulfill one of the most solemn pledges of the American Nation. Three Presidents—President Eisenhower, President Kennedy, and your present President—over 11 years have committed themselves and have promised to help defend this small and valiant nation.

Strengthened by that promise, the people of South Viet-Nam have fought for many long years. Thousands of them have died. Thousands more have been crippled and scarred by war. We just cannot now dishonor our word, or abandon our commitment, or leave those who believed us and who trusted us to the terror and repression and murder that would follow.

This, then, my fellow Americans, is why we are in Viet-Nam.

The Nation's Goals in Viet-Nam

What are our goals in that war-strained land?

First, we intend to convince the Communists that we cannot be defeated by force of arms or by superior power. They are not easily convinced. In recent months they have greatly increased their fighting forces and their attacks and the number of incidents.

I have asked the Commanding General, General Westmoreland, what more he needs to meet this mounting aggression. He has told me. We will meet his needs.

I have today ordered to Viet-Nam the Air Mobile Division and certain other forces which will raise our fighting strength from 75,000 to 125,000 men almost immediately. Additional forces will be needed later, and they will be sent as requested.

This will make it necessary to increase our active fighting forces by raising the monthly draft call from 17,000 over a period of time to 35,000 per month, and for us to step up our campaign for voluntary enlistments.

After this past week of deliberations, I have concluded that it is not essential to order Reserve units into service now. If that necessity should later be indicated, I will give the matter most careful consideration and I will give the country—you—an adequate notice before taking such action, but only after full preparations.

We have also discussed with the Government of South Viet-Nam lately, the steps that we will take to substantially increase their own effort, both on the battlefield and toward reform and progress in the villages. Ambassador Lodge is now formulating a new program to be tested upon his return to that area.

I have directed Secretary Rusk and Secretary McNamara to be available immediately to the Congress to review with these committees, the appropriate congressional committees, what we plan to do in these areas. I have asked them to be able to answer the questions of any Member of Congress.

Secretary McNamara, in addition, will ask the Senate Appropriations Committee to add a limited amount to present legislation to help meet part of this new cost until a supplemental measure is ready and hearings can be held when the Congress assembles in January. In the meantime, we will use the authority contained in the present Defense appropriation bill under consideration to transfer funds in addition to the additional money that we will ask.

These steps, like our actions in the past, are carefully measured to do what must be done to bring an end to aggression and a peaceful settlement.

We do not want an expanding struggle with consequences that no one can perceive, nor will we bluster or bully or flaunt our power, but we will not surrender and we will not retreat.

For behind our American pledge lies the determination and resources, I believe, of all of the American Nation.

Our Readiness to Negotiate

Second, once the Communists know, as we know, that a violent solution is impossible, then a peaceful solution is inevitable.

We are ready now, as we have always been, to move from the battlefield to the conference table. I have stated publicly and many times, again and again, America's willingness to begin unconditional discussions with any government, at any place, at any time. Fifteen efforts have been made to start these discussions with the help of 40 nations throughout the world, but there has been no answer.

But we are going to continue to persist, if persist we must, until death and desolation have led to the same conference table where others could now join us at a much smaller cost.

I have spoken many times of our objectives in Viet-Nam. So has the Government of South Viet-Nam. Hanoi has set forth its own proposals. We are ready to discuss their proposals and our proposals and any proposals of any government whose people may be affected, for we fear the meeting room no more than we fear the battlefield.

In this pursuit we welcome and we ask for the concern and the assistance of any nation and all nations. If the United Nations and its officials or any one of its 114 members can by deed or word, private initiative or public action, bring us nearer an honorable peace, then they will have the support and the gratitude of the United States of America.

Letter to U Thant

I have directed Ambassador Goldberg to go to New York today and to present immediately to Secretary General U Thant a letter from me requesting that all the resources, energy, and immense prestige of the United Nations be employed to find ways to halt aggression and to bring peace in Viet-Nam.

I made a similar request at San Francisco a few weeks ago, because we do not seek the destruction of any government, nor do we covet a foot of any territory. But we insist and we will always insist that the people of South Viet-Nam shall have the right of choice, the right to shape their own destiny in free elections in the South or throughout all Viet-Nam under international supervision, and they shall not have any government imposed upon them by force and terror so long as we can prevent it.

This was the purpose of the 1954 agreements which the Communists have now cruelly shattered. If the machinery of those agreements was tragically weak, its purposes still guide our action. As battle rages, we will continue as best we can to help the good people of South Viet-

Nam enrich the condition of their life, to feed the hungry and to tend the sick, and teach the young, and shelter the homeless, and to help the farmer to increase his crops, and the worker to find a job.

It is an ancient but still terrible irony that while many leaders of men create division in pursuit of grand ambitions, the children of man are really united in the simple, elusive desire for a life of fruitful and rewarding toil.

As I said at Johns Hopkins in Baltimore, I hope that one day we can help all the people of Asia toward that desire. Eugene Black has made great progress since my appearance in Baltimore in that direction—not as the price of peace, for we are ready always to bear a more painful cost, but rather as a part of our obligations of justice toward our fellow man.

The President's Personal Feelings
About War

[2.] Let me also add now a personal note. I do not find it easy to send the flower of our youth, our finest young men, into battle. I have spoken to you today of the divisions and the forces and the battalions and the units, but I know them all, every one. I have seen them in a thousand streets, of a hundred towns, in every State in this Union—working and laughing and building, and filled with hope and life. I think I know, too, how their mothers weep and how their families sorrow.

This is the most agonizing and the most painful duty of your President.

There is something else, too. When I was young, poverty was so common that we didn't know it had a name. An education was something that you had to fight for, and water was really life itself. I have now been in public life 35 years, more than three decades, and in each of those 35 years I have seen good men, and wise leaders, struggle to bring the blessings of this land to all of our people.

And now I am the President. It is now my opportunity to help every child get an education, to help every Negro and every American citizen have an equal opportunity, to have every family get a decent home, and to help bring healing to the sick and dignity to the old.

As I have said before, that is what I have lived for, that is what I have wanted all my life since I was a little boy, and I do not want to see all those hopes and all those dreams of so many people for so many years now drowned in the wasteful ravages of cruel wars. I am going to do all I can do to see that that never happens.

But I also know, as a realistic public servant, that as long as there are men who hate and destroy, we must have the courage to resist, or we will see it all, all that we have built, all that we hope to build, all of our dreams for freedom—all, *all* will be swept away on the flood of conquest.

So, too, this shall not happen. We will stand in Viet-Nam.

Voice of America Appointment;
John Chancellor

[3.] Now, what America is, and was, and hopes to stand for as an important national asset, telling the truth to this world, telling an exciting story, is the Voice of America. I classify this assignment in the front rank of importance to the freedom of the world, and that is why today I am proud to announce to you the name of the man who will direct the Voice of America.

He is a man whose voice and whose face and whose mind is known to this country and to most of the entire world. His name is John Chancellor.

Mr. Chancellor was born 38 years ago in Chicago. For more than 15 years he has been with the news department of the National Broadcasting Company. During that time he has covered the world—in Vienna, London, Moscow, New York, Brussels, Berlin, and Washington.

Since 1964 he has been with you, one of the White House correspondents.

This, I think, is the first time in the history of the Voice of America that a working newspaperman, a respected commentator, an experienced, independent reporter, has been given the responsibility of leadership and direction in this vital enterprise. I think he understands the challenges that are present and the achievements that are possible.

I am satisfied that the Voice of America will be in imaginative, competent, reliable, and always truthful hands.

Stand up, John, will you please?

Nomination of Abe Fortas to Supreme Court

[4.] The President has few responsibilities of greater importance or greater consequence to the country's future than the constitutional responsibility of nominating Justices for the Supreme Court of the United States.

I am happy today, here in the East Room, to announce that the distinguished American who was my first choice for the position now vacant on the Supreme Court, has agreed to accept this call to this vital duty. I will very shortly, this afternoon, send to the United States Senate my nomination of the Honorable Abe Fortas to be an Associate Justice of the Supreme Court.

For many, many years, I have regarded Mr. Fortas as one of this Nation's most able and most respected and most outstanding citizens, a scholar, a profound thinker, a lawyer of superior ability, and a man of humane and deeply compassionate feelings toward his fellow man—a champion of our liberties. That opinion is shared by the legal profession and by the bar of this country, by Members of the Congress and by the leaders of business and labor, and other sectors of our national life.

Mr. Fortas has, as you know, told me on numerous occasions in the last 20 months, that he would not be an applicant or a candidate, or would not accept any appointment to any public office. This is, I guess, as it should be, for in this instance the job has sought the man. Mr. Fortas agrees that the duty and the opportunity of service on the highest court of this great country, is not a call that any citizen can reject.

So I am proud for the country that he has, this morning, accepted this appointment and will serve his country as an Associate Justice of the Supreme Court.

I will be glad to take your questions now for a period.

Questions

Possibility of Escalation in Viet-Nam

[5.] Q. Mr. President, in the light of the decisions on Viet-Nam which you have just announced, is the United States prepared with additional plans should North Viet-Nam escalate its military effort, and how do you anticipate that the Chinese Communists will react to what you have announced today?

The President. I do not want to speculate on the reactions of other people. This Nation is prepared, and will always be prepared, to protect its national interest.

Duration of Fighting

Q. Mr. President, you have never talked about a timetable in connection with Viet-Nam. You have said, and you repeated today, that the United States will not be defeated, will not grow tired.

Donald Johnson, National Commander of the American Legion, went over to Viet-Nam in the spring and later called on you. He told White House reporters that he could imagine the war over there going on for 5, 6, or 7 years. Have you thought of that possibility, sir? And do you think the American people ought to think of that possibility?

The President. Yes, I think the American people ought to understand that there is no quick solution to the problem that we face there. I would not want to prophesy or predict whether it would be a matter of months or years or decades. I do not know that we had any accurate timetable on how long it would take to bring victory in World War I. I don't think anyone really knew whether it would be 2 years or 4 years or 6 years, to meet with success in World War II. I do think our cause is just. I do think our purposes and objectives are beyond any question.

I do believe that America will stand united behind her men that are there. I plan, as long as I am President, to see that our forces are strong enough to protect our national interest, our right hand constantly protecting that interest with our military, and that our diplomatic and political negotiations are constantly attempting to find some solution that would substitute words for bombs.

As I have said so many times, if anyone questions our good faith and will ask us to meet them to try to reason this matter out, they will find us at the appointed place, at the appointed time, in the proper chair. . . .

"Nervous Nellies"

Remarks at a Democratic Party Dinner
Chicago, Illinois
May 17, 1966

By mid-1966 the protest against the war had developed into a full-blown protest including not only students and professors and liberals, but Congressmen and Senators as well. In February, 1966 Senator William Fulbright had opened the Senate Foreign Relations Committee Hearings into the war, much to Johnson's displeasure. Johnson, therefore, used this occasion to criticize his critics. When he was done, the critics were outraged because he had not answered their arguments, but attacked their motives. Although he gained a short-term tactical advantage, Johnson provoked a deep-seated hostility among his critics, many of whom had supported him on domestic matters.

When I arrived in your city tonight, I was reminded of a remark I made several weeks ago to the mayors' convention in Washington. I told them that whenever the burdens of the Presidency seemed unusually heavy, I always remind myself that it could be worse. I just might have been a mayor of a city instead of President of the United States!

There is no more important job in public life. We in Washington can pass laws. We can develop forward-looking programs for all the people. But those laws and those programs have to be carried out by far-sighted and talented and capable leaders back in the local communities.

The people of this great city of Chicago are unusually fortunate. For more than a decade now you have enjoyed the steadfast leadership of a man who is recognized the world over as a great and talented municipal executive—your courageous and intelligent and hardworking mayor, Richard J. Daley—the number one mayor in all the United States of America.

Every time I visit Chicago, the progress that you have made impresses me. Your lakefront grows more beautiful, year by year. Your office buildings, your houses, your schools, and your thoroughfares are now being imitated by the city planners in the other cities throughout the land.

We are living tonight in what I have called the century of change—and in Chicago you are making certain that it is a change for the better. And that is the same goal that we are striving for in your National Capital in Washington.

And I want to remind you people of Illinois that you are equally fortunate in having an able, aggressive, and attractive Governor, my old friend, Otto Kerner. I know that none of the Governors will take any offense when I tell you that I believe him to be one of the best 50. And I am, too, so happy to have with me tonight another son of Illinois and Chicago, a brilliant scholar from this delightful city, the great Secretary of Labor, Willard Wirtz.

And when each of you votes for Adlai Stevenson III for State Treasurer, you will have your funds well-managed and well-secured. And I hope that you won't forget him when the election comes around.

And I don't want you to forget that a vote for Don Prince for State superintendent of public instruction will be a vote for better schools for every schoolchild in the State of Illinois.

You people are fortunate, you have much to be thankful for: You have one of the best and the most effective congressional delegations in all the House of Representatives—one which gives wholehearted support to the President of the United States and to the Democratic Party. And I just could not come to the city of Chicago and to Cook County without thanking you for each one of these men: first, Bill Dawson; Congressman Kluczynski; Congressman O'Hara; Congressman Murphy; Congressman Yates; Congressman Pucinski; Congressman Danny Rostenkowski; Congressman Annunzio; Congressman Ronan.

And that's a test for a fellow from Texas!

We have one man with us tonight who can testify to that from personal experience—my old friend, and one of the great Senators of our time, Paul Douglas. I was thinking about Senator Douglas as I was preparing these remarks on my way out here today—about his vision, about his capabilities, about his deep love and his deep devotion to this country for which he fought in World War II and for which he has fought every day of his public life.

Senator Douglas has spent his life in the service of humanity. For 28 years he was a great, outstanding teacher at your University of Chicago. And when the call of public service came, he went to Washington to help remake our country, remake it with the same enthusiasm and with the same wisdom with which he used to mold the minds of the young people of the Midwest.

I know how Senator Douglas must have felt while taking his seat in the Congress. I remember very well my own emotions when I caught a train to leave my State for the first time to go to Washington as a young man back in November 1931—some 35 years ago.

I took along on that train more than a suitcase. I took some dreams and some hopes and some ideas. All of them were based on my belief that we could do much to improve the lot of the average American. I have never forgotten those dreams or those hopes. And tonight, with the help of a wonderful Congress that the people have given us, I seem to see some of those dreams come true.

I remembered then—and I remember now—Edmund Burke's statement that was made more than 175 years ago, that "Government is a contrivance of human wisdom to provide for human wants. Men have a right that these wants should be provided for by this wisdom."

And that is what this administration and this Congress have been trying to do—provide for human wants.

I was working to provide for human wants back in the days of the National Youth Administration. And tonight one of the great pleasures that I get from coming to Chicago is to see that great Federal judge, Bill Campbell, who in those days was NYA Administrator of Illinois and I was NYA Administrator.

And I don't think it was Bill that said this, but I didn't really believe then that he would grace the bench as he has all these years, when I saw him as NYA Administrator, and I know he must not have ever envisioned me where I am tonight. As a matter of fact, after my television show the other night down at the ranch that some of you may have seen, one of my neighbors came up to me and he said, "Lyndon, you know I've heard all my life that a boy, any boy, born in America had a chance to someday grow up and be President. And now I believe it!"

Even in this day of prosperity, even in this day of great affluence, the needs of our people are deep and they are broad and they are wide.

I have seen a lot of changes in the 35 years that I have been in Washington. And that is exactly how it should have been. When we do not change we remain static and we do not go forward.

We have made progress in these 35 years. In three decades we have seen more progress in this great country than all of the civilizations in history could even imagine.

I saw the other day that one critic was complaining about how the 1958 dollar was worth more than the one that we've got today.

I wondered why he stopped at 1958. Look at what has happened since I went to Washington in 1931 and brought my hopes and my suitcase of the Nation's Capital.

The real question is not how much the dollar was worth then but how much the workingman could buy with his pay envelope.

I asked my economists when I heard of that statement—and I didn't have any when I got on the train to leave home from Texas—to take all the 1932 statistics and to convert them for me to 1965 prices.

And here is the story that those figures tell:

In 1932, the average factory worker made $17 a week when Roosevelt became President. Now, you're going to say that $17 bought more—and it did. But you convert that $17 into today's dollars, 1966 dollars, and it will buy only $39 worth of today's goods.

But today's factory worker does not get $39, today's factory worker buys $111 worth of goods. His true purchasing power has increased by 300 percent. Now that's what's been done for the average worker.

Now let's take the case of the farmer. In 1932, the average farmer cleared $304 a year. When you convert that in today's dollar, it will buy $869 worth of goods.

But the average farmer today can actually buy not $869 worth of goods but $4,280 worth of goods. He has a purchasing power 400 percent greater than he had in 1932. And that may be why the Democratic Party with the workers and the farmers carried 44 States in 1964 and are going to carry that many more in 1966.

Now what about the people that are not workers or not farmers. Well, I'll tell you what's happened to them.

Their dividends have multiplied threefold. They rose from 6.4 billion in 1932 to nearly 19 billion last year. And remember that these are dollars with the same purchasing power—from 6 to 19.

When I came to Washington, nearly 5 percent of all Americans were illiterate. We have cut that figure in half today.

The average American had only an eighth grade education. Today he gets almost four years of high school—and before the end of my lifetime I want to see him—the average American—get a college education. And that's what we are working for.

Back when I went to the Capital a newborn child could expect to live to be 62 years of age.

A child born today can expect to be around until the year 2036—a life expectancy of more than 70 years. And I hope that with the progress we're making with our cancer and our heart research—the law we passed last year—he just may be around a lot longer than 70.

In 1932 half of our retired people were living on less than $60 a month—and we're still now talking in terms of today's dollar.

If they got sick, the bills for the doctor and the hospital had to come out of that $60 a month. Tonight we have doubled their income and they have Medicare to help with their medical bills. I might add that a lot of people thought Medicare would never get on the books, but $3 billion will be paid out in it this year.

In 1932, 90 percent of our farm homes were lighted by kerosene lamps. Tonight 98 percent of our farm homes are lighted with electricity.

Not one of these changes came about without a long and bitter struggle.

Many of them were delayed far too long. Every time the President or a Congressman or a Senator presented a major piece of legislation to improve the welfare of the public, there was always somebody around to warn that we were spending ourselves into bankruptcy.

Some bankruptcy!

I say that because right now we are in the sixth year of our longest uninterrupted era of prosperity in the history of our Nation. Profits, sales, wages, incomes are higher than they have ever been before.

When the Democratic administration took office in 1961 the gross national product—that is the total value of all goods and all services we enjoy—was $504 billion. In the first quarter of 1966 it was not 504, it was $714 billion. This is an increase of more than $210 billion—or more than 41 percent. And tonight, May the 17th, it is even larger—and it is still going up and up.

In January, the Council of Economic Advisers estimated the gross national product of 1966 would not be $504 billion, but would fall within a range of $717 billion to $727 billion. And we might even exceed the top of this range. Some experts tonight believe that is will even go to $735 billion or higher.

In fiscal 1961 we took in Federal taxes of some $78 billion. This year we are taking in more than $100 billion, or 29 percent more.

From the time I became President until tonight we have increased our expenditures for health and education and training by $10 billion. And that is just a little over 2 years.

Since I came to Washington, this country has learned something important. We have learned that the right thing to do is usually the smart thing to do.

We have learned that the money we spend on health and education is not a gift but it is an investment. These investments come back in the form of higher earnings, they come back in more personal expenditures, they come back in additional taxes. In education, for example, we know that a college graduate will earn nearly $140,000 more than the high school graduate during his lifetime.

We know that the money we spend on health is just as much an investment. If we can reduce sick leave in this country by only one day per worker every year, we can add $3 billion to our gross national product.

We know that every child born in this country is entitled to have the fullest measure of freedom that we can provide and he should have every equality of opportunity.

And finally, we know that every citizen, according to his conscience, has a duty to work for the advancement of the greatest system of government ever known—the system that we call democracy—the system that we call our own free enterprise system.

We have worked for that advancement through both of our political parties and in spite of any temporary differences that we have had.

I remember very well some of the remarks I made the day before the election when I closed my campaign in my home State.

I said then—and I want to repeat them tonight— ''I have tried as best I could to lead this country to peace and to lead this country to prosperity.

"I have tried all the time to be President of all the people. I have tried to treat every man equally. I have tried to protect and make secure every man's constitutional rights."

Tonight I repeat that pledge. I was elected to my office as a Democrat.

As much as I love my dear Democratic Party, I love my America much more. The decisions I made last night and those that I made tonight transcend party considerations, because they involve the destiny of all of the people of America. The marines, the army, the airmen, and the sailors who man the carriers off the coast of Vietnam tonight—they know no parties. They wear no Republican jackets or no Democratic caps.

So I have tried to base my decisions and my thinking and all of my actions on what I think is really best for this country. I believe that is what my country expects me to do.

So tonight I ask each of you present here to give me a matching pledge. I ask you and I ask every American to put our country first if we want to keep it first. Put it above parties, if you want to seize the larger victories—the victories of freedom, and the victories of peace, and the victories of prosperity.

Put away all the childish divisive things, if you want the maturity and the unity that is the mortar of a nation's greatness.

I do not believe that those men who are out there fighting for us tonight think that we should enjoy the luxury of fighting each other back home.

So I ask you to carefully read the statements of every public official and of every candidate for every office and read them carefully, and then judge for yourself. Ask yourselves, "Is he helping the cause of his country or is he advancing the cause of himself?" Ask him, "Is he trying to draw us together and unite our land, or is he trying to pull us apart to promote himself?"

This is the measuring stick that I ask the people of America to judge us by.

I ask you, my friends, to put your faith in reason. I ask you to come together as a people and as a nation. I ask you to join hands and trust ourselves to God's hands, so that we can, together, bring peace to this world and a richer, better life to all who so earnestly desire it, and so urgently seek it.

A quarter of a century ago, a power-mad leader started marching through Poland engulfing free people. The courageous voice of Winston Churchill held that dictator until we could rally our forces, until we could unite our people, until we could bring relief to freedom's forces.

Following World War II, when our men returned and we had a chance to judge what we had been through, our Nation decided and our Congress decided that we should, as a matter of our Nation's highest policy, declare that all would-be adventurous conquerors who sought to engulf free people with power and with might and with force, and to conquer them with arms, these conquerors would have to meet and resist the forces of the United States of America in the various alliances of the world.

Our people and their representatives in the Congress decided that it was wiser to warn the dictators in advance that they would have to meet the United States if they took the road of aggression. And we did warn them. We did it in NATO, in collective security. We did it in SEATO, in the Southeast Asia Treaty Organization. We said that if any nation that is a part of this treaty—and there were 8 of them signed it—finds itself under attack and asks for our help, they will get it. And they are getting it tonight in Vietnam.

I do not genuinely believe that there is any single person anywhere in the world that wants peace as much as I want it.

I want the killing to stop.

I want us to join hands with others to do more in the fight against hunger and disease and ignorance.

But we all know from hard-won experience that the road to peace is not the road of concession and retreat.

A lot of our friends tell us how troubled they are and how frustrated they are. And we are troubled and we are frustrated, and we are seeking a way out. And we are trying to find a solution.

As Commander in Chief, I am neither a Democrat or Republican. The men fighting in Vietnam are simply Americans. Our policy in Vietnam is a national policy. It springs from every lesson that we have learned in this century. We fought in the First World War and then we failed to build a system of collective security which could have prevented the Second World War.

Standing in this great city of Chicago on October 5, 1937, one of the greatest leaders ever to be produced in America, Franklin D. Roosevelt said:

"When an epidemic of physical disease starts to spread, the community approves and joins in a quarantine of the patients in order to protect the health of the community against the spread of the disease. . . .

"War is a contagion, whether it be declared or undeclared. It can engulf states and peoples remote from the original scene of hostilities."

The country heard him, but did not listen.

The country failed to back him in that trying hour. And then we saw what happened when the aggressors felt confident that they could win while we sat by.

That was what President Truman remembered in 1947 in Greece and Turkey.

That is what he remembered during the blockade of Berlin and when the attack came in Korea.

That is what President Eisehower remembered in 1954 when he laid before the Senate the SEATO Treaty, and during the crisis over Quemoy and Matsu.

That is what President John F. Kennedy remembered when, in the face of Communist aggression in Laos and Vietnam, he began to send American forces there as early as 1962.

Yes, we have learned over the past half century that failure to meet aggression means war, not peace.

In carrying out that policy we have taken casualties in Berlin and Korea, and now in Vietnam.

We have had 160,000 American casualties from World War II up until Vietnam. Now every morning I look at those casualty figures. I measure them not as statistics, but man by man.

As of this morning, we lost 1,705 Americans in Vietnam in the year 1966—1,705. But we lost 49,000 last year on our highways.

But I tell you that if we fail in frustrating this aggression, the war that would surely come in Asia would produce casualties not in the hundreds or seventeen hundreds, but in the hundreds of thousands and perhaps in millions.

Your Government therefore, under your President, is determined to resist this aggression at the minimum cost to our people, and to our allies, and to the world.

I do not know what—who men may be trying to influence, and I do not seek to influence any tonight. But I do tell you here and now that we do not seek to enlarge this war, but we shall not run out of it.

America is determined to meet her commitments tonight, because those commitments are right.

As I said after a meeting yesterday with Ambassador Lodge just as he was returning to his post of duty:

—We shall continue to struggle against aggression and social misery in South Vietnam;
—We shall use our influence to help this young nation come together and move toward constitutional government;
—We shall seek an honorable peace.

Let those though who speak and write about Vietnam say clearly what other policy they would pursue.

And let them weigh their words carefully.

Let them remember that tonight there are 300,000 young Americans, our own boys, out there somewhere in Southeast Asia, on the land and on the sea and in the air. They are there fighting to quarantine another aggressor. They are there fighting for the peace of the world.

And let them remember that there are men on the other side who know well that their only hope for success in this aggression lies in a weakening of the fiber and the determination of the people of America. And so long as I am President, the policy of opposing aggression at minimum cost shall be continued.

I sent our ambassadors to more than 40 countries. I wrote letters to nearly 120 in the world asking for assistance, asking for peace. My plea was well received in all the nations of the world except the two most concerned, Red China and North Vietnam.

After 37 long days, while our men in uniform waited and while our planes were grounded on my orders, while our ambassadors went from nation to nation, we finally were forced to the conclusion that the time had not yet arrived when the Government of North Vietnam was willing or could even be persuaded to sit down at a peace table and try to reason these problems out. Therefore, our arguments need to be more persuasive and our determinations need to be more convincing and more compelling than they have been.

All I can say to you tonight is that the road ahead is going to be difficult. There will be some "Nervous Nellies" and some who will become frustrated and bothered and break ranks under the strain, and some will turn on their leaders, and on their country, and on our own fighting men. There will be times of trial and tension in the days ahead that will exact the best that is in all of us. But I have not the slightest doubt that the courage and the dedication and the good sense of the wise American people will ultimately prevail. They will stand united until every boy is brought home safely, until the gallant people of South Vietnam have their own choice of their own Government.

More than that, not just that one little country of 14 million people, but more than a hundred other little countries stand tonight and watch and wait. If America's commitment is dishonored in South Vietnam, it is dishonored in 40 other alliances or more that we have made.

So I leave you with the assurance that we love peace and we seek it every hour of every day. Any person who wishes to test us can give us the time and the date and the place, and he will find us occupying our peace chair at the negotiating table with any government who genuinely and who sincerely wants to talk instead of fight.

Perhaps my sentiments and my feelings are best expressed by the words of President Roosevelt when he prepared, only a day or so before he died in 1945, this speech and never had an opportunity to deliver it: "We seek peace—enduring peace. More than an end to war, we want an end to the beginnings of all wars—yes, an end to this brutal, inhuman and thoroughly impractical method of settling the differences between governments."

Somewhere tonight a great son of Wisconsin, Ambassador Gronouski, is winging his way across the waters to report to me in the Capital his conversations and his efforts to find a way to bring peace to this world.

The men who fight for us out there tonight in Vietnam—they are trying to find a way to peace. But they know—and I don't understand why we don't all recognize—that we can't get peace just for wishing for it. We must get on with the job until these men can come marching home, someday, when peace is secure not only for the people of America, but peace is secure for peace-loving people everywhere in this world.

The San Antonio Declaration
Address Before the National Legislative Conference
San Antonio, Texas
September 29, 1967

By 1967 protests in the United States reached violent proportions. During the summer riots broke out in Newark and Detroit over racial discord. The country was beginning to come apart. Johnson, therefore, chose this occasion to soften his position on negotiating a settlement of the American-Vietnamese War. It became his new platform for seeking someway out of the quicksand of the war.

I deeply appreciate this opportunity to appear before an organization whose members contribute every day such important work to the public affairs of our State and of our country.

This evening I came here to speak to you about Vietnam.

I do not have to tell you that our people are profoundly concerned about that struggle.

There are passionate convictions about the wisest course for our Nation to follow. There are many sincere and patriotic Americans who harbor doubts about sustaining the commitment that three Presidents and a half a million of our young men have made.

Doubt and debate are enlarged because the problems of Vietnam are quite complex. They are a mixture of political turmoil—of poverty—of religious and factional strife—of ancient servitude and modern longing for freedom. Vietnam is all of these things.

Vietnam is also the scene of a powerful aggression that is spurred by an appetite for conquest.

It is the arena where Communist expansionism is most aggressively at work in the world today—where it is crossing international frontiers in violation of international agreements;

where it is killing and kidnapping; where it is ruthlessly attempting to bend free people to its will.

Into this mixture of subversion and war, of terror and hope, America has entered—with its material power and with its moral commitment.

Why?

Why should three Presidents and the elected representatives of our people have chosen to defend this Asian nation more than 10,000 miles from American shores?

We cherish freedom—yes. We cherish self-determination for all people—yes. We abhor the political murder of any state by another, and the bodily murder of any people by gangsters of whatever ideology. And for 27 years—since the days of lend-lease—we have sought to strengthen free people against domination by aggressive foreign powers.

But the key to all that we have done is really our own security. At times of crisis—before asking Americans to fight and die to resist aggression in a foreign land—every American President has finally had to answer this question:

Is the aggression a threat—not only to the immediate victim—but to the United States of America and to the peace and security of the entire world of which we in America are a very vital part?

That is the question which Dwight Eisenhower and John Kennedy and Lyndon Johnson had to answer in facing the issue in Vietnam.

That is the question that the Senate of the United States answered by a vote of 82 to 1 when it ratified and approved the SEATO treaty in 1955, and to which the Members of the United States Congress responded in a resolution that it passed in 1964 by a vote of 504 to 2, ''. . . the United States is, therefore, prepared, as the President determines, to take all necessary steps, including the use of armed force, to assist any member or protocol state of the Southeast Asia Collective Defense Treaty requesting assistance in defense of its freedom.''

Those who tell us now that we should abandon our commitment—that securing South Vietnam from armed domination is not worth the price we are paying—must also answer this question. And the test they must meet is this: What would be the consequences of letting armed aggression against South Vietnam succeed? What would follow in the time ahead? What kind of world are they prepared to live in 5 months or 5 years from tonight?

For those who have borne the responsibility for decision during these past 10 years, the stakes to us have seemed clear—and have seemed high.

President Dwight Eisenhower said in 1959:

''Strategically, South Vietnam's capture by the Communists would bring their power several hundred miles into a hitherto free region. The remaining countries in Southeast Asia would be menaced by a great flanking movement. The freedom of 12 million people would be lost immediately, and that of 150 million in adjacent lands would be seriously endangered. The loss of South Vietnam would set in motion a crumbling process that could, as it progressed, have grave consequences for us and for freedom. . . .''

And President John F. Kennedy said in 1962:

''. . . withdrawal in the case of Vitenam and the case of Thailand might mean a collapse of the entire area.''

A year later, he reaffirmed that:

''We are not going to withdraw from that effort. In my opinion, for us to withdraw from that effort would mean a collapse not only of South Vietnam, but Southeast Asia. So we are going to stay there,'' said President Kennedy.

This is not simply an American viewpoint, I would have you legislative leaders know. I am going to call the roll now of those who live in that part of the world—in the great arc of Asian and Pacific nations—and who bear the responsibility for leading their people, and the responsibility for the fate of their people.

The President of the Philippines had this to say:

"Vietnam is the focus of attention now. . . . It may happen to Thailand or the Philippines, or anywhere, wherever there is misery, disease, ignorance. . . . For you to renounce your position of leadership in Asia is to allow the Red Chinese to gobble up all of Asia."

The Foreign Minister of Thailand said:

"(The American) decision will go down in history as the move that prevented the world from having to face another major conflagration."

The Prime Minister of Australia said:

"We are there because while Communist aggression persists the whole of Southeast Asia is threatened."

President Park of Korea said:

"For the first time in our history, we decided to dispatch our combat troops overseas . . . because in our belief any aggression against the Republic of Vietnam represented a direct and grave menace against the security and peace of free Asia, and therefore directly jeopardized the very security and freedom of our own people."

The Prime Minister of Malaysia warned his people that if the United States pulled out of South Vietnam, it would go to the Communists, and after that, it would be only a matter to time until they moved against neighboring states.

The Prime Minister of New Zealand said:

"We can thank God that America at least regards aggression in Asia with the same concern as it regards aggression in Europe—and is prepared to back up its concern with action."

The Prime Minister of Singapore said:

"I feel the fate of Asia—South and Southeast Asia—will be decided in the next few years by what happens in Vietnam."

I cannot tell you tonight as your President—with certainty—that a Communist conquest of South Vietnam would be followed by a Communist conquest of Southeast Asia. But I do know there are North Vietnamese troops in Laos. I do know that there are North Vietnamese trained guerrillas tonight in northeast Thailand. I do know that there are Communist-supported guerrilla forces operating in Burma. And a Communist coup was barely averted in Indonesia, the fifth largest nation in the world.

So your American President cannot tell you—with certainty—that a Southeast Asia dominated by Communist power would bring a third world war much closer to terrible reality. One could hope that this would not be so.

But all that we have learned in this tragic century strongly suggests to me that it would be so. As President of the United States, I am not prepared to gamble on the chance that it is not so. I am not prepared to risk the security—indeed, the survival—of this American Nation on mere hope and wishful thinking. I am convinced that by seeing this struggle through now, we are greatly reducing the chances of a much larger war—perhaps a nuclear war. I would rather stand in Vietnam, in our time, and by meeting this danger now, and facing up to it, thereby reduce the danger for our children and for our grandchildren.

I want to turn now to the struggle in Vietnam itself.

There are questions about this difficult war that must trouble every really thoughtful person. I am going to put some of these questions. And I am going to give you the very best answers that I can give you.

First, are the Vietnamese—with our help, and that of their other allies—really making any progress? Is there a forward movement? The reports I see make it clear that there is. Certainly there is a positive movement toward constitutional government. Thus far the Vietnamese have met the political schedule that they laid down in January 1966.

The people wanted an elected, responsive government. They wanted it strongly enough to brave a vicious campaign of Communist terror and assassination to vote for it. It has been said that they killed more civilians in 4 weeks trying to keep them from voting before the election than our American bombers have killed in the big cities of North Vietnam in bombing military targets.

On November 1, subject to the action, of course, of the Constituent Assembly, an elected government will be inaugurated and an elected Senate and Legislature will be installed. Their responsibility is clear: To answer the desires of the South Vietnamese people for self-determination and for peace, for an attack on corruption, for economic development, and for social justice.

There is progress in the war itself, steady progress considering the war that we are fighting; rather dramatic progress considering the situation that actually prevailed when we sent our troops there in 1965; when we intervened to prevent the dismemberment of the country by the Vietcong and the North Vietnamese.

The campaigns of the last year drove the enemy from many of their major interior bases. The military victory almost within Hanoi's grasp in 1965 has now been denied them. The grip of the Vietcong on the people is being broken.

Since our commitment of major forces in July 1965 the proportion of the population living under Communist control has been reduced to well under 20 percent. Tonight the secure proportion of the population has grown from about 45 percent to 65 percent—and in the contested areas, the tide continues to run with us.

But the struggle remains hard. The South Vietnamese have suffered severely, as have we—particularly in the First Corps area in the north, where the enemy has mounted his heaviest attacks, and where his lines of communication to North Vietnam are shortest. Our casualties in the war have reached about 13,500 killed in action, and about 85,000 wounded. Of those 85,000 wounded, we thank God that 79,000 of the 85,000 have been returned, or will return to duty shortly. Thanks to our great American medical science and the helicopter.

I know there are other questions on your minds, and on the minds of many sincere, troubled Americans: "Why not negotiate now?" so many ask me. The answer is that we and our South Vietnamese allies are wholly prepared to negotiate tonight.

I am ready to talk with Ho Chi Minh, and other chiefs of state concerned, tomorrow.

I am ready to have Secretary Rusk meet with their foreign minister tomorrow.

I am ready to send a trusted representative of America to any spot on this earth to talk in public or private with a spokesman of Hanoi.

We have twice sought to have the issue of Vietnam dealt with by the United Nations—and twice Hanoi has refused.

Our desire to negotiate peace—through the United Nations or out—has been made very, very clear to Hanoi—directly and many times through third parties.

As we have told Hanoi time and time and time again, the heart of the matter is really this: The United States is willing to stop all aerial and naval bombardment of North Vietnam when this will lead promptly to productive discussions. We, of course, assume that while discussions proceed, North Vietnam would not take advantage of the bombing cessation or limitation.

But Hanoi has not accepted any of these proposals.

So it is by Hanoi's choice—and not ours, and not the rest of the world's—that the war continues.

Why, in the face of military and political progress in the South, and the burden of our bombing in the North, do they insist and persist with the war?

From many sources the answer is the same. They still hope that the people of the United States will not see this struggle through to the very end. As one Western diplomat reported to me only this week—he had just been in Hanoi— "They believe their staying power is greater than ours and that they can't lose." A visitor from a Communist capital had this to say: "They expect the war to be long, and that the Americans in the end will be defeated by a breakdown in morale, fatigue, and psychological factors." The Premier of North Vietnam said as far back as 1962: "Americans do not like long, inconclusive war. . . . Thus we are sure to win in the end."

Are the North Vietnamese right about us?

I think not. No. I think they are wrong. I think it is the common failing to totalitarian regimes that they cannot really understand the nature of our democracy:

—They mistake dissent for disloyalty.
—They mistake restlessness for a rejection of policy.
—They mistake a few committees for a country.
—They misjudge individual speeches for public policy.

They are no better suited to judge the strength and perseverance of America than the Nazi and the Stalinist propagandists were able to judge it. It is a tragedy that they must discover these qualities in the American people, and discover them through a bloody war.

And, soon or late, they will discover them.

In the meantime, it shall be our policy to continue to seek negotiations—confident that reason will some day prevail; that Hanoi will realize that it just can never win; that it will turn away from fighting and start building for its own people.

Since World War II, this Nation has met and has mastered many challenges—challenges in Greece and Turkey, in Berlin, in Korea, in Cuba.

We met them because brave men were willing to risk their lives for their nation's security. And braver men have never lived than those who carry our colors in Vietnam at this very hour.

The price of these efforts, of course, has been heavy. But the price of not having made them at all, not having seen them through, in my judgment would have been vastly greater.

Our goal has been the same—in Europe, in Asia, in our own hemisphere. It has been—and it is now—peace.

And peace cannot be secured by wishes; peace cannot be preserved by noble words and pure intentions. "Enduring peace," Franklin D. Roosevelt said, "cannot be bought at the cost of other people's freedom."

The late President Kennedy put it precisely in November 1961, when he said: "We are neither warmongers nor appeasers, neither hard nor soft. We are Americans determined to defend the frontiers of freedom by an honorable peace if peace is possible but by arms if arms are used against us."

The true peace-keepers in the world tonight are not those who urge us to retire from the field in Vietnam—who tell us to try to find the quickest, cheapest exit from that tormented land, no matter what the consequences to us may be.

The true peace-keepers are those men who stand out there on the DMZ at this very hour, taking the worst that the enemy can give. The true peace-keepers are the soldiers who are breaking the terrorist's grip around the villages of Vietnam—the civilians who are bringing medical care and food and education to people who have already suffered a generation of war.

And so I report to you that we are going to continue to press forward. Two things we must do. Two things we shall do.

First, we must not mislead the enemy. Let him not think that debate and dissent will produce wavering and withdrawal. For I can assure you they won't. Let him not think that protests will produce surrender. Because they won't. Let him not think that he will wait us out. For he won't.

Second, we will provide all that our brave men require to do the job that must be done. And that job is going to be done.

These gallant men have our prayers—have our thanks—have our heart-felt praise—and our deepest gratitude.

Let the world know that the keepers of peace will endure through every trial—and that with the full backing of their countrymen, they are going to prevail.

Johnson Steps Down

Televised Address to the Nation
Washington, D.C.
March 31, 1968

In 1968 riots and protests had spread to almost every part of the United States. The President could not speak on a college campus. Many of those who supported him and sought to speak were shouted down. In March Johnson defeated Senator Eugene McCarthy by such a narrow margin in the New Hampshire Democratic primary that McCarthy's defeat became a "victory" for him. And Senator Robert Kennedy announced he was entering Presidential primaries to challenge the President on the war and for the nomination. Thus, Lyndon Johnson spoke to the nation on this evening outlining his new measures to disengage America from the American-Vietnamese War. But he caught the entire country by surprise with his announcement that he would not be a candidate for his party's nomination. He was, in essence, admitting defeat.

Tonight I want to speak to you of peace in Vietnam and Southeast Asia.

No other question so preoccupies our people. No other dream so absorbs the 250 million human beings who live in that part of the world. No other goal motivates American policy in Southeast Asia.

For years, representatives of our Government and others have traveled the world—seeking to find a basis for peace talks.

Since last September, they have carried the offer that I made public at San Antonio.

That offer was this:

That the United States would stop its bombardment of North Vietnam when that would lead promptly to productive discussions—and that we would assume that North Vietnam would not take military advantage of our restraint.

Hanoi denounced this offer, both privately and publicly. Even while the search for peace was going on, North Vietnam rushed their preparations for a savage assault on the people, the government, and the allies of South Vietnam.

Their attack—during the Tet holidays—failed to achieve its principal objectives.

It did not collapse the elected government of South Vietnam or shatter its army—as the Communists had hoped.

It did not produce a "general uprising" among the people of the cities as they had predicted.

The Communists were unable to maintain control of any of the more than 30 cities that they attacked. And they took very heavy casualties.

But they did compel the South Vietnamese and their allies to move certain forces from the countryside into the cities.

They caused widespread disruption and suffering. Their attacks, and the battles that followed, made refugees of half a million human beings.

The Communists may renew their attack any day.

They are, it appears, trying to make 1968 the year of decision in South Vietnam—the year that brings, if not final victory or defeat, at least a turning point in the struggle.

This much is clear:

If they do mount another round of heavy attacks, they will not succeed in destroying the fighting power of South Vietnam and its allies.

But tragically, this is also clear: Many men—on both sides of the struggle—will be lost. A nation that has already suffered 20 years of warfare will suffer once again. Armies on both sides will take new casualties. And the war will go on.

There is no need for this to be so.

There is no need to delay the talks that could bring an end to this long and this bloody war.

Tonight, I renew the offer I made last August—to stop the bombardment of North Vietnam. We ask that talks begin promptly, that they be serious talks on the substance of peace. We assume that during those talks Hanoi will not take advantage of our restraint.

We are prepared to move immediately toward peace through negotiations.

So, tonight, in the hope that this action will lead to early talks, I am taking the first step to deescalate the conflict. We are reducing—substantially reducing—the present level of hostilities.

And we are doing so unilaterally, and at once.

Tonight, I have ordered our aircraft and our naval vessels to make no attacks on North Vietnam, except in the area north of the demilitarized zone where the continuing enemy buildup directly threatens allied forward positions and where the movements of their troops and supplies are clearly related to that threat.

The area in which we are stopping our attacks includes almost 90 percent of North Vietnam's population, and most of its territory. Thus there will be no attacks around the principal populated areas, or in the food-producing areas of North Vietnam.

Even this very limited bombing of the North could come to an early end—if our restraint is matched by restraint in Hanoi. But I cannot in good conscience stop all bombing so long as to do so would immediately and directly endanger the lives of our men and our allies. Whether a complete bombing halt becomes possible in the future will be determined by events.

Our purpose in this action is to bring about a reduction in the level of violence that now exists.

It is to save the lives of brave men—and to save the lives of innocent women and children. It is to permit the contending forces to move closer to a political settlement.

And tonight, I call upon the United Kingdom and I call upon the Soviet Union—as cochairmen of the Geneva Conferences, and as permanent members of the United Nations Security Council—to do all they can to move from the unilateral act of deescalation that I have just announced toward genuine peace in Southeast Asia.

Now, as in the past, the United States is ready to send its representatives to any forum, at any time, to discuss the means of bringing this ugly war to an end.

I am designating one of our most distinguished Americans, Ambassador Averell Harriman, as my personal representative for such talks. In addition, I have asked Ambassador Llewellyn Thompson, who returned from Moscow for consultation, to be available to join Ambassador Harriman at Geneva or any other suitable place—just as soon as Hanoi agrees to a conference.

I call upon President Ho Chi Minh to respond positively, and favorably, to this new step toward peace.

But if peace does not come now through negotiations, it will come when Hanoi understands that our common resolve is unshakable, and our common strength is invincible.

Tonight, we and the other allied nations are contributing 600,000 fighting men to assist 700,000 South Vietnamese troops in defending their little country.

Our presence there has always rested on this basic belief: The main burden of preserving their freedom must be carried out by them—by the South Vietnamese themselves.

We and our allies can only help to provide a shield behind which the people of South Vietnam can survive and can grow and develop. On their efforts—on their determination and resourcefulness—the outcome will ultimately depend.

That small, beleaguered nation has suffered terrible punishment for more than 20 years.

I pay tribute once again tonight to the great courage and endurance of its people. South Vietnam supports armed forces tonight of almost 700,000 men—and I call your attention to the fact that this is the equivalent of more than 10 million in our own population. Its people maintain their firm determination to be free of domination by the North.

There has been substantial progress, I think, in building a durable government during these last 3 years. The South Vietnam of 1965 could not have survived the enemy's Tet offensive of 1968. The elected government of South Vietnam survived that attack—and is rapidly repairing the devastation that it wrought.

The South Vietnamese know that further efforts are going to be required:

—to expand their own armed forces,
—to move back into the countryside as quickly as possible,
—to increase their taxes,
—to select the very best men that they have for civil and military responsibility,
—to achieve a new unity within their constitutional government, and
—to include in the national effort all those groups who wish to preserve South Vietnam's control over its own destiny.

Last week President Thieu ordered the mobilization of 135,000 additional South Vietnamese. He plans to reach—as soon as possible—a total military strength of more than 800,000 men.

To achieve this, the Government of South Vietnam started the drafting of 19-year-olds on March 1st. On May 1st, the Government will begin the drafting of 18-year-olds.

Last month, 10,000 men volunteered for military service—that was two and a half times the number of volunteers during the same month last year. Since the middle of January, more than 48,000 South Vietnamese have joined the armed forces—and nearly half of them volunteered to do so.

All men in the South Vietnamese armed forces have had their tours of duty extended for the duration of the war, and reserves are now being called up for immediate active duty.

President Thieu told his people last week:

"We must make greater efforts and accept more sacrifices because, as I have said many times, this is our country. The existence of our nation is at stake, and this is mainly a Vietnamese responsibility."

He warned his people that a major national effort is required to root out corruption and incompetence at all levels of government.

We applaud this evidence of determination on the part of South Vietnam. Our first priority will be to support their effort.

We shall accelerate the reequipment of South Vietnam's armed forces—in order to meet the enemy's increased firepower. This will enable them progressively to undertake a larger share of combat operations against the Communist invaders.

On many occasions I have told the American people that we would send to Vietnam those forces that are required to accomplish our mission there. So, with that as our guide, we have previously authorized a force level of approximately 525,000.

Some weeks ago—to help meet the enemy's new offensive—we sent to Vietnam about

11,000 additional Marine and airborne troops. They were deployed by air in 48 hours, on an emergency basis. But the artillery, tank, aircraft, medical, and other units that were needed to work with and to support these infantry troops in combat could not then accompany them by air on that short notice.

In order that these forces may reach maximum combat effectiveness, the Joint Chiefs of Staff have recommended to me that we should prepare to send—during the next 5 months—support troops totaling approximately 13,500 men.

A portion of these men will be made available from our active forces. The balance will come from reserve component units which will be called up for service.

The actions that we have taken since the beginning of the year

—to reequip the South Vietnamese forces,
—to meet our responsibilities in Korea, as well as our responsibilities in Vietnam,
—to meet price increases and the cost of activating and deploying reserve forces,
—to replace helicopters and provide the other military supplies we need,

all of these actions are going to require additional expenditures.

The tentative estimate of those additional expenditures is $2.5 billion in this fiscal year, and $2.6 billion in the next fiscal year.

These projected increases in expenditures for our national security will bring into sharper focus the Nation's need for immediate action: action to protect the prosperity of the American people and to protect the strength and the stability of our American dollar.

On many occasions I have pointed out that, without a tax bill or decreased expenditures, next year's deficit would again be around $20 billion. I have emphasized the need to set strict priorities in our spending. I have stressed that failure to act and to act promptly and decisively would raise very strong doubts throughout the world about America's willingness to keep its financial house in order.

Yet Congress has not acted. And tonight we face the sharpest financial threat in the postwar era—at threat to the dollar's role as the keystone of international trade and finance in the world.

Last week, at the monetary conference in Stockholm, the major industrial countries decided to take a big step toward creating a new international monetary asset that will strengthen the international monetary system. I am very proud of the very able work done by Secretary Fowler and Chairman Martin of the Federal Reserve Board.

But to make this system work the United States just must bring its balance of payments to—or very close to—equilibrium. We must have a responsible fiscal policy in this country. The passage of a tax bill now, together with expenditure control that the Congress may desire and dictate, is absolutely necessary to protect this Nation's security, to continue our prosperity, and to meet the needs of our people.

What is at stake is 7 years of unparalleled prosperity. In those 7 years, the real income of the average American, after taxes, rose by almost 30 percent—a gain as large as that of the entire preceding 19 years.

So the steps that we must take to convince the world are exactly the steps we must take to sustain our own economic strength here at home. In the past 8 months, prices and interest rates have risen because of our inaction.

We must, therefore, now do everything we can to move from debate to action—from talking to voting. There is, I believe—I hope there is—in both Houses of the Congress—a growing sense of urgency that this situation just must be acted upon and must be corrected.

My budget in January was, we thought, a tight one. It fully reflected our evaluation of most of the demanding needs of this Nation.

But in these budgetary matters, the President does not decide alone. The Congress has the power and the duty to determine appropriations and taxes.

The Congress is now considering our proposals and they are considering reductions in the budget that we submitted.

As part of a program of fiscal restraint that includes the tax surcharge, I shall approve appropriate reductions in the January budget when and if Congress so decides that that should be done.

One thing is unmistakably clear, however: Our deficit just must be reduced. Failure to act could bring on conditions that would strike hardest at those people that all of us are trying so hard to help.

These times call for prudence in this land of plenty. I believe that we have the character to provide it, and tonight I plead with the Congress and with the people to act promptly to serve the national interest, and thereby serve all of our people.

Now let me give you my estimate of the chances for peace:

—the peace that will one day stop the bloodshed in South Vietnam,
—that will permit all the Vietnamese people to rebuild and develop their land,
—that will permit us to turn more fully to our own tasks here at home.

I cannot promise that the initiative that I have announced tonight will be completely successful in achieving peace any more than the 30 others that we have undertaken and agreed to in recent years.

But it is our fervent hope that North Vietnam, after years of fighting that have left the issue unresolved, will now cease its efforts to achieve a military victory and will join with us in moving toward the peace table.

And there may come a time when South Vietnamese—on both sides—are able to work out a way to settle their own differences by free political choice rather than by war.

As Hanoi considers its course, it should be in no doubt of our intentions. It must not miscalculate the pressures within our democracy in this election year.

We have no intention of widening this war.

But the United States will never accept a fake solution to this long and arduous struggle and call it peace.

No one can foretell the precise terms of an eventual settlement.

Our objective in South Vietnam has never been the annihilation of the enemy. It has been to bring about a recognition in Hanoi that its objective—taking over the South by force—could not be achieved.

We think that peace can be based on the Geneva Accords of 1954—under political conditions that permit the South Vietnamese—all the South Vietnamese—to chart their course free of any outside domination or interference, from us or from anyone else.

So tonight I reaffirm the pledge that we made at Manila—that we are prepared to withdraw our forces from South Vietnam as the other side withdraws its forces to the north, stops the infiltration, and the level of violence thus subsides.

Our goal of peace and self-determination in Vietnam is directly related to the future of all of Southeast Asia—where much has happened to inspire confidence during the past 10 years. We have done all that we knew how to do to contribute and to help build that confidence.

A number of its nations have shown what can be accomplished under conditions of security. Since 1966, Indonesia, the fifth largest nation in all the world, with a population of more than 100 million people, has had a government that is dedicated to peace with its neighbors and improved conditions for its own people. Political and economic cooperation between nations has grown rapidly.

I think every American can take a great deal of pride in the role that we have played in bringing this about in Southeast Asia. We can rightly judge—as responsible Southeast Asians themselves do—that the progress of the past 3 years would have been far less likely—if not completely impossible—if America's sons and others had not made their stand in Vietnam.

At Johns Hopkins University, about 3 years ago, I announced that the United States would take part in the great work of developing Southeast Asia, including the Mekong Valley, for all the people of that region. Our determination to help build a better land—a better land for men on both sides of the present conflict—has not diminished in the least. Indeed, the ravages of war, I think, have made it more urgent than ever.

So, I repeat on behalf of the United States again tonight what I said at Johns Hopkins—that North Vietnam could take its place in this common effort just as soon as peace comes.

Over time, a wider framework of peace and security in Southeast Asia may become possible. The new cooperation of the nations of the area could be a foundation-stone. Certainly friendship with the nations of such a Southeast Asia is what the United States seeks—and that is all that the United States seeks.

One day, my fellow citizens, there will be peace in Southeast Asia.

It will come because the people of Southeast Asia want it—those whose armies are at war tonight, and those who, though threatened, have thus far been spared.

Peace will come because Asians were willing to work for it—and to sacrifice for it—and to die by the thousands for it.

But let it never be forgotten: Peace will come also because America sent her sons to help secure it.

It has not been easy—far from it. During the past 4 1/2 years, it has been my fate and my responsibility to be Commander in Chief. I have lived—daily and nightly—with the cost of this war. I know the pain that it has inflicted. I know, perhaps better than anyone, the misgivings that it has aroused.

Throughout this entire, long period, I have been sustained by a single principle: that what we are doing now, in Vietnam, is vital not only to the security of Southeast Asia, but it is vital to the security of every American.

Surely we have treaties which we must respect. Surely we have commitments that we are going to keep. Resolutions of the Congress testify to the need to resist aggression in the world and in Southeast Asia.

But the heart of our involvement in South Vietnam—under three different Presidents, three separate administrations—has always been America's own security.

And the larger purpose of our involvement has always been to help the nations of Southeast Asia become independent and stand alone, self-sustaining, as members of a great world community—at peace with themselves, and at peace with all others.

With such an Asia, our country—and the world—will be far more secure than it is tonight.

I believe that a peaceful Asia is far nearer to reality because of what America has done in Vietnam. I believe that the men who endure the dangers of battle—fighting there for us tonight—are helping the entire world avoid far greater conflicts, far wider wars, far more destruction, than this one.

The peace that will bring them home someday will come. Tonight I have offered the first in what I hope will be a series of mutual moves toward peace.

I pray that it will not be rejected by the leaders of North Vietnam. I pray that they will accept it as a means by which the sacrifices of their own people may be ended. And I ask your help and your support, my fellow citizens, for this effort to reach across the battlefield toward an early peace.

Finally, my fellow Americans, let me say this:

Of those to whom much is given, much is asked. I cannot say and no man could say that no more will be asked of us.

Yet, I believe that now, no less than when the decade began, this generation of Americans is willing to "pay any price, bear any burden, meet any hardship, support any friend, oppose any foe to assure the survival and the success of liberty."

Since those words were spoken by John F. Kennedy, the people of America have kept that compact with mankind's noblest cause.

And we shall continue to keep it.

Yet, I believe that we must always be mindful of this one thing, whatever the trials and the tests ahead. The ultimate strength of our country and our cause will lie not in powerful weapons or infinite resources or boundless wealth, but will lie in the unity of our people.

This I believe very deeply.

Throughout my entire public career I have followed the personal philosophy that I am a free man, an American, a public servant, and a member of my party, in that order always and only.

For 37 years in the service of Our Nation, first as a Congressman, as a Senator, and as Vice President, and now as your President, I have put the unity of the people first. I have put it ahead of any divisive partisanship.

And in these times as in times before, it is true that a house divided against itself by the spirit of faction, of party, of region, of religion, of race, is a house that cannot stand.

There is division in the American house now. There is divisiveness among us all tonight. And holding the trust that is mine, as President of all the people, I cannot disregard the peril to the progress of the American people and the hope and the prospect of peace for all peoples.

So, I would ask all Americans, whatever their personal interests or concern, to guard against divisiveness and all its ugly consequences.

Fifty-two months and 10 days ago, in a moment of tragedy and trauma, the duties of this office fell upon me. I asked then for your help and God's, that we might continue America on its course, binding up our wounds, healing our history, moving forward in new unity, to clear the American agenda and to keep the American commitment for all of our people.

United we have kept that commitment. United we have enlarged that commitment.

Through all time to come, I think America will be a stronger nation, a more just society, and a land of greater opportunity and fulfillment because of what we have all done together in these years of unparalleled achievement

Our reward will come in the life of freedom, peace, and hope that our children will enjoy through ages ahead.

What we won when all of our people united just must not now be lost in suspicion, distrust, selfishness, and politics among any of our people.

Believing this as I do, I have concluded that I should not permit the Presidency to become involved in the partisan divisions that are developing in this political year.

With America's sons in the fields far away, with America's future under challenge right here at home, with our hopes and the world's hopes for peace in the balance every day, I do not believe that I should devote an hour or a day of my time to any personal partisan causes or to any duties other than the awesome duties of this office—the Presidency of your country.

Accordingly, I shall not seek, and I will not accept, the nomination of my party for another term as your President.

But let men everywhere know, however, that a strong, a confident, and a vigilant America stands ready tonight to seek an honorable peace—and stands ready tonight to defend an honored cause—whatever the price, whatever the burden, whatever the sacrifice that duty may require.

Thank you for listening.

Good night and God bless all of you.

The President and the Media

Remarks Before the National Association of Broadcasters.
Chicago, Illinois
April 1, 1968

The day after Johnson announced that he would not seek his party's nomination, he spoke before this gathering. He declared that his real problem as President had been one of "communication" and did little to conceal his belief that media had contributed to that problem.

Some of you might have thought from what I said last night that I had been taking elocution lessons from Lowell Thomas. One of my aides said this morning, "Things are really getting confused around Washington, Mr. President."

I said, "How is that?"

He said, "It looks to me like you are going to the wrong convention in Chicago."

I said, "Well, what you overlooked was that it is April Fool."

Once again we are entering the period of national festivity which Henry Adams called "the dance of democracy." At its best, that can be a time of debate and enlightenment. At its worst, it can be a period of frenzy. But always it is a time when emotion threatens to substitute for reason. Yet the basic hope of a democracy is that somehow—amid all the frenzy and all the emotion—in the end, reason will prevail. Reason just must prevail—if democracy itself is to survive.

As I said last evening, there are very deep and very emotional divisions in this land that we love today—domestic divisions, divisions over the war in Vietnam. With all of my heart, I just wish this were not so. My entire career in public life—some 37 years of it—has been devoted to the art of finding an area of agreement because generally speaking, I have observed that there are so many more things to unite us Americans than there are to divide us.

But somehow or other, we have a facility sometimes of emphasizing the divisions and the things that divide us instead of discussing the things that unite us. Sometimes I have been called a seeker of "consensus"—more often that has been criticism of my actions instead of praise of them. But I have never denied it. Because to heal and to build support, to hold people together, is something I think is worthy and I believe it is a noble task. It is certainly a challenge for all of us in this land and this world where there is restlessness and uncertainty and danger. In my region of the country where I have spent my life, where brother was once divided against brother, my heritage has burned this lesson and it has burned it deep in my memory.

Yet along the way I learned somewhere that no leader can pursue public tranquility as his first and only goal. For a President to buy public popularity at the sacrifice of his better judgment is too dear a price to pay. This Nation cannot afford such a price, and this Nation cannot long afford such a leader.

So, the things that divide our country this morning will be discussed throughout the land. I am certain that the very great majority of informed Americans will act, as they have always acted, to do what is best for their country and what serves the national interest.

But the real problem of informing the people is still with us. I think I can speak with some authority about the problem of communication. I understand, far better than some of my severe and perhaps intolerant critics would admit, my own shortcomings as a communicator.

How does a public leader find just the right word or the right way to say no more or no less than he means to say—bearing in mind that anything he says may topple governments and may involve the lives of innocent men?

How does that leader speak the right phrase, in the right way, under the right conditions, to suit the accuracies and contingencies of the moment when he is discussing questions of policy, so that he does not stir a thousand misinterpretations and leave the wrong connotation or impression?

How does he reach the immediate audience and how does he communicate with the millions of others who are out there listening from afar?

The President, who must call his people and summon them to meet their responsibilities as citizens in a hard and an enduring war, often ponders these questions and searches for the right course.

You men and women who are masters of the broadcast media surely must know what I am talking about. It was a long time ago when a President once said, "The printing press is the most powerful weapon with which man has ever armed himself.'' In our age, the electronic media have added immeasurably to man's power. You have within your hands the means to make our Nation as intimate and as informed as a New England town meeting.

Yet the use of broadcasting has not cleared away all of the problems that we still have of communications. In some ways, I think, sometimes it has complicated them, because it tends to put the leader in a time capsule. It requires him often to abbreviate what he has to say. Too often, it may catch a random phrase from his rather lengthy discourse and project it as the whole story.

How many men, I wonder, Mayor Daley, in public life have watched themselves on a TV newscast and then been tempted to exclaim, ''Can that really be me?''

Well, there is no denying it: You of the broadcast industry have enormous power in your hands. You have the power to clarify and you have the power to confuse. Men in public life cannot remotely rival your opportunity—day after day, night after night, hour after hour on the hour—and the half hour, sometimes—you shape the Nation's dialogue.

The words that you choose, hopefully always accurate, and hopefully always just, are the words that are carried out for all of the people to hear.

The commentary that you provide can give the real meaning to the issues of the day or it can distort them beyond all meaning. By your standards of what is news, you can cultivate wisdom—or you can nurture misguided passion.

Your commentary carries an added element of uncertainty. Unlike the printed media, television writes on the wind. There is no accumulated record which the historian can examine later with a 20-20 vision of hindsight, asking these questions: ''How fair was he tonight? How impartial was he today? How honest was he all along?''

Well, I hope the National Association of Broadcasters, with whom I have had a pleasant association for many years, will point the way to all of us in developing this kind of a record because history is going to be asking very hard questions about our times and the period through which we are passing.

I think that we all owe it to history to complete the record.

But I did not come here this morning to sermonize. In matters of fairness and judgment, no law or no set of regulations and no words of mine can improve you or dictate your daily responsibility.

All I mean to do, and what I am trying to do, is to remind you where there is great power, there must also be great responsibility. This is true for broadcasters just as it is true for Presidents—and seekers for the Presidency.

What we say and what we do now will shape the kind of a world that we pass along to our children and our grandchildren. I keep this thought constantly in my mind during the long days and the somewhat longer nights when crisis comes at home and abroad.

I took a little of your prime time last night. I would not have done that except for a very prime purpose.

I reported on the prospects for peace in Vietnam. I announced that the United States is taking a very important unilateral act of deescalation which could—and I fervently pray will—lead to mutual moves to reduce the level of violence and to deescalate the war.

As I sat in my office last evening, waiting to speak, I thought of the many times each week when television brings the war into the American home.

No one can say exactly what effect those vivid scenes have on American opinion. Historians must only guess at the effect that television would have had during earlier conflicts on the future of this Nation:

—during the Korean war, for example, at that time when our forces were pushed back there to Pusan;

—or World War II, the Battle of the Bulge, or when our men were slugging it out in Europe or when most of our Air Force was shot down that day in June 1942 off Australia.

But last night television was being used to carry a different message. It was a message of peace. It occurred to me that the medium may be somewhat better suited to conveying the actions of conflict than to dramatizing the words that the leaders use in trying and hoping to end the conflict.

Certainly, it is more "dramatic" to show policemen and rioters locked in combat than to show men trying to cooperate with one another.

The face of hatred and of bigotry comes through much more clearly—no matter what its color. The face of tolerance, I seem to find, is rarely "newsworthy."

Progress—whether it is a man being trained for a job or millions being trained or whether it is a child in Head Start learning to read or an older person of 72 in adult education or being cared for in Medicare—rarely makes the news, although more than 20 million of them are affected by it.

Perhaps this is because tolerance and progress are not dynamic events—such as riots and conflicts are events.

Peace, in the news sense, is a "condition." War is an "event."

Part of your responsibility is simply to understand the consequences of that fact—the consequences of your own acts, and part of that responsibility, I think, is to try—as very best we all can—to draw the attention of our people to the real business of society in our system—finding and securing peace in the world—at home and abroad. For all that you have done and that you are doing and that you will do to this end, I thank you and I commend you.

I pray that the message of peace that I tried so hard to convey last night will be accepted in good faith by the leaders of North Vietnam.

I pray that one time soon, the evening news show will have, not another battle in the scarred hills of Vietnam, but will show men entering a room to talk about peace.

That is the event that I think the American people are yearning and longing to see.

President Thieu of Vietnam and his Government are now engaged in very urgent political and economic tasks which I referred to last night—and which we regard as very constructive and hopeful. We hope the Government of South Vietnam makes great progress in the days ahead.

But some time in the weeks ahead—immediately, I hope—President Thieu will be in a position to accept my invitation to visit the United States so he can come here and see our people too, and together we can strengthen and improve our plans to advance the day of peace.

I pray that you and that every American will take to heart my plea that we guard against divisiveness. We have won too much, we have come too far, and we have opened too many doors of opportunity, for these things now to be lost in a divided country where brother is separated from brother. For the time that is allotted me, I shall do everything in one man's power to hasten the day when the world is at peace and Americans of all races—and all creeds—of all convictions—can live together—without fear or without suspicion or without distrust—in unity, and in common purpose.

United we are strong; divided we are in great danger.

In speaking as I did to the Nation last night, I was moved by the very deep convictions that I entertain about the nature of the office that it is my present privilege to hold. The Office of the Presidency is the only office in this land of all the people. Whatever may be the personal wishes or preferences of any man who holds it, a President of all the people can afford no thought of self.

At no time and in no way and for no reason can a President allow the integrity or the responsibility or the freedom of the office ever to be compromised or diluted or destroyed because when you destroy it, you destroy yourselves.

I hope and I pray that by not allowing the Presidency to be involved in divisions and deep partisanship, I shall be able to pass on to my successor a stronger office—strong enough to guard and defend all the people against all the storms that the future may bring us.

You men and women who have come here to this great progressive city of Chicago, led by this dynamic and great public servant, Dick Daley, are yourselves charged with a peculiar responsibility. You are yourselves trustees, legally accepted trustees and legally selected trustees of a great institution on which the freedom of our land utterly depends.

The security, the success of our country, what happens to us tomorrow—rests squarely upon the media which disseminate the truth on which the decisions of democracy are made.

An informed mind—and we get a great deal of our information from you—is the guardian genius of democracy.

So, you are the keepers of a trust. You must be just. You must guard and you must defend your media against the spirit of faction, against the works of divisiveness and bigotry, against the corrupting evils of partisanship in any guise.

For America's press, as for the American Presidency, the integrity and the responsibility and the freedom—the freedom to know the truth and let the truth make us free—must never be compromised or diluted or destroyed.

The defense of our media is your responsibility. Government cannot and must not and never will—as long as I have anything to do about it—intervene in that role.

But I do want to leave this thought with you as I leave you this morning: I hope that you will give this trust your closest care, acting as I know you can, to guard not only against the obvious, but to watch for the hidden—the sometimes unintentional, the often petty intrusions upon the integrity of the information by which Americans decide.

Men and women of the airways fully—as much as men and women of public service—have a public trust and if liberty is to survive and to succeed, that solemn trust must be faithfully kept. I do not want—and I don't think you want—to wake up some morning and find America changed because we slept when we should have been awake, because we remained silent when we should have spoken up, because we went along with what was popular and fashionable and "in" rather than what was necessary and what was right.

Being faithful to our trust ought to be the prime test of any public trustee in office or on the airways.

In any society, all you students of history know that a time of division is a time of danger. And in these times now we must never forget that "eternal vigilance is the price of liberty."

Thank you for wanting me to come. I've enjoyed it.

Richard Milhous Nixon
(1969–1974)

Nineteen sixty-eight was the year of the take-over of Columbia University, the assassinations of Dr. Martin Luther King, Jr. and Robert F. Kennedy, and the Chicago police riot. It was also the year Richard M. Nixon finally achieved his fondest dream and was elected 37th President of the United States.

But Nixon faced formidable political problems. He was a minority President having been elected by only 43.4% of the voting public. He had narrowly defeated Hubert Humphrey by only .7%. He entered the office as the first President in the twentieth-century to face both Houses of Congress in control of the opposition party. Finally, George Wallace of Alabama posed a serious threat to him on the right wing. It was in this context that Nixon's Presidency unfolded.

Nixon's Administration may be divided into 3 periods. The first period extended from 1969 to 1970 as he sought to transform his minority constituency into a majority. The second period was one in which Nixon "played Presidential" that is, he tried to stand above partisan politics. This period lasted from 1970-1972. The final time of his Presidency, 1972-August 9, 1974, found him devoting the majority of his time to the Watergate scandals.

Though Nixon announced the day after his election that he would "bring us together," he could hardly make good on that promise, given the margin of his victory. He had to define a majority constituency and cultivate it. Therefore, in June 1969 Nixon opened his drive at General Beadle State College to rally his supporters and others to his cause. Nixon carried the banner from June to November 3 in rallying supporters against student revolutionaries, "neo-isolationists," and those who advocated precipitate withdrawal from Vietnam. Furthermore, he finally settled on a name for his constituency: The Great Silent Majority. Vice President Agnew picked up the banner on November 13 and began travelling throughout the country railing against the Eastern liberal establishment, the "media," permissive students and professors, and eventually during the 1970 Congressional elections the "radic-libs" (radical-liberals). In that election Republicans picked up 2 seats in the Senate, but lost 9 seats in the House and 11 governorships.

But there were two weaknesses in the drive to build a majority constituency. First, Nixon suffered a severe set-back in May, 1970 when a nation-wide protest erupted in response to his invasion of Cambodia. The extremity of the protest caused the Nixon Administration to soften temporarily its attacks on its opponents. Second, Nixon himself entered the 1970 campaign and put his prestige on the line in a furious last ditch effort to purge those in Congress who had opposed his foreign policy. His efforts in terms of his Presidential image were counter-productive. In the words of one of his aides, Nixon looked like "he was running for sheriff."[1]

The frenetic campaigning of the first two years led to a decision that created the next period in the Administration: Nixon should portray himself as above partisan politics and should look "Presidential." That translated into Nixon remaining aloof from the public and the press and a rhetoric of announcements of actions or future actions, such as the historic visit to the People's Republic of China, the visit to the Soviet Union, and wage and price controls. This approach was continued right through the 1972 Presidential campaign as the President campaigned very little relying on surrogate speakers to carry his message to the American people for him. And in 1972 Nixon gained a "landslide" victory carrying all but one state.

But the drama for the third period of his Presidency had already commenced on June 17, 1972 when 5 men including James McCord, security chief for the Committee to Re-elect the President, were caught burglarizing the headquarters of the Democratic National Committee in the Watergate complex. Watergate did not catch fire during the campaign despite some intriguing revelations about links between the burglars and the Committee and even the White House. But in February, 1973 the Senate voted to establish a select committee to investigate campaign irregularities the previous year, and the trial of the men involved in Watergate continued in Judge John Sirica's courtroom. In March the cover-up of illegal activities by the Administration came apart forcing Nixon to deal with it fully for the first time.

Nixon began his defense of Watergate on April 17 with a statement saying new information had come to him and that he had launched a new investigation into the matter. On April 30 he devoted an entire speech broadcast over radio and television to the subject of Watergate. From that point to the end of his Presidency, Nixon found events out of his control, events such as: John Dean's accusations that Nixon had approved the paying of blackmail money to one of the burglars; Alexander Butterfield's revelation that Nixon had "bugged" the Oval Office and other Presidential offices; the "firestorm" of protest over the firing of Archibald Cox, the special prosecutor; the erased 18 1/2 minute tape recording; and so on and on. Finally, on August 5, 1974 Nixon released several tape recordings of his conversations with Haldeman that demonstrated the two had conspired to obstruct justice in covering up the ties between the burglary and the White House. Four days later Nixon formally resigned as President of the United States.

Richard Nixon's rhetoric, I believe, is as distinctive from that of other politicians as it is consistent throughout his career. His rhetoric is essentially a campaign rhetoric carried over into the art of governing where it is not always suitable. And it is based on a principal axiom of campaigning: people vote against, rather than for people or issues. In that sense, Nixon's rhetoric is consistently a negative rhetoric that divides the political world into either/or choices just as one limits the choices in a campaign to those between the two candidates. There are six constituents to this campaign rhetoric that Nixon took into the White House:

1. Anticipate your opposition in advance so you can put him on the defensive.
2. Be specific about what you are opposed to so supporters will have reasons to oppose your adversary.
3. Be general about what you stand for so you do not alienate supporters or potential supporters.
4. Present your opponents as extremists or as part only of a minority.

5. Predict dire consequences should your opponent triumph in this case before the public.
6. Strip away the pretence to show that the basic choice involved in the issue is a contest between two mutually exclusive moralities, or "life-styles."[2]

Thus, Nixon defines himself and his constituency in terms of what they are opposed to which gives him tremendous freedom to switch positions on what he stands for because his constituency supports him for what he is against.

More important, Nixon's rhetoric becomes his reality. What he says becomes the truth upon which actions are calculated and carried out.[3] The world then is manufactured by language and adjusted through policy to meet the requirements first established by rhetoric.

But, in the end, the White House tape recordings broke the spell of language for they provided evidence contrary to Nixon's assertions about his Presidency and his involvement in the cover-up of Watergate. And that doomed the unreal world of Richard Nixon's Presidency and thus forced him to become the first American President to resign from office in disgrace.

Notes

1. Cf. Rowland Evans, Jr. and Robert D. Novak, *Nixon in the White House: The Frustration of Power* (New York: Random House, 1971), pp. 245-353; and Jonathan Schell, *The Time of Illusion* (New York: Alfred A. Knopf, 1976), pp. 77-134.
2. The structure of Nixon's political rhetoric began in his first campaign against Jerry Voorhis in 1946 and was refined over the years. His mentor was Murray Chotiner and one should consult Chotiner's advice on campaigning found in his "Fundamentals of Campaign Organization" (n.p., n.d.) 24pp. To my knowledge, it has not been published in its entirety, but has been quoted extensively by writers on Nixon's career.
3. For only one of many examples, see his official word about the results of the 1970 campaign as described by Evans and Novak, pp. 347-352.

Student Revolutionaries
Address at the Dedication of the Karl E. Mundt Library at
General Beadle State College
Madison, South Dakota
June 3, 1969

President Nixon took the opportunity of this dedication to speak out on the problem of campus unrest that had plagued colleges and universities for the past several years. By omitting any reference to the war in Viet Nam, the President implicitly denied protest against the war was a cause for unrest. In fact, he appeared to eliminate government policy altogether as an underlying cause of the turmoil in academe. In so doing, he was refuting those who blamed the government for the outbursts of demonstrations and violence, a view expressed to the President by Calvin Plimpton, President of Amherst College, in his letter of 28 April. Plimpton wrote the President that demonstrations would continue until government leaders "attack more effectively, massively, persistently the major social and foreign problems of our country." Nixon rejected this analysis. Rather, he said, the cause of the current unrest lay in students' legitimate desire for honesty in American life and their "attempt to strip away sham and pretense, to puncture illusion, to get down to the basic nub of truth." The more imperative cause, Nixon stated, for the revolts could be found in "permissive professors" and a "vocal minority of young people" who hold democratic procedures in contempt. This second line of argument became the dominant rhetorical theme (especially in the speeches of Vice President Agnew) in the Administration's response to continued demonstrations.

I first want to begin with a personal note, responding to the very gracious remarks that have been made to me and about me by the Governor and by Karl Mundt, and, as I respond to them I want you to know that I feel very much at home here.

I feel at home here because I, too, grew up in a small town. I attended a small college, about the size of this one; and when I was in law school, at a much larger university, one of the ways that I helped work my way through that law school was to work in the law school library.

So I feel very much at home here before a great, new library, on the campus of a small college which is growing larger, and in a small town in the heartland of America.

I would like to relate what I have said a little more, perhaps, closely to this State. I suppose the best thing I could say would be that I was born in South Dakota. I was not. I was born in California. I could also say, possibly, that Mrs. Nixon was born in South Dakota. She was not. She was born in Nevada.

But I can go very close to that, because my wife's mother and father, Mr. and Mrs. Thomas [William] Ryan, were married and lived in their early years, before they moved to Nevada, in Lee, South Dakota. So we have a South Dakota background.

I should also point out that in the small estate that her father left was a mining claim in the Black Hills of South Dakota. We paid taxes on that in California for many, many years, and so we were South Dakota taxpayers.

No gold was ever discovered there, but when I returned to South Dakota as a candidate in 1960, I was presented with some Black Hills gold cuff links, and I am wearing them today to show my relationship to South Dakota.

Now an occasion like this does call for more than the usual informal remarks which, I think, are usually quite welcomed by an audience.

This is a solemn occasion. It is the beginning of a new institution as part of a larger institution.

I think as we dedicate this beautiful, new library, that this is the time and place to speak of some very basic things in American life. It is the time, because we find our fundamental values under bitter and even violent attack all over America. And it is the place, because so much that is basic to America is represented right here where we stand.

Opportunity for all is represented here.

This is a small college, not rich and famous like Yale and Harvard, and not a vast State university like Michigan and Berkeley. But for almost 90 years it has served the people of South Dakota, opening doors of opportunity for thousands of deserving young men and women. Like hundreds of other fine small colleges across this Nation, General Beadle State College—soon to be known as Dakota State College—has offered a chance to people who might otherwise not have had a chance for an education. And as one who had such a chance at a small college, I know what that means.

The pioneer spirit is represented here, and the progress that has shaped our heritage. Because here in South Dakota we still can sense the daring that converted a raw frontier into part of the vast heartland of America. The vitality of thought is represented here.

A college library is a place of living ideas; a place where timeless truths are collected to become the raw materials of discovery. In addition, the Karl E. Mundt Library will house the papers of a wise and dedicated man who for 30 years has been at the center of public events. Thus, more than most, this is a library of both thought and action, containing and combining the wisdom of past ages with a uniquely personal record of the present time.

So today, as we dedicate this place of ideas, I think we should reflect on some of the values we have inherited and which are now under challenge.

We live in a deeply troubled and profoundly unsettled time. Drugs and crime, campus revolts, racial discord, draft resistance—on every hand we find old standards violated, old values discarded, old precepts ignored. A vocal minority of our young people are opting out of the process by which a civilization maintains its continuity: the passing on of values from one generation to the next. Old and young across the Nation shout across a chasm of misunderstanding, and the louder they shout, the broader the chasm becomes.

As a result of all this, our institutions in America today are undergoing what may be the severest challenge of our history. I do not speak of the physical challenge, the force and threats of force that have racked our cities and now our colleges. Force can be contained. We have the power to strike back if need be, and we can prevail. The Nation has survived other attempts at insurrection. We can survive this one. It has not been a lack of civil power, but the reluctance of a free people to employ it, that so often has stayed the hand of authorities faced with confrontation.

But the challenge I speak of today is deeper—the challenge to our values and to the moral base of the authority that sustains those values.

At the outset, let me draw a very clear distinction. A great deal of today's debate about "values," or about "morality," centers on what essentially are private values and personal codes: patterns of dress and appearance, sexual mores, religious practices, the uses to which a person intends to put his own life.

Now these are immensely important, but they are not the values I mean to discuss here today.

My concern and our concern today is not with the length of a person's hair, but with his conduct in relation to the community; not with what he wears, but with his impact on the process by which a free society governs itself.

I speak not of private morality, but of public morality—and of "morality" in its broadest sense, as a set of standards by which the community chooses to judge itself.

Some critics call ours an "immoral" society because they disagree with its policies, or they refuse to obey its laws because they claim that those laws have no moral basis. Yet the structure of our laws has rested from the beginning on a foundation of moral purpose. That moral purpose embodies what is, above all, a deeply humane set of values—rooted in a profound respect for the individual, for the integrity of his person, for the dignity of his humanity.

At first glance, there is something homely and unexciting about basic values as we have long believed in them. And we feel apologetic about espousing them; even the profoundest truths become clichés with repetition. But these truths can be like sleeping giants: slow to rouse, but magnificent in their strength.

So today let us look at some of those values—so familiar now, and yet once so revolutionary in America and in the world:

—liberty, recognizing that liberties can only exist in balance, with the liberty of each stopping at that point at which it would infringe the liberty of another;

—freedom of conscience, meaning that each person has the freedom of his own conscience, and therefore none has the right to dictate the conscience of his neighbor;

—justice, recognizing that true justice is impartial and that no man can be judge in his own cause;

—human dignity, a dignity that inspires pride, is rooted in self-reliance, and provides the satisfaction of being a useful and respected member of the community;

—concern, concern for the disadvantaged and dispossessed, but a concern that neither panders nor patronizes;

—the right to participate in public decisions, which carries with it the duty to abide by those decisions when reached, recognizing that no one can have his own way all the time;

—human fulfillment, in the sense not of unlimited license, but of maximum opportunity;

—the right to grow, to reach upward, to be all that we can become, in a system that rewards enterprise, encourages innovation, and honors excellence.

In essence, these are aspects of freedom. They inhere in the concept of freedom; they aim at extending freedom; they celebrate the uses of freedom. They are not new, but they are as timeless and as timely as the human spirit, because they are rooted in the human spirit.

Our basic values concern not only what we seek, but how we seek it.

Freedom is a condition; it is also a process. And the process is essential to the freedom itself.

We have a Constitution that sets certain limits on what government can do, but that allows wide discretion within those limits. We have a system of divided powers, of checks and balances, of periodic elections, all of which are designed to insure that the majority has a chance to work its will but not to override the rights of the minority, or to infringe the rights of the individual.

What this adds up to is a democratic process, carefully constructed, stringently guarded. Now it is not perfect. No system could be. But it has served the Nation well, and nearly two centuries of growth and change testify to its strength and adaptability.

They testify, also, to the fact that avenues of peaceful change do exist in America. And those who can make a persuasive case for changes they want can achieve them through this orderly process.

To challenge a particular policy is one thing; to challenge the government's right to set that policy is another—for this denies the process of freedom itself.

Lately, however, a great many people have become impatient with this democratic process. Some of the more extreme even argue, with a rather curious logic, that there is no majority, because the majority has no right to hold opinions that they disagree with. Scorning persuasion they prefer coercion. Awarding themselves what they call a higher morality, they try to bully authorities into yielding to their "demands." On college campuses they draw support from faculty members who should know better; in the larger community, they find the usual apologists ready to excuse any tactic in the name of "progress."

It should be self-evident that this sort of self-righteous moral arrogance has no place in a free community in America, because it denies the most fundamental of all the values we hold—respect for the rights of others. This principle of mutual respect is the keystone of the entire structure of ordered liberty that makes freedom possible.

The student who invades an administration building, roughs up the dean, rifles the files, and issues "nonnegotiable demands" may have some of his demands met by a permissive university administration. But the greater his "victory," the more he will have undermined the security of his own rights. In a free society, the rights of none are secure unless the rights of all are respected. It is precisely the structure of law and custom that he has chosen to violate—the process of freedom—by which the rights of all are protected.

We have long considered our colleges and universities citadels of freedom, where the rule of reason prevails. Now both the process of freedom and the rule of reason are under assault. At the same time, our colleges are under pressure to reduce our educational standards, in the misguided belief that this would promote "opportunity."

Instead of attempting to raise the lagging students up to meet the college standards, the cry now is to lower the standards to meet the students. This is the old, familiar, self-indulgent cry for the easy way. It debases the integrity of the educational process because there is no easy way to excellence, no shortcuts to the truth, no magic wand that can produce a trained and disciplined mind without the hard discipline of learning. To yield to these demands would weaken the institution; more importantly, it would cheat the student of what he comes to college for, a good education.

Now, no group, as a group, should be more zealous defenders of the integrity of academic standards and the rule of reason in academic life than the faculties of our great colleges and universities. But if the teacher simply follows the loudest voices, parrots the latest slogan, yields to unreasonable demands, he will have won not the respect but the contempt of his students; and he will deserve that contempt. Students have some rights. They have a right to guidance, to leadership, and direction; they also have a right to expect their teachers to listen and to be reasonable, but also to stand for something—and most especially, to stand for the rule of reason against the rule of force.

Our colleges and universities have their weaknesses. Some have become too impersonal, or too ingrown, and curricula have lagged. But let us never forget that for all its faults, the American system of higher education is the best in this whole imperfect world, and it provides in the United States today a better education for more students of all economic levels than ever before anywhere in the history of the world.

And I submit this is no small achievement. We should be proud of it. We should defend it and we should never apologize for it.

Often the worst mischief is done in the name of the best cause. In our zeal for instant reform we should be careful not to destroy our educational standards and our educational system along with it, and not to undermine the process of freedom on which all else rests.

The process of freedom will be less threatened in America, however, if we pay more heed to one of the great cries of our young people today. I speak now of their demand for honesty: intellectual honesty, personal honesty, public honesty. Much of what seems to be revolt is really little more than this: an attempt to strip away sham and pretense, to puncture illusion, to get down to the basic nub of truth.

We should welcome this. We have seen too many patterns of deception in our lives:

—in political life, impossible promises;
—in advertising, extravagant claims;
—in business, shady deals.

In personal life, we all have witnessed deceits that ranged from the "little white lie" to moral hypocrisy; from cheating on income taxes to bilking the insurance company.

In public life, we have seen reputations destroyed by smear, and gimmicks paraded as panaceas. We have heard shrill voices of hate shouting lies and sly voices of malice twisting facts.

Even in intellectual life, we too often have seen logical gymnastics performed to justify a pet theory, and refusal to accept facts that fail to support it.

Of course, absolute honesty, on the other hand, would be ungenerous. Courtesy sometimes compels us to welcome the unwanted visitor, and kindness leads us to compliment the homely girl on how pretty she looks. But in our public discussions we sorely need a kind of honesty that too often has been lacking: the honesty of straight talk, a careful concern with the gradations of truth, a frank recognition of the limits of our knowledge about the problems we have to deal with. We have long demanded financial integrity in private life. We now need the most rigorous kind of intellectual integrity in public debate.

Unless we can find a way to speak plainly and truly, unselfconsciously, about the facts of public life, we may find that our grip on the forces of history is too loose to control our own destiny.

The honesty of straight talk leads us to the conclusion that some of our recent social experiments have worked and some have failed and that most have achieved something—but far less than their advance billing promised. This same honesty is concerned not with assigning blame, but with discovering what lessons can be drawn from that experience in order to design better programs next time. Perhaps the goals were unattainable; perhaps the means were inadequate; perhaps the program was based on an unrealistic assessment of human nature.

We can learn these lessons only to the extent that we can be candid with one another. We have and we face enormously complex choices. In approaching these, confrontation is no substitute for consultation; and passionate concern gets us nowhere without dispassionate analysis. More fundamentally, our structure of values depends on mutual faith, and faith depends on truth.

The values we cherish are sustained by a fabric of mutual self-restraint woven of ordinary civil decency, respect for the rights of others, respect for the laws of the community, and respect for the democratic process of orderly change. The purpose of these restraints, I submit, is not to protect an "establishment," but to establish the protection of liberty; not to prevent change, but to insure that change reflects the public will and respects the rights of all.

This process is our most precious resource as a nation, and it depends on public acceptance, public understanding, and public faith.

Whether our values are maintained depends ultimately not on government, but on people.

A nation can only be as great as the people want it to be.

A nation can only be as free as its people insist that it be.

A nation's laws are only as strong as the people's will to see them enforced.

A nation's freedoms are only as secure as the people's determination to see them maintained.

And a nation's values are only as lasting as the ability of each generation to pass them on to the next.

We often have a tendency to turn away from the familiar because it is familiar, and turn to the new because it is new.

To those intoxicated with the romance of violent revolution, the continuing revolution of democracy may sometimes seem quite unexciting. But no system has ever liberated the spirits of so many so fully. Nothing has ever "turned on" man's energies, his imagination, his unfettered creativity, the way the ideal of freedom has. We can be proud that we have that legacy and that we celebrate it today.

Now there are some who see America's vast wealth and protest that this has made us materialistic. But we should not be apologetic about our abundance. We should not fall into the easy trap of confusing the production of things with the worship of things. We produce abundantly, but our values turn not on what we have but on what we believe.

And what we believe very simply is this: We believe in liberty, in decency, and the process of freedom. On these beliefs we rest our pride as a nation. In these beliefs we rest our hopes for the future. And by our fidelity to the process of freedom we can assure to ourselves and our posterity the blessings of freedom.

I have spoken today of these basic values on this occasion because of the man we honor and also because of the place in which I stand. I know that many in this audience have shared the concern that I have shared, that in recent years, due to the fact that the spotlight has been turned on some public officials who have not reached the standard of integrity that we think they should have reached, we have tended to lose faith in the integrity of all of our institutions.

Let me, as one who for almost a quarter of a century has had the opportunity to meet Governors and Congressmen and Senators and State legislators and judges and public officials all over this land—as a matter of fact, I have probably met more than any living American—just let me say something based on my own observation.

There are men, some, who fail to meet the standards of integrity which should be met by a public servant, but I want this audience to know that as I look at the men who served in public life during my own generation, the great majority of Congressmen and Senators and Governors and State legislators and mayors and judges are honest, dedicated, decent men. And Karl Mundt represents that kind of honesty, decency, and honor. His public life stands for these values about which I have spoken. I am proud to have known him for 22 years. I am proud to have had his friendship and support in victory and also in defeat. And I am proud today to join with you in honoring him by dedicating in his name a library which will preserve those values for which and about which he has spoken so eloquently in 30 years of public life.

The Importance of Military Power
Address at Commencement Exercises at the Air Force Academy
Colorado Springs, Colorado
June 4, 1969

The Commencement Exercises at the Air Force Academy provided President Nixon an ideal symbolic setting to set forth his views on the proper place of military power in American defense policy and additionally to attack those who disagreed with him, the "neo-isolationists" as he termed them. The purpose of this speech was, as William Safire wrote, to "put his war critics on notice that he was ready to strike back, and that they were vulnerable to a charge of isolationism that could put them on the defensive."[1] The speech is vintage Nixon with its emphasis on an "either-or" choice reflecting the "us versus them" mentality that former Nixon aides have described as characteristic of the Administration.

Before addressing the members of the graduating class, I would like to be permitted a personal word to the people of Colorado and to the people of this city. I want to thank you for the very warm and gracious welcome you gave to me and the members of our family.

I well remember the conversations that I had with General Eisenhower in the months before he died. He often reminisced about the past and among his fondest memories were his visits to Colorado. These were some of the happiest days of his life.

Yesterday when we arrived in Colorado Springs, we stepped out of the aircraft; we breathed this wonderfully fresh air; we looked off across the mountains 50 miles away; and as we stood there we knew what he meant when he spoke of Colorado, its people, and also the climate—everything that all of you who live here know and love so much.

I should just like to give you one impression that shows you there is some continuity in history. Dwight David Eisenhower II, the grandson of General Eisenhower, and his namesake, as he saw this beautiful country and looked to the mountains off to the distance, said, "Gee, this is great country." I want you to know that I agree, and I congratulate the Air Force for having the good judgment to locate the Air Force Academy here in Colorado Springs.

One other personal note: I had the opportunity before coming to this stadium to take a tour of some of the campus facilities and particularly the chapel. Now, there has been some controversy about that chapel. This is the first time that I have seen it. I am not an architectural expert, but I think it is magnificent, and I think you can be very proud of that chapel at the Air Force Academy.

Now, if I could address the members of the graduating class. For each of you, and your parents, and your countrymen, this is a moment of quiet pride. After years of study and training, you have earned the right to be saluted.

But you are beginning your careers at a difficult time in military life. On a fighting front, you are asked to be ready to make unlimited sacrifice in a limited war. On the home front, you are under attack from those who question the need for a strong national defense, and indeed see a danger in the power of the defenders.

You are entering the military service of your country when the Nation's potential adversaries abroad have never been stronger and when your critics at home have never been more numerous.

It is open season on the Armed Forces. Military programs are ridiculed as needless if not deliberate waste. The military profession is derided in some of the so-called best circles of America. Patriotism is considered by some to be a backward fetish of the uneducated and the unsophisticated. Nationalism is hailed and applauded as a panacea for the ills of every nation—except the United States of America.

This paradox of military power is a symptom of something far deeper that is stirring in our body politic. It goes beyond the dissent about the war in Vietnam. It goes behind the fear of the "military-industrial complex."

The underlying questions are really these: What is America's role in the world? What are the responsibilities of a great nation toward protecting freedom beyond its shores? Can we ever be left in peace if we do not actively assume the burden of keeping the peace?

When great questions are posed, fundamental differences of opinion come into focus. It serves no purpose to gloss over these differences, or to try to pretend that they are mere matters of degree. Because there is one school of thought that holds that the road to understanding with the Soviet Union and Communist China lies through a downgrading of our own alliances and what amounts to a unilateral reduction of our arms in order to demonstrate our "good faith."

They believe that we can be conciliatory and accommodating only if we do not have the strength to be otherwise. They believe that America will be able to deal with the possibility of peace only when we are unable to cope with the threat of war.

Those who think that way have grown weary of the weight of free world leadership that fell upon us in the wake of World War II. They argue that we—that the United States is as much responsible for the tensions in the world as the adversaries we face.

They assert that the United States is blocking the road to peace by maintaining its military strength at home and its defenses abroad. If we would only reduce our forces, they contend, tensions would disappear and the chances for peace would brighten.

America's powerful military presence on the world scene, they believe, makes peace abroad improbable and peace at home impossible.

Now we should never underestimate the appeal of the isolationist school of thought. Their slogans are simplistic and powerful: "Charity begins at home. Let's first solve our problems at home and then we can deal with the problems of the world."

This simple formula touches a responsive chord with many an overburdened taxpayer. It would be easy, easy for a President of the United States to buy some popularity by going along with the new isolationists. But I submit to you that it would be disastrous for our Nation and the world.

I hold a totally different view of the world, and I come to a different conclusion about the direction America must take.

Imagine for a moment, if you will, what would happen to this world if America were to become a dropout in assuming the responsibility for defending peace and freedom in the world. As every world leader knows, and as even the most outspoken critics of America would admit, the rest of the world would live in terror.

Because if America were to turn its back on the world, there would be peace that would settle over this planet, but it would be the kind of peace that suffocated freedom in Czechoslovakia.

The danger to us has changed, but it has not vanished. We must revitalize our alliances, not abandon them.

We must rule out unilateral disarmament, because in the real world it wouldn't work. If we pursue arms control as an end in itself, we will not achieve our end. The adversaries in the world are not in conflict because they are armed. They are armed because they are in conflict, and have not yet learned peaceful ways to resolve their conflicting national interests.

The aggressors of this world are not going to give the United States a period of grace in which to put our domestic house in order—just as the crises within our society cannot be put on a back burner until we resolve the problem of Vietnam.

The most successful solutions that we can possibly imagine for our domestic programs will be meaningless if we are not around to enjoy them. Nor can we conduct a successful peace policy abroad if our society is at war with itself at home.

There is no advancement for Americans at home in a retreat from the problems of the world. I say that America has a vital national interest in world stability, and no other nation can uphold that interest for us.

We stand at a crossroad in our history. We shall reaffirm our destiny for greatness or we shall choose instead to withdraw into ourselves. The choice will affect far more than our foreign policy; it will determine the quality of our lives.

A nation needs many qualities, but it needs faith and confidence about all. Skeptics do not build societies; the idealists are the builders. Only societies that believe in themselves can rise to their challenges. Let us not, then, pose a false choice between meeting our responsibilities abroad and meeting the needs of our people at home. We shall meet both or we shall meet neither.

That is why my disagreement with the skeptics and the isolationists is fundamental. They have lost the vision indispensable to great leadership. They observe the problems that confront us; they measure our resources and then they despair. When the first vessels set out from Europe for the New World these men would have weighed the risks and they would have stayed behind. When the colonists on the eastern seaboard started across the Appalachians to the unknown reaches of the Ohio Valley, these men would have counted the costs and they would have stayed behind.

Our current exploration of space makes the point vividly; here is testimony to man's vision and to man's courage. The journey of the astronauts is more than a technical achievement; it is a reaching-out of the human spirit. It lifts our sights; it demonstrates that magnificent conceptions can be made real.

They inspire us and at the same time they teach us true humility. What could bring home to us more the limitations of the human scale than the hauntingly beautiful picture of our earth seen from the moon?

When the first man stands on the moon next month every American will stand taller because of what he has done, and we should be proud of this magnificent achievement.

We will know then that every man achieves his own greatness by reaching out beyond himself, and so it is with nations. When a nation believes in itself—as Athenians did in their Golden Age, as Italians did in the Renaissance—that nation can perform miracles. Only when a nation means something to itself can it mean something to others.

That is why I believe a resurgence of American idealism can bring about a modern miracle, and that modern miracle is a world order of peace and justice.

I know that every member of this graduating class is, in that sense, an idealist.

However, I must warn you that in the years to come you may hear your commitment to the American responsibility in the world derided as a form of militarism. It is important that you recognize that strawman issue for what it is, the outward sign of a desire by some to turn America inward and to have America turn away from greatness. I am not speaking about those responsible critics who reveal waste and inefficiency in our defense establishment, who demand clear answers on procurement problems, who want to make sure new weapons systems will truly add to our defense. On the contrary, you should be in the vanguard of that movement. Nor do I speak of those with sharp eyes and sharp pencils who are examining our post-Vietnam planning with other pressing national priorities in mind. I count myself as one of those.

But as your Commander in Chief, I want to relay to you as future officers of our Armed Forces some of my thoughts on these great issues of national moment.

I worked closely with President Eisenhower for 8 years. I know what he meant when he said: ". . . we must guard against the acquisition of unwarranted influence, whether sought or unsought, by the military-industrial complex."

Many people conveniently forget that he followed that warning with another: ". . . we must also be alert to the equal and opposite danger that public policy could itself become the captive of a scientific-technological elite."

We sometimes forget that in the same farewell address, President Eisenhower spoke of the need for national security. He said: "A vital element in keeping the peace is our military establishment. Our arms must be mighty, ready for instant action, so that no potential aggressor may be tempted to risk his own destruction."[1]

I say to you, my fellow Americans, let us never forget those wise words of one of America's greatest leaders.

The American defense establishment should never be a sacred cow, but on the other hand, the American military should never be anybody's scapegoat.

America's wealth is enormous, but it is not limitless. Every dollar available in the Federal Government has been taken from the American people in taxes, and a responsible government has a duty to be prudent when it spends the people's money. There is no more justification for wasting money on unnecessary military hardware than there is for wasting it on unwarranted social programs.

There can be no question that we should not spend unnecessarily for defense. But we must also not confuse our priorities.

The question, I submit, in defense spending is a very simple one: "How much is necessary?" The President of the United States is the man charged with making that judgment. After a complete review of our foreign and defense policies I have submitted requests to the Congress for military appropriations. Some of these are admittedly controversial. These requests represent the minimum I believe essential for the United States to meet its current and long-range obligations to itself and to the free world. I have asked only for those programs and those expenditures that I believe are necessary to guarantee the security of this country and to honor our obligations. I will bear the responsibility for those judgments. I do not consider my recommendations infallible. But if I have made a mistake, I pray that it is on the side of too much and not too little. If we do too much it will cost us our money. If we do too little, it may cost us our lives.

Mistakes in military policy today can be irretrievable. Time lost in this age of science can never be regained. America had months in order to prepare and to catch up in order to wage World War I. We had months and even years in order to catch up so we could play a role in winning World War II. When a war can be decided in 20 minutes, the nation that is behind will have no time to catch up.

I say: Let America never fall behind in maintaining the defenses necessary for the strength of this Nation.

I have no choice in my decisions but to come down on the side of security, because history has dealt harshly with those nations who have taken the other course.

So, in that spirit, to the members of this graduating class, let me offer this credo for the defenders of our Nation:

I believe that we must balance our need for survival as a nation with our need for survival as a people. Americans, soldiers and civilians, must remember that defense is not an end in itself; it is a way of holding fast to the deepest values known to civilized men.

I believe that our defense establishment will remain the servants of our national policy of bringing about peace in the world and that those in any way connected with the military must scrupulously avoid even the appearance of becoming the master of that policy.

I believe that every man in uniform is a citizen first and a serviceman second, and that we must resist any attempt to isolate or separate the defenders from the defended. So you can see that in this regard, those who agitate for the removal of the ROTC [Reserve Officers' Training Corps] from college campuses contribute to an unwanted militarism.

I believe that the basis for decisions on defense spending must be "What do we do; what do we need for our security?" and not "What will this mean for business and employment?" The Defense Department must never be considered as a modern WPA [Work Projects Administration]. There are far better ways for government to help insure a sound prosperity and high employment.

I feel that moderation has a moral significance only in those who have another choice. The weak can only plead. Magnanimity and restraint gain moral meaning coming from the strong.

I believe that defense decisions must be made on the hard realities of the offensive capabilities of our potential adversaries, and not on the fervent hopes about their intentions. With Thomas Jefferson, we can prefer "the flatteries of hope" to the gloom of despair, but we cannot survive in the real world if we plan our defense in a dream world.

I believe we must take risks for peace—but calculated risks, not foolish risks. We shall not trade our defenses for a disarming smile or charming words. We are prepared for new initiatives in the control of arms in the context of other specific moves to reduce tensions around the world.

I believe that America is not going to become a "garrison state," or a "welfare state," or a "police state"—simply because the American people will defend our values from those forces, external or internal, that would challenge or erode them.

And I believe this above all: That this Nation shall continue to be a source of world leadership, a source of freedom's strength, in creating a just world order that will bring an end to war.

Members of the graduating class and your colleagues in the Academy, a President shares a special bond with the men and women in the Nation's Armed Forces. He feels that bond strongly at moments like these, facing all of you who have pledged your lives, your fortunes, and your sacred honor to the service of your country. He feels that bond most strongly when he presents the Medal of Honor to an 8-year-old boy who will never see his father again. Because of that bond, let me say this to you:

In the past generation, since 1941, this Nation has paid for 14 years of peace with 14 years of war. The American war dead of this generation has been far greater than all of the preceding generations in America's history. In terms of human suffering, this has been the costliest generation in the two centuries of our history.

Perhaps this is why my generation is so determined to pass on a different legacy. We want to redeem that sacrifice. We want to be remembered, not as the generation that suffered in war, but as the generation that was tempered in its fire for a great purpose: to make the kind of peace that the next generation will be able to keep.

This is a challenge worthy of the idealism which I know motivates every man who will receive his diploma today.

I am proud to have served in the Armed Forces of this Nation in a war which ended before the members of this class were born.

It is my deepest hope and my belief that each of you will be able to look back on your military career with pride, not because of the wars in which you have fought, but because of the peace and freedom which your service will make possible for America and the world.

Notes

1. William Safire, *Before the Fall* (New York: Belmont Towers Books, 1975) p. 141.

The War in Viet Nam
Televised Address to the Nation
Washington, D.C.
November 3, 1969

By Fall, 1969 Nixon's political honeymoon with Congress and with some segments of the American public was over. Congressional critics were demanding concrete details of his "secret plan" to end the war and calling for a public time-table for American withdrawal from Viet Nam. At roughly the same time the anti-war movement revived itself and scheduled a Moratorium demonstration for October 15th. On October 23, the White House announced that the President would speak to the nation about Viet Nam on November 3, a mid-point between the October and November demonstrations. For the two weeks before the speech many muted their criticism of Nixon in hopes that he had gotten the message that Americans were weary of the war and ready to get out of Viet Nam as soon as possible. They were in for a surprise. In his speech the President refused to set a time-table for withdrawal, contended that the major obstacle to peace lay in the North Vietnamese refusal to negotiate seriously, and outlined his policy of continued negotiations and Vietnamization of the military struggle. He gave no quarter to his critics. Rather, he called upon "the great silent majority" of Americans to support him vis-a-vis the vocal minority that advocated "precipitate withdrawal" with its attendant tragic consequences. This speech was Nixon's most effective. A telephone survey after the speech indicated that 77% of those polled supported his policy. A Gallup poll a week later revealed that President Nixon's approval rating among the public had risen by 12% over the previous month to a high of 68%. The November demonstration was held with one of the largest gatherings of anti-war sentiment assembled to that time. However, in December at the Moratorium the attendance dwindled, and by early 1970 massive protest seemed a historical relic, a thing of the by-gone past. In April the Mobilization Committee announced it was closing its Washington headquarters.

Tonight I want to talk to you on a subject of deep concern to all Americans and to many people in all parts of the world—the war in Vietnam.

I believe that one of the reasons for the deep division about Vietnam is that many Americans have lost confidence in what their Government has told them about our policy. The American people cannot and should not be asked to support a policy which involves the overriding issues of war and peace unless they know the truth about that policy.

Tonight, therefore, I would like to answer some of the questions that I know are on the minds of many of you listening to me.

How and why did America get involved in Vietnam in the first place?

How has this administration changed the policy of the previous administration?

What has really happened in the negotiations in Paris and on the battlefront in Vietnam?

What choices do we have if we are to end the war?

What are the prospects for peace?

Let me begin by describing the situation I found when I was inaugurated on January 20.

—The war had been going on for 4 years.

—31,000 Americans had been killed in action.

—The training program for the South Vietnamese was behind schedule.

—540,000 Americans were in Vietnam with no plans to reduce the number.

—No progress had been made at the negotiations in Paris and the United States had not put forth a comprehensive peace proposal.

—The war was causing deep division at home and criticism from many of our friends as well as our enemies abroad.

In view of these circumstances there were some who urged that I end the war at once by ordering the immediate withdrawal of all American forces.

From a political standpoint this would have been a popular and easy course to follow. After all, we became involved in the war while my predecessor was in office. I could blame the defeat which would be the result of my action on him and come out as the peacemaker. Some put it to me quite bluntly: This was the only way to avoid allowing Johnson's war to become Nixon's war.

But I had a greater obligation than to think only of the years of my administration and the next election. I had to think of the effect of my decision on the next generation and on the future of peace and freedom in America and in the world.

Let us all understand that the question before us is not whether some Americans are for peace and some Americans are against peace. The question at issue is not whether Johnson's war becomes Nixon's war.

The great question is: How can we win America's peace?

Let us turn now to the fundamental issue. Why and how did the United States become involved in Vietnam in the first place?

Fifteen years ago North Vietnam, with the logistical support of Communist China and the Soviet Union, launched a campaign to impose a Communist government on South Vietnam by instigating and supporting a revolution.

In response to the request of the Government of South Vietnam, President Eisenhower sent economic aid and military equipment to assist the people of South Vietnam in their efforts to prevent a Communist takeover. Seven years ago, President Kennedy sent 16,000 military personnel to Vietnam as combat advisers. Four years ago, President Johnson sent American combat forces to South Vietnam.

Now, many believe that President Johnson's decision to send American combat forces to South Vietnam was wrong. And many others—I among them—have been strongly critical of the way the war has been conducted.

But the question facing us today is—now that we are in the war, what is the best way to end it?

In January I could only conclude that the precipitate withdrawal of American forces from Vietnam would be a disaster not only for South Vietnam but for the United States and for the cause of peace.

For the South Vietnamese, our precipitate withdrawal would inevitably allow the Communists to repeat the massacres which followed their takeover in the North 15 years before.

—They then murdered more than 50,000 people and hundreds of thousands more died in slave labor camps.

—We saw a prelude of what would happen in South Vietnam when the Communists entered the city of Hue last year. During their brief rule there, there was a bloody reign of terror in which 3,000 civilians were clubbed, shot to death, and buried in mass graves.

—With the sudden collapse of our support, these atrocities of Hue would become the nightmare of the entire nation—and particularly for the million and a half Catholic refugees who fled the South Vietnam when the Communists took over in the North.

For the United States, this first defeat in our Nation's history would result in a collapse of confidence in American leadership, not only in Asia but throughout the world.

Three American Presidents have recognized the great stakes involved in Vietnam and understood what had to be done.

—In 1963, President Kennedy, with his characteristic eloquence and clarity, said, ". . . we want to see a stable government there, carrying on a struggle to maintain its national independence.

"We believe strongly in that. We are not going to withdraw from that effort. In my opinion, for us to withdraw from that effort would mean a collapse not only of South Vietnam, but Southeast Asia. So we are going to stay there."

President Eisenhower and President Johnson expressed the same conclusion during their terms of office.

For the future of peace, precipitate withdrawal would thus be a disaster of immense magnitude.

—A nation cannot remain great if it betrays its allies and lets down its friends.

—Our defeat and humiliation in South Vietnam without question would promote recklessness in the councils of those great powers who have not yet abandoned their goals of world conquest.

—This would spark violence wherever our commitments help maintain the peace—in the Middle East, in Berlin, eventually even in the Western Hemisphere.

Ultimately, this would cost more lives.

It would not bring peace; it would bring more war.

For these reasons, I rejected the recommendation that I should end the war by immediately withdrawing all our forces. I chose instead to change American policy on both the negotiating front and battlefront.

In order to end a war fought on many fronts, I initiated a pursuit for peace on many fronts.

In a television speech on May 14, in a speech before the United Nations, and one a number of other occasions I set forth our peace proposals in great detail.

—We have offered the complete withdrawal of all outside forces within 1 year.

—We have proposed a cease-fire under international supervision.

—We have offered free elections under international supervision with the Communists participating in the organization and conduct of the elections as an organized political force. The Saigon Government has pledged to accept the result of the elections.

We have not put forth our proposals on a take-it-or-leave-it basis. We have indicated that we are willing to discuss the proposals that have been put forth by the other side. We have declared that anything is negotiable except the right of the people of South Vietnam to determine their own future. At the Paris peace conference, Ambassador Lodge has demonstrated our flexibility and good faith in 40 public meetings.

Hanoi has refused even to discuss our proposals. They demand our unconditional acceptance of their terms, which are that we withdraw all American forces immediately and unconditionally and that we overthrow the Government of South Vietnam as we leave.

We have not limited our peace initiatives to public forums and public statements. I recognized, in January, that a long and bitter war like this usually cannot be settled in a public forum. That is why in addition to the public statements and negotiations I have explored every possible private avenue that might lead to a settlement.

Tonight I am taking the unprecedented step of disclosing to you some of our other initiatives for peace—initiatives we undertook privately and secretly because we thought that we thereby might open a door which publicly would be closed.

I did not wait for my inauguration to begin my quest for peace.

—Soon after my election through an individual who is directly in contact on a personal basis with the leaders of North Vietnam I made two private offers for a rapid, comprehensive settlement. Hanoi's replies called in effect for our surrender before negotiations.

—Since the Soviet Union furnishes most of the military equipment for North Vietnam, Secretary of State Rogers, my Assistant for National Security Affairs, Dr. Kissinger, Ambassador Lodge, and I, personally, have met on a number of occasions with representatives of the Soviet Government to enlist their assistance in getting meaningful negotiations started. In addition we have had extended discussions directed toward that same end with representatives of other governments which have diplomatic relations with North Vietnam. None of the initiatives have to date produced results.

—In mid-July, I became convinced that it was necessary to make a major move to break the deadlock in the Paris talks. I spoke directly in this office, where I am now sitting, with an individual who had known Ho Chi Minh on a personal basis for 25 years. Through him I sent a letter to Ho Chi Minh.

I did this outside of the usual diplomatic channels with the hope that with the necessity of making statements for propaganda removed, there might be constructive progress toward bringing the war to an end. Let me read from that letter:

"Dear Mr. President:

" I realize that it is difficult to communicate meaningfully across the gulf of four years of war. But precisely because of this gulf, I wanted to take this opportunity to reaffirm in all solemnity my desire to work for a just peace. I deeply believe that the war in Vietnam has gone on too long and delay in bringing it to an end can benefit no one—least of all the people of Vietnam. . . .

"The time has come to move forward at the conference table toward an early resolution of this tragic war. You will find us forthcoming and open-minded in a common effort to bring the blessings of peace to the brave people of Vietnam. Let history record that at this critical juncture, both sides turned their face toward peace rather than toward conflict and war."

I received Ho Chi Minh's reply on August 30, 3 days before his death. It simply reiterated the public position North Vietnam had taken at Paris and flatly rejected my initiative.

The full text of both letters is being released to the press.

—In addition to the public meetings that I have referred to, Ambassador Lodge has met with Vietnam's chief negotiator in Paris in 11 private sessions.

—We have taken other significant initiatives which must remain secret to keep open some channels of communication which may still prove to be productive.

But the effect of all the public, private, and secret negotiations which have been undertaken since the bombing halt a year ago and since this administration came into office on January 20, can be summed up in one sentence: No progress whatever has been made except agreement on the shape of the bargaining table.

Now who is at fault?

It has become clear that the obstacle in negotiating an end to the war is not the President of the United States. It is not the South Vietnamese Government.

The obstacle is the other side's absolute refusal to show the least willingness to join us in seeking a just peace. It will not do so while it is convinced that all it has to do is to wait for our next concession, and our next concession after that one, until it gets everything it wants.

There can not be no longer any question that progress in negotiation depends only on Hanoi's deciding to negotiate, to negotiate seriously.

I realize that this report on our efforts on the diplomatic front is discouraging to the

American people, but the American people are entitled to know the truth—the bad news as well as the good news, where the lives of our young men are involved.

Now let me turn, however, to a more encouraging report on another front.

At the time we launched our search for peace I recognized we might not succeed in bringing an end to the war through negotiation. I, therefore, put into effect another plan to bring peace—a plan which will bring the war to an end regardless of what happens on the negotiating front.

It is in line with a major shift in U.S. foreign policy which I described in my press conference at Guam on July 25. Let me briefly explain what has been described as the Nixon Doctrine—a policy which not only will help end the war in Vietnam, but which is an essential element of our program to prevent future Vietnams.

We Americans are a do-it-yourself people. We are an impatient people. Instead of teaching someone else to do a job, we like to do it ourselves. And this trait has been carried over into our foreign policy.

In Korea and again in Vietnam, the United States furnished most of the money, most of the arms, and most of the men to help the people of those countries defend their freedom against Communist aggression.

Before any American troops were committed to Vietnam, a leader of another Asian country expressed this opinion to me when I was traveling in Asia as a private citizen. He said, "When you are trying to assist another nation defend its freedom, U.S. policy should be to help them fight the war but not to fight the war for them."

Well, in accordance with this wise counsel, I laid down in Guam three principles as guidelines for future American policy toward Asia:

First, the United States will keep all of its treaty commitments.

Second, we shall provide a shield if a nuclear power threatens the freedom of a nation allied with us or of a nation whose survival we consider vital to our security.

Third, in cases involving other types of aggression, we shall furnish military and economic assistance when requested in accordance with our treaty commitments. But we shall look to the nation directly threatened to assume the primary responsibility of providing the manpower for its defense.

After I announced this policy, I found that the leaders of the Philippines, Thailand, Vietnam, South Korea, and other nations which might be threatened by Communist aggression, welcomed this new direction in American foreign policy.

The defense of freedom is everybody's business—not just America's business. And it is particularly the responsibility of the people whose freedom is threatened. In the previous administration, we Americanized the war in Vietnam. In this administration, we are Vietnamizing the search for peace.

The policy of the previous administration not only resulted in our assuming the primary responsibility for fighting the war but even more significantly did not adequately stress the goal of strengthening the South Vietnamese so that they could defend themselves when we left.

The Vietnamization plan was launched following Secretary Laird's visit to Vietnam in March. Under the plan, I ordered first a substantial increase in the training and equipment of South Vietnamese forces.

In July, on my visit to Vietnam, I changed General Abrams' orders so that they were consistent with the objectives of our new policies. Under the new orders, the primary mission of our troops is to enable the South Vietnamese forces to assume the full responsibility for the security of South Vietnam.

Our air operations have been reduced by over 20 percent.

And now we have begun to see the results of this long overdue change in American policy in Vietnam.

— After 5 years of Americans going into Vietnam, we are finally bringing American men home. By December 15, over 60,000 men will have been withdrawn from South Vietnam—including 20 percent of all of our combat forces.

— The South Vietnamese have continued to gain in strength. As a result they have been able to take over combat responsibilities from our American troops.

Two other significant developments have occurred since this administration took office.

— Enemy infiltration, infiltration which is essential if they are to launch a major attack, over that last 3 months is less than 20 percent of what it was over the same period last year.

— Most important—United States casualties have declined during the last 2 months to the lowest point in 3 years.

Let me now turn to our program for the future.

We have adopted a plan which we have worked out in cooperation with the South Vietnamese for the complete withdrawal of all U.S. combat ground forces, and their replacement by South Vietnamese forces on an orderly scheduled timetable. This withdrawal will be made from strength and not from weakness. As South Vietnamese forces become stronger, the rate of American withdrawal can become greater.

I have not and do not intend to announce the timetable for our program. There are obvious reasons for this decision which I am sure you will understand. As I have indicated on several occasions, the rate of withdrawal will depend on developments on three fronts.

One of these is the progress which can be or might be made in the Paris talks. An announcement of a fixed timetable for our withdrawal would completely remove any incentive for the enemy to negotiate an agreement. They would simply wait until our forces had withdrawn and then move in.

The other two factors on which we will base our withdrawal decisions are the level of enemy activity and the progress of the training program of the South Vietnamese forces. I am glad to be able to report tonight progress on both of these fronts has been greater than we anticipated when we started the program in June for withdrawal. As a result, our timetable for withdrawal is more optimistic now than when we made our first estimates in June. This clearly demonstrates why it is not wise to be frozen in on a fixed timetable.

We must retain the flexibility to base each withdrawal decision on the situation as it is at that time rather than on estimates that are no longer valid.

Along with this optimistic estimate, I must—in all candor—leave one note of caution.

If the level of enemy activity significantly increases we might have to adjust our timetable accordingly.

However, I want the record to be completely clear on one point.

At the time of the bombing halt just a year ago, there was some confusion as to whether there was an understanding on the part of the enemy that if we stopped the bombing of North Vietnam they would stop the shelling of cities in South Vietnam. I want to be sure that there is no misunderstanding on the part of the enemy with regard to our withdrawal program.

We have noted the reduced level of infiltration, the reduction of our casualties, and are basing our withdrawal decisions partially on those factors.

If the level of infiltration or our casualties increase while we are trying to scale down the fighting, it will be the result of a conscious decision by the enemy.

Hanoi could make no greater mistake than to assume that an increase in violence will be to its advantage. If I conclude that increased enemy action jeopardizes our remaining forces in Vietnam, I shall not hesitate to take strong and effective measures to deal with that situation.

This is not a threat. This is a statement of policy which as Commander in Chief of our Armed Forces I am making in meeting my responsibility for the protection of American fighting men wherever they may be.

My fellow Americans, I am sure you can recognize from what I have said that we really only have two choices open to us if we want to end this war.

—I can order an immediate, precipitate withdrawal of all Americans from Vietnam without regard to the effects of that action.
—Or we can persist in our search for a just peace through a negotiated settlement if possible, or through continued implementation of our plan for Vietnamization if necessary—a plan in which we will withdraw all of our forces from Vietnam on a schedule in accordance with our program, as the the South Vietnamese become strong enough to defend their own freedom.

I have chosen this second course.

It is not the easy way.

It is the right way.

It is a plan which will end the war and serve the cause of peace—not just in Vietnam but in the Pacific and in the world.

In speaking of the consequences of a precipitate withdrawal, I mentioned that our allies would lose confidence in America.

Far more dangerous, we would lose confidence in ourselves. Oh, the immediate reaction would be a sense of relief that our men were coming home. But as we saw the consequences of what we had done, inevitable remorse and divisive recrimination would scar our spirit as a people.

We have faced other crises in our history and have become stronger by rejecting the easy way out and taking the right way in meeting our challenges. Our greatness as a nation has been our capacity to do what had to be done when we knew our course was right.

I recognize that some of my fellow citizens disagree with the plan for peace I have chosen. Honest and patriotic Americans have reached different conclusions as to how peace should be achieved.

Strategically brilliant - thought Ashbury Center for 8 days

In San Francisco a few weeks ago, I saw demonstrators carrying signs reading: "Lose in Vietnam, bring the boys home."

Well, one of the strengths of our free society is that any American has a right to reach that conclusion and to advocate that point of view. But as President of the United States, I would be untrue to my oath of office if I allowed the policy of this Nation to be dictated by the minority who hold that point of view and who try to impose it on the Nation by mounting demonstrations in the street.

For almost 200 years, the policy of this Nation has been made under our Constitution by those leaders in the Congress and in the White House elected by all of the people. If a vocal minority, however fervent its cause, prevails over reason and the will of the majority this Nation has no future as a free society.

And now I would like to address a word if I may to the young people of this Nation who are particularly concerned, and I understand why they are concerned, about this war.

I respect your idealism.

I share your concern for peace.

I want peace as much as you do.

There are powerful personal reasons I want to end this war. This week I will have to sign 83 letters to mothers, fathers, wives, and loved ones of men who have given their lives for America in Vietnam. It is very little satisfaction to me that this is only one-third as many letters as I signed the first week in office. There is nothing I want more than to see the day come when I do not have to write any of those letters.

—I want to end the war to save the lives of those brave young men in Vietnam.

—But I want to end it in a way which will increase the chance that their younger brothers and their sons will not have to fight in some future Vietnam someplace in the world.

—And I want to end the war for another reason. I want to end it so that the energy and dedication of you, our young people, now too often directed into bitter hatred against those responsible for the war, can be turned to the great challenges of peace, a better life for all Americans, a better life for all people on this earth.

I have chosen a plan for peace. I believe it will succeed.

If it does succeed, what the critics say now won't matter. If it does not succeed, anything I say then won't matter.

I know it may not be fashionable to speak of patriotism or national destiny these days. But I feel it is appropriate to do so on this occasion.

Two hundred years ago this Nation was weak and poor. But even then, America was the hope of millions in the world. Today we have become the strongest and richest Nation in the world. The wheel of destiny has turned so that any hope the world has for the survival of peace and freedom will be determined by whether the American people have the moral stamina and the courage to meet the challenge of free world leadership.

Let historians not record that when America was the most powerful nation in the world we *good Samaritan Allusion is set off* passed on the other side of the road and allowed the last hopes for peace and freedom of millions of people to be suffocated by the forces of totalitarianism.

And so tonight—to you, the great silent majority of my fellow Americans—I ask for your support.

I pledged in my campaign for the Presidency to end the war in a way that we could win the peace. I have initiated a plan of action which will enable me to keep that pledge.

The more support I can have from the American people, the sooner that pledge can be redeemed; for the more divided we are at home, the less likely the enemy is to negotiate at Paris.

Let us be united for peace. Let us also be united against defeat. Because let us understand: North Vietnam cannot defeat or humiliate the United States. Only Americans can do that.

Fifty years ago, in this room and at this very desk, President Woodrow Wilson spoke words which caught the imagination of a war-weary world. He said, "This is the war to end wars." His dream for peace after World War I was shattered on the hard realities of great power politics and Woodrow Wilson died a broken man.

Tonight I do not tell you that the war in Vietnam is the war to end wars. But I do say this:

I have initiated a plan which will end this war in a way that will bring us closer to that great goal to which Woodrow Wilson and every American President in our history has been dedicated—the goal of a just and lasting peace.

As President I hold the responsibility for choosing the best path to that goal and then leading the Nation along it.

I pledge to you tonight that I shall meet this responsibility with all of the strength and wisdom I can command in accordance with your hopes, mindful of your concerns, sustained by your prayers.

The Cambodian Invasion
Televised Address to the Nation
Washington, D.C.
April 30, 1970

On April 20 President Nixon announced the withdrawal of an additional 150,000 troops from Viet Nam. It seemed as if his disengagement from the war was proceeding orderly in accordance with his own private schedule. Then, ten days later Nixon shocked the American public and indeed the world with this apocalyptic announcement of a joint American-South Vietnamese invasion of Cambodia, a neutral country. Opposition formed immediately. Protests erupted on campuses throughout the country and spread. Nixon's reference to protestors as "bums" on the next day only fueled the flames of dissent. On May 4, four white students were killed by National Guardsmen at Kent State University, and all hell broke loose. More than 300 colleges and universities closed. Nixon responded with a public relations campaign. Certain government officials were designated to meet with protestors who descended upon Washington. The President conferred with university presidents. At his May 8 press conference the President pledged an early return of the troops from Cambodia. And in a not very well camouflaged reference to the hard-line statements coming from Agnew, Nixon said he hoped members of his Administration would remember one of his cardinal rules of politics: "When the action is hot, keep the rhetoric cool." Eventually, as American troops returned from Cambodia, the furor cooled down. But the invasion and the rhetoric justifying it left a nation deeply scarred and even more divided than before.

Ten days ago, in my report to the Nation on Vietnam, I announced a decision to withdraw an additional 150,000 Americans from Vietnam over the next year. I said then that I was making that decision despite our concern over increased enemy activity in Laos, in Cambodia, and in South Vietnam.

At that time, I warned that if I concluded that increased enemy activity in any of these areas endangered the lives of Americans remaining in Vietnam, I would not hesitate to take strong and effective measures to deal with that situation.

Despite that warning, North Vietnam has increased its military aggression in all these areas, and particularly in Cambodia.

After full consultation with the National Security Council, Ambassador Bunker, General Abrams, and my other advisers, I have concluded that the actions of the enemy in the last 10 days clearly endanger the lives of Americans who are in Vietnam now and would constitute an unacceptable risk to those who will be there after withdrawal of another 150,000.

To protect our men who are in Vietnam and to guarantee the continued success of our withdrawal and Vietnamization programs, I have concluded that the time has come for action.

Tonight, I shall describe the actions of the enemy, the actions I have ordered to deal with that situation, and the reasons for my decision.

Cambodia, a small country of 7 million people, has been a neutral nation since the Geneva Agreement of 1954—an agreement, incidentally, which was signed by the Government of North Vietnam.

American policy since then has been to scrupulously respect the neutrality of the Cambodian people. We have maintained a skeleton diplomatic mission of fewer than 15 in Cambodia's capital, and that only since last August. For the previous 4 years, from 1965 to 1969, we did not have any diplomatic mission whatever in Cambodia. And for the past 5 years, we have provided no military assistance whatever and no economic assistance to Cambodia.

North Vietnam, however, has not respected that neutrality.

For the past 5 years—as indicated on this map that you see here—North Vietnam has occupied military sanctuaries all along the Cambodian frontier with South Vietnam. Some of these extend up to 20 miles into Cambodia. The sanctuaries are in red and, as you note, they are on both sides of the border. They are used for hit and run attacks on American and South Vietnamese forces in South Vietnam.

These Communist occupied territories contain major base camps, training sites, logistics facilities, weapons and ammunition factories, air strips, and prisoner-of-war compounds.

For 5 years, neither the United States nor South Vietnam has moved against these enemy sanctuaries because we did not wish to violate the territory of a neutral nation. Even after the Vietnamese Communists began to expand these sanctuaries 4 weeks ago, we counseled patience to our South Vietnamese allies and imposed restraints on our own commanders.

In contrast to our policy, the enemy in the past 2 weeks has stepped up his guerrilla actions and he is concentrating his main forces in these sanctuaries that you see on this map where they are building up to launch massive attacks on our forces and those of South Vietnam.

North Vietnam in the last 2 weeks has stripped away all pretense of respecting the sovereignty or the neutrality of Cambodia. Thousands of their soldiers are invading the country from the sanctuaries; they are encircling the capital of Phnom Penh. Coming from these sanctuaries, as you see here, they have moved into Cambodia and are encircling the capital.

Cambodia, as a result of this, has sent out a call to the United States, to a number of other nations, for assistance. Because if this enemy effort succeeds, Cambodia would become a vast enemy staging area and a springboard for attacks on South Vietnam along 600 miles of frontier—a refuge where enemy troops could return from combat without fear of retaliation.

North Vietnamese men and supplies could then be poured into that country, jeopardizing not only the lives of our own men but the people of South Vietnam as well.

Now confronted with this situation, we have three options.

First, we can do nothing. Well, the ultimate result of that course of action is clear. Unless we indulge in wishful thinking, the lives of Americans remaining in Vietnam after our next withdrawal of 150,000 would be gravely threatened.

Let us go to the map again. Here is South Vietnam. Here is North Vietnam. North Vietnam already occupies this part of Laos. If North Vietnam also occupied this whole band in Cambodia, or the entire country, it would mean that South Vietnam was completely outflanked and the forces of Americans in this area, as well as the South Vietnamese, would be in an untenable military position.

Our second choice is to provide massive military assistance to Cambodia itself. Now unfortunately, while we deeply sympathize with the plight of 7 million Cambodians whose country is being invaded, massive amounts of military assistance could not be rapidly and effectively utilized by the small Cambodian Army against the immediate threat.

With other nations, we shall do our best to provide the small arms and other equipment which the Cambodian Army of 40,000 needs and can use for its defense. But the aid we will provide will be limited to the purpose of enabling Cambodia to defend its neutrality and not for the purpose of making it an active belligerent on one side or the other.

Our third choice is to go to the heart of the trouble. That means cleaning out major North Vietnamese and Vietcong occupied territories, these sanctuaries which serve as bases for attacks on both Cambodia and American and South Vietnamese forces in South Vietnam. Some of these, incidentally, are as close to Saigon as Baltimore is to Washington.

This one, for example is called the Parrot's Beak. It is only 33 miles from Saigon.

Now faced with these three options, this is the decision I have made.

In cooperation with the armed forces of South Vietnam, attacks are being launched this week to clean out major enemy sanctuaries on the Cambodian-Vietnam border.

A major responsibility for the ground operations is being assumed by South Vietnamese forces. For example, the attacks in several areas, including the Parrot's Beak that I referred to a moment ago, are exclusively South Vietnamese ground operations under South Vietnamese command with the United States providing air and logistical support.

There is one area, however, immediately above Parrot's Beak, where I have concluded that a combined American and South Vietnamese operation is necessary.

Tonight, American and South Vietnamese units will attack the headquarters for the entire Communist military operation in South Vietnam. This key control center has been occupied by the North Vietnamese and Vietcong for 5 years in blatant violation of Cambodia's neutrality.

This is not an invasion of Cambodia. The areas in which these attacks will be launched are completely occupied and controlled by North Vietnamese forces. Our purpose is not to occupy the areas. Once enemy forces are driven out of these sanctuaries and once their military supplies are destroyed, we will withdraw.

These actions are in no way directed at the security interests of any nation. Any government that chooses to use these actions as a pretext for harming relations with the United States will be doing so on its own responsibility, and on its own initiative, and we will draw the appropriate conclusions.

Now let me give you the reasons for my decision.

A majority of the American people, a majority of you listening to me, are for the withdrawal of our forces from Vietnam. The action I have taken tonight is indispensable for the continuing success of that withdrawal program.

A majority of the American people want to end this war rather than to have it drag on interminably. The action I have taken tonight will serve that purpose.

A majority of the American people want to keep the casualties of our brave men in Vietnam at an absolute minimum. The action I take tonight is essential if we are to accomplish that goal.

We take this action not for the purpose of expanding the war into Cambodia but for the purpose of ending the war in Vietnam and winning the just peace we all desire. We have made and we will continue to make every possible effort to end this war through negotiation at the conference table rather than through more fighting on the battlefield.

Let us look again at the record. We have stopped the bombing of North Vietnam. We have cut air operations by over 20 percent. We have announced withdrawal of over 250,000 of our men. We have offered to withdraw all of our men if they will withdraw theirs. We have offered to negotiate all issues with only one condition—and that is that the future of South Vietnam be determined not by North Vietnam, not by the United States, but by the people of South Vietnam themselves.

The answer of the enemy has been intransigence at the conference table, belligerence in Hanoi, massive military aggression in Laos and Cambodia, and stepped-up attacks in South Vietnam, designed to increase American casualties.

This attitude has become intolerable. We will not react to this threat to American lives merely by plaintive diplomatic protests. If we did, the credibility of the United States would be destroyed in every area of the world where only the power of the United States deters aggression.

personalizes

Tonight, I again warn the North Vietnamese that if they continue to escalate the fighting when the United States is withdrawing its forces, I shall meet my responsibility as Commander in Chief of our Armed Forces to take the action I consider necessary to defend the security of our American men.

The action that I have announced tonight puts the leaders of North Vietnam on notice that we will be patient in working for peace, we will be conciliatory at the conference table, but we will not be humiliated. We will not be defeated. We will not allow American men by the thousands to be killed by an enemy from privileged sanctuaries.

The time came long ago to end this war through peaceful negotiations. We stand ready for those negotiations. We have made major efforts, many of which must remain secret. I say tonight that all the offers and approaches made previously remain on the conference table whenever Hanoi is ready to negotiate seriously.

But if the enemy response to our most conciliatory offers for peaceful negotiation continues to be to increase its attacks and humiliate and defeat us, we shall react accordingly.

My fellow Americans, we live in an age of anarchy both abroad and at home. We see mindless attacks on all the great institutions which have been created by free civilizations in the last 500 years. Even here in the United States, great universities are being systematically destroyed. Small nations all over the world find themselves under attack from within and from without.

If, when the chips are down, the world's most powerful nation, the United States of America, acts like a pitiful, helpless giant, the forces of totalitarianism and anarchy will threaten free nations and free institutions throughout the world.

It is not our power but our will and character that is being tested tonight. The question all Americans must ask and answer tonight is this: Does the richest and strongest nation in the history of the world have the character to meet a direct challenge by a group which rejects every effort to win a just peace, ignores our warning, tramples on solemn agreements, violates the neutrality of an unarmed people, and uses our prisoners as hostages?

If we fail to meet this challenge, all other nations will be on notice that despite its overwhelming power the United States, when a real crisis comes, will be found wanting.

During my campaign for the Presidency, I pledged to bring Americans home from Vietnam. They are coming home.

I promised to end this war. I shall keep that promise.

I promised to win a just peace. I shall keep that promise.

We shall avoid a wider war. But we are also determined to put an end to this war.

In this room, Woodrow Wilson made the great decisions which led to victory in World War I. Franklin Roosevelt made the decisions which led to our victory in World War II. Dwight D. Eisenhower made decisions which ended the war in Korea and avoided war in the Middle East. John F. Kennedy, in his finest hour, made the great decision which removed Soviet nuclear missiles from Cuba and the Western Hemisphere.

I have noted that there has been a great deal of discussion with regard to this decision that I have made and I should point out that I do not contend that it is in the same magnitude as these decisions that I have just mentioned. But between those decisions and this decision there is a difference that is very fundamental. In those decisions, the American people were not assailed by counsels of doubt and defeat from some of the most widely known opinion leaders of the Nation.

I have noted, for example, that a Republican Senator has said that this action I have taken means that my party has lost all chance of winning the November elections. And others are saying today that this move against enemy sanctuaries will make me a one-term President.

No one is more aware than I am of the political consequences of the action I have taken. It is tempting to take the easy political path: to blame this war on previous administrations and to bring all of our men home immediately, regardless of the consequences, even though that would mean defeat for the United States; to desert 18 million South Vietnamese people, who have put their trust in us and to expose them to the same slaughter and savagery which the leaders of North Vietnam inflicted on hundreds of thousands of North Vietnamese who chose freedom when the Communists took over North Vietnam in 1954; to get peace at any price now, even though I know that a peace of humiliation for the United States would lead to a bigger war or, surrender later.

trying to heighten ethos

I have rejected all political considerations in making this decision.

personalities

Whether my party gains in November is nothing compared to the lives of 400,000 brave Americans fighting for our country and for the cause of peace and freedom in Vietnam. Whether I may be a one-term President is insignificant compared to whether by our failure to act in this crisis the United States proves itself to be unworthy to lead the forces of freedom in this critical period in world history. I would rather be a one-term President and do what I believe is right than to be a two-term President at the cost of seeing America become a second-rate power and to see this Nation accept the first defeat in its proud 190-year history.

I realize that in this war there are honest and deep differences in this country about whether we should have become involved, that there are differences as to how the war should have been conducted. But the decision I announce tonight transcends those differences.

For the lives of American men are involved. The opportunity for 150,000 Americans to come home in the next 12 months is involved. The future of 18 million people in South Vietnam and 7 million people in Cambodia is involved. The possibility of winning a just peace in Vietnam and in the Pacific is at stake.

It is customary to conclude a speech from the White House by asking support for the President of the United States. Tonight, I depart from that precedent. What I ask is far more important. I ask for your support for our brave men fighting tonight halfway around the world—not for territory—not for glory—but so that their younger brothers and their sons and your sons can have a chance to grow up in a world of peace and freedom and justice.

"I've Studied the Lives of All the Presidents. . . ."

Remarks at Dr. Billy Graham's East Tennessee Crusade
Knoxville, Tennessee
May 28, 1970

Nixon's appearance at the Billy Graham rally proved embarrassing to the officials of the University of Tennessee, for they had leased the football stadium to Graham for religious purposes. Still reeling from the fury of opposition to the Cambodian invasion, Nixon flew to the rally apparently to comfort himself in the midst of an audience more sympathetic than those he had faced during the previous four weeks. In addition, it was Youth Night. The young people attending this rally represented Nixon's constituency among the young, in sharp contrast to those the public had seen on television denouncing the invasion and his Administration. No doubt Nixon intended this comparison to be drawn between the clean-cut youth at the rally and the screaming, long-haired protestors at the Capitol. Nixon's speech is filled with non sequiturs, exaggerated claims, and nonsensical statements. Yet, it represents certain values—particularly a strong belief in patriotism and civil religion—that bound Nixon's constituency to him.

May I say very briefly to you, first, how deeply honored Mrs. Nixon and I are to be here in Tennessee and to receive such a wonderfully warm and friendly welcome from our friends in Tennessee.

And we also want you to know that it is a very great privilege to be on the campus of the largest university in the South—the University of Tennessee.

And if I may add a personal note as one who warmed the bench for 4 years, it is finally good to get out on the football field here at Volunteer Stadium. And even if we are on the 20-yard line, we are going to be over that goal line before we are through.

Billy Graham, when he invited me to come here, said that this was to be Youth Night. He told me that there would be youth from the university, from other parts of the State, representing different points of view. I am just glad that there seems to be a rather solid majority on one side rather than the other side tonight.

Could I say to you, too, that I think that, if I could have your attention for just a moment, perhaps America needs to know something about America's youth and perhaps America's youth needs to know something about America.

I want to tell you that I am very proud that on our White House staff we have the largest proportion of staff members in responsible positions below the age of 30 of any White House staff in history. The reason we have is that I believe in the young people of America. I think they have something to say and I want them in the high counsels of the government of this country.

The reason that they are there is because I believe America also needs to know that the great majority of our young people are people who go to college and universities for the purpose of getting a good education. It is a well-educated generation. It is a very dedicated generation. It is also a generation, I know, that is enormously interested, not simply in the pursuit of a good living, but also in those causes that are beyond self. And for this I am most grateful that the young who will be leading this country when we are gone is one that is interested in America's future, and is so dedicated to those goals.

And also I am proud to say that the great majority of America's young people do not approve of violence; the great majority of America's young people, as I do, do approve of dissent. But they say they want the right to be heard and when they speak they think other people should be silent so that they can be heard.

And so it is a generation that is not the lost generation, as some Americans think. It isn't the beat generation. It isn't the beat-up generation. It can be and will become the great young generation. That is what I believe and that is what you are going to make it become.

And now if I could say a word about what perhaps we should know about America. I don't tell you that everything about America is what I want it to be. I can understand why so many of our young people speak of their desire for peace. I want that. You want it. The man who will address you tonight represents a religious faith that has been dedicated to peace.

I recognize that a great number of our young people are concerned about the fact that in our great cities the air is dirty; that some places the water is polluted; that there aren't enough parks; that education is inferior; that health is inadequate; that there is alienation between the races in this country; and that there is also alienation between the generations.

I know there are things about America that are wrong. But I also know this: that this is a country where a young person knows that there is a peaceful way he can change what he doesn't like about America and that is why it is a great country. And I also know that of all the nations in the world, that this is the one country where a young person knows that not only do we have the power, but we have the ability to clean up the air and clean up the water and provide better jobs and better opportunity and all of these things for our people. And that is because we are so fortunate to be so rich in those things that are material.

And now one other thought: I speak from the field of government and the man who follows me will speak from another field. As one who works in the field of government, I can tell you my life is dedicated to the cause that I know you are dedicated to, all of you. I want this Nation to be at peace, and we shall be. I want the air to be clean, and it will be clean. I want the water to be pure, and it will be pure. I want better education for all Americans, whatever their race or religion or whatever it may be, and an equal opportunity for all, and that shall be.

But I can tell you, my friends, that while government can bring peace, that while government can clean up the air, that while government can clean up the streets and while government can clean up the water and bring better education and better health, there is one thing that government cannot do because, you see, we can have what can be described as complete cleanliness and yet have a sterile life unless we have the spirit, a spirit that cannot come from a man in government, a spirit that will be represented by the man who follows me.

I conclude with one thought: I have studied the lives of all the Presidents of this country, of both parties. They came from different religions. Some were better church-goers than others, but there is one thing I have noted about every man who has occupied this office, and that is by the time he ended his term in office he was more dedicated and more dependent on his religious faith than when he entered it. And that tells me something.

This is a great office and I am proud and humble to hold it. This is enormous responsibility and I accept the responsibility without fear but with also great respect.

But I can also tell you America would not be what it is today, the greatest nation in the world, if this were not a nation which has made progress under God. This nation would not be the great nation that it was unless those who have led this nation had each in his own way turned for help beyond himself for these causes that we all want for our young people, a better life, the things that we may not have had ourselves but we want for them.

And I simply want to tell the people here in Tennessee and those listening on television and radio that I respect those who disagree with me.

No one can be sure what decision is right. I have to make it. I thank those who send in their criticisms and those who send in their support, but above all, I want you to know that I have appreciated the fact that in the few months I have been in this office I have received thousands of letters from people who say, "I pray for this country and I pray for the President in the exercise of the powers of his office."

With that kind of spiritual guidance and spiritual assistance there is no question in my view about the long-range future of America.

And I can only say in conclusion to all of those gathered here today that government can provide, as I have indicated, peace, clean water, clean air, clean streets, and all the rest, but we must remember that that quality of the spirit that each one of us needs, that each one of us hungers for must come from a man who will address you in a moment.

Some will not share his religious convictions, but all with me will share respect for the message that he brings because what he will say to you is what America and the world needs to hear, and that is that man does not live by bread alone, that the material things are not enough, that if we are going to bring people together as we must bring them together, if we are going to have peace in the world, if our young people are going to have a fulfillment beyond simply those material things, they must turn to those great spiritual sources that have made America the great country that it is.

I am proud to be here, and I am proud to have your warm reception.

"Speak Up for America"
Sky Harbor Airport
Phoenix, Arizona
October 31, 1970

In the 1970 Congressional elections, the Nixon administration pinpointed certain Democrats (and at least one Republican, Charles Goodell of New York) to defeat. The central issue the administration hammered at was "the social issue," violence and permissiveness in America. Vice President Agnew came forth as principal spokesman for the administration, and he attacked opponents as "radic-libs" (radical-liberals) and associated them with violence, extremists, and permissiveness. However, Nixon decided late in the campaign to put his prestige on the line by campaigning also. From October 17 to Election Eve he spoke in 23 different states. This speech followed a rock-throwing incident at San Jose a few days before, and it is representative of Nixon's use of the "the social issue." Its importance lies in the fact that an edited 15 minute version of it was broadcast on Election Eve. It was a disaster. The print of the speech was in black and white with a very poor audio sound track. Furthermore in an age of "cool" television, the President came off as frenetic and "hot." To top it off, he was followed on television that evening by Senator Edmund Muskie, speaking for the Democrats from his living room, quietly and in living color. The edited television version was generally admitted to be a mistake, and one Nixon aide—the one responsible for the tape—calculated it cost the Republicans 2 or 3 Senate seats in the Election.

I appreciate very much your wonderful reception. I understand, incidentally, that traffic is backed up for 3 miles. We saw it as we came in. I hope, incidentally, that our friends in radio and television have this on the radio, so that the poeple in the cars can hear on the radio, and my greetings to you.

I am very happy to be back in Arizona. I remember my very young years when I was in Prescott on three different summers. I have very warm feelings about this. As Barry Goldwater says, too, I was raised on Arizona's water, so we share something in common.

I am particularly impressed by the size of this group and I realize what we are competing with today, the Homecoming of the University of Arizona at Tucson. I understand the Arizona State Fair—is that right?—it is going on right now, and the opening of deer season.

And also, I am very appreciative of the fact that we have had some wonderful musical organizations that have been entertaining us and entertaining you before we were here. If I can just mention them briefly. I want all of those listening on television and radio to hear it, too. I understand we have, from the choral groups, and let's give them all a hand: the Phoenix Boys' Club Chorus, the Coronado High School Choral group, the Phoenicians Barbershop Chorus, the Scottsdale High School Band, and the Arizona State University Band.

After that reception from the band, I can't resist just saying something to you that is going to get me in trouble someplace else. When I was in Texas a few days ago, they told me that Texas was number one. When I was in Ohio the other day, they told me that Ohio State was going to be number one. When I was in Indiana, they told me Notre Dame was going to be number one. When I was in Northern California, they told me that Stanford was number one.

But, boy, when I am in Arizona, Arizona State is number one.

I am glad to be in the State of champions, a champion United States Senator and a man that belongs not only to Arizona but the whole Nation—Barry Goldwater.

And a champion in the form of the man that I am proud here to endorse, a very great Governor, one who has served this State and one who is among the top ranks of the Governors of the Nation, Governor Williams, of Arizona.

And champion Congressmen, too, Johnny Rhodes, who serves in the leadership with me, and Congressman Steiger. Let me say for our Congressional candidates, let's give them the hand that they deserve, too.

And finally, your United States Senator, the man who is up for reelection, the man who is among those for whom I am particularly campaigning across this country, because what happens in the Senate this year is perhaps the most important Senate race in the 190-year history of this country.

I simply want to say this about Paul Fannin: I have known him as you have known him for a number of years. I have known him as a fine Senator and as a fine man.

I also know this, that he is a man upon whom I depend. I value his advice. I know that he fights for Arizona, but I also know that he fights for the defense of the United States of America, and we need that, too, in the United States Senate.

I am proud to endorse him. I don't know what I would do without him. Give him back, will you? How about it? We want him back.

Now, ladies and gentlemen, you are all standing here and I know you have been standing for a long time, jammed up, and I don't want you to get tired. But I have selected this particular occasion for a major statement. A major statement that needs to be made, needs to be made now, not because it is the end of a political campaign, but because this problem has been building up in America.

It is time for the President of the United States to speak out clearly to the American people, not because he personally has been affected by it, but because all of America is affected by what happened a couple of days ago in my home State of California, in San Jose.

You saw some of it on television. You saw the crowd inside, a crowd like this, 3,000 people, listening, cheering, indicating their interest in who might be the Governor, who might be the Senator and, of course, showing respect for the office of the President of the United States. You saw also the crowd outside.

The crowd inside were exercising their right to peaceable assembly, as you are today. They were listening to political speakers. They were weighing the issues in the campaign of 1970.

And outside the hall there was a mob of about 1,000, maybe a few more. We could see the hate in their faces as we drove into the hall, and the obscenities they waved. We could hear the hate in their voices as they chanted their obscenities.

And inside the hall, we could hear them pounding on the doors as if they could not bear the thought of people listening respectfully to the Governor of the State of California, the senior Senator, and the President of the United States.

Along the campaign trail we have seen and heard demonstrators, but never before in this campaign was there such an atmosphere of hatred. As we came out of the hall and entered the motorcade, the haters surged past the barricades.

They began throwing rocks. These were not small stones; they were large rocks. They were heavy enough to smash windows, windows in the press bus, windows in the staff cars. They weren't directed at me, though some did hit the Presidential car. Most of the rocks hit the buses and the other cars behind.

What is the reaction of the people who came—people like you? They are at a rally, peaceably at a rally. Many who brought their children were terrified. Others were incensed at the insult to elected leaders. And all were repelled by the atmosphere of violence and hatred that marred the event. And they thought to themselves, "Is this America? Is this the land where reason and peaceful discussion is the hallmark of a free society?"

Some say that the violent dissent is caused by the war in Vietnam. Well, ladies and gentlemen, my fellow Americans, it is about time we branded this line of thinking, this alibi for violence, for what it is: pure nonsense.

Those who carry a "peace" sign in one hand and throw a bomb or a brick with the other are the super hypocrites of our time.

My friends, the war is ending. Instead of sending men to Vietnam, we are bringing them home. Instead of casualties going up, they are coming down. The peace plan is on the table. And we are ending the war in a way that will discourage aggressors so that we can have not just peace for the next election, but peace for the next generation. That is what is happening.

And yet, as the war ends, the violence continues, and this is proof that these alibis are worthless.

Others say that the cause of violence is repression, but the people who came peaceably to the rally in San Jose—they were not repressing the haters outside. There is more freedom in the United States than anywhere else in the world, and it is about time that we cut out the nonsense—it is simply pure nonsense—that repression is the cause of violence in the United States of America.

Violence in America today is not caused by the war, it is not caused by repression. There is no romantic ideal involved. Let's recognize these people for what they are. They are not romantic revolutionaries. They are the same thugs and hoodlums that have always plagued the good people.

And now the reason, a major reason, that they have gained such prominence in our national life, the major reason they dominate our television screens as they do night after night, the reason that they increasingly terrorize decent citizens, can be summed up in a single word: appeasement. When you permit an imbalance to exist that favors the accused over the victim, you are inviting more violence and breeding more bullies.

For too long, and this needs to be said and said now and here, the strength of freedom in our society has been eroded by a creeping permissiveness in our legislatures, in our courts, in our family life, and in our colleges and universities.

For too long, we have appeased aggression here at home, and as with all appeasement, the result has been more aggression and more violence. The time has come to draw the line. The time has come for the great silent majority of Americans of all ages, of every political persuasion, to stand up and be counted against the appeasement of the rock throwers and the obscenity shouters in America.

My fellow Americans, let us understand this is not a partisan issue. There is no candidate of either party that is for crime, that is for violence. The choice before the American people next week is not so simple as picking between the pro-violent and the anti-violent. Everyone denounces violence.

The choice is between approaches to the same goal. One approach holds that violence will end as we end the war; that violence will end as we give more power to those who demand more power; that violence will end as we end hunger and poverty in America.

The people who believe in this approach are sincere Americans. They have every right to this point of view. But I believe that their approach has led us down a path of appeasement that has resulted in the very thing that they abhor most: the increase in violence, the limiting of personal freedom.

For years now, it has been fashionable to portray ourselves, this great country of America, as a sick society; to belittle its successes and breastbeat about its shortcomings; to make automatic heroes out of those who protest as if the act of protest, regardless of what was being protested or how it was done, or whose rights were being infringed, or even whether the protesters had anything better to offer, as if this itself were the mark of higher virtue, and when rituals of protest began to establish a tyranny of their own, there were many who somehow forgot that tyranny was wrong, whatever its form—whether the tyranny of government, the tyranny of terrorists, the tyranny of those who shout down speakers, the tyranny of those who would shut down colleges or blockade streets in an effort to impose their own views on others.

That way is not the American way and that way will not be the American way as long as those who care about freedom, decency, and respect for the rights of one another stand up and be counted.

For a decade, now, this approach dominated America. It has obviously failed. The time has come to try a new approach.

Let me first point out what this new approach, our approach, is not. The answer to bluster is not more bluster. The answer to bluster is firmness. The answer to a wave of violence is not a wave of repression. This is exactly what the violent few want so that they can enlist the sympathies of the moderates.

The answer to violence is the strong application of fair American justice.

And the answer to violent dissent is not oppression of legitimate dissent. The great danger to dissent today comes not from the forces of law, but from the organized tyranny of some dissenters.

Now, let me spell out what the new approach, our approach, is:

First, the new approach to violence calls for new and strong laws that will give the peace forces new muscle to deal with the criminal forces in the United States of America. And in the United States Senate, Paul Fannin, and in the House of Representatives, Johnny Rhodes and Sam Steiger, have stood firmly with the President for that proposition and we need them back.

I have called for a whole series of laws. But because we have not had enough support in the House and the Senate, Congress has dilly-dallied; Congress has bottled them up in committee; Congress has passed only part of a program I asked for; and then they waited until just before the election.

The new approach to violence requires men in Congress who will work for and fight for laws that will put the terrorists where they belong—not roaming around civil society, but behind bars. That is where they belong.

And our new approach calls for a new approach to the interpretation of the laws we already have. I will continue to appoint judges to the Supreme Court and to all the courts who have an awareness of the rights of the victim as well as the rights of the accused.

And I need men in the United States Senate like Paul Fannin who will back me up when I send those recommendations for such judges to the United States Senate.

Third, our new approach to violence calls for a new attitude on the part of the American people—on your part, all of us. "Law and order" are not code words for racism or repression. "Law and order" are code words for freedom from fear in America.

This new attitude means that parents must exercise their responsibility for moral guidance. It means that college administrators and college faculties must stop caving in to the demands of a radical few. It means that moderate students must take a position that says to the violent: "Hit the books or hit the road."

This new attitude means that all Americans should stand with the men who are assigned to carry out the laws. After all, my friends, the first step toward respect for law is respect for the lawman. Let's give him the respect that he deserves.

Today I have been describing two approaches to violence in America. While the goal of ending violence is the same, the two approaches are very different. But don't let anybody tell you everybody is against violence, it is not an issue. The two approaches are deeply different. It is an issue, one of the central issues in America today.

If we do not act now to protect our freedom, we will lose our freedom. If we do not choose the tough-minded approach to violence, we will allow violence to gain a terrible momentum. If a man chooses to dress differently, to wear his hair differently—if he has any—or to talk in a way that repels decent people, that is his business. But when he picks up a rock, then it becomes your business and my business to stop him. Because, you see, that is what American freedom is all about.

When a man cannot bring his child—and I see so many wonderful children here today—when he can't bring his child to a political rally for fear that the person in the next seat is going to start yelling some filthy obscenity; when a man can't bring his wife to a rally for fear she is going to be pushed around by an unruly mob; and when any American faces the risk of a rock being thrown at him when he rises to speak, then I say appeasement has gone too far and it is time to draw the line.

Since 1776, this great Nation of ours has never knuckled under to the tactics of terror, abroad or at home, and we are not about to start in the year 1970.

And now could I add a personal note? The terrorists, the far left, would like nothing better than to make the President of the United States a prisoner in the White House. Well, let me just set them straight. As long as I am President, no band of violent thugs is going to keep me from going out and speaking with the American people wherever they want to hear me and wherever I want to go. This is a free country, and I fully intend to share that freedom with my fellow Americans. This President is not going to be cooped up in the White House.

To keep this country free, to adopt the new approach to violence, to answer those who shout their four-letter words and abuse the right of free speech, what can you do, particularly you of voting age, as an individual? I will tell you what.

You don't have to shout back the same obscenities. You don't have to pick up a rock or a stone or a bomb. You have your vote. That is more powerful than any obscenity, any word; more powerful than a bomb. That vote of yours is what makes this Government respond. That vote of yours can bring about the new tough-minded approach to violence that threatens freedom.

Many people have asked me why I have been campaigning so hard in the past few weeks when my own name isn't on the ballot. "You are risking your prestige," they say. "After all, if some of the people you campaign for lose, you are going to be hurt." I am a lot less interested in my prestige than I am in the future of this country that we all love.

The American people, and the people of Arizona joining with them, elected me 2 years ago to do a job. I am trying to do that job, and I need help. I need help in the Congress to put across the programs that will make America strong enough to bring a full generation of peace abroad and strong enough to turn back the threat to peace and order at home.

My fellow Americans, America is a great country. Americans are a great people. And Americans together share a great future. I have seen this. I have felt this from an airplane hangar in Vermont to the warmth and goodwill of that vast majority of the people in San Jose.

I want to say, too, to young Americans, as I said last night and I repeat here with so many young Americans: Night after night on the television screen you get an inaccurate picture of young Americans. You see the bomb throwers, the rock throwers, those shouting out the filthy words, trying to shout down speakers. And you get the impression that they are a majority of young Americans or maybe the leaders of the future.

Well, I have news for you. I have seen young Americans all over the country and those that appear on the television screens night after night, they are not a majority of young Americans today and they will not be the leaders of America tomorrow.

My fellow Americans, the message in the campaign of 1970 is very simple. It is this: Have faith in this great country. Have faith in your ability to improve this country with your vote.

And have faith in a system that has resisted attack from the violent few for almost two centuries.

Nobody is going to tear this country down as long as you are ready to cast your vote to build this country up.

A New American Revolution

State of the Union Address
Washington, D.C.
January 22, 1971

Nixon abandoned the partisanship that had marked the first two years in this State of the Union Address. He also departed from tradition somewhat by not presenting a "laundry-list" of proposals he wanted enacted in the next year. Rather, he outlined 6 goals that he wanted to achieve. Generally, journalists and other commentators greeted the speech with praise, and in some cases, enthusiasm.

Mr. Speaker, before I begin my formal address, I want to use this opportunity to congratulate all of those who were winners in the rather spirited contest for leadership positions in the House and the Senate, and also to express my condolences to the losers. I know how both of you feel.

And I particularly want to join with all of the Members of the House and the Senate as well in congratulating the new Speaker of the United States Congress.

To those new Members of this House who may have some doubts about the possibilities for advancement in the years ahead, I would remind you that the Speaker and I met just 24 years ago in this Chamber as freshmen Members of the 80th Congress. As you see, we both have come up in the world a bit since then.

Mr. Speaker, this 92d Congress has a chance to be recorded as the greatest Congress in America's history.

In these troubled years just past, America has been going through a long nightmare of war and division, of crime and inflation. Even more deeply, we have gone through a long, dark night of the American spirit. But now that night is ending. Now we must let our spirits soar again. Now we are ready for the lift of a driving dream.

The people of this Nation are eager to get on with the quest for new greatness. They see challenges, and they are prepared to meet those challenges. It is for us here to open the doors that will set free again the real greatness of this Nation—the genius of the American people.

Now shall we meet this challenge? How can we truly open the doors, and set free the full genius of our people?

The way in which the 92d Congress answers these questions will determine its place in history. More importantly, it can determine this Nation's place in history as we enter the third century of our independence.

Tonight I shall present to the Congress six great goals. I shall ask not simply for more new programs in the old framework. I shall ask to change the framework of government itself—to reform the entire structure of American government so we can make it again fully responsive to the needs and the wishes of the American people.

If we act boldly—if we seize this moment and achieve these goals—we can close the gap between promise and performance in American government. We can bring together the resources of this Nation and the spirit of the American people.

In discussing these great goals, I shall deal tonight only with matters on the domestic side of the Nation's agenda. I shall make a separate report to the Congress and the Nation next month on developments in foreign policy.

The first of these great goals is already before the Congress.

I urge that the unfinished business of the 91st Congress be made the first priority business of the 92d Congress.

Over the next 2 weeks, I will call upon Congress to take action on more than 35 pieces of proposed legislation on which action was not completed last year.

The most important is welfare reform.

The present welfare system has become a monstrous, consuming outrage—an outrage against the community, against the taxpayer, and particularly against the children it is supposed to help.

We may honestly disagree, as we do, on what to do about it. But we can all agree that we do-but must meet the challenge, not by pouring more money into a bad program but by abolishing the present welfare system and adopting a new one.

So let us place a floor under the income of every family with children in America—and without those demeaning, soul-stifling affronts to human dignity that so blight the lives of do-but welfare children today. But let us also establish an effective work incentive and an effective work requirement.

Let us provide the means by which more *can* help themselves. This shall be our goal.

Let us generously help those who are not able to help themselves. But let us stop helping do-but those who are able to help themselves but refuse to do so.

The second great goal is to achieve what Americans have not enjoyed since 1957—full prosperity in peacetime. ~ economic issues

The tide of inflation has turned. The rise in the cost of living, which had been gathering dangerous momentum in the late sixties, was reduced last year. Inflation will he further reduced this year.

But as we have moved from runaway inflation toward reasonable price stability, and at the same time as we have been moving from a wartime economy to a peacetime economy, we have paid a price in increased unemployment.

We should take no comfort from the fact that the level of unemployment in this transition from a wartime to a peacetime economy is lower than in any peacetime year of the sixties.

This is not good enough for the man who is unemployed in the seventies. We must do better for workers in peacetime and we will do better.

To achieve this, I will submit an expansionary budget this year—one that will help stimulate the economy and thereby open up new job opportunities for millions of Americans.

It will be a full employment budget, a budget designed to be in balance if the economy were operating at its peak potential. By spending as if we were *at* full employment, we will help to *bring about* full employment.

I ask the Congress to accept these expansionary policies—to accept the concept of a full employment budget. At the same time, I ask the Congress to cooperate in resisting expenditures that go beyond the limits of the full employment budget. For as we wage a campaign to bring about a widely shared prosperity, we must not reignite the fires of inflation and so undermine that prosperity.

With the stimulus and the discipline of a full employment budget, with the commitment of the independent Federal Reserve System to provide fully for the monetary needs of a growing economy, and with a much greater effort on the part of labor and management to make their wage and price decisions in the light of the national interest and their own self-interest—then for the worker, the farmer, the consumer, for Americans everywhere we shall gain the goal of a new prosperity: more jobs, more income, more profits, without inflation and without war.

This is a great goal, and one that we can achieve together.

The third great goal is to continue the effort so dramatically begun last year, to restore and enhance our natural environment.

Building on the foundation laid in the 37-point program that I submitted to Congress last year, I will propose a strong new set of initiatives to clean up our air and water, to combat noise, and to preserve and restore our surroundings.

I will propose programs to make better use of our land, to encourage a balanced national growth—growth that will revitalize our rural heartland and enhance the quality of life in America.

And not only to meet today's needs but to anticipate those of tomorrow, I will put forward the most extensive program ever proposed by a President of the United States to expand the Nation's parks, recreation areas, open spaces, in a way that truly brings parks to the people where the people are. For only if *we* leave a legacy of parks will the next generation have parks to enjoy.

As a fourth great goal, I will offer a far-reaching set of proposals for improving America's health care and making it available more fairly to more people.

I will propose:

—A program to insure that no American family will be prevented from obtaining basic medical care by inability to pay.

—I will propose a major increase in and redirection of aid to medical schools, to greatly increase the number of doctors and other health personnel.

—Incentives to improve the delivery of health services, to get more medical care resources into those areas that have not been adequately served, to make greater use of medical assistants, and to slow the alarming rise in the costs of medical care.

—New programs to encourage better preventive medicine, by attacking the causes of disease and injury, and by providing incentives to doctors to keep people well rather than just to treat them when they are sick.

I will also ask for an appropriation of an extra $100 million to launch an intensive campaign to find a cure for cancer, and I will ask later for whatever additional funds can effectively be used. The time has come in America when the same kind of concentrated effort that split the atom and took man to the moon should be turned toward conquering this dread disease. Let us make a total national commitment to achieve this goal.

America has long been the wealthiest nation in the world. Now it is time we became the healthiest nation in the world.

The fifth great goal is to strengthen and to renew our State and local governments.

As we approach our 200th anniversary in 1976, we remember that this Nation launched itself as a loose confederation of separate States, without a workable central government. At that time, the mark of its leaders' vision was that they quickly saw the need to balance the separate powers of the States with a government of central powers.

And so they gave us a Constitution of balanced powers, of unity with diversity—and so clear was their vision that it survives today as the oldest written Constitution still in force in the world.

For almost two centuries since—and dramatically in the 1930's—at those great turning points when the question has been between the States and the Federal Government, that question has been resolved in favor of a stronger central Federal Government.

During this time the Nation grew and the Nation prospered. But one thing history tells us is that no great movement goes in the same direction forever. Nations change, they adapt, or they slowly die.

The time has now come in America to reverse the flow of power and resources from the States and communities to Washington, and start power and resources flowing back from Washington to the States and communities and, more important, to the people all across America.

The time has come for a new partnership between the Federal Government and the States and localities—a partnership in which we entrust the States and localities with a larger share of the Nation's responsibilities, and in which we share our Federal revenues with them so that they can meet those responsibilities.

To achieve this goal, I propose to the Congress tonight that we enact a plan of revenue sharing historic in scope and bold in concept.

All across America today, States and cities are confronted with a financial crisis. Some have already been cutting back on essential services—for example, just recently San Diego and Cleveland cut back on trash collections. Most are caught between the prospects of bankruptcy on the one hand and adding to an already crushing tax burden on the other.

As one indication of the rising costs of local government, I discovered the other day that my home town of Whittier, California—which has a population of 67,000—has a larger budget for 1971 than the entire Federal budget was in 1791.

Now the time has come to take a new direction, and once again to introduce a new and more creative balance to our approach to government.

So let us put the money where the needs are. And let us put the power to spend it where the people are.

I propose that the Congress make a $16 billion investment in renewing State and local government. $5 billion of this will be in new and unrestricted funds to be used as the States and localities see fit. The other $11 billion will be provided by allocating $1 billion of new funds and converting one-third of the money going to the present narrow-purposes—for urban development, rural development, education, transportation, job training and law enforcement—but with the States and localities making their own decisions on how it should be spent within each category.

For the next fiscal year, this would increase total Federal aid to the States and localities more than 25 percent over the present level.

The revenue-sharing proposals I send to the Congress will include the safeguards against discrimination that accompany all other Federal funds allocated to the States. Neither the President nor the Congress nor the conscience of this Nation can permit money which comes from *all* the people to be used in a way which discriminates against *some* of the people.

The Federal Government will still have a large and vital role to play in achieving our national progress. Established functions that are clearly and essentially Federal in nature will still be performed by the Federal Government. New functions that need to be sponsored or performed by the Federal Government—such as those I have urged tonight in welfare and health—will be added to the Federal agenda. Whenever it makes the best sense for us to act as a whole nation, the Federal Government should and will lead the way. But where States or local governments can better do what needs to be done, let us see that they have the resources to do it there.

Under this plan, the Federal Government will provide the States and localities with more money and less interference—and by cutting down the interference the same amount of money will go a lot further.

Let us share our resources.

Let us share them to rescue the States and localities from the brink of financial crisis.

Let me share them to give homeowners and wage earners a chance to escape from ever-higher property taxes and sales taxes.

Let us share our resources for two other reasons as well.

The first of these reasons has to do with government itself, and the second has to do with each of us, with the individual.

Let's face it. Most Americans today are simply fed up with government at all levels. They will not—and they should not—continue to tolerate the gap between promise and performance in government.

The fact is that we have made the Federal Government so strong it grows muscle-bound and the States and localities so weak they approach impotence.

If we put more power in more places, we can make government more creative in more places. That way we multiply the number of people with the ability to make things happen—and we can open the way to a new burst of creative energy throughout America.

The final reason I urge this historic shift is much more personal, for each and for every one of us.

As everything seems to have grown bigger and more complex in America, as the forces that shape our lives seem to have grown more distant and more impersonal, a great feeling of frustration has crept across this land.

Whether it is the workingman who feels neglected, the black man who feels oppressed, or the mother concerned about her children, there has been a growing feeling that "things are in the saddle, and ride mankind."

Millions of frustrated young Americans today are crying out—asking not what will government do for me, but what can *I* do, how can *I* contribute, how can *I* matter?

And so let us answer them. Let us say to them and let us say to all Americans: "We hear you. We will give you a chance. We are going to give you a new chance to have more to say about the decisions that affect your future—a chance to participate in government—because we are going to provide more centers of power where what you do can make a difference that you can see and feel in your own life and the life of your whole community."

The further away government is from people, the stronger government becomes and the weaker people become. And a nation with a strong government and a weak people is an empty shell.

I reject the patronizing idea that government in Washington, D.C., is inevitably more wise, more honest and more efficient than government at the local or State level. The honesty and efficiency of government depends on people. Government at all levels has good people and bad people. And the way to get more good people into government is to give them more opportunity to do good things.

The idea that a bureaucratic elite in Washington knows best what is best for people everywhere and that you cannot trust local government is really a contention that you cannot trust people to govern themselves. This notion is completely foreign to the American experience. Local government is the government closest to the *people,* it is most responsive to the individual *person.* It is people's government in a far more intimate way than the government in Washington can ever be.

People came to America because they wanted to determine their own future rather than to live in a country where others determined their future for them.

What this change means is that once again in America we are placing our trust in people.

I have faith in people. I trust the judgment of people. Let us give the people of America a chance, a bigger voice in deciding for themselves those questions that so greatly affect their lives.

The sixth great goal is a complete reform of the Federal Government itself.

Based on a long and intensive study with the aid of the best advice obtainable, I have concluded that a sweeping reorganization of the executive branch is needed if the Government is to keep up with the times and with the needs of the people.

I propose, therefore, that we reduce the present 12 Cabinet Departments to eight.

I propose that the Departments of State, Treasury, Defense and Justice remain, but that all the other departments be consolidated into four: Human Resources, Community Development, Natural Resources, and Economic Development.

Let us look at what these would be:

—First, a department dealing with the concerns of *people*—as individuals, as members of a family—a department focused on human needs.
—Second, a department concerned with the *community*—rural communities and urban communities—and with all that it takes to make a community function as a community.
—Third, a department concerned with our *physical environment,* with the preservation and balanced use of those great natural resources on which our Nation depends.
—And fourth, a department concerned with our *prosperity*—with our jobs, our businesses, and those many activities that keep our economy running smoothly and well.

Under this plan, rather than dividing up our departments by narrow subjects, we would organize them around the great purposes of government. Rather than scattering responsibility by adding new levels of bureaucracy, we would focus and concentrate the responsibility for getting problems solved.

With these four departments, when we have a problem we will know where to go—and the department will have the authority and the resources to do something about it.

Over the years we have added departments and created agencies at the Federal level, each to serve a new constituency, to handle a particular task—and these have grown and multiplied in what has become a hopeless confusion of form and function.

The time has come to match our structure to our purposes—to look with a fresh eye, to organize the Government by conscious, comprehensive design to meet the new needs of a new era.

One hundred years ago, Abraham Lincoln stood on a battlefield and spoke of a government of the people, by the people, for the people. Too often since then, we have become a nation of the Government, by the Government, for the Government.

By enacting these reforms, we can renew that principle that Lincoln stated so simply and so well.

By giving everyone's voice a chance to be heard, we will have government that truly is *of* the people.

By creating more centers of meaningful power, more places where decisions that really count can be made, by giving more people a chance to do something, we can have government that truly is *by* the people.

And by setting up a completely modern, functional system of government at the national level, we in Washington will at last be able to provide government that is truly *for* the people.

I realize that what I am asking is that not only the executive branch in Washington but that even this Congress will have to change by giving up some of its power.

Change is hard. But without change there can be no progress. And for each of us the question then becomes, not "Will change cause me inconvenience?" but "Will change bring progress for America?"

Giving up power is hard. But I would urge all of you, as leaders of this country, to remember that the truly revered leaders in world history are those who gave power to people, and not those who took it away.

As we consider these reforms we will be acting, not for the next 2 years or for the next 10 years, but for the next hundred years.

So let us approach these six great goals with a sense, not only of this moment in history but also of history itself.

Let us act with the willingness to work together and the vision and the boldness and the courage of those great Americans who met in Philadelphia almost 190 years ago to write a Constitution.

Let us leave a heritage as they did—not just for our children but for millions yet unborn—of a nation where every American will have a chance not only to live in peace and to enjoy prosperity and opportunity but to participate in a system of government where he knows not only his votes but his ideas count—a system of government which will provide the means for America to reach heights of achievement undreamed of before.

Those men who met at Philadelphia left a great heritage because they had a vision—not only of what the Nation was but of what it could become.

As I think of that vision, I recall that America was founded as the land of the open door—as a haven for the oppressed, a land of opportunity, a place of refuge, of hope.

When the first settlers opened the door of America three and a half centuries ago, they came to escape persecution and to find opportunity—and they left wide the door of welcome for others to follow.

When the Thirteen Colonies declared their independence almost two centuries ago, they opened the door to a new vision of liberty and of human fulfillment—not just for an elite but for all.

To the generations that followed, America's was the open door that beckoned millions from the old world to the new in search of a better life, a freer life, a fuller life, and in which, by their own decisions, they could shape their own destinies.

For the black American, the Indian, the Mexican-American, and for those others in our land who have not had an equal chance, the Nation at last has begun to confront the need to press open the door of full and equal opportunity, and of human dignity.

For all Americans, with these changes I have proposed tonight we can open the door to a new era of opportunity. We can open the door to full and effective participation in the decisions that affect their lives. We can open the door to a new partnership among governments at all levels, between those governments and the people themselves. And by so doing, we can open wide the doors of human fulfillment for millions of people here in America now and in the years to come.

In the next few weeks I will spell out in greater detail the way I propose that we achieve these six great goals. I ask this Congress to be responsive. If it is, then the 92d Congress, your Congress, our Congress, at the end of its term, will be able to look back on a record more splendid than any in our history.

This can be the Congress that helped us end the longest war in the Nation's history, and end it in a way that will give us at last a genuine chance to enjoy what we have not had in this century—a full generation of peace.

This can be the Congress that helped achieve an expanding economy, with full employment and without inflation—and without the deadly stimulus of war.

This can be the Congress that reformed a welfare system that has robbed recipients of their dignity and robbed States and cities of their resources.

This can be the Congress that pressed forward the rescue of our environment, and established for the next generation an enduring legacy of parks for the people.

This can be the Congress that launched a new era in American medicine, in which the quality of medical care was enhanced while the costs were made less burdensome.

But above all, what this Congress can be remembered for is opening the way to a New American Revolution—a peaceful revolution in which power was turned back to the people—in which government at all levels was refreshed and renewed, and made truly responsive. This can be a revolution as profound, as far-reaching, as exciting as that first revolution almost 200 years ago—and it can mean that just 5 years from now America will enter its third century as a young nation new in spirit, with all the vigor and the freshness with which it began its first century.

My colleagues in the Congress, these are great goals. They can make the sessions of this Congress a great moment for America. So let us pledge together to go forward together—by achieving these goals to give America the foundation today for a new greatness tomorrow and in all the years to come, and in so doing to make this the greatest Congress in the history of this great and good country.

"Four More Years"
Acceptance Speech
Miami, Florida
August 23, 1972

Nixon's acceptance speech presents what he believed were the accomplishments of his first 4 years and sets the tone for the campaign he intended to wage against the Democrats in the election.

Four years ago, standing in this very place, I proudly accepted your nomination for President of the United States.

With your help and with the votes of millions of Americans, we won a great victory in 1968.

Tonight, I again proudly accept your nomination for President of the United States.

Let us pledge ourselves to win an even greater victory this November in 1972.

I congratulate Chairman Ford. I congratulate Chairman Dole, Anne Armstrong, and the hundreds of others who have laid the foundation for that victory by their work at this great convention.

Our platform is a dynamic program for progress for America and for peace in the world.

Speaking in a very personal sense, I express my deep gratitude to this convention for the tribute you have paid to the best campaigner in the Nixon family—my wife Pat. In honoring her, you have honored millions of women in America who have contributed in the past and will contribute in the future so very much to better government in this country.

Again, as I did last night, when I was not at the convention, I express the appreciation of all of the delegates and of all America for letting us see young America at its best at our convention. As I express my appreciation to you, I want to say that you have inspired us with your enthusiasm, with your intelligence, with your dedication at this convention. You have made us realize that this is a year when we can prove the experts' predictions wrong, because we can set as our goal winning a majority of the new voters for *our* ticket this November.

I pledge to you, all of the new voters in America who are listening on television and listening here in this convention hall, that I will do everything that I can over these next 4 years to make your support be one that you can be proud of, because, as I said to you last night, and I feel it very deeply in my heart: Years from now I want you to look back and be able to say that your first vote was one of the best votes you ever cast in your life.

Mr. Chairman, I congratulate the delegates to this convention for renominating as my running-mate the man who has just so eloquently and graciously introduced me, Vice President Ted Agnew.

I thought he was the best man for the job 4 years ago.

I think he is the best man for the job today.

And I am not going to change my mind tomorrow.

Finally, as the Vice President has indicated, you have demonstrated to the Nation that we can have an open convention without dividing Americans into quotas.

Let us commit ourselves to rule out every vestige of discrimination in this country of ours. But my fellow Americans, the way to end discrimination against some is not to begin discrimination against others.

Dividing Americans into quotas is totally alien to the American traditions.

Americans don't want to be part of a quota. They want to be part of America. This Nation proudly calls itself the United States of America. Let us reject any philosophy that would make us the divided people of America.

In that spirit, I address you tonight, my fellow Americans, not as a partisan of party, which would divide us, but as a partisan of principles which can unite us.

Six weeks ago our opponents at their convention rejected many of the great principles of the Democratic Party. To those millions who have been driven out of their home in the Democratic Party, we say come home. We say come home not to another party, but we say come home to the great principles we Americans believe in together.

And I ask you, my fellow Americans, tonight to join us not in a coalition held together only by a desire to gain power. I ask you to join us as members of a new American majority bound together by our common ideals.

I ask everyone listening to me tonight—Democrats, Republicans, Independents, to join our new majority—not on the basis of the party label you wear in your lapel, but on the basis of what you believe in your hearts.

In asking for your support I shall not dwell on the record of our Administration which has been praised perhaps too generously by others at this convention.

We have made great progress in these past 4 years.

It can truly be said that we have changed America and that America has changed the world. As a result of what we have done, America today is a better place and the world is a safer place to live in than was the case 4 years ago.

We can be proud of that record, but we shall never be satisfied. A record is not something to stand on; it is something to build on.

Tonight I do not ask you to join our new majority because of what we have done in the past. I ask your support of the principles I believe should determine America's future.

The choice in this election is not between radical change and no change. The choice in this election is between change that works and change that won't work.

I begin with an article of faith.

It has become fashionable in recent years to point up what is wrong with what is called the American system. The critics contend it is so unfair, so corrupt, so unjust, that we should tear it down and substitute something else in its place.

I totally disagree. I believe in the American system.

I have traveled to 80 countries in the past 25 years, and I have seen Communist systems, I have seen Socialist systems, I have seen systems that are half Socialist and half free.

Every time I come home to America, I realize how fortunate we are to live in this great and good country.

Every time I am reminded that we have more freedom, more opportunity, more prosperity than any people in the world; that we have the highest rate of growth of any industrial nation; that Americans have more jobs at higher wages than in any country in the world; that our rate of inflation is less than that of any industrial nation; that the incomparable productivity of America's farmers has made it possible for us to launch a winning war against hunger in the United States; and that the productivity of our farmers also makes us the best fed people in the world with the lowest percentage of the family budget going to food of any country in the world.

We can be very grateful in this country that the people on welfare in America would be rich in most of the nations of the world today.

Now, my fellow Americans, in pointing up those things, we do not overlook the fact that our system has its problems.

Our Administration, as you know, has provided the biggest tax cut in history, but taxes are still too high.

That is why one of the goals of our Administration is to reduce the property tax which is such an unfair and heavy burden on the poor, the elderly, the wage earner, the farmer, and those on fixed incomes.

As all of you know, we have cut inflation in half in this Administration, but we have got to cut it further. We must cut it further so that we can continue to expand on the greatest accomplishment of our new economic policy: For the first time in 5 years wage increases in America are not being eaten up by price increases.

As a result of the millions of new jobs created by our new economic policies, unemployment today in America is less than the peacetime average of the sixties, but we must continue the unparalleled increase in new jobs so that we can achieve the great goal of our new prosperity—a job for every American who wants to work, without war and without inflation. The way to reach this goal is to stay on the new road we have charted to move America forward and not to take a sharp detour to the left, which would lead to a dead end for the hopes of the American people.

This points up one of the clearest choices in this campaign. Our opponents believe in a different philosophy.

Theirs is the politics of paternalism, where master planners in Washington make decisions for people.

Ours is the politics of people—where people make decisions for themselves.

The proposal that they have made to pay $1,000 to every person in America insults the intelligence of the American voters.

Because you know that every politician's promise has a price—the taxpayer pays the bill.

The American people are not going to be taken in by any scheme where Government gives money with one hand and then takes it away with the other.

Their platform promises everything to everybody, but at an increased net in the budget of $144 billion, but listen to what it means to you, the taxpayers of the country. That would mean an increase of 50 percent in what the taxpayers of America pay. I oppose any new spending programs which will increase the tax burden on the already overburdened American taxpayer.

And they have proposed legislation which would add 82 million people to the welfare rolls.

I say that instead of providing incentives for millions of more Americans to go on welfare, we need a program which will provide incentives for people to get off of welfare and to get to work.

We believe that it is wrong for anyone to receive more on welfare than for someone who works. Let us be generous to those who can't work without increasing the tax burden of those who do work.

And while we are talking about welfare, let us quit treating our senior citizens in this country like welfare recipients. They have worked hard all of their lives to build America. And as the builders of America, they have not asked for a handout. What they ask for is what they have earned—and that is retirement in dignity and self-respect. Let's give that to our senior citizens.

Now, when you add up the cost of all of the programs our opponents have proposed, you reach only one conclusion: They would destroy the system which has made America number one in the world economically.

Listen to these facts: Americans today pay one-third of all of their income in taxes. If their programs were adopted, Americans would pay over one-half of what they earn in taxes. This means that if their programs are adopted, American wage earners would be working more for the government than they would for themselves.

Once we cross this line, we cannot turn back because the incentive which makes the American economic system the most productive in the world would be destroyed.

Theirs is not a new approach. It has been tried before in countries abroad, and I can tell you that those who have tried it have lived to regret it.

We cannot and we will not let them do this to America.

Let us always be true to the principle that has made America the world's most prosperous nation—that here in America a person should get what he works for and work for what he gets.

Let me illustrate the difference in our philosophies. Because of our free economic system, what we have done is to build a great building of economic wealth and money in America. It is by far the tallest building in the world and we are still adding to it. Now because some of the windows are broken, they say tear it down and start again. We say, replace the windows and keep building. That is the difference.

Let me turn now to a second area where my beliefs are totally different from those of our opponents.

Four years ago crime was rising all over America at an unprecedented rate. Even our Nation's Capital was called the crime capital of the world. I pledged to stop the rise in crime. In order to keep that pledge, I promised in the election campaign that I would appoint judges to the Federal courts, and particularly to the Supreme Court, who would recognize that the first civil right of every American is to be free from domestic violence.

I have kept that promise. I am proud of the appointments I have made to the courts, and particularly proud of those I have made to the Supreme Court of the United States. And I pledge again tonight, as I did 4 years ago, that whenever I have the opportunity to make more appointments to the courts, I shall continue to appoint judges who share my philosophy that we must strengthen the peace forces as against the criminal forces in the United States.

We have launched an all-out offensive against crime, against narcotics, against permissiveness in our country.

I want the peace officers across America to know that they have the total backing of their President in their fight against crime.

My fellow Americans, as we move toward peace abroad, I ask you to support our programs which will keep the peace at home.

Now, I turn to an issue of overriding importance not only to this election, but for generations to come—the progress we have made in building a new structure of peace in the world.

Peace is too important for partisanship. There have been five Presidents in my political lifetime—Franklin D. Roosevelt, Harry Truman, Dwight Eisenhower, John F. Kennedy, and Lyndon Johnson.

They had differences on some issues, but they were united in their belief that where the security of America or the peace of the world is involved we are not Republicans, we are not Democrats. We are Americans, first, last, and always.

These five Presidents were united in their total opposition to isolation for America and in their belief that the interests of the United States and the interests of world peace require that America be strong enough and intelligent enough to assume the responsibilities of leadership in the world.

They were united in the conviction that the United States should have a defense second to none in the world.

They were all men who hated war and were dedicated to peace.

But not one of these five men and no President in our history believed that America should ask an enemy for peace on terms that would betray our allies and destroy respect for the United States all over the world.

As your President, I pledge that I shall always uphold that proud bipartisan tradition. Standing in this Convention Hall 4 years ago, I pledged to seek an honorable end to the war in Vietnam. We have made great progress toward that end. We have brought over half a million men home and more will be coming home. We have ended America's ground combat role. No draftees are being sent to Vietnam. We have reduced our casualties 98 percent. We have gone the extra mile, in fact, we have gone tens of thousands of miles trying to seek a negotiated settlement of the war. We have offered a cease-fire, a total withdrawal of all American forces, an exchange of all prisoners of war, internationally supervised free elections with the Communists participating in the elections and in the supervision.

There are three things, however, that we have not and that we will not offer.

We will never abandon our prisoners of war.

Second, we will not join our enemies in imposing a Communist government on our allies—the 17 million people of South Vietnam.

And we will never stain the honor of the United States of America.

Now I realize that many, particularly in this political year, wonder why we insist on an honorable peace in Vietnam. From a political standpoint they suggest that since I was not in office when over a half million American men were sent there, that I should end the war by agreeing to impose a Communist government on the people of South Vietnam and just blame the whole catastrophe on my predecessors.

This might be good politics, but it would be disastrous to the cause of peace in the world. If, at this time, we betray our allies, it will discourage our friends abroad and it will encourage our enemies to engage in aggression.

In areas like the Mideast, which are danger areas, small nations who rely on the friendship and support of the United States would be in deadly jeopardy.

To our friends and allies in Europe, Asia, the Mideast, and Latin America, I say the United States will continue its great bipartisan tradition—to stand by our friends and never to desert them.

Now in discussing Vietnam, I have noted that in this election year there has been a great deal of talk about providing amnesty for those few hundred Americans who chose to desert their country rather than to serve it in Vietnam. I think it is time that we put the emphasis where it belongs. The real heroes are two and one-half million young Americans who chose to serve their country rather than desert it. I say to you tonight, in these times when there is so much of a tendency to run down those who have served America in the past and who serve it today, let us give those who serve in our Armed Forces and those who have served in Vietnam the honor and the respect that they deserve and that they have earned.

Finally, in this connection, let one thing be clearly understood in this election campaign: The American people will not tolerate any attempt by our enemies to interfere in the cherished right of the American voter to make his own decision with regard to what is best for America without outside intervention.

Now it is understandable that Vietnam has been a major concern in foreign policy. But we have not allowed the war in Vietnam to paralyze our capacity to initiate historic new policies to construct a lasting and just peace in the world.

When the history of this period is written, I believe it will be recorded that our most significant contributions to peace resulted from our trips to Peking and to Moscow.

The dialogue that we have begun with the People's Republic of China has reduced the danger of war and has increased the chance for peaceful cooperation between two great peoples.

Within the space of 4 years in our relations with the Soviet Union we have moved from confrontation to negotiation, and then to cooperation in the interest of peace.

We have taken the first step in limiting the nuclear arms race.

We have laid the foundation for further limitations on nuclear weapons and eventually of reducing the armaments in the nuclear area.

We can thereby not only reduce the enormous cost of arms for both our countries, but we can increase the chances for peace.

More than on any other single issue, I ask you, my fellow Americans, to give us the chance to continue these great initiatives that can contribute so much to the future of peace in the world.

It can truly be said that as a result of our initiatives, the danger of war is less today than it was; the chances for peace are greater.

But a note of warning needs to be sounded. We cannot be complacent. Our opponents have proposed massive cuts in our defense budget which would have the inevitable effect of making the United States the second strongest nation in the world.

For the United States unilaterally to reduce its strength with the naive hope that other nations would do likewise would increase the danger of war in the world.

It would completely remove any incentive of other nations to agree to a mutual limitation or reduction of arms.

The promising initiatives we have undertaken to limit arms would be destroyed.

The security of the United States and all the nations in the world who depend upon our friendship and support would be threatened.

Let's look at the record on defense expenditures. We have cut spending in our Administration. It now takes the lowest percentage of our national product in 20 years. We should not spend more on defense than we need. But we must never spend less than we need.

What we must understand is, spending what we need on defense will cost us money. Spending less than we need could cost us our lives or our freedom.

So tonight, my fellow Americans, I say, let us take risks for peace, but let us never risk the security of the United States of America.

It is for that reason that I pledge that we will continue to seek peace and the mutual reduction of arms. The United States, during this period, however, will always have a defense second to none.

There are those who believe that we can entrust the security of America to the good will if our adversaries.

Those who hold this view do not know the real world. We can negotiate limitation of arms and we have done so. We can make agreements to reduce the danger of war, and we have done so.

But one unchangeable rule of international diplomacy that I have learned over many, many years is that, in negotiations between great powers, you can only get something if your have something to give in return.

That is why I say tonight: Let us always be sure that when the President of the United States goes to the conference table, he never has to negotiate from weakness.

There is no such thing as a retreat to peace.

My fellow Americans, we stand today on the threshold of one of the most exciting and challenging eras in the history of relations between nations.

We have the opportunity in our time to be the peacemakers of the world, because the world trusts and respects us, and because the world knows that we shall only use our power to defend freedom, never to destroy it; to keep the peace, never to break it.

A strong America is not the enemy of peace; it is the guardian of peace.

The initiatives that we have begun can result in reducing the danger of arms, as well as the danger of war which hangs over the world today.

Even more important, it means that the enormous creative energies of the Russian people and the Chinese people and the American people and all the great peoples of the world can be turned away from production of war and turned toward production for peace.

In America it means that we can undertake programs for progress at home that will be just as exciting as the great initiatives we have undertaken in building a new structure of peace abroad.

My fellow Americans, the peace dividend that we hear so much about has too often been described solely in monetary terms—how much money we could take out of the arms budget and apply to our domestic needs. By far the biggest dividend, however, is that achieving our goal of a lasting peace in the world would reflect the deepest hopes and ideals of all of the American people.

Speaking on behalf of the American people, I was proud to be able to say in my television address to the Russian people in May: "We covet no one else's territory. We seek no dominion over any other nation. We seek peace not only for ourselves, but for all the people of the world."

This dedication to idealism runs through America's history.

During the tragic War Between the States, Abraham Lincoln was asked whether God was on his side. He replied, "My concern is not whether God is on our side, but whether we are on God's side."

May that always be our prayer for America.

We hold the future of peace in the world and our own future in our hands. Let us reject therefore the policies of those who whine and whimper about our frustrations and call on us to turn inward.

Let us not turn away from greatness.

The chance America now has to lead the way to a lasting peace in the world may never come again.

With faith in God and faith in ourselves and faith in our country, let us have the vision and the courage to seize the moment and meet the challenge before it slips away.

On your television screen last night, you saw the cemetery in Leningrad I visited on my trip to the Soviet Union—where 300,000 people died in the siege of that city during World War II.

At the cemetery I saw the picture of a 12-year-old girl. She was a beautiful child. Her name was Tanya.

I read her diary. It tells the terrible story of war. In the simple words of a child she wrote of the deaths of the members of her family. Zhenya in December. Grannie in January. Then Leka. Then Uncle Vasya. Then Uncle Lyosha. Then Mama in May. And finally—these were the last words in her diary: "All are dead. Only Tanya is left."

Let us think of Tanya and of the other Tanyas and their brothers and sisters everywhere in Russia, in China, in America, as we proudly meet our responsibilities for leadership in the world in a way worthy of a great people.

I ask you, my fellow Americans, to join our new majority not just in the cause of winning an election, but in achieving a hope that mankind has had since the beginning of civilization. Let us build a peace that our children and all the children of the world can enjoy for generations to come.

The Watergate Investigation

Televised Address to the Nation
Washington, D.C.
April 30, 1973

On April 17 Nixon read a brief statement in the White House press room in which he announced that "serious charges" had been brought to his attention on March 21st causing him to begin "intensive new inquiries" into the Watergate scandal. He further reported that this investigation had produced "major developments" and "real progress . . . in finding the truth" about the break-in. After the announcement Ron Ziegler, White House press secretary, declared all previous statements on Watergate by the Administration "inoperative." As we know from the transcripts of Nixon's tapes, the situation was more serious than he let on. The "cover-up" had begun to come apart, and Nixon was casting about for ways to save himself from his aides, especially John Dean, Counsel to the President, who was already talking to Federal Prosecutors about his role and the roles of others in the conspiracy. On April 30 President Nixon, flanked by a bust of Lincoln and a picture of his family, spoke to the American people in his first speech devoted solely to Watergate. He announced the resignations of H. R. Haldeman and John Ehrlichman, "two of the finest public servants it has been my privilege to know," the resignations of Attorney General Kleindienst and John Dean, and the appointment of Elliot Richardson as his nominee for Kleindienst's replacement. Nixon then stated that he knew nothing about illegal activities by his aides until March 21, that he had been too busy with trying to achieve peace in 1972 to monitor campaign activities, and he fully intended to get to the truth about what happened now that new information had come to his attention. The speech was not as successful as Nixon had hoped. A Gallup Poll taken soon after the speech showed that about half the respondents believed Nixon had participated in the cover-up. A poll several weeks later showed 45% disapproved of Nixon's performance in office to 44% approval, the first time since 1969 that the disapproval percentage was greater than the approval percentage.

I want to talk to you tonight from my heart on a subject of deep concern to every American.

In recent months, members of my Administration and officials of the Committee for the Re-election of the President—including some of my closest friends and most trusted aides— have been charged with involvement in what has come to be known as the Watergate Affair. These include charges of illegal activity during the preceding the 1972 Presidential election and charges that responsible officials participated in efforts to cover up that illegal activity.

The inevitable result of these charges has been to raise serious questions about the integrity of the White House itself. Tonight I wish to address those questions.

Last June 17, while I was in Florida trying to get a few days rest after my visit to Moscow, I first learned from news reports of the Watergate break-in. I was appalled at this senseless, illegal action, and I was shocked to learn that employees of the Re-election Committee were apparently among those guilty. I immediately ordered an investigation by appropriate Government authorities. On September 15, as you will recall, indictments were brought against seven defendants in the case.

As the investigations went forward, I repeatedly asked those conducting the investigation whether there was any reason to believe that members of my Administration were in any way involved. I received repeated assurances that there were not. Because of these continuing reassurances, because I believed the reports I was getting, because I had faith in the persons from whom I was getting them, I discounted the stories in the press that appeared to implicate members of my Administration or other officials of the campaign committee.

Until March of this year, I remained convinced that the denials were true and that the charges of involvement by members of the White House Staff were false. The comments I made during this period, and the comments made by my Press Secretary in my behalf, were based on the information provided to us at the time we made those comments. However, new information then came to me which persuaded me that there was a real possibility that some of these charges were true, and suggesting further that there had been an effort to conceal the facts both from the public, from you, and from me.

As a result, on March 21, I personally assumed the responsibility for coordinating intensive new inquiries into the matter, and I personally ordered those conducting the investigations to get all the facts and to report them directly to me, right here in this office.

I again ordered that all persons in the Government or at the Re-election Committee should cooperate fully with the FBI, the prosecutors, and the grand jury. I also ordered that anyone who refused to cooperate in telling the truth would be asked to resign from government service. And, with ground rules adopted that would preserve the basic constitutional separation of powers between the Congress and the Presidency, I directed that members of the White House Staff should appear and testify voluntarily under oath before the Senate committee which was investigating Watergate.

I was determined that we should get to the bottom of the matter, and that the truth should be fully brought out—no matter who was involved.

At the same time, I was determined not to take precipitate action, and to avoid, if at all possible, any action that would appear to reflect on innocent people. I wanted to be fair. But I knew that in the final analysis, the integrity of this office—public faith in the integrity of this office—would have to take priority over all personal considerations.

Today, in one of the most difficult decisions of my Presidency, I accepted the resignations of two of my closest associates in the White House—Bob Haldeman, John Ehrlichman—two of the finest public servants it has been my privilege to know.

I want to stress that in accepting these resignations, I mean to leave no implication whatsoever of personal wrongdoing on their part, and I leave no implication tonight of implication on the part of others who have been charged in this matter. But in matters as sensitive as guarding the integrity of our democratic process, it is essential not only that rigorous legal and ethical standards be observed, but also that the public, you, have total confidence that they are both being observed and enforced by those in authority and particularly by the President of the United States. They agree with me that this move was necessary in order to restore that confidence.

Because Attorney General Kleindienst—though a distinguished public servant, my personal friend for 20 years, with no personal involvement whatever in this matter—has been a close personal and professional associate of some of those who are involved in this case, he and I both felt that it was also necessary to name a new Attorney General.

The Counsel to the President, John Dean, has also resigned.

As the new Attorney General, I have today named Elliot Richardson, a man of unimpeachable integrity and rigorously high principle. I have directed him to do everything necessary to ensure that the Department of Justice has the confidence and the trust of every law abiding person in this country.

I have given him absolute authority to make all decisions bearing upon the prosecution of the Watergate case and related matters. I have instructed him that if he should consider it appropriate, he has the authority to name a special supervising prosecutor for matters arising out of the case.

Whatever may appear to have been the case before, whatever improper activities may yet be discovered in connection with this whole sordid affair, I want the American people, I want you to know beyond the shadow of a doubt that during my term as President, justice will be pursued fairly, fully, and impartially, no matter who is involved. This office is a sacred trust and I am determined to be worthy of that trust.

Looking back at the history of this case, two questions arise:

How could it have happened?

Who is to blame?

Political commentators have correctly observed that during my 27 years in politics I have always previously insisted on running my own campaigns for office.

But 1972 presented a very different situation. In both domestic and foreign policy, 1972 was a year of crucially important decisions, of intense negotiations, of vital new directions, particularly in working toward the goal which has been my overriding concern throughout my political career—the goal of bringing peace to America, peace to the world.

That is why I decided, as the 1972 campaign approached, that the Presidency should come first and politics second. To the maximum extent possible, therefore, I sought to delegate campaign operations, to remove the day-to-day campaign decisions from the President's office and from the White House. I also, as you recall, severely limited the number of my own campaign appearances.

Who, then, is to blame for what happened in this case?

For specific criminal actions by specific individuals, those who committed those actions must, of course, bear the liability and pay the penalty.

For the fact that alleged improper actions took place within the White House or within my campaign organization, the easiest course would be for me to blame those to whom I delegated the responsibility to run the campaign. But that would be a cowardly thing to do.

I will not place the blame on subordinates—on people whose zeal exceeded their judgment, and who may have done wrong in a cause they deeply believed to be right.

In any organization, the man at the top must bear the responsibility. That responsibility, therefore, belongs here, in this office. I accept it. And I pledge to you tonight, from this office, that I will do everything in my power to ensure that the guilty are brought to justice, and that such abuses are purged from our political processes in the years to come, long after I have left this office.

Some people, quite properly appalled at the abuses that occurred, will say that Watergate demonstrates the bankruptcy of the American political system. I believe precisely the opposite is true. Watergate represented a series of illegal acts and bad judgments by a number of individuals. It was the system that has brought the facts to light and that will bring those guilty to justice—a system that in this case has included a determined grand jury, honest prosecutors, a courageous judge, John Sirica, and a vigorous free press.

It is essential now that we place our faith in that system—and especially in the judicial system. It is essential that we let the judicial process go forward, respecting those safeguards that are established to protect the innocent as well as to convict the guilty. It is essential that in reacting to the excesses of others, we not fall into excesses ourselves.

It is also essential that we not be so distracted by events such as this that we neglect the vital work before us, before this Nation, before America, at a time of critical importance to America and the world.

Since March, when I first learned that the Watergate affair might, in fact, be far more serious than I had been led to believe, it has claimed far too much of my time and my attention.

Whatever may now transpire in the case, whatever the actions of the grand jury, whatever the outcome of any eventual trials, I must now turn my full attention—and I shall do so—once again to the larger duties of this office. I owe it to this great office that I hold, and I owe it to you—to my country.

I know that as Attorney General, Elliot Richardson will be both fair and he will be fearless in pursuing this case wherever it leads. I am confident that with him in charge, justice will be done.

There is vital work to be done toward our goal of a lasting structure of peace in the world—work that cannot wait, work that I must do.

Tomorrow, for example, Chancellor Brandt of West Germany will visit the White House for talks that are a vital element of "The Year of Europe," as 1973 has been called. We are already preparing for the next Soviet-American summit meeting later this year.

This is also a year in which we are seeking to negotiate a mutual and balanced reduction of armed forces in Europe, which will reduce our defense budget and allow us to have funds for other purposes at home so desperately needed. It is the year when the United States and Soviet negotiators will seek to work out the second and even more important round of our talks on limiting nuclear arms, and of reducing the danger of a nuclear war that would destroy civilization as we know it. It is a year in which we confront the difficult tasks of maintaining peace in Southeast Asia and in the potentially explosive Middle East.

There is also vital work to be done right here in America: to ensure prosperity, and that means a good job for everyone who wants to work; to control inflation, that I know worries every housewife, everyone who tries to balance a family budget in America; to set in motion new and better ways of ensuring progress toward a better life for all Americans.

When I think of this office—of what it means—I think of all the things that I want to accomplish for this Nation, of all the things I want to accomplish for you.

On Christmas Eve, during my terrible personal ordeal of the renewed bombing of North Vietnam, which after 12 years of war, finally helped to bring America peace with honor, I sat down just before midnight. I wrote out some of my goals for my second term as President.

Let me read them to you.

"To make it possible for our children, and for our children's children, to live in a world of peace.

"To make this country be more than ever a land of opportunity—of equal opportunity, full opportunity for every American.

"To provide jobs for all who can work, and generous help for those who cannot work.

"To establish a climate of decency, and civility, in which each person respects the feelings and the dignity and the God-given rights of his neighbor.

"To make this a land in which each person can dare to dream, can live his dreams—not in fear, but in hope—proud of his community, proud of his country, proud of what America has meant to himself and to the world."

These are great goals. I believe we can, we must work for them. We can achieve them. But we cannot achieve these goals unless we dedicate ourselves to another goal.

We must maintain the integrity of the White House, and that integrity must be real, not transparent. There can be no whitewash at the White House.

We must reform our political process—ridding it not only of the violations of the law, but also of the ugly mob violence, and other inexcusable campaign tactics that have been too often practiced and too readily accepted in the past, including those that may have been a response by one side to the excesses or expected excesses of the other side. Two wrongs do not make a right.

I have been in public life for more than a quarter of a century. Like any other calling, politics has good people, and bad people. And let me tell you, the great majority in politics—in the Congress, in the Federal Government, in the State Government—are good people. I know that it can be very easy, under the intensive pressures of a campaign, for even well-intentioned people to fall into shady tactics—to rationalize this on the grounds that what is at stake is of such importance to the Nation that the end justifies the means. And both of our great parties have been guilty of such tactics in the past.

In recent years, however, the campaign excesses that have occurred on all sides have provided a sobering demonstration of how far this false doctrine can take us. The lesson is clear: America, in its political campaigns, must not again fall into the trap of letting the end, however great that end is, justify the means.

I urge the leaders of both political parties, I urge citizens, all of you, everywhere, to join in working toward a new set of standards, new rules and procedures to ensure that future elections will be as nearly free of such abuses as they possibly can be made. This is my goal. I ask you to join in making it America's goal.

When I was inaugurated for a second term this past January 20, I gave each member of my Cabinet and each member of my senior White House Staff a special 4-year calendar, with each day marked to show the number of days remaining to the Administration. In the inscription on each calendar, I wrote these words: "The Presidential term which begins today consists of 1,461 days—no more, no less. Each can be a day of strengthening and renewal for America; each can add depth and dimension to the American experience. If we strive together, if we make the most of the challenge and the opportunity that these days offer us, they can stand out as great days for America, and great moments in the history of the world."

I looked at my own calendar this morning up at Camp David as I was working on this speech. It showed exactly 1,361 days remaining in my term. I want these to be the best days in America's history, because I love America. I deeply believe that America is the hope of the world. And I know that in the quality and wisdom of the leadership America gives lies the only hope for millions of people all over the world, that they can live their lives in peace and freedom. We must be worthy of that hope, in every sense of the word. Tonight, I ask for your prayers to help me in everything that I do throughout the days of my Presidency to be worthy of their hopes and of yours.

God bless America and God bless each and every one of you.

"The White House Horrors"
Statement by the President
Washington, D.C.
May 22, 1973

By May, Nixon faced grave political dangers from both the Special Watergate Prosecutor, Archibald Cox whom he had appointed, and the Senate Select Committee on Presidential Campaign Activities, the "Ervin" or "Watergate" Committee. He undoubtedly feared one of the two would uncover other White House covert activities that would further damage him. Therefore, he apparently decided to get out in "front of the curve" by releasing this four thousand word statement about those activities so as to put them in the best light possible—national security. In an attempt to minimize the importance of these covert and in some cases illegal acts, he issued a statement rather than holding a press conference or making a speech. It was John Mitchell, former U.S. Attorney General, who in his testimony before the Senate Committee, described these acts as the "White House horrors." It was apt and stuck.

Recent news accounts growing out of testimony in the Watergate investigations have given grossly misleading impressions of many of the facts, as they relate both to my own role and to certain unrelated activities involving national security.

Already, on the basis of second-hand and third-hand hearsay testimony by persons either convicted or themselves under investigation in the case, I have found myself accused of involvement in activities I never heard of until I read about them in news accounts.

These impressions could also lead to a serious misunderstanding of those national security activities which, though totally unrelated to Watergate, have become entangled in the case. They could lead to further compromise of sensitive national security information.

I will not abandon my responsibilities. I will continue to do the job I was elected to do.

In the accompanying statement, I have set forth the facts as I know them as they relate to my own role.

With regard to the specific allegations that have been made, I can and do state categorically:

1. I had no prior knowledge of the Watergate operation.
2. I took no part in, nor was I aware of, any subsequent efforts that may have been made to cover up Watergate.
3. At no time did I authorize any offer of executive clemency for the Watergate defendants, nor did I know of any such offer.

4. I did not know, until the time of my own investigation, of any effort to provide the Watergate defendants with funds.
5. At no time did I attempt, or did I authorize others to attempt, to implicate the CIA in the Watergate matter.
6. It was not until the time of my own investigation that I learned of the break-in at the office of Mr. Ellsberg's psychiatrist, and I specifically authorized the furnishing of this information to Judge Byrne.
7. I neither authorized nor encouraged subordinates to engage in illegal or improper campaign tactics.

In the accompanying statement, I have sought to provide the background that may place recent allegations in perspective. I have specifically stated that executive privilege will not be invoked as to any testimony concerning possible criminal conduct or discussions of possible criminal conduct, in the matters under investigation. I want the public to learn the truth about Watergate and those guilty of any illegal actions brought to justice.

Allegations surrounding the Watergate affair have so escalated that I feel a further statement from the President is required at this time.

A climate of sensationalism has developed in which even second- or third-hand hearsay charges are headlined as fact and repeated as fact.

Important national security operations which themselves had no connection with Watergate have become entangled in the case.

As a result, some national security information has already been made public through court orders, through the subpoenaing of documents, and through testimony witnesses have given in judicial and Congressional proceedings. Other sensitive documents are now threatened with disclosure. Continued silence about those operations would compromise rather than protect them, and would also serve to perpetuate a grossly distorted view—which recent partial disclosures have given—of the nature and purpose of those operations.

The purpose of this statement is threefold:

—First, to set forth the facts about my own relationship to the Watergate matter;

—Second, to place in some prespective some of the more sensational—and inaccurate—of the charges that have filled the headlines in recent days, and also some of the matters that are currently being discussed in Senate testimony and elsewhere;

—Third, to draw the distinction between national security operations and the Watergate case. To put the other matters in perspective, it will be necessary to describe the national security operations first.

In citing these national security matters, it is not my intention to place a national security "cover" on Watergate, but rather to separate them out from Watergate—and at the same time to explain the context in which certain actions took place that were later misconstrued or misused.

Long before the Watergate break-in, three important national security operations took place which have subsequently become entangled in the Watergate case.

—The first operation, begun in 1969, was a program of wiretaps. All were legal, under the authorities then existing. They were undertaken to find and stop serious national security leaks.

—The second operation was a reassessment, which I ordered in 1970, of the adequacy of internal security measures. This resulted in a plan and a directive to strengthen our intelligence operations. They were protested by Mr. Hoover, and as a result of his protest they were not put into effect.

—The third operation was the establishment, in 1971, of a Special Investigations Unit in the White House. Its primary mission was to plug leaks of vital security information. I also directed this group to prepare an accurate history of certain crucial national security matters which occured under prior administrations, on which the Government's records were incomplete.

Here is the background of these three security operations initiated in my Administration.

1969 Wiretaps

By mid-1969, my Administration had begun a number of highly sensitive foreign policy initiatives. They were aimed at ending the war in Vietnam, achieving a settlement in the Middle East, limiting nuclear arms, and establishing new relationships among the great powers. These involved highly secret diplomacy. They were closely interrelated. Leaks of secret information about any one could endanger all.

Exactly that happened. News accounts appeared in 1969, which were obviously based on leaks—some of them extensive and detailed—by people having access to the most highly classified security materials.

There was no way to carry forward these diplomatic initiatives unless further leaks could be prevented. This required finding the source of the leaks.

In order to do this, a special program of wiretaps was instituted in mid-1969 and terminated in February 1971. Fewer than 20 taps, of varying duration, were involved. They produced important leads that made it possible to tighten the security of highly sensitive materials. I authorized this entire program. Each individual tap was undertaken in accordance with procedures legal at the time and in accord with longstanding precedent.

The persons who were subject to these wiretaps were determined through coordination among the Director of the FBI, my Assistant for National Security Affairs, and the Attorney General. Those wiretapped were selected on the basis of access to the information leaked, material in security files, and evidence that developed as the inquiry proceeded.

Information thus obtained was made available to senior officials responsible for national security matters in order to curtail further leaks.

The 1970 Intelligence Plan

In the spring and summer of 1970, another security problem reached critical proportions. In March a wave of bombings and explosions struck college campuses and cities. There were 400 bomb threats in one 24-hour period in New York City. Rioting and violence on college campuses reached a new peak after the Cambodiàn operation and the tragedies at Kent State and Jackson State. The 1969-70 school year brought nearly 1,800 campus demonstrations and nearly 250 cases of arson on campus. Many colleges closed. Gun battles between guerrilla-style groups and police were taking place. Some of the disruptive activities were receiving foreign support.

Complicating the task of maintaining security was the fact that, in 1966, certain types of undercover FBI operations that had been conducted for many years had been suspended. This also had substantially impaired our ability to collect foreign intelligence information. At the same time, the relationships beteeen the FBI and other intelligence agencies had been deteriorating. By May 1970, FBI Director Hoover shut off his agency's liaison with the CIA altogether.

On June 5, 1970, I met with the Director of the FBI (Mr. Hoover), the Director of the Central Intelligence Agency (Mr. Richard Helms), the Director of the Defense Intelligence Agency (Gen. Donald V. Bennett), and the Director of the National Security Agency (Adm. Noel Gayler). We discussed the urgent need for better intelligence operations. I appointed Director Hoover as chairman of an interagency committee to prepare recommendations.

On June 25, the committee submitted a report which included specific options for expanded intelligence operations, and on July 23 the agencies were notified by memorandum of the options approved. After reconsideration, however, prompted by the opposition of Director Hoover, the agencies were notified 5 days later, on July 28, that the approval had been rescinded. The options initially approved had included resumption of certain intelligence operations which had been suspended in 1966. These in turn had included authorization for surreptitious entry— breaking and entering, in effect—on specified categories of targets in specified situations related to national security.

Because the approval was withdrawn before it had been implemented, the net result was that the plan for expanded intelligence activities never went into effect.

The documents spelling out this 1970 plan are extremely sensitive. They include—and are based upon—assessments of certain foreign intelligence capabilities and procedures, which of course must remain secret. It was this unused plan and related documents that John Dean removed from the White House and placed in a safe deposit box giving the keys to Judge Sirica. The same plan, still unused, is being headlined today.

Coordination among our intelligence agencies continued to fall short of our national security needs. In July 1970, having earlier discontinued the FBI's liaison with the CIA, Director Hoover ended the FBI's normal liaison with all other agencies except the White House. To help remedy this, an Intelligence Evaluation Committee was created in December 1970. Its members included representatives of the White House, CIA, FBI, NSA, the Departments of Justice, Treasury, and Defense, and the Secret Service.

The Intelligence Evaluation Committee and its staff were instructed to improve coordination among the intelligence community and to prepare evaluations and estimates of domestic intelligence. I understand that its activities are now under investigation. I did not authorize nor do I have any knowledge of any illegal activity by this Committee. If it went beyond its charter and did engage in any illegal activities, it was totally without my knowledge or authority.

kept oath
g office

The Special Investigations Unit

On Sunday, June 13, 1971, The New York Times published the first installment of what came to be known as "The Pentagon Papers." Not until a few hours before publication did any responsible Government official know that they had been stolen. Most officials did not know they existed. No senior official of the Government had read them or knew with certainty what they contained.

All the Government knew, at first, was that the papers comprised 47 volumes and some 7,000 pages, which had been taken from the most sensitive files of the Departments of State and Defense and the CIA, covering military and diplomatic moves in a war that was still going on.

Moreover, a majority of the documents published with the first three installments in The Times had not been included in the 47-volume study—raising serious questions about what and how much else might have been taken.

There was every reason to believe this was a security leak of unprecedented proportions.

It created a situation in which the ability of the Government to carry on foreign relations even in the best of circumstances could have been severely compromised. Other governments no longer knew whether they could deal with the United States in confidence. Against the background of the delicate negotiations the United States was then involved in on a number of fronts—with regard to Vietnam, China, the Middle East, nuclear arms limitations, U.S.-Soviet relations, and others—in which the utmost degree of confidentiality was vital, it posed a threat so grave as to require extraordinary actions.

Therefore during the week following the Pentagon Papers publication, I approved the creation of a Special Investigations Unit within the White House—which later came to be known as the "plumbers." This was a small group at the White House whose principal purpose was to stop security leaks and to investigate other sensitive security matters. I looked to John Ehrlichman for the supervision of this group.

Egil Krogh, Mr. Ehrlichman's assistant, was put in charge. David Young was added to this unit, as were E. Howard Hunt and G. Gordon Liddy.

The unit operated under extremely tight security rules. Its existence and functions were known only to a very few persons at the White House. These included Messrs. Haldeman, Ehrlichman, and Dean.

At about the time the unit was created, Daniel Ellsberg was identified as the person who had given the Pentagon Papers to The New York Times. I told Mr. Krogh that as a matter of first priority, the unit should find out all it could about Mr. Ellsberg's associates and his motives. Because of the extreme gravity of the situation, and not then knowing what additional national secrets Mr. Ellsberg might disclose, I did impress upon Mr. Krogh the vital importance to the national security of his assignment. I did not authorize and had no knowledge of any illegal means to be used to achieve this goal.

However, because of the emphasis I put on the crucial importance of protecting the national security, I can understand how highly motivated individuals could have felt justified in engaging in specific activities that I would have disapproved had they been brought to my attention.

Consequently, as President, I must and do assume responsibility for such actions despite the fact that I at no time approved or had knowledge of them.

I also assigned the unit a number of other investigatory matters, dealing in part with compiling an accurate record of events related to the Vietnam war, on which the Government's records were inadequate (many previous records having been removed with the change of administrations) and which bore directly on the negotiations then in progress. Additional assignments included tracing down other national security leaks, including one that seriously compromised the U.S. negotiating position in the SALT talks.

The work of the unit tapered off around the end of 1971. The nature of its work was such that it involved matters that, from a national security standpoint, were highly sensitive then and remain so today.

These intelligence activities had no connection with the break-in of the Democratic headquarters, or the aftermath.

I considered it my responsibility to see that the Watergate investigation did not impinge adversely upon the national security area. For example, on April 18, 1973, when I learned that Mr. Hunt, a former member of the Special Investigations Unit at the White House, was to be questioned by the U.S. Attorney, I directed Assistant Attorney General Petersen to pursue every issue involving Watergate but to confine his investigation to Watergate and related matters and to stay out of national security matters. Subsequently, on April 25, 1973, Attorney General Kleindienst informed me that because the Government had clear evidence that Mr. Hunt was involved in the break-in of the office of the psychiatrist who had treated Mr. Ellsberg, he, the Attorney General, believed that despite the fact that no evidence had been obtained from Hunt's acts, a report should nevertheless be made to the court trying the Ellsberg case. I concurred, and directed that the information be transmitted to Judge Byrne immediately.

Watergate

The burglary and bugging of the Democratic National Committee headquarters came as a complete surprise to me. I had no inkling that any such illegal activities had been planned by persons associated with my campaign; if I had known, I would not have permitted it. My immediate reaction was that those guilty should be brought to justice, and, with the five burglars themselves already in custody, I assumed that they would be.

Within a few days, however, I was advised that there was a possibility of CIA involvement in some way.

It did seem to me possible that, because of the involvement of former CIA personnel, and because of some of their apparent associations, the investigation could lead to the uncovering of covert CIA operations totally unrelated to the Watergate break-in.

In addition, by this time, the name of Mr. Hunt had surfaced in connection with Watergate, and I was alerted to the fact that he had previously been a member of the Special Investigations Unit in the White House. Therefore, I was also concerned that the Watergate investigation might well lead to an inquiry into the activities of the Special Investigations Unit itself.

In this area, I felt it was important to avoid disclosure of the details of the national security matters with which the group was concerned. I knew that once the existence of the group became known, it would lead inexorably to a discussion of these matters, some of which remain, even today, highly sensitive.

I wanted justice done with regard to Watergate; but in the scale of national priorities with which I had to deal—and not at that time having any idea of the extent of political abuse which Watergate reflected—I also had to be deeply concerned with ensuring that neither the covert operations of the CIA nor the operations of the Special Investigations Unit should be compromised. Therefore, I instructed Mr. Haldeman and Mr. Ehrlichman to ensure that the investigation of the break-in not expose either an unrelated covert operation of the CIA or the activities of the White House investigations unit—and to see that this was personally coordinated between General Walters, the Deputy Director of the CIA, and Mr. Gray of the FBI. It was certainly not my intent, nor my wish, that the investigation of the Watergate break-in or of related acts be impeded in any way.

On July 6, 1972, I telephoned the Acting Director of the FBI, L. Patrick Gray, to congratulate him on his successful handling of the hijacking of a Pacific Southwest Airlines plane the previous day. During the conversation Mr. Gray discussed with me the progress of the Watergate investigation, and I asked him whether he had talked with General Walters. Mr. Gray said that he had, and that General Walters had assured him that the CIA was not involved. In the discussion, Mr. Gray suggested that the matter of Watergate might lead higher. I told him to press ahead with his investigation.

It now seems that later, through whatever complex of individual motives and possible misunderstandings, there were apparently wide-ranging efforts to limit the investigation or to conceal the possible involvement of members of the Administration and the campaign committee.

I was not aware of any such efforts at the time. Neither, until after I began my own investigation, was I aware of any fundraising for defendants convicted of the break-in at Democratic headquarters, much less authorize any such fundraising. Nor did I authorize any offer of executive clemency for any of the defendants.

In the weeks and months that followed Watergate, I asked for, and received, repeated assurances that Mr. Dean's own investigation (which included reviewing files and sitting in on FBI interviews with White House personnel) had cleared everyone then employed by the White House of involvement.

In summary, then:

(1) I had no prior knowledge of the Watergate bugging operation, or of any illegal surveillance activities for political purposes.

(2) Long prior to the 1972 campaign, I did set in motion certain internal security measures, including legal wiretaps, which I felt were necessary from a national security standpoint and, in the climate then prevailing, also necessary from a domestic security standpoint.

(3) People who had been involved in the national security operations later, without my knowledge or approval, undertook illegal activities in the political campaign of 1972.

(4) Elements of the early post-Watergate reports led me to suspect, incorrectly, that the CIA had been in some way involved. They also led me to surmise, correctly, that since persons

originally recruited for covert national security activities had participated in Watergate, an unrestricted investigation of Watergate might lead to and expose those covert national security operations.

(5) I sought to prevent the exposure of these covert national security activities, while encouraging those conducting the investigation to pursue their inquiry into the Watergate itself. I so instructed my staff, the Attorney General, and the Acting Director of the FBI.

(6) I also specifically instructed Mr. Haldeman and Mr. Ehrlichman to ensure that the FBI would not carry its investigation into areas that might compromise these covert national security activities, or those of the CIA.

(7) At no time did I authorize or know about any offer of executive clemency for the Watergate defendants. Neither did I know until the time of my own investigation of any efforts to provide them with funds.

Conclusion

With hindsight, it is apparent that I should have given more heed to the warning signals I received along the way about a Watergate cover-up and less to the reassurances.

With hindsight, several other things also become clear:

—With respect to campaign practices, and also with respect to campaign finances, it should now be obvious that no campaign in history has ever been subjected to the kind of intensive and searching inquiry that has been focused on the campaign waged in my behalf in 1972.

It is clear that unethical, as well as illegal, activities took place in the course of that campaign.

None of these took place with my specific approval or knowledge. To the extent that I may in any way have contributed to the climate in which they took place, I did not intend to; to the extent that I failed to prevent them, I should have been more vigilant.

It was to help ensure against any repetition of this in the future that last week I proposed the establishment of a top-level, bipartisan, independent commission to recommend a comprehensive reform of campaign laws and practices. Given the priority I believe it deserves, such reform should be possible before the next Congressional elections in 1974.

—It now appears that there were persons who may have gone beyond my directives, and sought to expand on my efforts to protect the national security operations in order to cover up any involvement they or certain others might have had in Watergate. The extent to which this is true, and who may have participated and to what degree, are questions that it would not be proper to address here. The proper forum for settling these matters is in the courts.

—To the extent that I have been able to determine what probably happened in the tangled course of this affair, on the basis of my own recollections and of the conflicting accounts and evidence that I have seen, it would appear that one factor at work was that at critical points various people, each with his own perspective and his own responsibilities, saw the same situation with different eyes and heard the same words with different ears. What might have seemed insignificant to some seemed significant to another; what one saw in terms of public responsibility, another saw in terms of political opportunity; and mixed through it all, I am sure, was a concern on the part of many that the Watergate scandal should not be allowed to get in the way of what the Administration sought to achieve.

The truth about Watergate should be brought out—in an orderly way, recognizing that the safeguards of judicial procedure are designed to find the truth, not to hide the truth.

With his selection of Archibald Cox—who served both President Kennedy and President Johnson as Solicitor General—as the special supervisory prosecutor for matters related to the case, Attorney General-designate Richardson has demonstrated his own determination to see the truth brought out. In this effort he has my full support.

Considering the number of persons involved in this case whose testimony might be subject to a claim of executive privilege, I recognize that a clear definition of that claim has become central to the effort to arrive at the truth.

Accordingly, executive privilege will not be invoked as to any testimony concerning possible criminal conduct or discussions of possible criminal conduct, in the matters presently under investigation, including the Watergate affair and the alleged cover-up.

I want to emphasize that this statement is limited to my own recollections of what I said and did relating to security and to the Watergate. I have specifically avoided any attempt to explain what other parties may have said and done. My own information on those other matters is fragmentary, and to some extent contradictory. Additional information may be forthcoming of which I am unaware. It is also my understanding that the information which has been conveyed to me has also become available to those prosecuting these matters. Under such circumstances, it would be prejudicial and unfair of me to render my opinions on the activities of others; those judgments must be left to the judicial process, our best hope for achieving the just result that we all seek.

Defending Against Watergate

News Conference
San Clemente, California
August 22, 1973

On August 4 the Senate Watergate Committee recessed. By this time, John Dean, former Counsel to the President, had accused Nixon of participation in the cover-up of Watergate. Alexander Butterfield, former Deputy Assistant to the President, had revealed the existence of Nixon's taping system. Both the Committee and the Special Prosecutor had subpoenaed the recordings only to have the President refuse to release them. Now, all three branches of government were locked in what can only be called a "Constitutional crisis" over possession of the tapes. All the while Nixon kept silent except for extemporaneous remarks about people "wallowing in Watergate" and for statements refusing to hand over the tapes. After the Committee recess, Nixon spoke to the American people on television on August 15 once again proclaiming his innocence. Five days later he held his first press conference in 5 months, the first time he had faced the press since the scandal broke wide open. Although his opening statement contained important announcements—the resignation of William P. Rogers as Secretary of State and the nomination of Dr. Henry Kissinger to replace him—the press was interested only in Watergate.

The President. [1.] Ladies and gentlemen, I have an announcement before going to your questions.

It is with the deep sense of not only official regret but personal regret, that I announce the resignation of Secretary of State William Rogers, effective September 3. A letter, which will be released to the press after this conference, will indicate my appraisal of his work as Secretary of State.

I will simply say at this time that he wanted to leave at the conclusion of the first 4 years. He agreed to stay on, because we had some enormously important problems coming up, including the negotiations which resulted in the end of the war in Vietnam, the Soviet summit, the European Security Conference, as well as in other areas—Latin America and in Asia—where the Secretary of State, as you know, has been quite busy over these past 8 months.

As he returns to private life, we will not only miss him, in terms of his official service, but I shall particularly miss him because of his having been, through the years, a very close personal friend and adviser.

That personal friendship and advice, however, I hope still to have the benefit of, and I know that I will.

As his successor, I shall nominate and send to the Senate for confirmation the name of Dr. Henry Kissinger. Dr. Kissinger will become Secretary of State, assume the duties of the office after he is confirmed by the Senate. I trust the Senate will move expeditiously on the confirmation hearings, because there are a number of matters of very great importance that are coming up.

There are, for example, some matters that might even involve some foreign travel by Dr. Kissinger that will have to be delayed in the event that the Senate hearings are delayed.

Dr. Kissinger's qualifications for this post, I think, are well known by all of you ladies and gentlemen, as well as those looking to us and listening to us on television and radio.

He will retain the position, after he becomes Secretary of State, of Assistant to the President for National Security Affairs. In other words, he will have somewhat a parallel relationship to the White House which George Shultz has. George Shultz, as you know, is Secretary of the Treasury, but is also an Assistant to the President in the field of economic affairs.

The purpose of this arrangement is to have a closer coordination between the White House and the departments, and in this case, between the White House, the national security affairs, the NSC, and the State Department, which carries a major load in this area.

And also, another purpose is to get the work out in the departments where it belongs, and I believe that this change in this respect, with Dr. Kissinger moving in as Secretary of State and still retaining the position as Assistant to the President for National Security Affairs, will serve the interest not only of coordination but also of the interests of an effective foreign policy.

I will simply say, finally, with regard to Secretary Rogers, that he can look back on what I think, and I suppose it is a self-serving statement but I will say it about him rather than about myself at the moment, one of the most successful eras of foreign policy in any administration in history—an era in which we ended a war, the longest war in America's history; an era, in addition, in which we began to build a structure of peace, particularly involving the two great powers, the People's Republic of China and the Soviet Union, where before there had been nothing but ugly and, at some times, very, very difficult confrontation.

We still have a long way to go. There are trouble spots in the area of the Mideast, others—Southeast Asia, which we could go into in detail.

But as Secretary Rogers looks back on his years—4 1/2 years of service as Secretary of State—he can be very proud that he was one of the major architects of what I think was a very successful foreign policy.

Questions

Recording of Presidential Conversations

[2.] And now, we will go to the questions. I think AP, Miss Lewine [Frances L. Lewine, Associated Press] has the first question.

Q. Mr. President, on Watergate, you have said that disclosure of the tapes could jeopardize and cripple the functions of the Presidency. Two questions: If disclosure carries such a risk, why did you make the tapes in the first place, and what is your reaction to surveys that show three out of four Americans believe you were wrong to make the tapes?

The President. Well, with regard to the questions as to why Americans feel we were wrong to make the tapes, that is not particularly surprising. I think that most Americans do not like the idea of the taping of conversations, and frankly, it is not something that particularly appeals to me.

As a matter of fact, that is why, when I arrived in the White House and saw this rather complex situation set up where there was a taping capacity, not only in the President's office, the room outside of his office, but also in the Cabinet Room and at Camp David and in other areas, that I had the entire system dismantled.

It was put into place again in June of 1970 (1971), because my advisers felt it was important in terms particularly of national security affairs to have a record for future years that would be an accurate one, but a record which would only be disclosed at the discretion of the President or according to directives that he would set forth.

As you know, of course, this kind of capability not only existed during the Johnson Administration, it also existed in the Kennedy Administration, and I can see why both President Johnson and President Kennedy did have the capability because—not because they wanted to infringe upon the privacy of anybody, but because they felt that they had some obligation, particularly in the field of foreign policy and some domestic areas, to have a record that would be accurate.

As far as I am concerned, we now do not have that capability, and I am just as happy that we don't. As a matter of fact, I have a practice, whenever I am not too tired at night, of dictating my own recollections of the day. I think that, perhaps, will be the more accurate record of history in the end.

The Watergate Investigation

[3.] I think we go to the UP now, and then we will come to the television.

Q. Mr President, on July 6, 1972, you were warned by Patrick Gray that you were being mortally wounded by some of your top aides. Can you explain why you did not ask who they were, why, what was going on?

The President. Well, in the telephone conversation that you refer to that has been, of course, quite widely reported in the press as well as on television, Mr. Gray said that he was concerned that as far as the investigation that he had responsibility for, that some of my top aides were not cooperating.

Whether the term was used as "mortally wounded" or not, I don't know. Some believe that it was, some believe that it was not, that is irrelevant. He could have said that.

The main point was, however, I asked him whether or not he had discussed this matter with General Walters, because I knew that there had been meetings between General Walters, representing the CIA, to be sure that the CIA did not become involved in the investigation, and between the Director of the FBI.

He said that he had. He told me that General Walters agreed that the investigation should be pursued, and I told him to go forward with a full press on the investigation to which he has so testified.

It seemed to me that with that kind of a directive to Mr. Gray, that that was adequate for the purpose of carrying out the responsibilities.

As far as the individuals were concerned, I assume that the individuals that he was referring to involved this operation with the CIA. That is why I asked him the Walters question. When he cleared that up, he went forward with the investigation, and he must have thought it was a very good investigation because when I sent his name down to the Senate for confirmation the next year, I asked him about his investigation. He said he was very proud of it. He said it was the most thorough investigation that had ever taken place since the assassination of President Kennedy, that he could defend it with enthusiasm, and that under the circumstances, therefore, he had carried out the directive that I had given him on July 6.

So, there was no question about Mr. Gray having direct orders from the President to carry out an investigation that was thorough.

Access to Presidential Tape Recordings

[4.] Mr. Jarriel [Tom Jarriel, ABC News].

Q. Mr. President, Assistant Attorney General Henry Petersen has testified that on April 15 of this year he met with you and warned you at that time there might be enough evidence to warrant indictments against three of your top aides, Messrs. Ehrlichman, Haldeman, and Dean. You accepted their resignations on April 30, calling Mr. Haldeman and Mr. Ehrlichman two of the finest public servants you had known. After that, you permitted Mr. Haldeman, after he had left the White House, to hear confidential tapes of conversations you had had in your office with Mr. Dean. My question is, why did you permit a man who you knew might be indicted to hear those tapes which you now will not permit the American public or the Federal prosecutors handling the case to listen to?

The President. The only tape that has been referred to, that Mr. Haldeman has listened to, he listened to at my request, and he listened to that tape—that was the one on September 15, Mr. Jarriel—because he had been present and was there. I asked him to listen to it in order to be sure that as far as any allegations that had been made by Mr. Dean with regard to that conversation is concerned, I wanted to be sure that we were absolutely correct in our response. That is all he listened to. He did not listen to any tapes in which only Mr. Dean and I participated. He listened only to the tape on September 15—this is after he left office—in which he had participated in the conversation throughout.

Principle of Confidentiality

[5.] Q. Mr. President, one of the lingering doubts about your denial of any involvement is concerning your failure to make the tapes available either to the Senate committee or the Special Prosecutor. You have made it perfectly clear you don't intend to release those tapes.

The President. Perfectly clear?

Q. Perfectly clear. But is there any way that you could have some group listen to tapes and give a report so that that might satisfy the public mind?

The President. I don't believe, first, it would satisfy the public mind, and it should not. The second point is that as Mr. Wright, who argued the case, I understand very well, before Judge Sirica this morning, has indicated, to have the tapes listened to—he indicated this also in his brief—either by a prosecutor or by a judge or *in camera* or in any way, would violate the principle of confidentiality, and I believe he is correct. That is why we are standing firm on the proposition that we will not agree to the Senate committee's desire to have, for example, its chief investigator listen to the tapes, or the Special Prosecutor's desire to hear the tapes, and also why we will oppose, as Mr. Wright did in his argument this morning, any compromise of the principle of confidentiality.

Let me explain very carefully that the principle of confidentiality either exists or it does not exist. Once it is compromised, once it is known that a conversation that is held with the President can be subject to a subpoena by a Senate committee, by a grand jury, by a prosecutor, and be listened to by anyone, the principle of confidentiality is thereby irreparably damaged. Incidentally, let me say that now that tapes are no longer being made, I suppose it could be argued that, what difference does it make now, now that these tapes are also in the past. What is involved here is not only the tapes; what is involved, as you ladies and gentlemen well know, is the request on the part of the Senate committee, and the Special Prosecutor as well, that we turn over Presidential papers—in other words, the records of conversations with the President made by his associates. Those papers, and the tapes as well, cannot be turned over without breaching the principle of confidentiality. It was President Truman that made that argument very effectively in his letter to a Senate committee—or his response to a Congressional committee, a House committee it was, in 1953—when they asked him to turn over his papers. So, whether it is a paper or whether it is a tape, what we have to bear in mind is that for a President to conduct the affairs of this office and conduct them effectively, he must be able to do so with the principle of confidentiality intact. Otherwise, the individuals who come to talk to him, whether it is his advisers, or whether it is a visitor in the domestic field, or whether it is someone in a foreign field, will always be speaking in a eunuch-like way, rather than laying it on the line, as it has to be laid on the line if you are going to have the creative kind of discussion that we have often had, and it has been responsible for some of our successes in the foreign policy period, particularly in the past few years.

Administration Participants in the Investigation

[6.] Q. Mr. President, could you tell us who you personally talked to in directing that investigations be made both in June of '72, shortly after the Watergate incident, and last March 21, when you got new evidence and ordered a more intensive investigation?

The President. Certainly. In June, I, of course, talked to Mr. MacGregor first of all, who was the new chairman of the committee. He told me that he would conduct a thorough investigation as far as his entire committee staff was concerned. Apparently that investigation was very effective except for Mr. Magruder, who stayed on. But Mr. MacGregor does not have to assume responsibility for that. I say not responsibility for it, because basically what happened there was that he believed Mr. Magruder, and many others have believed him, too. He proved, however, to be wrong.

In the White House, the investigation's responsibility was given to Mr. Ehrlichman at the highest level, and in turn, he delegated them to Mr. Dean, the White House Counsel, something of which I was aware and of which I approved.

Mr. Dean, as White House Counsel, therefore sat in on the FBI interrogations of the members of the White House Staff, because what I wanted to know was whether any member of the White House Staff was in any way involved. If he was involved, he would be fired. And when we met on September 15, and again throughout our discussions in the month of March, Mr. Dean insisted that there was not—and I use his words—"a scintilla of evidence" indicating that anyone on the White House Staff was involved in the planning of the Watergate break-in.

Now, in terms of after March 21, Mr. Dean first was given the responsibility to write his own report, but I did not rest it there. I also had a contact made with the Attorney General himself, Attorney General Kleindienst, told him—it was on the 27th of March—to report to me directly anything that he found in this particular area. And I gave the responsibility to Mr. Ehrlichman on the 29th of March to continue the investigation that Mr. Dean was unable to conclude, having spent a week at Camp David and unable to finish the report.

Mr. Ehrlichman questioned a number of people in that period at my direction, including Mr. Mitchell, and I should also point out that as far as my own activities were concerned, I was not leaving it just to them. I met at great length with Mr. Ehrlichman, Mr. Haldeman, Mr. Dean, and Mr. Mitchell on the 22d. I discussed the whole matter with them. I kept pressing for the view that I had had throughout, that we must get this story out, get the truth out, whatever and whoever it is going to hurt, and it was there that Mr. Mitchell suggested that all the individuals involved in the White House appear in an executive session before the Ervin committee. We never got that far, but at least that is an indication of the extent of my own investigation.

Testimony of Former Attorney General Mitchell

[7.] I think we will go to Mr. Lisagor now [Peter Lisagor, Chicago Daily News].

Q. Mr. President, you have said repeatedly that you tried to get all the facts, and just now you mentioned the March 22 meeting. Yet former Attorney General John Mitchell said that if you had ever asked him at any time about the Watergate matter, he would have told you the whole story, chapter and verse. Was Mr. Mitchell not speaking the truth when he said that before the committee?

The President. Now, Mr. Lisagor, I am not going to question Mr. Mitchell's veracity, and I will only say that throughout I had confidence in Mr. Mitchell. Mr. Mitchell, in a telephone call that I had with him immediately after it occurred, expressed great chagrin that he had not run a tight enough shop and that some of the boys, as he called them, got involved in this kind of activity, which he knew to be very, very embarrassing, apart from its illegality, to the campaign. Throughout, I would have expected Mr. Mitchell to tell me in the event that he was involved or that anybody else was. He did not tell me. I don't blame him for not telling me. He has given his reasons for not telling me. I regret that he did not, because he is exactly right. Had he told me, I would have blown my stack, just as I did at Ziegler the other day. [*Laughter*]

The President's Responsibility

[8.] Q. Mr. President, I wonder, sir, how much personal blame, to what degree of personal blame do you accept for the climate in the White House, and at the Re-election Committee, for the abuses of Watergate?

The President. I accept it all.

The Ellsberg Case; Meetings with Judge Byrne

[9.] Q. Mr. President, I want to state this question with due respect to your office, but also as directly as possible.

The President. That would be unusual. [*Laughter*]

Q. I would like to think not, sir. It concerns——

The President. You are always respectful, Mr. Rather [Dan Rather, CBS News]. You know that.

Q. Thank you, Mr. President. It concerns the events surrounding Mr. Ehrlichman's contact and, on one occasion, your own contact with the judge in the Pentagon Papers case, Judge Byrne.

The President. Yes.

Q. As I understand your own explanation of events, and putting together your statement with Mr. Ehrlichman's testimony and what Judge Byrne has said, what happened here is that sometime late in March—March 17, I believe you said—you first found out about the break-in at the psychiatrist's office of Mr. Ellsberg, that you asked to have that looked into and that you later, I think in late April, instructed Attorney General Kleindienst to inform the judge.

Now, my question is this: that, while the Pentagon Papers trial was going on, Mr. Ehrlichman secretly met once with the judge in that case, you secretly met another time the judge with Mr. Ehrlichman. Now, you are a lawyer, and given the state of the situation and what you knew, could you give us some reason why the American people should not believe that that was at least a subtle attempt to bribe the judge in that case, and it gave at least the appearance of a lack of moral leadership?

The President. Well, I would say the only part of your statement that is perhaps accurate is that I am a lawyer. Now, beyond that, Mr. Rather, let me say that with regard to the "secret" meeting that we had with the judge, as he said, I met the judge briefly—after all, I had appointed him to the position—I met him for perhaps one minute outside my door here in full view of the whole White House Staff and everybody else who wanted to see. I asked him how he liked his job—so did not discuss the case—and he went on for his meeting with Mr. Ehrlichman.

Now, why did the meeting with Mr. Ehrlichman take place? Because we had determined that Mr. Gray could not be confirmed, as you will recall. We were on a search for a Director of the FBI. Mr. Kleindienst had been here, and I asked him what he would recommend with regard to a Director, and I laid down certain qualifications.

I said I wanted a man preferably with FBI experience, and preferably with prosecutor's experience, and preferably, if possible, a Democrat so that we would have no problem on confirmation. He said, "The man for the job is Byrne." He said, "He is the best man." I said, "Would you recommend him?" He said, "Yes."

Under those circumstances then, Mr. Ehrlichman called Mr. Byrne. He said: Under no circumstances will we talk to you—he, Ehrlichman, will talk to you—if he felt that it would in any way compromise his handling of the Ellsberg case.

Judge Byrne made the decision that he would talk to Mr. Ehrlichman, and he did talk to him privately, here. And on that occasion, he talked to him privately, the case was not discussed at all—only the question of whether or not, at the conclusion of this case, Mr. Byrne would like to be considered as Director of the FBI.

I understand, incidentally, that he told Mr. Ehrlichman that he would be interested. Of course, the way the things broke eventually, we found another name with somewhat the same qualifications, although, in this case, not a judge—in this case, a chief of police with former FBI experience.

Now, with regard to the Ellsberg break-in, let me explain that in terms of that, I discussed that on the telephone with Mr. Henry Petersen on the 18th of April. It was on the 18th of April that I learned that the grand jury was going away from some of its Watergate investigation and moving into national security areas.

I told Mr. Petersen at that time about my concern about the security areas, and particularly about the break-in as far as the Ellsberg case is concerned.

And then he asked me a very critical question which you, as a nonlawyer, will not understand, and lawyers probably will, too. He said, "Was any evidence developed out of this break-in?" And I said, "No, it was a dry hole." He said, "Good."

Now, what he meant by that was that in view of the fact that no evidence was developed as a result of the break-in—which is, incidentally, illegal, unauthorized, as far as I was concerned, and completely deplorable—but since no evidence was developed, there was no requirement that it be presented to the jury that was hearing the case. That was why Mr. Petersen, a man of impeccable credentials in the law enforcement field, did not, at that time on the 18th, at a time that I told him what I had known about the Ellsberg break-in, say "Let's present it then to the grand jury," because nothing had been accomplished, nothing had been obtained that would taint the case.

It was approximately 10 days later that Mr. Kleindienst came in and said that, after a review of the situation in the prosecutor's office in Washington, in which Mr. Petersen had also participated, that they believed that it was best that we bend over backwards in this case and send this record of the Ellsberg break-in, even though there was no evidence obtained from it that could have affected the jury one way or another, sent it to the judge.

When they made that recommendation to me, I directed that it be done, instantly. It was done. Incidentally, the prosecutor argued this case just the way that I have argued it to you, and whether or not it had an effect on the eventual outcome, I do not know.

At least, as far as we know, Mr. Ellsberg went free, this being one of the factors. But that is the explanation of what happened and obviously, you, in your commentary tonight, can attach anything you want to it.

I hope you will be just as fair and objective as I try to be in giving you the answer. And I know you will be, sir.

Vice President Agnew

[10.] Q. Mr. President, what is the state of your confidence in your Vice President at this point in time?

The President. I have noted some press speculation to the effect that I have not expressed confidence in the Vice President, and therefore, I welcome this question because I want to set the record straight. I had confidence in the integrity of the Vice President when I selected him as Vice President when very few knew him, as you may recall back in 1968—knew him nationally. My confidence in his integrity has not been shaken, and in fact, it has been strengthened by his courageous conduct and his ability—even though he is controversial at times, as I am—over the past 4 1/2 years. So I have confidence in the integrity of the Vice President and particularly in the performance of the duties that he has had as Vice President and as a candidate for Vice President.

Now obviously the question arises as to charges that have been made about activities that occurred before he became Vice President. He would consider it improper—I would consider it improper—for me to comment on those charges, and I shall not do so. But I will make a comment on another subject that I think needs to be commented upon, and that is the outrageous leak of information from either the grand jury, or the prosecutors, or the Department of Justice, or all three. And, incidentally, I am not going to put the responsibility on all three until I learn from the Attorney General, who, at my request, is making a full investigation of this at the present time. I am not going to put the responsibility—but the leak of information with regard to charges that have been made against the Vice President and leaking them all in the press.

Convicting an individual—not only trying him but convicting him—in the headlines and on television before he has had a chance to present his case in court is completely contrary to the American tradition. Even a Vice President has a right to some, shall I say, consideration in this respect, let alone the ordinary individual. And I will say this—and the Attorney General, I know, has taken note of this fact: Any individual in the Justice Department or in the prosecutor's office who is in the employ of the United States who has leaked information in this case to the press or to anybody else will be summarily dismissed from Government service. That is how strongly I feel about it, and I feel that way, because I would make this ruling whether it was the Vice President or any individual.

We have to remember that a hearing before a grand jury—and that determination in the American process is one that is supposed to be in confidence—is supposed to be in secret, because all kinds of charges are made which will not stand up in open court, and it is only when the case gets to open court that the press and the TV have a right to cover it—well, they have a right to cover it, but, I mean, have a right, it seems to me, to give such broad coverage to the charges.

The President's Capacity to Govern

[11.] Q. Mr. President, at any time during the Watergate crisis did you ever consider resigning, and would you consider resigning if you felt that your capacity to govern had been seriously weakened? And in that connection, how much do you think your capacity to govern has been weakened?

The President. The answer to the first two questions is no; the answer to the third question is that it is true that as far as the capacity to govern is concerned, that to be under a constant barrage—12 to 15 minutes a night on each of the three major networks for 4 months—tends to raise some questions in the people's mind with regard to the President, and it may raise some questions with regard to the capacity to govern. But I also know this: I was elected to do a job. Watergate is an episode that I deeply deplore, and had I been running the campaign rather than trying to run the country, and particularly the foreign policy of this country at this time, it would never have happened. But that is water under the bridge, it is gone now.

The point that I make now is that we are proceeding as best we know how to get all those guilty brought to justice in Watergate. But now we must move on from Watergate to the business of the people, and the business of the people is continuing with initiatives we began in the first Administration.

Q. Mr. President.

The President. Just a moment.

We have had 30 minutes of this press conference. I have yet to have, for example, one question on the business of the people, which shows you how we are consumed with this. I am not criticizing the members of the press, because you naturally are very interested in this issue, but let me tell you, years from now people are going to perhaps be interested in what happened in terms of the efforts of the United States to build structure of peace in the world. They are perhaps going to be interested in the efforts of this Administration to have a kind of prosperity that we have not had since 1955—that is, prosperity without war and without inflation— because throughout the Kennedy years and throughout the Johnson years, whatever prosperity we had was at the cost of either inflation or war or both. I don't say that critically of them, I am simply saying we have got to do better than that.

Now, our goal is to move forward then, to move forward to build a structure of peace. And when you say, do I consider resigning, the answer is no, I shall not resign. I have 3 1/2 years to go, or almost 3 1/2 years, and I am going to use every day of those 3 1/2 years trying to get the people of the United States to recognize that, whatever mistakes we have made, that in the long run this Administration, by making this world safer for their children, and this Administration, by making their lives better at home for themselves and their children, deserves high marks rather than low marks. Now, whether I succeed or not, we can judge them.

Surveillance in National Security Matters

[12.] We always have to have Mr. Deakin [James Deakin, St. Louis Post-Dispatch] for one.

Q. As long as we are on the subject of the American tradition, and following up Mr. Rather's question, what was authorized, even if the burglary of Dr. Fielding's office was not— what was authorized was the 1970 plan which by your own description permitted illegal acts, illegal breaking and entering, mail surveillance, and the like.

Now, under the Constitution you swore an oath to execute the laws of the United States faithfully. If you were serving in Congress, would you not be considering impeachment proceedings and discussing impeachment possibility against an elected public official who had violated his oath of office?

The President. I would if I had violated the oath of office. I would also, however, refer you to the recent decision of the Supreme Court, or at least an opinion that even last year—which indicates inherent power in the Presidency to protect the national security in cases like this. I should also point out to you that in the 3 Kennedy years and the 3 Johnson years through 1966, when burglarizing of this type did take place, when it was authorized on a very large scale, there was no talk of impeachment, and it was quite well known.

I shall also point out that when you ladies and gentlemen indicate your great interest in wiretaps, and I understand that, that the height of the wiretaps was when Robert Kennedy was Attorney General in 1963. I don't criticize it, however. He had over 250 in 1963, and of course, the average in the Eisenhower Administration and the Nixon Administration is about 110. But if he had had 10 more and, as a result of wiretaps, had been able to discover the Oswald plan, it would have been worth it.

So, I will go to another question.

Former Assistants to the President Haldeman and Ehrlichman

[13.] Q. Mr. President, do you still consider Haldeman and Ehrlichman two of the finest public servants you have ever known?

The President. I certainly do. I look upon public servants as men who have got to be judged by their entire record, not by simply parts of it. Mr. Ehrlichman and Mr. Haldeman, for 4 1/2 years, have served with great distinction, with great dedication, and like everybody in this deplorable Watergate business, at great personal sacrifice and with no personal gain.

We admit the scandalous conduct. Thank God there has been no personal gain involved. That would be going much too far, I suppose.

But the point that I make with regard to Mr. Haldeman and Mr. Ehrlichman is that I think, too, that as all the facts come out, that—and when they have an opportunity to have their case heard in court and not simply to be tried before a committee and tried in the press and tried in television—they will be exonerated.

Funds for the Watergate Defendants

[14.] Mr. Horner [Garnett D. Horner, Washington Star-News].

Q. Mr. President, could you tell us your recollection of what you told John Dean on March 21 on the subject of raising funds for the Watergate defendants?

The President. Certainly. Mr. Haldeman has testified to that, and his statement is accurate. Basically, what Mr. Dean was concerned about on March 21 was not so much the raising of money for the defendants, but the raising of money for the defendants for the purpose of keeping them still—in other words, so-called hush money. The one would be legal—in other words, raising a defense fund for any group, any individual, as you know, is perfectly legal, and it is done all the time. But if you raise funds for the purpose of keeping an individual from talking, that is obstruction of justice.

Mr. Dean said also on March 21 that there was an attempt, as he put it, to blackmail the White House, to blackmail the White House by one of the defendants. Incidentally, that defendant has denied it, but at least this was what Mr. Dean had claimed, and that unless certain amounts of money were paid—I think it was $120,000 for attorneys fees and other support—that this particular defendant would make a statement, not with regard to Watergate, but with regard to some national security matters in which Mr. Ehrlichman had particular responsibility.

My reaction, very briefly, was this: I said, "As you look at this," I said, "isn't it quite obvious, first, that if it is going to have any chance to succeed, that these individuals aren't going to sit there in jail for 4 years? They are going to have clemency; isn't that correct?"

He said, "Yes." I said, "We can't give clemency." He agreed. Then, I went to another point. I said, "The second point is that isn't it also quite obvious, as far as this is concerned, that while we could raise the money"—and he indicated in answer to my question, it would probably take a million dollars over 4 years to take care of this defendant, and others, on this kind of basis—the problem was, how do you get the money to them, and also, how do you get around the problem of clemency, because they are not going to stay in jail simply because their families are being taken care of. And so, that was why I concluded, as Mr. Haldeman recalls perhaps and did testify very effectively, one, when I said, "John, it is wrong, it won't work. We can't give clemency, and we have got to get this story out. And therefore, I direct you, and I direct Haldeman, and I direct Ehrlichman, and I direct Mitchell to get together tomorrow and then meet with me as to how we get this story out."

And that is how the meeting on the 22d took place.

Plans for Defense Against Charges

[15.] Q. Mr. President, earlier in the news conference you said that you gave Mr. Haldeman the right to listen to one tape because you wanted to be sure that "we are correct"—I think I am quoting you correctly.

Now, you have indicated that you still feel that Mr. Haldeman and Mr. Ehrlichman are two of the finest public servants that you have ever known. You have met with their lawyer at least twice that we know of. Are you and Mr. Haldeman and Mr. Ehrlichman coordinating their and your defense and, if so, why?

The President. No. No, as far as my defense is concerned, I make it myself. As far as their defense is concerned, their lawyer has demonstrated very well before the committee that he can handle it very well without any assistance from me.

The Vice President

[16.] Mr. Theis [J. William Theis, Hearst Newspapers and Hearst Headline Service].

Q. Mr. President, a follow-up question on the Agnew situation. You have said in the past that any White House official who was indicted would be suspended and that anyone convicted would be dismissed. Should Vice President Agnew be indicted, would you expect him to resign or somehow otherwise stand down temporarily until cleared?

The President. Now, Mr. Theis, that is a perfectly natural question and one that any good newsman, as you are, would ask. But as you know, it is one that it would be most inappropriate for me to comment upon. The Vice President has not been indicted; charges have been thrown out by innuendo, and otherwise, which he has denied to me personally and which he has denied publicly. And to talk about indictment and to talk about resignation, even now—I am not questioning your right to ask the question, understand—but for me to talk about it would be totally inappropriate, and I make no comment in answer to that question.

Executive Privilege

[17.] I will take the big man. [*Laughter*]

Q. Thank you, Mr. President.

The President. I know my troubles if I don't take him—or if I do. [*Laughter*]

Q. Mr. President, looking to the future on executive privilege, there are a couple of questions that come to mind——

The President. I thought we got past that, Clark [Clark R. Mollenhoff, Des Moines Register and Tribune], that was a year ago.

Q. But we have it for the future——

The President. All right, fine.

Q. Where is the check on authoritarianism by the executive if the President is to be the sole judge of what the executive branch makes available and suppresses? And will you obey a Supreme Court order if you are asked and directed to produce the tapes or other documents for the Senate committee or for the Special Prosecutor? And, if this is not enough—[*laughter*]—is there any limitation on the President, short of impeachment, to compel the production of evidence of a criminal nature?

The President. Is there anything else?

Q. No, I think that would be enough.[*Laughter*]

The President. No, I was not being facetious, but I realize it is a complicated question. The answer to the first question is that the limitation on the President in almost all fields like this is, of course, the limitation of public opinion and, of course, Congressional and other pressures that may arise. As far as executive privilege is concerned in the Watergate matter and, I must say, the ITT file and so forth, that this Administration has, I think, gone further in terms of waiving executive privilege than any Administration in my memory, certainly a lot further than Mr. Truman was willing to go when I was on the other side, as you recall, urging that he waive executive privilege.

Now, with regard to what the Supreme Court will do or say, the White House Press Secretary—assistant Press Secretary, Mr. Warren, has responded to that already. I won't make any statement on that at this time while the matter is still being considered by Judge Sirica. I understand his decision will come down on Wednesday, and then we will make a determination. But as far as the statement that Mr. Warren has made with regard to the President's position of complying with a definitive order of the Supreme Court is concerned, that statement stands.

Motivations of Watergate Critics

[18.] Q. Sir, last week in your speech you referred to those who would exploit Watergate to keep you from doing your job. Could you specifically detail who "those" are?

The President. I would suggest that where the shoe fits, people should wear it. I would think that some political figures, some members of the press, perhaps, some members of the television, perhaps would exploit it. I don't impute, interestingly enough, motives, however, that are improper, because here is what is involved. There are a great number of people in this country that would prefer that I do resign. There are a great number of people in this country that didn't accept the mandate of 1972. After all, I know that most of the members of the press corps were not enthusiastic—and I understand that—about either my election in '63 or '72. That is not unusual.

Frankly, if I had always followed what the press predicted or the polls predicted, I would have never been elected President. But what I am saying is this: People who did not accept the mandate of '72, who do not want the strong America that I want to build, who do not want the foreign policy leadership that I want to give, who do not want to cut down the size of this government bureaucracy that burdens us so greatly and to give more of our government back to the people, people who do not want these things, naturally, would exploit any issue—if it weren't Watergate, anything else—in order to keep the President from doing his job.

And so I say I impute no improper motives to them; I think they would prefer that I fail. On the other hand, I am not going to fail. I am here to do a job, and I am going to do the best I can, and I am sure the fair-minded members of this press corps—and that is most of you—will report when I do well, and I am sure you will report when I do badly.

Wiretaps and Protection of the Presidents

[19.] Q. Mr. President, you recently suggested today that if the late Robert Kennedy had initiated 10 more wiretaps he would have been able to discover the Oswald plan, as you described it, and thereby presumably prevent the assassination of President Kennedy.

The President. Let me correct you, sir. I want to be sure that the assumption is correct. I said if 10 more wiretaps could have found the conspiracy, if it was a conspiracy, or the individual, then it would have been worth it. As far as I am concerned, I am no more of an expert on that assassination than anybody else, but my point is that wiretaps in the national security area were very high in the Kennedy Administration for a very good reason; because there were many threats on the President's life, because there were national security problems, and that is why that in that period of 1961 to'63, there were wiretaps on news organizations, on news people, on civil rights leaders, and on other people. And I think they were perfectly justified, and I am sure that President Kennedy and his brother, Robert Kennedy, would never have authorized them, as I would never have authorized them, unless he thought they were in the national interest.

Q. Do you think then that threats to assassinate the President merit more national security wiretaps particularly?

The President. No. No, as far as I am concerned, I was only suggesting that in terms of those times,—of those times—to have the Oswald thing happen just seemed so unbelievable. With his record—with his record—that with everything that everybody had on him, that that fellow could have been where he was, in a position to shoot the President of the United States, seems to me to have been a terrible breakdown in our protective security areas.

I would like to say, however, that as far as protection generally is concerned, I don't like it, and my family does not like it. Both of my daughters would prefer to have no Secret Service. I discussed it with the Secret Service. They say they have too many threats, and so they have to have it. My wife does not want to have Secret Service, and I would prefer—and I recommended this just 3 days ago—to cut my detail by one third, because I noticed there were criticisms of how much the Secret Service is spending.

Let me say that we always are going to have threats against the President, but I frankly think that one man probably is as good against a threat as a hundred. That is my view, but my view does not happen to be in a majority there, and it does not happen to agree with the Congress— so I will still have a great number of Secret Service around me, more than I want, more than my family wants.

Watergate Investigation

[20.] Q. Mr. President, during March and April, you received from your staff on several occasions information about criminal wrongdoing and some indication that members of your staff might have been involved. My question, sir, is why didn't you turn this information over immediately to the prosecutors instead of having your own staff continue to make these investigations?

The President. Well, for the very obvious reason that in March, for example, the man that was in constant contact with the prosecutors was my Counsel, Mr. Dean. Mr. Dean was talking to Mr. Petersen. I assumed that anything he was telling me he was telling the prosecutors. And in April, after Mr. Dean left the investigation, Mr. Ehrlichman was in charge. I would assume—and incidentally, Mr. Ehrlichman did talk to Mr. Kleindienst—that is why it was done that way. The President does not pick up the phone and call the Attorney General every time something comes up on a matter; he depends on his Counsel or whoever he has given the job to—or he has given that assignment to do the job. And that is what I expected in this instance.

U.S. Bombing of Cambodia

[21.] Q. Mr. President, in your Cambodian invasion speech of April 1970, you reported to the American people that the United States has been strictly observing the neutrality of Cambodia. I am wondering if you in light of what we now know, that there were 15 months of bombing of Cambodia previous to your statement, whether you owe an apology to the American people?

The President. Certainly not, and certainly not to the Cambodian people, because as far as this area is concerned, the area of approximately 10 miles which was bombed during this period, no Cambodians had been in it for years. It was totally occupied by the North Vietnamese Communists. They were using this area for the purpose of attacking and killing American Marines and soldiers by the thousands. The bombing took place against those North Vietnamese forces in enemy-occupied territory, and as far as the American people are concerned, I think the American people are very thankful that the President ordered what was necessary to save the lives of their men and shorten this war which he found when he got here, and which he ended.

Helen Thomas (United Press International). Thank you, Mr. President.

Firestorm
News Conference
Washington, D.C.
October 26, 1973

October, 1973 was one of the most dramatic months in American history. A new Arab-Israeli war erupted resulting in an Arab boycott of oil to the United States. Against that international background was played out our domestic drama. On October 10, Vice President Agnew pleaded no contest to one charge of income-tax evasion and resigned the Vice Presidency. Two days later the Court of Appeals ruled that Nixon had to turn over his tapes relating to Watergate to Judge John Sirica for examination. That same evening the President announced his choice of Gerald Ford to succeed Agnew as Vice President. But the bombshell hit on October 20. President Nixon ordered Special Prosecutor Cox fired. Attorney General Elliot Richardson and Deputy Attorney General William Ruckelshaus resigned rather than do it. It fell to Solicitor General Robert Bork to carry the assignment. That evening Press Secretary Ronald Ziegler announced the dismissal and resignations as well as the abolishment of the office of the Watergate Special Prosecutor. It immediately became known as the "Saturday Night Massacre." The public response was immediate. Thousands of letters, telegrams and telephone calls poured in. Democrats in the House of Representatives prepared impeachment resolutions. Even Republicans deserted the President. Faced with this thunderous outcry, Nixon reversed himself and agreed to comply with the Court order to turn the Watergate tapes over to Judge Sirica. Even as these domestic matters held the headlines, Nixon had also ordered an American military alert as a warning to the Soviet Union not to enter directly the Arab-Israeli dispute. On October 22, a cease-fire was announced in the Middle-East. Against this background of tumultuous events, Nixon held a news conference on October 26.

The Situation in the Middle East

The President. [1.] Ladies and gentlemen, before going to your questions, I have a statement with regard to the Mideast which I think will anticipate some of the questions, because this will update the information which is breaking rather fast in that area, as you know, for the past 2 days.

The cease-fire is holding. There have been some violations, but generally speaking it can be said that it is holding at this time. As you know, as a result of the U.N. resolution which was agreed to yesterday by a vote of 14 to 0, a peacekeeping force will go to the Mideast, and this force, however, will not include any forces from the major powers, including, of course, the United States and the Soviet Union.

The question, however, has arisen as to whether observers from major powers could go to the Mideast. My up-to-the-minute report on that, and I just talked to Dr. Kissinger 5 minutes before coming down, is this: We will send observers to the Mideast if requested by the Secretary General of the United Nations, and we have reason to expect that we will receive such a request.

With regard to the peacekeeping force, I think it is important for all of you ladies and gentlemen, and particularly for those listening on radio and television, to know why the United States has insisted that major powers not be part of the peacekeeping force and that major powers not introduce military forces into the Mideast. A very significant and potentially explosive crisis developed on Wednesday of this week. We obtained information which led us to believe that the Soviet Union was planning to send a very substantial force into the Mideast, a military force.

When I received that information, I ordered, shortly after midnight on Thursday morning, an alert for all American forces around the world. This was a precautionary alert. The purpose of that was to indicate to the Soviet Union that we could not accept any unilateral move on their part to move military forces into the Mideast. At the same time, in the early morning hours, I also proceeded on the diplomatic front. In a message to Mr. Brezhnev—an urgent message—I indicated to him our reasoning, and I urged that we not proceed along that course and that, instead, we join in the United Nations in supporting a resolution which would exclude any major powers from participating in a peacekeeping force.

As a result of that communication and the return that I received from Mr. Brezhnev—we had several exchanges, I should say—we reached the conclusion that we would jointly support the resolution which was adopted in the United Nations.

We now come, of course, to the critical time in terms of the future of the Mideast. And here, the outlook is far more hopeful than what we have been through this past week. I think I could safely say that the chances for not just a cease-fire—which we presently have and which, of course, we have had in the Mideast for some time—but the outlook for a permanent peace is the best that it has been in 20 years.

The reason for this is that the two major powers, the Soviet Union and the United States, have agreed—this was one of the results of Dr. Kissinger's trip to Moscow—have agreed that we would participate in trying to expedite the talks between the parties involved. That does not mean that the two major powers will impose a settlement. It does mean, however, that we will use our influence with the nations in the area to expedite a settlement.

The reason we feel this is important is that first, from the standpoint of the nations in the Mideast, none of them—Israel, Egypt, Syria, none of them—can or should go through the agony of another war.

The losses in this war on both sides have been very, very high. And the tragedy must not occur again. There have been four of these wars, as you ladies and gentlemen know, over the past 20 years. But beyond that, it is vitally important to the peace of the world that this potential trouble spot, which is really one of the most potentially explosive areas in the world, that it not become an area in which the major powers come together in confrontation.

What the developments of this week should indicate to all of us is that the United States and the Soviet Union, who admittedly have very different objectives in the Mideast, have now agreed that it is not in their interest to have a confrontation there, a confrontation which might lead to a nuclear confrontation, and neither of the two major powers wants that.

We have agreed, also, that if we are to avoid that, it is necessary for us to use our influence more than we have in the past, to get the negotiating track moving again, but this time, moving to a conclusion—not simply a temporary truce but a permanent peace.

I do not mean to suggest that it is going to come quickly, because the parties involved are still rather far apart. But I do say that now there are greater incentives within the area to find a peaceful solution, and there are enormous incentives as far as the United States is concerned, and the Soviet Union and other major powers, to find such a solution.

Turning now to the subject of our attempts to get a cease-fire on the home front, that is a bit more difficult.

Presidential Tape Recordings

[2.] Today, White House Counsel contacted Judge Sirica—we tried yesterday, but he was in Boston, as you know—and arrangements were made to meet with Judge Sirica on Tuesday to work out the delivery of the tapes to Judge Sirica.

Watergate Special Prosecutor

[3.] Also, in consultations that we have had in the White House today, we have decided that next week the Acting Attorney General, Mr. Bork, will appoint a new Special Prosecutor for what is called the Watergate matter. The Special Prosecutor will have independence. He will have total cooperation from the executive branch, and he will have as his primary responsibility to bring this matter which has so long concerned the American people, bring it to an expeditious conclusion, because we have to remember that under our Constitution, it has always been held that justice delayed is justice denied. It is time for those who are guilty to be prosecuted and for those who are innocent to be cleared. And I can assure you ladies and gentlemen, and all of our listeners tonight, that I have no greater interest than to see that the new Special Prosecutor has the cooperation from the executive branch and the independence that he needs to bring about that conclusion.

Questions

The Special Prosecutor

[4.] And now I will go to Mr. Cormier [Frank Cormier, Associated Press].

Q. Mr. President, would the new Special Prosecutor have your go-ahead to go to court if necessary to obtain evidence from your files that he felt were vital?

The President. Well, Mr. Cromier, I would anticipate that that would not be necessary. I believe that as we look at the events which led to the dismissal of Mr. Cox, we find that these are matters that can be worked out and should be worked out in cooperation and not by having a suit filed by a Special Prosecutor within the executive branch against the President of the United States.

This, incidentally, is not a new attitude on the part of a President. Every President since George Washington has tried to protect the confidentiality of Presidential conversations, and you remember the famous case involving Thomas Jefferson where Chief Justice Marshall, then sitting as a trial judge, subpoenaed the letter which Jefferson had written which Marshall thought or felt was necessary evidence in the trial of Aaron Burr. Jefferson refused to do so, but it did not result in a suit. What happened was, of course, a compromise in which a summary of the contents of the letter which was relevant to the trial was produced by Jefferson, and the Chief Justice of the United States, acting in his capacity as Chief Justice, accepted that.

That is exactly, of course, what we tried to do in this instant case.

I think it would be well if I could take just a moment, Mr. Cormier, in answering your question to point out what we tried to do and why we feel it was the proper solution to a very aggravating and difficult problem.

The matter of the tapes has been one that has concerned me because of my feeling that I have a constitutional responsibility to defend the Office of the Presidency from any encroachments on confidentiality which might affect future Presidents in their abilities to conduct the kind of conversations and discussions they need to conduct to carry on the responsibilities of this office. And of course, the Special Prosecutor felt that he needed the tapes for the purpose of his prosecution.

That was why, working with the Attorney General, we worked out what we thought was an acceptable compromise, one in which Judge Stennis, now Senator Stennis, would hear the tapes and would provide a complete and full disclosure, not only to Judge Sirica but also to the Senate committee.

Attorney General Richardson approved of this proposition. Senator Baker, Senator Ervin approved of the proposition. Mr. Cox was the only one that rejected it.

Under the circumstances, when he rejected it and indicated that despite the approval of the Attorney General, of course, of the President and of the two major Senators on the Ervin committee, when he rejected the proposal, I had no choice but to dismiss him.

Under those circumstances, Mr. Richardson, Mr. Ruckelshaus felt that because of the nature of their confirmation that their commitment to Mr. Cox had to take precedence over any commitment they might have to carry out an order from the President.

Under those circumstances, I accepted with regret the resignations of two fine public servants.

Now we come to a new Special Prosecutor. We will cooperate with him, and I do not anticipate that we will come to the time when he would consider it necessary to take the President to court. I think our cooperation will be adequate.

Q. This is perhaps another way of asking Frank's question, but if the Special Prosecutor considers that information contained in Presidential documents is needed to prosecute the Watergate case, will you give him the documents, beyond the nine tapes which you have already given him?

The President. I have answered that question before. We will not provide Presidential documents to a Special Prosecutor. We will provide, as we have in great numbers, all kinds of documents from the White House, but if it is a document involving a conversation with the President, I would have to stand on the principle of confidentiality. However, information that is needed from such documents would be provided. That is what we have been trying to do.

Q. Mr. President, you know in the Congress there is a great deal of suspicion over any arrangement which will permit the executive branch to investigate itself or which will establish a

Special Prosecutor which you may fire again. And 53 Senators, a majority, have now cosponsored a resolution which would permit Judge Sirica to establish and name an independent prosecutor, separate and apart from the White House and the executive branch. Do you believe this arrangement would be constitutional, and would you go along with it?

The President. Well, I would suggest that the action that we are going to take, appointing a Special Prosecutor, would be satisfactory to the Congress and that they would not proceed with that particular matter.

Thoughts on Questions of Impeachment or Resignation

[5.] Mr. Rather [Dan Rather, CBS News].

Q. Mr. President, I wonder if you could share with us your thoughts, tell us what goes through your mind when you hear people, people who love this country and people who believe in you, say reluctantly that perhaps you should resign or be impeached.

The President. Well, I am glad we don't take the vote of this room, let me say. And I understand the feelings of people with regard to impeachment and resignation. As a matter of fact, Mr. Rather, you may remember that when I made the rather difficult decision—I thought the most difficult decision of my first term—on December 18, the bombing by B-52's of North Vietnam, that exactly the same words were used on the networks—I don't mean by you, but they were quoted on the networks—that were used now: tyrant, dictator, he has lost his senses, he should resign, he should be impeached.

But I stuck it out, and as a result of that, we not only got our prisoners of war home, as I have often said, on their feet rather than on their knees, but we brought peace to Vietnam, something we haven't had and didn't for over 12 years.

It was a hard decision, and it was one that many of my friends in the press who had consistently supported me on the war up to that time disagreed with. Now, in this instance I realize there are people who feel that the actions that I have taken with regard to the dismissal of Mr. Cox are grounds for impeachment.

I would respectfully suggest that even Mr. Cox and Mr. Richardson have agreed that the President had the right, constitutional right, to dismiss anybody in the Federal Government. And second, I should also point out that as far as the tapes are concerned, rather than being in defiance of the law, I am in compliance with the law.

As far as what goes through my mind, I would simply say that I intend to continue to carry out, to the best of my ability, the responsibilities I was elected to carry out last November. The events of this past week—I know, for example, in your head office in New York, some thought that it was simply a blown-up exercise; there wasn't a real crisis. I wish it had been that. It was a real crisis. It was the most difficult crisis we have had since the Cuban confrontation of 1962.

But because we had had our initiative with the Soviet Union, because I had a basis of communication with Mr. Brezhnev, we not only avoided a confrontation but we moved a great step forward toward real peace in the Mideast.

Now, as long as I can carry out that kind of responsibility, I am going to continue to do this job.

Motives of Mr. Cox

[6.] Mr. Lisagor [Peter Lisagor, Chicago Daily News].

Q. There have been reports that you felt that Mr. Cox was somehow out to get you. I would like to ask you if you did feel that, and if so, what evidence did you have?

The President. Mr. Lisagor, I understand Mr. Cox is going to testify next week under oath before the Judiciary Committee, and I would suggest that he perhaps would be better qualified to answer that question.

As far as I am concerned, we had cooperated with the Special Prosecutor. We tried to work out in a cooperative way this matter of the production of the tapes. He seemed to be more interested in the issue than he was in a settlement, and under the circumstances, I had no choice but to dismiss him. But I am not going to question his motives as to whether or not he was out to get me. Perhaps the Senators would like to ask that question.

The Nation's Confidence

[7.] Q. Mr. President, in 1968, before you were elected, you wrote that too many shocks can drain a nation of its energy and even cause a rebellion against creative change and progress. Do you think America is at that point now?

The President. I think that many would speculate—I have noted a lot on the networks, particularly, and sometimes even in the newspapers. But this is a very strong country, and the American people, I think, can ride through the shocks that they have—the difference now from what it was in the days of shocks, even when Mr. Lisagor and I first met 25 years ago, is the electronic media.

I have never heard or seen such outrageous, vicious, distorted reporting in 27 years of public life. I am not blaming anybody for that. Perhaps what happened is that what we did brought it about, and therefore, the media decided that they would have to take that particular line.

But when people are pounded night after night with that kind of frantic, hysterical reporting, it naturally shakes their confidence. And yet, I should point out that even in this week, when many thought that the President was shell-shocked, unable to act, the President acted decisively in the interests of peace, in the interests of the country, and I can assure you that whatever shocks gentlemen of the press may have, or others, political people, these shocks will not affect me in my doing my job.

The Middle East Crisis

[8.] Q. Mr. President, getting back to the Middle East crisis for a moment, do you consider that the crisis is over now, and how much longer will the American forces be kept on alert around the world?

The President. With regard to the alert, the alert has already been discontinued with regard to NORAD, that is the North American [Air Defense] Command, and with regard to SAC [Strategic Air Command]. As far as other forces are concerned, they are being maintained in a state of readiness, and obviously, Soviet Union forces are being maintained in a state of readiness.

Now, as far as the crisis in the Mideast is concerned, I don't want to leave any impression that we aren't going to continue to have problems with regard to the cease-fire. There will be outbreaks because of the proximity of the antagonistic forces, and there will be some very, very tough negotiating in attempting to reach a diplomatic settlement. But I think now that all parties are going to approach this problem of trying to reach a settlement with a more sober and a more determined attitude than ever before, because the Mideast can't afford—Israel can't afford, Egypt can't afford, Syria can't afford—another war. The world cannot afford a war in that part of the world. And because the Soviet Union and the United States have potentially conflicting interests there, we both now realize that we cannot allow our differences in the Mideast to jeopardize even greater interests that we have, for example, in continuing a détente in Europe, in continuing the negotiations which can lead to a limitation of nuclear arms and eventually reducing the burden of nuclear arms, and in continuing in other ways that can contribute to the peace of the world.

As a matter of fact, I would suggest that with all of the criticism of détente, that without détente, we might have had a major conflict in the Middle East. With détente, we avoided it.

Oil and the Middle East

[9.] Q. Mr. President, a question from the electronic media, related to the Middle East—
The President [to Forrest J. Boyd, Mutual Broadcasting System]. Radio.

Q. Radio, yes. I have heard that there was a meeting at the State Department this afternoon of major oil company executives on the fuel shortage. Whether or not you can confirm that, has this confrontation in the Middle East caused a still more severe oil problem, and is there any thinking now of gasoline rationing?

The President. Well, we have contingency plans for gasoline rationing and so forth, which I hope never have to be put into place.

But with regard to the oil shortage, which you referred to, one of the major factors which gave enormous urgency to our efforts to settle this particular crisis was the potential of an oil cutoff.

Let me say that I have also noted that in the State Department—or from the State Department—today a statement raised a little difficulty in Europe to the effect that our European friends hadn't been as cooperative as they might have been in attempting to help us work out the Middle East settlement or at least the settlement to the extent that we have worked it out as of the resolution of yesterday.

I can only say on that score that Europe, which gets 80 percent of its oil from the Mideast, would have frozen to death this winter unless there had been a settlement, and Japan, of course, is in that same position. The United States, of course, gets only approximately 10 percent of its oil from the Mideast.

What I am simply suggesting is this: that with regard to the fuel shortage, potentially, in the United States and in the world, it is indispensable at this time that we avoid any further Mideast crisis so that the flow of oil to Europe, to Japan, and to the United States can continue.

Exchanges with General Secretary Brezhnev

[10.] Q. Mr. President, against this background of détente, Mr. Brezhnev's note to you has been described as rough or perhaps brutal by one Senator. Can you characterize it for us and for history in any way?

The President. Yes, I could characterize it, but, Mr. Theis [J. William Theis, Hearst Newspapers and Hearst Headline Service], it wouldn't be in the national interest to do so. My notes to him he might characterize as being rather rough. However, I would rather—perhaps it would be best to characterize it. Rather than saying, Mr. Theis, that his note to me was rough and brutal, I would say that is was very firm, and it left very little to the imagination as to what he intended.

And my response was also very firm and left little to the imagination of how we would react. And it is because he and I know each other, and it is because we have had this personal contact, that notes exchanged in that way result in a settlement rather than a confrontation.

Mr. Rebozo and Campaign Contributions

[11.] Mr. Deakin?

Q. Yes, Mr. Deakin [James Deakin, St. Louis Post-Dispatch]. Is it credible, can the American people believe that your close friend, Mr. Rebozo, for 3 years, during which time you saw him weekly sometimes, kept from you the fact that he had $100,000 in cash from Mr. Howard Hughes? Is that credible? Is it credible that your personal attorney, Mr. Kalmbach, knew about this money for at least a year and never told you about it?

And if this was a campaign contribution, as your press secretaries say, who authorized Mr. Rebozo to collect campaign contributions for your reelection or for the Republican Party?

What campaign committee was he an official of?

The President. Well, it is obviously not credible to you, and I suppose that it would sound incredible to many people who do not know how I operate. In terms of campaign contributions, I have had a rule, Mr. Deakin, which Mr. Stans, Mr. Kalmbach, Mr. Rebozo, and every contributor will agree has been the rule—I have refused always to accept contributions myself. I have refused to have any discussion of contributions. As a matter of fact, my orders to Mr. Stans were that after the campaign was over, I would then send notes of appreciation to those that contributed, but before the election, I did not want to have any information from anybody with regard to campaign contributions.

Now, with regard to Mr. Rebozo, let me say that he showed, I think, very good judgment in doing what he did. He received a contribution. He was prepared to turn it over to the finance chairman when the finance chairman was appointed. But in the interlude, after he received the contribution and before the finance chairman was appointed, the Hughes company, as you all know, had an internal fight of massive proportions, and he felt that such a contribution to the campaign might prove to be embarrassing.

At the conclusion of the campaign, he decided that it would be in the best interests of everybody concerned rather than to turn the money over then, to be used in the '74 campaigns, to return it intact. And I would say that any individual, and particularly a banker, who would have a contribution of $100,000 and not touch it—because it was turned back in exactly the form it was received—I think that is a pretty good indication that he is a totally honest man, which he is.

Presidential Tape Recordings

[12.] Q. Mr. President, after the tapes are presented to Judge Sirica and they are processed under the procedure outlined by the U.S. Court of Appeals, will you make those tapes public?

The President. No, that is not the procedure that the court has ordered, and it would not be proper. Judge Sirica, under the circuit court's order, is to listen to the tapes and, then, is to present to the grand jury the pertinent evidence with regard to its investigation. Publication of the tapes has not been ordered by the circuit court of appeals, and Judge Sirica, of course, would not do anything that would be in contravention of what the circuit court of appeals has ordered.

Presidential Stress

[13.] Mr. terHorst [J.F. terHorst, Detroit News].

Q. Mr. President, Harry Truman used to talk about the heat in the kitchen——

The President. I know what he meant.

Q. ——and a lot of people have been wondering how you are bearing up emotionally under the stress of recent events. Can you discuss that?

The President. Well, those who saw me during the Middle East crisis thought I bore up rather well, and, Mr. terHorst, I have a quality which is—I guess I must have inherited it from my Midwestern mother and father—which is that the tougher it gets, the cooler I get. Of course, it isn't pleasant to get criticism. Some of it is justified, of course. It isn't pleasant to find your honesty questioned. It isn't pleasant to find, for example, that, speaking of my friend Mr. Rebozo, that despite the fact that those who printed it, and those who said it, knew it was untrue—said that he had a million-dollar trust fund for me that he was handling—it was nevertheless put on one of the networks, knowing it was untrue. It isn't pleasant, for example, to hear or read that a million dollars in campaign funds went into my San Clemente property and, even after we had a complete audit, to have it repeated.

Those are things which, of course, do tend to get under the skin of the man who holds this office. But as far as I am concerned, I have learned to expect it. It has been my lot throughout my political life, and I suppose because I have been through so much, that may be one of the reasons that when I have to face an international crisis, I have what it takes.

Watergate Influence on Middle East Crisis

[14.] Q. Mr. President, I would like to ask you a question about the Mideast. To what extent do you think your Watergate troubles influenced Soviet thinking about your ability to respond in the Mideast, and did your Watergate problems convince you that the United States needed a strong response in the Mideast to convince other nations that you have not been weakened?

The President. Well, I have noted speculation to the effect that the Watergate problems may have led the Soviet Union to miscalculate. I tend to disagree with that, however.

I think Mr. Brezhnev probably can't quite understand how the President of the United States wouldn't be able to handle the Watergate problems. He would be able to handle it all right, if he had them. [*Laughter*] But I think what happens is that what Mr. Brezhnev does understand is the power of the United States. What he does know is the President of the United States.

What he also knows is that the President of the United States, when he was under unmerciful assault at the time of Cambodia at the time of May 8, when I ordered the bombing and the mining of North Vietnam, at the time of December 18, still went ahead and did what he thought was right; the fact that Mr. Brezhnev knew that regardless of the pressures at home, regardless of what people see and hear on television night after night, he would do what was right. That is what made Mr. Brezhnev act as he did.

Presidential Views on Television Coverage

[15.] Q. Mr. President, you have lambasted the television networks pretty well. Could I ask you, at the risk of reopening an obvious wound, you say after you have put on a lot of heat that you don't blame anyone. I find that a little puzzling. What is it about the television coverage of you in these past weeks and months that has so aroused your anger?

The President [to Robert C. Pierpoint, CBS News]. Don't get the impression that you arouse my anger. [*Laughter*]

Q. I'm afraid, sir, that I have that impression. [*Laughter*]

The President. You see, one can only be angry with those he respects.

Regaining the Confidence of the People

[16.] Q. Mr. President, businessmen increasingly are saying that many chief executive officers of corporations do not get the latitude you have had, if they have the personnel problems that you have had, to stay in the job and correct them. You have said you are going to stay. Do you have any plan set out to regain confidence of people across the country and these businessmen who are beginning to talk about this matter? Do you have any plans besides the Special Prosecutor, which looks backward; do you have any plan that looks forward for regaining confidence of people?

The President. I certainly have. First, to move forward in building a structure of peace in the world, in which we have made enormous progress in the past and which we are going to make more progress in, in the future; our European initiative, our continued initiative with the Soviet Union, with the People's Republic of China. That will be the major legacy of this Administration.

Moving forward at home in our continuing battle against the high cost of living, in which we are now finally beginning to make some progress, and moving forward also on the matters that you referred to, it is true that what happened in Watergate, the campaign abuses, were deplorable. They have been very damaging to this Administration; they have been damaging certainly to the country as well.

Let me say, too, I didn't want to leave an impression with my good friend from CBS over here that I don't respect the reporters. What I was simply saying was this: that when a commentator takes a bit of news and then, with knowledge of what the facts are, distorts it, viciously, I have no respect for that individual.

Executive Privilege

[17.] Q. Mr. President!

The President [to Clark R. Mollenhoff, Des Moines Register and Tribune]. You are so loud, I will have to take you.

Q. I have to be, because you happen to dodge my questions all of the time.

The President. You had three last time.

Q. Last May, you went before the American people, and you said executive privilege will not be invoked as to any testimony concerning possible criminal conduct or discussing of possible criminal conduct, including the Watergate affair and the alleged coverup.

If you have revised or modified this position, as you seem to have done, could you explain the rationale of a law-and-order Administration covering up evidence, prima facie evidence, of high crimes and misdemeanors?

The President. Well, I should point out that perhaps all the other reporters in the room are aware of the fact that we have waived executive privilege on all individuals within the Administration. It has been the greatest waiver of executive privilege in the whole history of this Nation.

And as far as any other matters are concerned, the matters of the tapes, the matters of Presidential conversations, those are matters in which the President has a responsibility to defend this office, which I shall continue to do.

Mr. Cromier. Thank you, Mr. President.

Downfall: The Release of the White House Transcripts
Televised Address to the Nation
Washington, D.C.
April 29, 1974

Since Alexander Butterfield revealed the recording system in the White House, the tapes had loomed large in the resolution of the Watergate scandal. Nixon's counter-offensive ("Operation Candor") in November, 1973 had been torpedoed by the revelation that a crucial tape—a conversation between him and Haldeman on June 20—contained an 18 1/2 minute erasure. Now in April Nixon faced additional subpoenas from the Special Prosecutor as well as a April 30 deadline from the House Judiciary Committee that was considering his impeachment. Thus, Nixon delivered this address to announce the release of edited transcripts of those tapes both to the proper authorities and to the public. The transcripts were quickly published in paperback and became an over-night best-seller. But they were a disaster for the President. Most Americans were appalled by the substance and tone of the tapes. Senator Hugh Scott, Senate Minority leader, called the transcripts "deplorable, disgusting, shabby, immoral." A new phrase, "expletive deleted," came into our political vocabulary. Moreover, the House Judiciary Committee found some intriguing omissions. For example, the edited transcript of March 22 omitted a section in which the President said to John Mitchell: "I don't give a shit what happens. I want you all to stonewall it, let them plead the Fifth Amendment, cover-up, or anything else, if it'll save it—save the plan.'' The transcripts were a disaster for the President. Republicans joined calls for his resignation. Newspapers that had previously been staunch supporters echoed that chorus. Nixon's public approval rating fell even further.

I have asked for this time tonight in order to announce my answer to the House Judiciary Committee's subpoena for additional Watergate tapes, and to tell you something about the actions I shall be taking tomorrow—about what I hope they will mean to you and about the very difficult choices that were presented to me.

These actions will at last, once and for all, show that what I knew and what I did with regard to the Watergate break-in and coverup were just as I have described them to you from the very beginning.

I have spent many hours during the past few weeks thinking about what I would say to the American people if I were to reach the decision I shall announce tonight. And so, my words have not been lightly chosen; I can assure you they are deeply felt.

It was almost 2 years ago, in June 1972 that five men broke into the Democratic National Committee headquarters in Washington. It turned out that they were connected with my reelection committee, and the Watergate break-in became a major issue in the campaign.

The full resources of the FBI and the Justice Department were used to investigate the incident thoroughly. I instructed my staff and campaign aides to cooperate fully with the investigation. The FBI conducted nearly 1,500 interviews. For 9 months—until March 1973—I was assured by those charged with conducting and monitoring the investigations that no one in the White House was involved.

Nevertheless, for more than a year, there have been allegations and insinuations that I knew about the planning of the Watergate break-in and that I was involved in an extensive plot to cover it up. The House Judiciary Committee is now investigating these charges.

On March 6, I ordered all materials that I had previously furnished to the Special Prosecutor turned over to the committee. These included tape recordings of 19 Presidential conversations and more than 700 documents from private White House files.

On April 11, the Judiciary Committee issued a subpoena for 42 additional tapes of conversations which it contended were necessary for its investigation. I agreed to respond to that subpoena by tomorrow.

In these folders that you see over here on my left are more than 1,200 pages of transcripts of private conversations I participated in between September 15, 1972, and April 27 of 1973 with my principal aides and associates with regard to Watergate. They include all the relevant portions of all the subpoenaed conversations that were recorded, that is, all portions that relate to the question of what I knew about Watergate or the coverup and what I did about it.

They also include transcripts of other conversations which were not subpoenaed, but which have a significant bearing on the question of Presidential actions with regard to Watergate. These will be delivered to the committee tomorrow.

In these transcripts, portions not relevant to my knowledge or actions with regard to Watergate are not included, but everything that is relevant is included—the rough as well as the smooth—the strategy sessions, the exploration of alternatives, the weighing of human and political costs.

As far as what the President personally knew and did with regard to Watergate and the coverup is concerned, these materials—together with those already made available—will tell it all.

I shall invite Chairman Rodino and the committee's ranking minority member, Congressman Hutchinson of Michigan, to come to the White House and listen to the actual, full tapes of these conversations, so that they can determine for themselves beyond question that the transcripts are accurate and that everything on the tapes relevant to my knowledge and my actions on Watergate is included. If there should be any disagreement over whether omitted material is relevant, I shall meet with them personally in an effort to settle the matter. I believe this arrangement is fair, and I think it is appropriate.

For many days now, I have spent many hours of my own time personally reviewing these materials and personally deciding questions of relevancy. I believe it is appropriate that the committee's review should also be made by its own senior elected officials, and not by staff employees.

The task of Chairman Rodino and Congressman Hutchinson will be made simpler than was mine by the fact that the work of preparing the transcripts has been completed. All they will need to do is to satisfy themselves of their authenticity and their completeness.

Ever since the existence of the White House taping system was first made known last summer, I have tried vigorously to guard the privacy of the tapes. I have been well aware that my effort to protect the confidentiality of Presidential conversations has heightened the sense of mystery about Watergate and, in fact, has caused increased suspicions of the President. Many people assume that the tapes must incriminate the President, or that otherwise, he would not insist on their privacy.

But the problem I confronted was this: Unless a President can protect the privacy of the advice he gets, he cannot get the advice he needs.

This principle is recognized in the constitutional doctrine of executive privilege, which has been defended and maintained by every President since Washington and which has been recognized by the courts, whenever tested, as inherent in the Presidency. I consider it to be my constitutional responsibility to defend this principle.

Three factors have now combined to persuade me that a major unprecedented exception to the principle is now necessary:

First, in the present circumstances, the House of Representatives must be able to reach an informed judgment about the President's role in Watergate.

Second, I am making a major exception to the principle of confidentiality because I believe such action is now necessary in order to restore the principle itself, by clearing the air of the central question that has brought such pressures upon it—and also to provide the evidence which will allow this matter to be brought to a prompt conclusion.

Third, in the context of the current impeachment climate, I believe all the American people, as well as their representatives in Congress, are entitled to have not only the facts but also the evidence that demonstrates those facts.

I want there to be no question remaining about the fact that the President has nothing to hide in this matter.

The impeachment of a President is a remedy of last resort; it is the most solemn act of our entire constitutional process. Now, regardless of whether or not it succeeded, the action of the

House, in voting a formal accusation requiring trial by the Senate, would put the Nation through a wrenching ordeal it has endured only once in its lifetime, a century ago, and never since America has become a world power with global responsibilities.

The impact of such an ordeal would be felt throughout the world, and it would have its effect on the lives of all Americans for many years to come.

Because this is an issue that profoundly affects all the American people, in addition to turning over these transcripts to the House Judiciary Committee, I have directed that they should all be made public—all of these that you see here.

To complete the record, I shall also release to the public transcripts of all those portions of the tapes already turned over to the Special Prosecutor and to the committee that relate to Presidential actions or knowledge of the Watergate affair.

During the past year, the wildest accusations have been given banner headlines and ready credence as well. Rumor, gossip, innuendo, accounts from unnamed sources of what a prospective witness might testify to, have filled the morning newspapers and then are repeated on the evening newscasts day after day.

Time and again, a familiar pattern repeated itself. A charge would be reported the first day as what it was—just an allegation. But it would then be referred back to the next day and thereafter as if it were true.

The distinction between fact and speculation grew blurred. Eventually, all seeped into the public consciousness as a vague general impression of massive wrongdoing, implicating everybody, gaining credibility by its endless repetition.

The basic question at issue today is whether the President personally acted improperly in the Watergate matter. Month after month of rumor, insinuation, and charges by just one Watergate witness—John Dean—suggested that the President did act improperly.

This sparked the demands for an impeachment inquiry. This is the question that must be answered. And this is the question that will be answered by these transcripts that I have ordered published tomorrow.

These transcripts cover hour upon hour of discussion that I held with Mr. Haldeman, John Ehrlichman, John Dean, John Mitchell, former Attorney General Kleindienst, Assistant General Petersen, and others with regard to Watergate.

They were discussions in which I was probing to find out what had happened, who was responsible, what were the various degrees of responsibilities, what were the legal culpabilities, what were the political ramifications, and what actions were necessary and appropriate on the part of the President.

I realize that these transcripts will provide grist for many sensational stories in the press. Parts will seem to be contradictory with one another, and parts will be in conflict with some of the testimony given in the Senate Watergate committee hearings.

I have been reluctant to release these tapes, not just because they will embarrass me and those with whom I have talked—which they will—and not just because they will become the subject of speculation and even ridicule—which they will—and not just because certain parts of them will be seized upon by political and journalistic opponents—which they will.

I have been reluctant because, in these and in all the other conversations in this office, people have spoken their minds freely, never dreaming that specific sentences or even parts of sentences would be picked out as the subjects of national attention and controversy.

I have been reluctant because the principle of confidentiality is absolutely essential to the conduct of the Presidency. In reading the raw transcripts of these conversations, I believe it will be more readily apparent why that principle is essential and must be maintained in the future. These conversations are unusual in their subject matter, but the same kind of uninhibited discussion—and it is that—the same brutal candor is necessary in discussing how to bring warring factions to the peace table or how to move necessary legislation through the Congress.

Names are named in these transcripts. Therefore, it is important to remember that much that appears in them is no more than hearsay or speculation, exchanged as I was trying to find out what really had happened, while my principal aides were reporting to me on rumors and reports that they had heard, while we discussed the various, often conflicting stories that different persons were telling.

As the transcripts will demonstrate, my concerns during this period covered a wide range. The first and obvious one was to find out just exactly what had happened and who was involved.

A second concern was for the people who had been, or might become, involved in Watergate. Some were close advisers, valued friends, others whom I had trusted. And I was also concerned about the human impact on others, especially some of the young people and their families who had come to Washington to work in my Administration, whose lives might be suddenly ruined by something they had done in an excess of loyalty or in the mistaken belief that it would serve the interests of the President.

And then, I was quite frankly concerned about the political implications. This represented potentially a devastating blow to the Administration and to its programs, one which I knew would be exploited for all it was worth by hostile elements in the Congress as well as in the media. I wanted to do what was right, but I wanted to do it in a way that would cause the least unnecessary damage in a highly charged political atmosphere to the Administration.

And fourth, as a lawyer, I felt very strongly that I had to conduct myself in a way that would not prejudice the rights of potential defendants.

And fifth, I was striving to sort out a complex tangle, not only of facts but also questions of legal and moral responsibility. I wanted, above all, to be fair. I wanted to draw distinctions, where those were appropriate, between persons who were active and willing participants on the one hand, and on the other, those who might have gotten inadvertently caught up in the web and be technically indictable but morally innocent.

Despite the confusions and contradictions, what does come through clearly is this:

John Dean charged in sworn Senate testimony that I was "fully aware of the coverup" at the time of our first meeting on September 15, 1972. These transcripts show clearly that I first learned of it when Mr. Dean himself told me about it in this office on March 21—some 6 months later.

Incidentally, these transcripts—covering hours upon hours of conversations—should place in somewhat better perspective the controversy over the 18 1/2 minute gap in the tape of a conversation I had with Mr. Haldeman back in June of 1972.

Now, how it was caused is still a mystery to me and, I think, to many of the experts as well. But I am absolutely certain, however, of one thing: that it was not caused intentionally by my secretary, Rose Mary Woods, or any of my White House assistants. And certainly, if the theory were true that during those 18 1/2 minutes, Mr. Haldeman and I cooked up some sort of a

Watergate coverup scheme, as so many have been quick to surmise, it hardly seems likely that in all of our subsequent conversations—many of them are here—which neither of us ever expected would see the light of day, there is nothing remotely indicating such a scheme; indeed, quite the contrary.

From the beginning, I have said that in many places on the tapes there were ambiguities—a statement and comments that different people with different perspectives might interpret in drastically different ways—but although the words may be ambiguous, though the discussions may have explored many alternatives, the record of my actions is totally clear now, and I still believe it was totally correct then.

A prime example is one of the most controversial discussions, that with Mr. Dean on March 21—the one in which he first told me of the coverup, with Mr. Haldeman joining us midway through the conversation.

His revelations to me on March 21 were a sharp surprise, even though the report he gave to me was far from complete, especially since he did not reveal at that time the extent of his own criminal involvement.

I was particularly concerned by his report that one of the Watergate defendants, Howard Hunt, was threatening blackmail unless he and his lawyer were immediately given $120,000 for legal fees and family support, and that he was attempting to blackmail the White House, not by threatening exposure on the Watergate matter, but by threatening to reveal activities that would expose extremely sensitive, highly secret national security matters that he had worked on before Watergate.

I probed, questioned, tried to learn all Mr. Dean knew about who was involved, what was involved. I asked more than 150 questions of Mr. Dean in the course of that conversation.

He said to me, and I quote from the transcripts directly: "I can just tell from our conversation that these are things that you have no knowledge of."

It was only considerably later that I learned how much there was that he did not tell me then—for example, that he himself had authorized promises of clemency, that he had personally handled money for the Watergate defendants, and that he had suborned perjury of a witness.

I knew that I needed more facts. I knew that I needed the judgments of more people. I knew the facts about the Watergate coverup would have to be made public, but I had to find out more about what they were before I could decide how they could best be made public.

I returned several times to the immediate problem posed by Mr. Hunt's blackmail threat, which to me was not a Watergate problem, but one which I regarded, rightly or wrongly, as a potential national security problem of very serious proportions. I considered long and hard whether it might in fact be better to let the payment go forward, at least temporarily, in the hope that this national security matter would not be exposed in the course of uncovering the Watergate coverup.

I believe then, and I believe today, that I had a responsibility as President to consider every option, including this one, where production of sensitive national security matters was at issue—protection of such matters. In the course of considering it and of "just thinking out loud," as I put it at one point, I several times suggested that meeting Hunt's demands might be necessary.

But then I also traced through where that would lead. The money could be raised. But money demands would lead inescapably to clemency demands, and clemency could not be granted. I said, and I quote directly from the tape: "It is wrong, that's for sure." I pointed out, and I quote again from the tape: "But in the end we are going to be bled to death. And in the end it is all going to come out anyway. Then you get the worst of both worlds. We are going to lose, and people are going to——"

And Mr. Haldeman interrupts me and says: "And look like dopes!"

And I responded, "And in effect look like a coverup. So that we cannot do."

Now, I recognize that this tape of March 21 is one which different meanings could be read in by different people. But by the end of the meeting, as the tape shows, my decision was to convene a new grand jury and to send everyone before the grand jury with instructions to testify.

Whatever the potential for misinterpretation there may be as a result of the different options that were discussed at different times during the meeting, my conclusion at the end of the meeting was clear. Any my actions and reactions as demonstrated on the tapes that follow that date show clearly that I did not intend the further payment to Hunt or anyone else be made. These are some of the actions that I took in the weeks that followed in my effort to find the truth, to carry out my responsibilities to enforce the law:

As a tape of our meeting on March 22, the next day, indicates, I directed Mr. Dean to go to Camp David with instructions to put together a written report. I learned 5 days later, on March 26, that he was unable to complete it. And so on March 27, I assigned John Ehrlichman to try to find out what had happened, who was at fault, and in what ways and to what degree.

One of the transcripts I am making public is a call that Mr. Ehrlichman made to the Attorney General on March 28, in which he asked the Attorney General to report to me, the President, directly, any information he might find indicating possible involvement of John Mitchell or by anyone in the White House. I had Mr. Haldeman separately pursue other, independent lines of inquiry.

Throughout, I was trying to reach determinations on matters of both substance and procedure on what the facts were and what was the best way to move the case forward. I concluded that I wanted everyone to go before the grand jury and testify freely and fully. This decision, as you will recall, was publicly announced on March 30, 1973. I waived executive privilege in order to permit everybody to testify. I specifically waived executive privilege with regard to conversations with the President, and I waived the attorney-client privilege with John Dean in order to permit him to testify fully and, I hope, truthfully.

Finally, on April 14—3 weeks after I learned of the coverup from Mr. Dean—Mr. Ehrlichman reported to me on the results of his investigation. As he acknowledged, much of what he had gathered was hearsay, but he had gathered enough to make it clear that the next step was to make his findings completely available to the Attorney General, which I instructed him to do.

And the next day, Sunday, April 15, Attorney General Kleindienst asked to see me, and he reported new information which had come to his attention on this matter. And although he was in no way whatever involved in Watergate, because of his close personal ties, not only to John Mitchell but to other potential people who might be involved, he quite properly removed himself from the case.

We agreed that Assistant Attorney General Henry Petersen, the head of the Criminal Division, a Democrat and career prosecutor, should be placed in complete charge of the investigation.

Later that day, I met with Mr. Petersen. I continued to meet with him, to talk with him, to consult with him, to offer him the full cooperation of the White House—as you will see from these transcripts—even to the point of retaining John Dean on the White House Staff for an extra 2 weeks after he admitted his criminal involvement, because Mr. Petersen thought that would make it easier for the prosecutor to get his cooperation in breaking the case if it should become necessary to grant Mr. Dean's demand for immunity.

On April 15, when I heard that one of the obstacles to breaking the case was Gordon Liddy's refusal to talk, I telephoned Mr. Petersen and directed that he should make clear not only to Mr. Liddy but to everyone that—and now I quote directly from the tape of that telephone call— "As far as the President is concerned, everybody in this case is to talk and to tell the truth." I told him if necessary I would personally meet with Mr. Liddy's lawyer to assure him that I wanted Liddy to talk and to tell the truth.

From the time Mr. Petersen took charge, the case was solidly within the criminal justice system, pursued personally by the Nation's top professional prosecutor with the active, personal assistance of the President of the United States.

I made clear there was to be no coverup.

Let me quote just a few lines from the transcripts—you can read them to verify them—so that you can hear for yourself the orders I was giving in this period.

Speaking to Haldeman and Ehrlichman, I said: ". . . It is ridiculous to talk about clemency. They all knew that."

Speaking to Ehrlichman, I said: "We all have to do the right thing . . . We just cannot have this kind of a business . . ."

Speaking to Haldeman and Ehrlichman, I said: "The boil had to be pricked . . . We have to prick the boil and take the heat. Now that's what we are doing here."

Speaking to Henry Petersen, I said: "I want you to be sure to understand that you know we are going to get to the bottom of this thing."

Speaking to John Dean, I said: "Tell the truth. That is the thing I have told everybody around here."

And then speaking to Haldeman: "And you tell Magruder, 'now Jeb, this evidence is coming in, you ought to go to the grand jury. Purge yourself if you're perjured and tell this whole story.' "

I am confident that the American people will see these transcripts for what they are, fragmentary records from a time more than a year ago that now seems very distant, the records of a President and of a man suddenly being confronted and having to cope with information which, if true, would have the most far-reaching consequences, not only for his personal reputation but, more important, for his hopes, his plans, his goals for the people who had elected him as their leader.

If read with an open and a fair mind and read together with the record of the actions I took, these transcripts will show that what I have stated from the beginning to be the truth has been the truth: that I personally had no knowledge of the break-in before it occurred, that I had no knowledge of the coverup until I was informed of it by John Dean on March 21, that I never offered clemency for the defendants, and that after March 21, my actions were directed toward finding the facts and seeing that justice was done, fairly and according to the law.

The facts are there. The conversations are there. The record of actions is there.

To anyone who reads his way through this mass of materials I have provided, it will be totally, abundantly clear that as far as the President's role with regard to Watergate is concerned, the entire story is there.

As you will see, now that you also will have this mass of evidence I have provided, I have tried to cooperate with the House Judiciary Committee. And I repeat tonight the offer that I have made previously: to answer written interrogatories under oath and, if there are then issues still unresolved, to meet personally with the chairman of the committee and with Congressman Hutchinson to answer their questions under oath.

As the committee conducts its inquiry, I also consider it only essential and fair that my counsel, Mr. St. Clair, should be present to cross-examine witnesses and introduce evidence in an effort to establish the truth.

I am confident that for the overwhelming majority of those who study the evidence that I shall release tomorrow—those who are willing to look at it fully, fairly, and objectively—the evidence will be persuasive and, I hope, conclusive.

We live in a time of very great challenge and great opportunity for America.

We live at a time when peace may become possible in the Middle East for the first time in a generation.

We are at last in the process of fulfilling the hope of mankind for a limitation on nuclear arms—a process that will continue when I meet with the Soviet leaders in Moscow in a few weeks.

We are well on the way toward building a peace that can last, not just for this but for other generations as well.

And here at home, there is vital work to be done in moving to control inflation, to develop our energy resources, to strengthen our economy so that Americans can enjoy what they have not had since 1956: full prosperity without war and without inflation.

Every day absorbed by Watergate is a day lost from the work that must be done—by your President and by your Congress—work that must be done in dealing with the great problems that affect your prosperity, affect your security, that could affect your lives.

The materials I make public tomorrow will provide all the additional evidence needed to get Watergate behind us and to get it behind us now.

Never before in the history of the Presidency have records that are so private been made so public.

In giving you these records—blemishes and all—I am placing my trust in the basic fairness of the American people.

I know in my own heart that through the long, painful, and difficult process revealed in these transcripts, I was trying in that period to discover what was right and to do what was right.

I hope and I trust that when you have seen the evidence in its entirety, you will see the truth of that statement.

As for myself, I intend to go forward, to the best of my ability, with the work that you elected me to do. I shall do so in a spirit perhaps best summed up a century ago by another President when he was being subjected to unmerciful attack. Abraham Lincoln said:

"I do the very best I know how—the very best I can; and I mean to keep doing so until the end. If the end brings me out all right, what is said against me won't amount to anything. If the end brings me out wrong, ten angels swearing I was right would make no difference."

Resignation
Televised Address to the Nation
Washington, D.C.
August 8, 1974

On August 5, the White House released the transcripts of three conversations the President had with H. R. Haldeman on June 23, 1972, six days after the Watergate break-in. These showed that Nixon ordered a halt to the F.B.I. investigation primarily for political reasons, as he admitted in a statement accompanying the transcripts. This admission showed that he had lied for a year and a half. During that time he had steadfastly maintained that he had intervened in the investigation solely to protect national security. His support in Congress evaporated practically over-night. Thus, four days later, one of the largest audiences in television history gathered for an historical occasion: the first resignation of a President in American history. The speech consists of two directly conflicting genres: a statement of resignation and his reasons for being forced to leave office; and a farewell to the American people in which he recounts the major achievements of his administration.

This is the 37th time I have spoken to you from this office, where so many decisions have been made that shaped the history of this Nation. Each time I have done so to discuss with you some matter that I believe affected the national interest.

In all the decisions I have made in my public life, I have always tried to do what was best for the Nation. Throughout the long and difficult period of Watergate, I have felt it was my duty to persevere, to make every possible effort to complete the term of office to which you elected me.

In the past few days, however, it has become evident to me that I no longer have a strong enough political base in the Congress to justify continuing that effort. As long as there was such a base, I felt strongly that it was necessary to see the constitutional process through to its conclusion, that to do otherwise would be unfaithful to the spirit of that deliberately difficult process and a dangerously destabilizing precedent for the future.

But with the disappearance of that base, I now believe that the constitutional purpose has been served, and there is no longer a need for the process to be prolonged.

I would have preferred to carry through to the finish, whatever the personal agony it would have involved, and my family unanimously urged me to do so. But the interests of the Nation must always come before any personal considerations.

From the discussions I have had with Congressional and other leaders, I have concluded that because of the Watergate matter, I might not have the support of the Congress that I would consider necessary to back the very difficult decisions and carry out the duties of this office in the way the interests of the Nation will require.

I have never been a quitter. To leave office before my term is completed is abhorrent to every instinct in my body. But as President, I must put the interests of America first. America needs a full-time President and a full-time Congress, particularly at this time with problems we face at home and abroad.

To continue to fight through the months ahead for my personal vindication would almost totally absorb the time and attention of both the President and the Congress in a period when our entire focus should be on the great issues of peace abroad and prosperity without inflation at home.

Therefore, I shall resign the Presidency effective at noon tomorrow. Vice President Ford will be sworn in as President at that hour in this office.

As I recall the high hopes for America with which we began this second term, I feel a great sadness that I will not be here in this office working on your behalf to achieve those hopes in the next 2 1/2 years. But in turning over direction of the Government to Vice President Ford, I know, as I told the Nation when I nominated him for the office 10 months ago, that the leadership of America will be in good hands.

In passing this office to the Vice President, I also do so with the profound sense of the weight of responsibility that will fall on his shoulders tomorrow and, therefore, of the understanding, the patience, the cooperation he will need from all Americans.

As he assumes that responsibility, he will deserve the help and the support of all of us. As we look to the future, the first essential is to begin healing the wounds of this Nation, to put the bitterness and divisions of the recent past behind us and to rediscover those shared ideals that lie at the heart of our strength and unity as a great and as a free people.

By taking this action, I hope that I will have hastened the start of that process of healing which is so desperately needed in America.

I regret deeply any injuries that may have been done in the course of the events that led to this decision. I would say only that if some of my judgments were wrong—and some were wrong—they were made in what I believed at the time to be the best interest of the Nation.

To those who have stood with me during these past difficult months—to my family, my friends, to many others who joined in supporting my cause because they believed it was right—I will be eternally grateful for your support.

And to those who have not felt able to give me your support, let me say I leave with no bitterness toward those who have opposed me, because all of us, in the final analysis, have been concerned with the good of the country, however our judgments might differ.

So, let us all now join together in affirming that common commitment and in helping our new President succeed for the benefit of all Americans.

I shall leave this office with regret at not completing my term, but with gratitude for the privilege of serving as your President for the past 5 1/2 years. These years have been a momentous time in the history of our Nation and the world. They have been a time of achievement in which we can all be proud, achievements that represent the shared efforts of the Administration, the Congress, and the people.

But the challenges ahead are equally great, and they, too, will require the support and the efforts of the Congress and the people working in cooperation with the new Administration.

We have ended America's longest war, but in the work of securing a lasting peace in the world, the goals ahead are even more far-reaching and more difficult. We must complete a structure of peace so that it will be said of this generation, our generation of Americans, by the people of all nations, not only that we ended one war but that we prevented future wars.

We have unlocked the doors that for a quarter of a century stood between the United States and the People's Republic of China.

We must now ensure that the one quarter of the world's people who live in the People's Republic of China will be and remain not our enemies, but our friends.

In the Middle East, 100 million people in the Arab countries, many of whom have considered us their enemy for nearly 20 years, now look on us as their friends. We must continue to build on that friendship so that peace can settle at last over the Middle East and so that the cradle of civilization will not become its grave.

Together with the Soviet Union, we have made the crucial breakthroughs that have begun the process of limiting nuclear arms. But we must set as our goal not just limiting but reducing and, finally, destroying these terrible weapons so that they cannot destroy civilization and so that the threat of nuclear war will no longer hand over the world and the people.

We have opened the new relation with the Soviet Union. We must continue to develop and expand that new relationship so that the two strongest nations of the world will live together in cooperation, rather than confrontation.

Around the world—in Asia, in Africa, in Latin America, in the Middle East—there are millions of people who live in terrible poverty, even starvation. We must keep as our goal turning away from production for war and expanding production for peace so that people everywhere on this Earth can at last look forward in their children's time, if not in our own time, to having the necessities for a decent life.

Here in America, we are fortunate that most of our people have not only the blessings of liberty but also the means to live full and good and, by the world's standards, even abundant lives. We must press on, however, toward a goal, not only of more and better jobs but of full opportunity for every American and of what we are striving so hard right now to achieve, prosperity without inflation.

For more than a quarter of a century in public life, I have shared in the turbulent history of this era. I have fought for what I believed in. I have tried, to the best of my ability, to discharge those duties and meet those responsibilities that were entrusted to me.

Sometimes I have succeeded and sometimes I have failed, but always I have taken heart from what Theodore Roosevelt once said about the man in the arena, "whose face is marred by dust and sweat and blood, who strives valiantly, who errs and comes short again and again because there is not effort without error and short-coming, but who does actually strive to do the deed, who knows the great enthusiams, the great devotions, who spends himself in a worthy cause, who at the best knows in the end the triumphs of high achievements and who at the worst, if he fails, at least fails while daring greatly."

I pledge to you tonight that as long as I have a breath of life in my body, I shall continue in that spirit. I shall continue to work for the great causes to which I have been dedicated throughout my years as a Congressman, a Senator, Vice President, and President, the cause of peace, not just for America but among all nations—prosperity, justice, and opportunity for all of our people.

There is one cause above all to which I have been devoted and to which I shall always be devoted for as long as I live.

When I first took the oath of office as President 5 1/2 years ago, I made this sacred commitment: to "consecrate my office, my energies, and all the wisdom I can summon to the cause of peace among nations."

I have done my very best in all the days since to be true to that pledge. As a result of these efforts, I am confident that the world is a safer place today, not only for the people of America but for the people of all nations, and that all of our children have a better chance than before of living in peace rather than dying in war.

This, more than anything, is what I hoped to achieve when I sought the Presidency. This, more than anything, is what I hope will be my legacy to you, to our country, as I leave the Presidency.

To have served in this office is to have felt a very personal sense of kinship with each and every American. In leaving it, I do so with this prayer: May God's grace be with you in all the days ahead.

Farewell
Televised Remarks to the White House Staff
Washington, D.C.
August 9, 1974

At 9:36 A.M. in the East Room of the White House President Nixon spoke for the last time as President of the United States. His audience was his White House staff. Unlike the formal speech of the night before, his words were impromptu and revealed a curious admixture of some of his private thoughts: one last sneering reference to the press, words of praise and encouragement to the staff, an admission of mistakes in his administration, memories of his father and mother, and finally the drawing of an incongruous parallel between Theodore Roosevelt's loss of his wife and his own loss of power. And then he was gone.

I think the record should show that this is one of those spontaneous things that we always arrange whenever the President comes in to speak, and it will be so reported in the press, and we don't mind, because they have to call it as they see it.

But on our part, believe me, it is spontaneous.

You are here to say goodby to us, and we don't have a good word for it in English—the best is *au revoir*. We will see you again.

I just met with the members of the White House staff, you know, those who serve here in the White House day in and day out, and I asked them to do what I ask all of you to do to the extent that you can and, of course, are requested to do so: to serve our next President as you have served me and previous Presidents—because many of you have been here for many years—with devotion and dedication, because this office, great as it is, can only be as great as the men and women who work for and with the President.

This house, for example—I was thinking of it as we walked down this hall, and I was comparing it to some of the great houses of the world that I have been in. This isn't the biggest house. Many, and most, in even smaller countries, are much bigger. This isn't the finest house. Many in Europe, particularly, and in China, Asia, have paintings of great, great value, things that we just don't have here and, probably, will never have until we are 1,000 years old or older.

But this is the best house. It is the best house, because it has something far more important than numbers of people who serve, far more important than numbers of rooms or how big it is, far more important than number of magnificent pieces of art.

This house has a great heart, and that heart comes from those who serve. I was rather sorry they didn't come down. We said goodby to them upstairs. But they are really great. And I recall after so many times I have made speeches, and some of them pretty tough, yet, I always come back, or after a hard day—and my days usually have run rather long—I would always get a lift from them, because I might be a little down but they always smiled.

And so it is with you. I look around here, and I see so many on this staff that, you know, I should have been by your offices and shaken hands, and I would love to have talked to you and found out how to run the world—everybody wants to tell the President what to do, and boy, he needs to be told many times—but I just haven't had the time. But I want you to know that each and every one of you, I know, is indispensable to this Government.

I am proud of this Cabinet. I am proud of all the members who have served in our Cabinet. I am proud of our sub-Cabinet. I am proud of our White House Staff. As I pointed our last night, sure, we have done some things wrong in this Administration, and the top man always takes the responsibility, and I have never ducked it. But I want to say one thing: We can be proud of it—5 1/2 years. No man or no woman came into this Administration and left it with more of this world's goods than when he came in. No man or no woman ever profited at the public expense or the public till. That tells something about you.

Mistakes, yes. But for personal gain, never. You did what you believed in. Sometimes right, sometimes wrong. And I only wish that I were a wealthy man—at the present time, I have got to find a way to pay my taxes—[*laughter*]—and if I were, I would like to recompense you for the sacrifices that all of you have made to serve in government.

But you are getting something in government—and I want you to tell this to your children, and I hope the Nation's children will hear it, too—something in government service that is far more important than money. It is a cause bigger than yourself. It is the cause of making this the greatest nation in the world, the leader of the world, because without our leadership, the world will know nothing but war, possibly starvation or worse, in the years ahead. With our leadership it will know peace, it will know plenty.

We have been generous, and we will be more generous in the future as we are able to. But most important, we must be strong here, strong in our hearts, strong in our souls, strong in our belief, and strong in our willingness to sacrifice, as you have been willing to sacrifice, in a pecuniary way, to serve in government.

There is something else I would like for you to tell your young people. You know, people often come in and say, "What will I tell my kids?" They look at government and say, sort of a rugged life, and they see the mistakes that are made. They get the impression that everybody is here for the purpose of feathering his nest. That is why I made this earlier point—not in this Administration, not one single man or woman.

And I say to them, there are many fine careers. This country needs good farmers, good businessmen, good plumbers, good carpenters.

I remember my old man. I think that they would have called him sort of a little man, common man. He didn't consider himself that way. You know what he was? He was a streetcar motorman first, and then he was a farmer, and then he had a lemon ranch. It was the poorest lemon ranch in California, I can assure you. He sold it before they found oil on it. [*Laughter*] And then he was a grocer. But he was a great man, because he did his job, and every job counts up to the hilt, regardless of what happens.

Nobody will ever write a book, probably, about my mother. Well, I guess all of you would say this about your mother—my mother was a saint. And I think of her, two boys dying of tuberculosis, nursing four others in order that she could take care of my older brother for 3 years in Arizona, and seeing each of them die, and when they died, it was like one of her own.

Yes, she will have no books written about her. But she was a saint.

Now, however, we look to the future. I had a little quote in the speech last night from T.R. As you know, I kind of like to read books. I am not educated, but I do read books—[*laughter*]—and the T.R. quote was a pretty good one.

Here is another one I found as I was reading, my last night in the White House, and this quote is about a young man. He was a young lawyer in New York. He had married a beautiful girl, and they had a lovely daughter, and then suddenly she died, and this is what he wrote. This was in his diary.

He said, "She was beautiful in face and form and lovelier still in spirit. As a flower she grew and as a fair young flower she died. Her life had been always in the sunshine. There had never come to her a single great sorrow. None ever knew her who did not love and revere her for her bright and sunny temper and her saintly unselfishness. Fair, pure and joyous as a maiden, loving, tender and happy as a young wife. When she had just become a mother, when her life seemed to be just begun and when the years seemed so bright before her, then by a strange and terrible fate death came to her. And when my heart's dearest died, the light went from my life forever."

There was T.R. in his twenties. He thought the light had gone from his life forever—but he went on. And he not only became President but, as an ex-President, he served his country, always in the arena, tempestuous, strong, sometimes wrong, sometimes right, but he was a man.

And as I leave, let me say, that is an example I think all of us should remember. We think sometimes when things happen that don't go the right way; we think that when you don't pass the bar exam the first time—I happened to, but I was just lucky; I mean, my writing was so poor the bar examiner said, "We have just got to let the guy through." We think that when someone dear to us dies, we think that when we lose an election, we think that when we suffer a defeat that all is ended. We think, as T.R. said, that the light had left his life forever.

Not true. It is only a beginning, always. The young must know it; the old must know it. It must always sustain us, because the greatness comes not when things go always good for you, but the greatness comes and you are really tested, when you take some knocks, some disappointments, when sadness comes, because only if you have been in the deepest valley can you ever know how magnificent it is to be on the highest mountain.

And so I say to you on this occasion, as we leave, we leave proud of the people who have stood by us and worked for us and served this country.

We want you to be proud of what you have done. We want you to continue to serve in government, if that is your wish. Always give your best, never get discouraged, never be petty; always remember, others may hate you, but those who hate you don't win unless you hate them, and then you destroy yourself.

And so, we leave with high hopes, in good spirit, and with deep humility, and with very much gratefulness in our hearts. I can only say to each and every one of you, we come from many faiths, we pray perhaps to different gods—but really the same God in a sense—but I want to say for each and every one of you, not only will we always remember you, not only will we always be grateful to you but always you will be in our hearts and you will be in our prayers.

Thank you very much.

Gerald R. Ford
(1974–1977)

Gerald R. Ford entered the Presidency under extraordinary circumstances. He was truly an "accidental" President. When Vice President Spiro Agnew pleaded *nolo contendere* to one count of income tax evasion, Richard Nixon, under his power granted by the 25th amendment, first sought to nominate John Connolly as his new Vice President. Political advisors told him it would be practically impossible to get Connolly approved in Congress. Thus, on October 12 and with considerable fanfare Nixon surprised his immediate audience and people watching at home on television sets by naming Jerry Ford as his choice to occupy the second ranking executive office in the United States. Less than a year later, Nixon became the first President in American history to resign his office, and Ford became the first President in American history to assume that office without being elected to either it or the Vice Presidency.

At the outset of his Presidency, Ford offered a welcomed relief from the turbulent last month of the Nixon administration. He was open, not secretive; homey, not pompous. Even his occasional fumbling with words stood him in good stead. By the beginning of September more than 70% of the American people approved of his handling of the Presidency. Then, with one sweep of the pen he destroyed that atmosphere of good feeling. On a Sunday morning, September 8, Ford granted a "full and free" pardon to Richard Nixon for any and all crimes he might have committed during his tenure as President. The reaction was swift and devastating. Protests mounted. His approval rating dropped 21 percentage points. He eventually found himself testifying before a Congressional sub-committee about the circumstances that led up to this extraordinary pardon.

After the pardon his troubles continued. His nomination of Nelson Rockefeller to be his Vice President angered the conservative wing of the Republican party, and that anger was doubled when he announced an amnesty for Vietnam draft evaders. His Whip Inflation Now campaign (with the accompanying WIN buttons) became more a topic for comedians' jokes than a serious program to confront a serious problem. Ford appeared to be a "caretaker" President, and he seemed to accept this role.

President Ford presided over one of the most painful periods in American history: the fall of South Vietnam to the North Vietnamese and the capture of Cambodia by the Khmer Rouge. But misfortune had a way of presenting new opportunities for Ford. On March 12, 1975 the Khmer Rouge seized an American merchant ship, the *Mayaguez,* and took possession of its crew of forty. Ford acted (many would say over-reacted) immediately. He approved a military plan to recapture the ship and set the crew free. In subsequent military action 41 American servicemen were killed and another 49 wounded. Nonetheless, the ship and crew were eventually returned, and Americans—frustrated by the Vietnam years—rejoiced. Little matter that we lost more men than we recovered. The symbol of action meant more than its results. And it transformed Ford overnight into a tough leader, a man of action, a Presidential candidate for 1976.

In the 1976 Republican primaries Ronald Reagan challenged Ford for the nomination. Though Ford eventually beat Reagan, he did so at a price. Reagan forced Ford to take more conservative positions than he had previously. Ford had to drop Rockefeller from his ticket. He had to back away from his support for a new Panama Canal treaty. And he generally moved to the right on other issues agitating the conservative wing of the party. All these combined with his pardon of Nixon and his major slip in the second television debate with Carter on eastern Europe not being under Soviet domination cost him the Presidential election in 1976.

What can one say of Gerald R. Ford, this accidental President? He was basically a decent man who offended few and inspired few. He aroused no great passions, except when he pardoned Nixon. He brought no real innovations either to the office or to policy. As a speaker, he was bland. William Safire somewhere remarked that Ford was unique among 20th century Presidents because he uttered not one memorable phrase during his entire tenure in office. He served as a transition, a transition from an unwelcomed past to an uncertain future.

"Our Long National Nightmare Is Over"

Washington, D.C.
August 9, 1974

At 11:35 A.M. Secretary of State Henry Kissinger received a formal letter that read: "Dear Mr. Secretary: I hereby resign the office of President of the United States. Sincerely, Richard Nixon." At that moment Gerald Ford became President. At 12:03 P.M. he was formally sworn in by Chief Justice Warren E. Burger in the East Room of the White House.

The oath that I have taken is the same oath that was taken by George Washington and by every President under the Constitution. But I assume the Presidency under extraordinary circumstances, never before experienced by Americans. This is an hour of history that troubles our minds and hurts our hearts.

Therefore, I feel it is my first duty to make an unprecedented compact with my countrymen. Not an inaugural address, not a fireside chat, not a campaign speech—just a little straight talk among friends. And I intend it to be the first of many.

I am acutely aware that you have not elected me as your President by your ballots, and so I ask you to confirm me as your President with your prayers. And I hope that such prayers will also be the first of many.

If you have not chosen me by secret ballot, neither have I gained office by any secret promises. I have not campaigned either for the Presidency or the Vice Presidency. I have not subscribed to any partisan platform. I am indebted to no man, and only to one woman—my dear wife—as I begin this very difficult job.

I have not sought this enormous responsibility, but I will not shirk it. Those who nominated and confirmed me as Vice President were my friends and are my friends. They were of both parties, elected by all the people and acting under the Constitution in their name. It is only fitting then that I should pledge to them and to you that I will be the President of all the people.

Thomas Jefferson said the people are the only sure reliance for the preservation of our liberty. And down the years, Abraham Lincoln renewed this American article of faith asking, "Is there any better way or equal hope in the world?"

I intend, on Monday next, to request of the Speaker of the House of Representatives and the President pro tempore of the Senate the privilege of appearing before the Congress to share with my former colleagues and with you, the American people, my views on the priority business of the Nation and to solicit your views and their views. And may I say to the Speaker and the others, if I could meet with you right after these remarks, I would appreciate it.

Even though this is late in an election year, there is no way we can go forward except together and no way anybody can win except by serving the people's urgent needs. We cannot stand still or slip backwards. We must go forward now together.

To the peoples and the governments of all friendly nations, and I hope that could encompass the whole world, I pledge an uninterrupted and sincere search for peace. America will remain strong and united, but its strength will remain dedicated to the safety and sanity of the entire family of man, as well as to our own precious freedom.

I believe that truth is the glue that holds government together, not only our Government, but civilization itself. That bond, though strained, is unbroken at home and abroad.

In all my public and private acts as your President, I expect to follow my instincts of openness and candor with full confidence that honesty is always the best policy in the end.

My fellow Americans, our long national nightmare is over.

Our Constitution works; our great Republic is a Government of laws and not of men. Here the people rule. But there is a higher power, by whatever name we honor Him, who ordains not only righteousness but love, not only justice but mercy.

As we bind up the internal wounds of Watergate, more painful and more poisonous than those of foreign wars, let us restore the golden rule to our political process, and let brotherly love purge our hearts of suspicion and of hate.

In the beginning, I asked you to pray for me. Before closing, I ask again your prayers, for Richard Nixon and for his family. May our former President, who brought peace to millions, find it for himself. May God bless and comfort his wonderful wife and daughters, whose love and loyalty will forever be a shining legacy to all who bear the lonely burdens of the White House.

I can only guess at those burdens, although I have witnessed at close hand the tragedies that befell three Presidents and the lesser trials of others.

With all the strength and all the good sense I have gained from life, with all the confidence my family, my friends, and my dedicated staff impart to me, and with the good will of countless Americans I have encountered in recent visits to 40 States, I now solemnly reaffirm my promise I made to you last December 6: to uphold the Constitution, to do what is right as God gives me to see the right, and to do the very best I can for America.

God helping me, I will not let you down.

Thank you.

The Pardon of Richard Nixon

Televised Remarks on Signing the Proclamation Granting the Pardon
Washington, D.C.
September 8, 1974

Precisely one month after President Nixon announced his decision to resign, President Ford granted him a "full, free, and absolute pardon." He did so in these brief televised remarks from the Oval Office at 11:00 A.M. on a Sunday morning.

The reaction from the country was swift and devastating. The telegrams and phone calls that poured into the White House overwhelmingly opposed the pardon. The Gallup Poll recorded that Ford dropped from a 71% approval rating to a 50% approval after the pardon. Jerald terHorst, Ford's press secretary, resigned in protest. Congress cut into Ford's request for a $850,000 appropriation for Nixon's transition expenses by reducing it to $200,000. Congress also set aside an agreement reached between Ford and Nixon to return the Watergate tapes to Nixon. Congress placed them in the custody of the Special Prosecutor's Office. And finally, President Ford became the first President since Abraham Lincoln to testify before a Congressional committee to explain his reasons for the pardon.

I have come to a decision which I felt I should tell you and all of my fellow American citizens, as soon as I was certain in my own mind and in my own conscience that it is the right thing to do.

I have learned already in this office that the difficult decisions always come to this desk. I must admit that many of them do not look at all the same as the hypothetical questions that I have answered freely and perhaps too fast on previous occasions.

My customary policy is to try and get all the facts and to consider the opinions of my countrymen and to take counsel with my most valued friends. But these seldom agree, and in the end, the decision is mine. To procrastinate, to agonize, and to wait for a more favorable turn of events that may never come or more compelling external pressures that may as well be wrong as right, is itself a decision of sorts and a weak and potentially dangerous course for a President to follow. *Less than compelling external events*

I have promised to uphold the Constitution, to do what is right as God gives me to see the right, and to do the very best that I can for America.

I have asked your help and your prayers, not only when I became President but many times since. The Constitution is the supreme law of our land and it governs our actions as citizens. Only the laws of God, which govern our consciences, are superior to it.

As we are a nation under God, so I am sworn to uphold our laws with the help of God. And I have sought such guidance and searched my own conscience with special diligence to determine the right thing for me to do with respect to my predecessor in this place, Richard Nixon, and his loyal wife and family. *how? what part did ford play*

Theirs is an American tragedy in which we all have played a part. It could go on and on and on, or someone must write the end to it. I have concluded that only I can do that, and if I can, I must. *Theodore Deisen book / Oedipus parallel is crazy*

There are no historic or legal precedents to which I can turn in this matter, none that precisely fit the circumstances of a private citizen who has resigned the Presidency of the United States.

[Handwritten margin notes at top: "Sword of executioner", "story of Damacles", "? / fragility / complexity of political power", "not Fate, he committed crimes"]

But it is common knowledge that serious allegations and accusations hang like a sword over our former President's head, threatening his health as he tries to reshape his life, a great part of which was spent in the service of this country and by the mandate of its people.

After years of bitter controversy and divisive national debate, I have been advised, and I am compelled to conclude that many months and perhaps more years will have to pass before Richard Nixon could obtain a fair trial by jury in any jurisdiction of the United States under governing decisions of the Supreme Court.

I deeply believe in equal justice for all Americans, whatever their station or former station. The law, whether human or divine, is no respecter of persons; but the law is a respecter of reality.

The facts, as I see them, are that a former President of the United States, instead of enjoying equal treatment with any other citizen accused of violating the law, would be cruelly and excessively penalized either in preserving the presumption of his innocence or in obtaining a speedy determination of his guilt in order to repay a legal debt to society.

During this long period of delay and potential litigation, ugly passions would again be aroused. And our people would again be polarized in their opinions. And the credibility of our free institutions of government would again be challenged at home and abroad.

In the end, the courts might well hold that Richard Nixon had been denied due process, and the verdict of history would even more be inconclusive with respect to those charges arising out of the period of his Presidency, of which I am presently aware. *It's now inconclusive*

But it is not the ultimate fate of Richard Nixon that most concerns me, though surely it deeply troubles every decent and every compassionate person. My concern is the immediate future of this great country.

In this, I dare not depend upon my personal sympathy as a long-time friend of the former *wants to depend on it, too* President, nor my professional judgment as a lawyer, and I do not. *[margin: out of proxy role]*

As President, my primary concern must always be the greatest good of all the people of the United States whose servant I am. As a man, my first consideration is to be true to my own convictions and my own conscience.

My conscience tells me clearly and certainly that I cannot prolong the bad dreams that continue to reopen a chapter that is closed. My conscience tells me that only I, as President, have the constitutional power to firmly shut and seal this book. My conscience tells me it is my duty, not merely to proclaim domestic tranquility but to use every means that I have to insure it. *[margin: undermines his own investigation]*

I do believe that the buck stops here, that I cannot rely upon public opinion polls to tell me what is right.

I do believe that right makes might and that if I am wrong, 10 angels swearing I was right would make no difference. *Quoting Nixon Quoting Lincoln — we know* *[margin: he lied]* *[left margin: odd]*

I do believe, with all my heart and mind and spirit, that I, not as President but as a humble servant of God, will receive justice without mercy if I fail to show mercy. *[margin: step out of role]*

Finally, I feel that Richard Nixon and his loved ones have suffered enough and will continue to suffer, no matter what I do, no matter what we, as a great and good nation, can do together to make his goal of peace come true. *What does this mean? odd language*

[At this point, the President began reading from the proclamation granting the pardon.]

perhaps, peace of mind

Constitut. is vehicle to do what he personally wants

"Now, therefore, I, Gerald R. Ford, President of the United States, pursuant to the pardon power conferred upon me by Article II, Section 2, of the Constitution, have granted and by these presents do grant a full, free, and absolute pardon unto Richard Nixon for all offenses against the United States which he, Richard Nixon, has committed or may have committed or taken part in during the period from July (January) 20, 1969 through August 9, 1974."

[The President signed the proclamation and then resumed reading.]

"In witness whereof, I have hereunto set my hand this eighth day of September, in the year of our Lord nineteen hundred and seventy-four, and of the Independence of the United States of America the one hundred and ninety-ninth."

Excerpts from **The Second Ford-Carter Presidential Campaign Debate**

Palace of Fine Arts Theatre
San Francisco, California
October 6, 1976

In the 1976 Presidential campaign the two candidates agreed to engage in 3 televised "debates." The first dealt with domestic policy, and, according to many observers, President Ford demonstrated greater command of the subject than his opponent. The second debate concerned foreign affairs, an area in which candidate Carter was presumed to be less knowledgeable than the President. Whether he was or not was obscured by a major "faux pax" by Ford when he contended that Eastern European countries were not under the domination of the Soviet Union.

Mr. Frankel, you have the first question for Governor Carter.

Mr. Frankel. Governor, since the Democrats last ran our foreign policy, including many of the men who are advising you, the country has been relieved of the Vietnam agony and the military draft; we've started arms control negotiations with the Russians; we've opened relations with China; we've arranged the disengagement in the Middle East; we've regained influence with the Arabs without deserting Israel. Now, maybe, we've even begun a process of peaceful change in Africa.

Now, you've objected in this campaign to the style with which much of this was done, and you've mentioned some other things that you think ought to have been done. But do you really have a quarrel with this Republican record? Would you not have done any of those things?

Mr. Carter. Well, I think this Republican administration has been almost all style and spectacular and not substance. We've got a chance tonight to talk about, first of all, leadership, the character of our country, and a vision of the future. In every one of these instances, the Ford administration has failed. And I hope tonight that I and Mr. Ford will have a chance to discuss the reason for those failures.

Our country is not strong any more; we're not respected any more. We can only be strong overseas if we're strong at home, and when I become President, we'll not only be strong in those areas but also in defense—a defense capability second to none.

We've lost, in our foreign policy, the character of the American people. We've ignored or excluded the American people and the Congress from participation in the shaping of our foreign policy. It's been one of secrecy and exclusion.

In addition to that, we've had a chance to become now, contrary to our long-standing beliefs and principles, the arms merchant of the whole world. We've tried to buy success from our enemies, and at the same time we've excluded from the process the normal friendship of our allies.

In addition to that, we've become fearful to compete with the Soviet Union on an equal basis. We talk about détente. The Soviet Union knows what they want in détente, and they've been getting it. We have not known what we've wanted, and we've been out-traded in almost every instance.

The other point I want to make is about our defense. We've got to be a nation blessed with the defense capability that's efficient, tough, capable, well organized, narrowly focused fighting capability. The ability to fight if necessary is the best way to avoid the chance for or the requirement to fight.

And the last point I want to make is this: Mr. Ford, Mr. Kissinger have continued on with the policies and failures of Richard Nixon. Even the Republican platform has criticized the lack of leadership in Mr. Ford, and they've criticized the foreign policy of this administration. This is one instance where I agree with the Republican platform.

I might say this in closing, and that is, that as far as foreign policy goes, Mr. Kissinger has been the President of this country. Mr. Ford has shown an absence of leadership and an absence of a grasp of what this country is and what it ought to be. That's got to be changed, and that is one of the major issues in this campaign of 1976.

The Moderator. President Ford, would you like to respond?

The President. Governor Carter again is talking in broad generalities. Let me take just one question that he raises—the military strength and capability of the United States. Governor Carter, in November of 1975, indicated that he wanted to cut the defense budget by $15 billion. A few months later he said he wanted to cut the defense budget by $8 billion or $9 billion. And more recently he talks about cutting the defense budget by $5 billion to $7 billion. There is no way you can be strong militarily and have those kinds of reductions in our military appropriations.

Now let me just tell you a little story. About late October of 1975, I asked the then Secretary of Defense, Mr. Schlesinger, to tell me what had to be done if we were going to reduce the defense budget by $3 to $5 billion. A few days later Mr. Schlesinger came back and said if we cut the defense budget by $3 to $5 billion, we will have to cut military personnel by 250,000, civilian personnel by 100,000, jobs in America by 100,000. We would have to stretch out our aircraft procurement. We would have to reduce our naval construction program. We would have to reduce the research and development for the Army, the Navy, the Air Force, and Marines by 8 percent. We would have to close 20 military bases in the United States immediately. That's the kind of a defense program that Mr. Carter wants.

Let me tell you this straight from the shoulder: You don't negotiate with Mr. Brezhnev from weakness. And the kind of a defense program that Mr. Carter wants will mean a weaker defense and a poorer negotiating position.

The Moderator. Mr. Trewhitt, a question for President Ford.

Mr. Trewhitt. Mr. President, my question really is the other side of the coin from Mr. Frankel's. For a generation the United States had had a foreign policy based on containment of communism; yet we have lost the first war in Vietnam, we lost a shoving match in Angola, Communists threaten to come to power by peaceful means in Italy, and relations generally have cooled with the Soviet Union in the last few months. So, let me ask you, first, what do you do about such cases as Italy, and, secondly, does this general drift mean that we're moving back toward something like an old cold war relationship with the Soviet Union?

The President. I don't believe we should move to a cold war relationship. I think it's in the best interest of the United States and the world as a whole that the United States negotiate rather than go back to the cold war relationship with the Soviet Union.

I don't look at the picture as bleakly as you have indicated in your question, Mr. Trewhitt. I believe that the United States has had many successes in recent years and recent months as far as the Communist movement is concerned. We have been successful in Portugal where, a year ago, it looked like there was a very great possibility that the Communists would take over in Portugal. It didn't happen. We have a democracy in Portugal today.

A few months ago—or I should say maybe 2 years ago—the Soviet Union looked like they had continued strength in the Middle East. Today, according to Prime Minister Rabin, the Soviet Union is weaker in the Middle East than they have been in many, many years. The facts are the Soviet Union relationship with Egypt is at a low level; the Soviet Union relationship with Syria is at a very low point. The United States today, according to Prime Minister Rabin of Israel, is at a peak in its influence and power in the Middle East.

But let's turn for a minute to the southern African operations that are now going on. The United States of America took the initiative in southern Africa. We wanted to end the bloodshed in southern Africa. We wanted to have the right of self-determination in southern Africa. We wanted to have majority rule with the full protection of the rights of the minority. We wanted to preserve human dignity in southern Africa. We have taken initiative, and in southern Africa today the United States is trusted by the black frontline nations and black Africa. The United States is trusted by the other elements in southern Africa.

The United States foreign policy under this administration has been one of progress and success. And I believe that instead of talking about Soviet progress, we can talk about American successes.

And may I make an observation—part of the question you asked, Mr. Trewhitt—I don't believe that it's in the best interests of the United States and the NATO nations to have a Communist government in NATO. Mr. Carter has indicated he would look with sympathy to a Communist government in NATO. I think that would destroy the integrity and the strength of NATO, and I am totally opposed to it.

Mr. Carter. Well, Mr. Ford, unfortunately, has just made a statement that's not true. I have never advocated a Communist government for Italy; that would, obviously, be a ridiculous thing for any one to do who wanted to be President of the country. I think that this is an instance for deliberate distortion, and this has occurred also in the question about defense. As a matter of fact, I've never advocated any cut of $15 billion in our defense budget. As a matter of fact, Mr. Ford has made a political football out of the defense budget.

About a year ago, he cut the Pentagon budget $6.8 billion. After he fired James Schlesinger the political heat got so great that he added back about $3 billion. When Ronald Reagan won the Texas primary election, Mr. Ford added back another $1½ billion. Immediately before the Kansas City convention he added back another $1.8 billion in the defense budget. And his own Office of Management and Budget testified that he had a $3 billion cut insurance added to the defense budget under the pressure from the Pentagon. Obviously, this is another indication of trying to use the defense budget for political purposes, which he's trying to do tonight.

Now, we went into South Africa late, after Great Britian, Rhodesia, the black nations had been trying to solve this problem for many, many years. We didn't go in until right before the election, similar to what was taking place in 1972, when Mr. Kissinger announced peace is at hand just before the election at that time.

And we have weakened our position in NATO, because the other countries in Europe supported the democratic forces in Portugal long before we did. We stuck to the Portugal dictatorships much longer than other democracies did in this world.

The Moderator. Mr. Valeriani, a question for Governor Carter.

Mr. Valeriani. Governor Carter, much of what the United States does abroad is done in the name of the national interest. What is your concept of the national interest? What should the role of the United States in the world be? And in that connection, considering your limited experience in foreign affairs and the fact that you take some pride in being a Washington outsider, don't you think it would be appropriate for you to tell the American voters, before the election, the people that you would like to have in key positions such as Secretary of State, Secretary of Defense, national security affairs adviser at the White House?

Mr. Carter. Well, I'm not going to name my Cabinet before I get elected; I've got a little ways to go before I start doing that. But I have an adequate background, I believe. I am a graduate of the U.S. Naval Academy, the first military graduate since Eisenhower. I've served as Governor of Georgia and have traveled extensively in foreign countries—in South America, Central America, Europe, the Middle East, and in Japan.

I've traveled the last 21 months among the people of this country. I've talked to them, and I've listened. And I've seen at firsthand, in a very vivid way, the deep hurt that's come to this country in the aftermath of Vietnam and Cambodia and Chile and Pakistan and Angola and Watergate, CIA revelations.

What we were formerly so proud of—the strength of our country, its moral integrity, the representation in foreign affairs of what our people are, what our Constitution stands for—has been gone. And in the secrecy that has surrounded our foreign policy in the last few years, the American people and the Congress have been excluded.

I believe I know what this country ought to be. I've been one who's loved my Nation, as many Americans do. And I believe that there is no limit placed on what we can be in the future if we can harness the tremendous resources—militarily, economically—and the stature of our people, the meaning of our Constitution in the future.

Every time we've made a serious mistake in foreign affairs, it's been because the American people have been excluded from the process. If we can just tap the intelligence and ability, the sound commonsense, and the good judgment of the American people, we can once again have a foreign policy to make us proud instead of ashamed. And I'm not going to exclude the American people from that process in the future, as Mr. Ford and Kissinger have done.

0

3

This is what it takes to have a sound foreign policy; strong at home, strong defense, permanent commitments, not betray the principles of our country, and involve the American people and the Congress in the shaping of our foreign policy.

Every time Mr. Ford speaks from a position of secrecy—in negotiations and secret treaties that have been pursued and achieved, in supporting dictatorships, in ignoring human rights—we are weak and the rest of the world knows it.

So these are the ways that we can restore the strength of our country. And they don't require long experience in foreign policy—nobody has that except a President who served a long time or a Secretary of State. But my background, my experience, my knowledge of the people of this country, my commitment to our principles that don't change—those are the best bases to correct the horrible mistakes of this administration and restore our own country to a position of leadership in the world.

Mr. Valeriani. How, specifically, Governor, are you going to bring the American people into the decisionmaking process in foreign policy? What does that mean?

Mr. Carter. First of all, I would quit conducting the decisionmaking process in secret, as has been a characteristic of Mr. Kissinger and Mr. Ford. In many instances we've made agreements, like in Vietnam, that have been revealed later on to our embarrassment.

Recently, Ian Smith, the President of Rhodesia, announced that he had unequivocal commitments from Mr. Kissinger that he could not reveal. The American people don't know what those commitments are. We've seen in the past a destruction of elected governments, like in Chile, and the strong support of military dictatorship there. These kinds of things have hurt us very much.

I would restore the concept of the fireside chat, which was an integral part of the administration of Franklin Roosevelt. And I would also restore the involvement of the Congress. When Harry Truman was President, he was not afraid to have a strong Secretary of Defense—Dean Acheson, George Marshall were strong Secretaries of State—excuse me, State. But he also made sure that there was a bipartisan support. The Members of Congress, Arthur Vandenburg, Walter George, were part of the process. And before our Nation made a secret agreement and before we made a bluffing statement, we were sure that we had the backing not only of the President and the Secretary of State but also of the Congress and the people. This is a responsibility of the President, and I think it's very damaging to our country for Mr. Ford to have turned over this responsibility to the Secretary of State.

The Moderator. President Ford, do you have a response?

The President. Governor Carter again contradicts himself. He complains about secrecy, and yet he is quoted as saying that in the attempt to find a solution in the Middle East, that he would hold unpublicized meetings with the Soviet Union—I presume for the purpose of imposing a settlement of Israel and the Arab nations.

But let me talk just a minute about what we've done to avoid secrecy in the Ford administration. After the United States took the initiative in working with Israel and with Egypt and achieving the Sinai II agreement—and I am proud to say that not a single Egyptian or Israeli soldier has lost his life since the signing of the Sinai agreement—but at the time that I submitted the Sinai agreement to the Congress of the United States, I submitted every single document that was applicable to the Sinai II agreement. It was the most complete documentation by any President of any agreement signed by a President on behalf of the United States.

Now, as far as meeting with the Congress is concerned, during the 24 months that I've been the President of the United States, I have averaged better than one meeting a month with responsible groups or committees of the Congress, both House and Senate.

The Secretary of State has appeared, in the several years that he's been the Secretary, before 80 different committee hearings in the House and in the Senate. The Secretary of State has made better than 50 speeches all over the United States explaining American foreign policy. I have made, myself, at least 10 speeches in various parts of the country, where I have discussed with the American people defense and foreign policy.

The Moderator. Mr. Frankel, a question for President Ford.

Mr. Frankel. Mr. President, I'd like to explore a little more deeply our relationship with the Russians. They used to brag, back in Khrushchev's day, that because of their greater patience and because of our greed for business deals, that they would sooner or later get the better of us. Is it possible that, despite some setbacks in the Middle East, they've proved their point? Our allies in France and Italy are now flirting with communism; we've recognized a permanent Communist regime in East Germany; we virtually signed, in Helsinki, an agreement that the Russians have dominance in Eastern Europe; we bailed out Soviet agriculture with our huge grain sales, we've given them large loans, access to our best technology, and if the Senate hadn't interfered with the Jackson Amendment, maybe you would have given them even larger loans. Is that what you call a two-way street of traffic in Europe?

The President. I believe that we have negotiated with the Soviet Union since I've been President from a position of strength. And let me cite several examples.

Shortly after I became President, in December of 1974, I met with General Secretary Brezhnev in Valdivostok. And we agreed to a mutual cap on the ballistic missile launchers at a ceiling of 2,400, which means that the Soviet Union, if that becomes a permanent agreement, will have to make a reduction in their launchers that they now have or plan to have. I negotiated at Vladivostok with Mr. Brezhnev a limitation on the MIRVing of their ballistic missles at a figure of 1,320, which is the first time that any President has achieved a cap either on launchers or on MIRV's.

It seems to me that we can go from there to the grain sales. The grain sales have been a benefit to American agriculture. We have achieved a 5¾-year sale of a minimum of 6 million metric tons, which means that they have already bought about 4 million metric tons this year and are bound to buy another 2 million metric tons, to take the grain and corn and wheat that the American farmers have produced in order to have full production. And these grain sales to the Soviet Union have helped us tremendously in meeting the cost of the additional oil and the oil that we have bought from overseas.

If we turn to Helsinki—I am glad you raised it, Mr. Frankel—in the case of Helsinki, 35 nations signed an agreement, including the Secretary of State for the Vatican. I can't under any circumstances believe that His Holiness the Pope would agree, by signing that agreement, that the 35 nations have turned over to the Warsaw Pact nations the domination of Eastern Europe. It just isn't true. And if Mr. Carter alleges that His Holiness, by signing that, has done it, he is totally inaccurate.

Now, what has been accomplished by the Helsinki agreement? Number one, we have an agreement where they notify us and we notify them of any military maneuvers that are to be undertaken. They have done it in both cases where they've done so. There is no Soviet domination of Eastern Europe, and there never will be under a Ford administration.

Mr. Frankel. I'm sorry, could I just follow—did I understand you to say, sir, that the Russians are not using Eastern Europe as their own sphere of influence and occupying most of the countries there and making sure with their troops that it's a Communist zone, whereas on our side of the line the Italians and the French are still flirting with the possibility of communism?

The President. I don't believe, Mr. Frankel, that the Yugoslavians consider themselves dominated by the Soviet Union. I don't believe that the Romanians consider themselves dominated by the Soviet Union. I don't believe that the Poles consider themselves dominated by the Soviet Union. Each of those countries is independent, autonomous; it has its own territorial integrity. And the United States does not concede that those countries are under the domination of the Soviet Union. As a matter of fact, I visited Poland, Yugoslavia, and Romania, to make certain that the people of those countries understood that the President of the United States and the people of the United States are dedicated to their independence, their autonomy, and their freedom.

The Moderator. Governor Carter, have you a response?

Mr. Carter. Well, in the first place, I am not criticizing His Holiness the Pope. I was talking about Mr. Ford.

The fact is that secrecy has surrounded the decisions made by the Ford administration. In the case of the Helsinki agreement, it may have been a good agreement at the beginning, but we have failed to enforce the so-called Basket 3 part, which ensures the right of people to migrate, to join their families, to be free to speak out. The Soviet Union is still jamming Radio Free Europe. Radio Free Europe is being jammed.

We've also seen a very serious problem with the so-called Sonnenfeldt document which, apparently, Mr. Ford has just endorsed, which said that there is an organic linkage between the Eastern European countries and the Soviet Union. And I would like to see Mr. Ford convince the Polish Americans and the Czech Americans and the Hungarian Americans in this county that those countries don't live under the domination and supervision of the Soviet Union behind the Iron Curtain.

We also have seen Mr. Ford exclude himself from access to the public. He hasn't had a tough, cross-examination-type press conference in over 30 days. One press conference he had without sound.

He's also shown a weakness in yielding to pressure. The Soviet Union, for instance, put pressure on Mr. Ford, and he refused to see a symbol of human freedom recognized around the world—Alexander Solzhenitsyn.

The Arabs have put pressure on Mr. Ford—and he's yielded and he has permitted a boycott by the Arab countries of American businesses who trade with Israel, who have American Jews owning or taking part in the management of American companies. His own Secretary of Commerce had to be subpoenaed by the Congress to reveal the names of businesses who were subject to this boycott. They didn't volunteer the information; he had to be subpoenaed.

And the last thing I'd like to say is this: This grain deal with the Soviet Union in '72 was terrible, and Mr. Ford made up for it with three embargoes—one against our own ally in Japan. That's not the way to run our foreign policy, including international trade.

• • •

Mr. Trewhitt. Governor Carter, before this event the most communication I received concerned Panama. Would you, as President, be prepared to sign a treaty which at a fixed date yielded administrative and economic control of the Canal Zone and shared defense which, as I understand it, is the position the United States took in 1974?

Mr. Carter. Well, here again, the Panamanian question is one that has been confused by Mr. Ford. He had directed his diplomtic representative to yield to the Panamanians full sovereignty over the Panama Canal Zone at the end of a certain period of time. When Mr. Reagan raised this question in Florida, Mr. Ford not only disavowed his instructions but he also even dropped, parenthetically, the use of the word "détente."

I would never give up complete control or practical control of the Panama Canal Zone, but I would continue to negotiate with the Panamanians. When the original treaty was signed back in the early 1900's, when Theodore Roosevelt was President, Panama retained sovereignty over the Panama Canal Zone. We retained control as though we had sovereignty.

Now, I would be willing to go ahead with negotiations. I believe that we could share more fully responsibilities for the Panama Canal Zone with Panama. I would be willing to continue to raise the payment for shipment of goods through the Panama Canal Zone. I might even be willing to reduce to some degree our military emplacements in the Panama Canal Zone, but I would not relinquish practical control of the Panama Canal Zone any time in the foreseeable future.

The Moderator. President Ford.

The President. The United States must and will maintain complete access to the Panama Canal. The United States must maintain a defense capability of the Panama Canal, and the United States will maintain our national security interests in the Panama Canal.

The negotiations for the Panama Canal started under President Johnson and have continued up to the present time. I believe those negotiations should continue. But there are certain guidelines that must be followed, and I've just defined them.

• • •

Jimmy Carter
(1977–1981)

Jimmy Carter literally came out of nowhere to become the 39th President of the United States. As a one-term Governor of Georgia, he had attracted national attention when he hung a portrait of Dr. Martin Luther King, Jr. in the State capitol. But that was only momentary. At the beginning of the 1976 Presidential primaries he was Jimmy who? Yet, he turned his lack of national recognition into an asset by campaigning against Washington. And he caught hold of the national mood, of a country yearning for decency, honesty, and compassion. "I will never lie to you," he repeated throughout his campaign. In November, 1976 Jimmy Carter, former Governor and peanut farmer, was elected President.

Carter's administration can be divided into three periods: (1) a progressive "honeymoon" period from his inauguration to the end of 1977; (2) a period from 1978–November 1979 marked by indecision, reversals and decline; and (3) a re-emergence as he began to run for renomination.

He moved quickly to stamp his personal imprint upon the Presidency. The day after his inauguration, he issued a pardon for draft evaders and resisters from the Vietnam War. Soon thereafter he called for a new cabinet-level Department of Energy and a comprehensive energy program. He introduced zero-based budgeting. He demanded welfare reform, social security and labor law reform. He developed a plan for reorganizing the executive branch of government. All these as well as a number of other important bills were sent to Congress within the first 6 months after he took office. But he did so without stressing priorities, with the possible exception of his energy bill. His task became more complicated because his staff was unfamiliar with Washington, an asset in the campaign but a serious defect in running the government. They often alienated people in Congress rather than persuading them.

The Bert Lance affair symbolized the change from good feelings to antagonism, from promise to decline. Lance, Director of the Office of Management and Budget, was accused of mishandling certain transactions at the bank he managed before joining the White House. Though Carter stood behind him, Lance was forced to resign, a resignation that tarnished the administration. The inevitable decline in popularity that accompanies any Presidency soon set in.[1] Through 1978 and much of 1979, energy costs rose dramatically. Inflation began to climb reaching an annual rate of 13.5% in 1979. Though Carter scored occasional triumphs, such as the 1978 Camp David Summit, people began to lose confidence in his leadership.

By the summer of 1979 polls showed that Democrats preferred Senator Edward Kennedy as the Presidential candidate for the next election. Upon Carter's return from the Economic Summit meeting held in Tokyo in June, Carter was greeted with a somber memorandum from Stuart Eizenstat, his chief domestic advisor, warning him of the political dangers he faced, particularly in regard to the energy crisis. Carter retreated to Camp David for a series of discussions with national leaders about how best to attack the problem. He returned from Camp David to address the American people in one of his best speeches on July 15, 1979 calling once again for enactment of a comprehensive energy program. It caused a small improvement in his standing among Americans, but only momentarily.

Then, on November 4, militant Iranian students seized the American Embassy in Tehran and began holding Americans hostages. This was followed by a Soviet invasion of Afghanistan in December. These two events caused the American people to "rally around" their President. Furthermore, Carter, particularly in his 1980 State of the Union Address, took a turn to the right on foreign affairs, assuming a much harder stance against the Soviet Union than he had previously shown. This new stance was never more vividly demonstrated than on April 24. After months of patient diplomacy in attempting to get our hostages away from the students in the Embassy, Carter approved a dare-devil plan to have commandos rescue them. The plan ended in disaster, a failure equal in magnitude to Kennedy's Bay of Pigs. Within days, his Secretary of State, Cyrus Vance, resigned in protest and criticism of his leadership mounted.

Why this roller-coaster ride in Carter's Presidency? I believe there are two reasons, one political, one rhetorical. Neither the politicians in Washington nor the nation at large was prepared for a Southern liberal to assume the Presidency. Since the days of Franklin Roosevelt Democratic liberalism had found its sustenance in the belief in a strong and growing centralized federal government. It had its roots in the large, northern urban areas of the country and took from them its values. Deficit spending practically became an article of faith among northern liberals. In foreign policy pragmatism replaced moralism (except for the moralism of anti-communism).[2]

Carter comes from a different liberal tradition, one not heard in Washington since Woodrow Wilson left the White House in 1921. His values come, as did Jefferson's, from the small towns and farms of the South. His early insistence on human rights as the cornerstone of American foreign policy—made specific and more than irritating to the Russians in his letter to Sakharov—shocked jaded northern liberals as much as sophisticated conservatives.[3] Then, in a press conference on the eve of Secretary Vance's trip to Moscow to begin negotiating the Vladivostok agreements, Carter announced for all the world to hear our negotiating position as well as our "fall back" position. He appeared to have taken Wilson's call for "open covenants, openly made" literally. These and a number of other positions taken over the next 3 years confounded his supporters and adversaries alike. They were unprepared politically and historically for this revival of this long-forgotten tradition.

Carter compounded this confusion because he has been a rhetorical failure. And there are several reasons for this. Carter prefers press conferences (by February, 1980, he had held 54), town meetings, phone-ins to the White House to oratory. These allow him to respond to people one-on-one. Each question is separate, often unrelated to what has been asked or gone before. In these formats Carter is often very effective. But such encounters only explain policies, they do not usually contribute to a larger vision of how they fit together for the future. James Fallows, his chief speech-writer for 3 years, commented: "He holds explicit, thorough positions on every issue under the sun, but he has no large view of the relations between them, no line indicating which goals . . . will take precedence over which . . . ? Spelling out these choices makes the difference between a position and a philosophy, but it is an act foreign to Carter's mind."[4] Instead of ideas, Carter thinks in lists.[5]

Furthermore, Fallows has said the Carter "didn't think it important to give effective speeches."[6] He seems to have no sense of the importance of leading the country through careful and articulate expressions of our national goals. Jody Powell admitted as much when the administration was totally surprised by the reactions to Carter's letter to Sakharov: "It might be the best example of how we had not fully appreciated the significance of public statements by the President on international affairs."[7] Judging from other rhetorical efforts since then, neither President Carter nor his advisors has yet learned. Whether they will learn in the future that rhetoric is not only a source of inspiration but also a source of power remains to be seen. But now in April, 1980 one has to conclude that one reason for President Carter's various problems as President has been his failure in rhetoric.

Notes

1. Cf. John E. Mueller, "Presidential Popularity from Truman to Johnson," *American Political Science Review* (March, 1970).
2. Much of this tradition of liberalism was confiscated by Richard Nixon as Garry Wills pointed out in his chapter "Nixon Agonistes: The Last Liberal?" in *Nixon Agonistes. The Crisis of the Self-Made Man* (Boston: Houghton Mifflin Company, 1970), pp. 589–602.
3. Carter's early insistence on human rights had positive international repercussions for the United States. After almost a decade of being on the defensive because of our war in Vietnam and Cambodia, we moved to the offensive and placed the Soviet Union on the defensive. Secretary Brezhnev appeared to realize this and wasted no time in replying to Carter's human rights offensive in a speech on March 21.
4. James Fallows, "The Passionless Presidency," *Atlantic* (May, 1979), p. 42.
5. *Ibid.*
6. Fallows in an interview with Mark Schreiber, "News Talk," KQV radio, Pittsburgh, Pennsylvania, July 24, 1979.
7. Quoted in Robert Shogan, *Promises to Keep* (New York: Thomas Y. Crowell, 1977), p. 220.

The Energy Problem: I

Washington, D.C.
April 18, 1977

The day after his inauguration, President Carter issued a statement on the urgent need for initiatives to deal with the energy crisis. He said: "Today's crisis is a painful reminder that our energy problems are real and cannot be ignored. This Nation needs a coherent energy policy and such a program of energy action will be formulated promptly." Soon thereafter, the Federal Energy Agency sponsored a number of citizens' meetings, federal and state governments conducted miniconferences on energy, and the White House mailed letters to 450,000 people asking for their views.

During the week of April 18 the President began a media blitz—all on prime time—with a three pronged rhetorical attack on this problem. On the 18th he addressed the American people attempting to convince them that the problem was quite real and that they would have to conserve energy in the future. The President appeared on television dressed casually in a sweater and before a fireplace to symbolize this need to conserve. On the 20th he spoke to a joint session of Congress to detail his legislative proposals. And on the 22nd he held a televised press conference to answer any questions that could not be handled in formal speeches. Though these constituted a virtuoso performance, the President would have to wait for 3 years before any substantive measures would be passed.

Tonight I want to have an unpleasant talk with you about a problem that is unprecedented in our history. With the exception of preventing war, this is the greatest challenge that our country will face during our lifetime.

The energy crisis has not yet overwhelmed us, but it will if we do not act quickly. It's a problem that we will not be able to solve in the next few years, and it's likely to get progressively worse through the rest of this century.

We must not be selfish or timid if we hope to have a decent world for our children and our grandchildren. We simply must balance our demand for energy with our rapidly shrinking resources. By acting now we can control our future instead of letting the future control us.

Two days from now, I will present to the Congress my energy proposals. Its Members will be my partners, and they have already given me a great deal of valuable advice.

Many of these proposals will be unpopular. Some will cause you to put up with inconveniences and to make sacrifices. The most important thing about these proposals is that the alternative may be a national catastrophe. Further delay can affect our strength and our power as a Nation.

Our decision about energy will test the character of the American people and the ability of the President and the Congress to govern this Nation. This difficult effort will be the moral equivalent of war, except that we will be uniting our efforts to build and not to destroy.

Now, I know that some of you may doubt that we face real energy shortages. The 1973 gas lines are gone and with this springtime weather, our homes are warm again. But our energy problem is worse tonight than it was in 1973 or a few weeks ago in the dead of winter. It's worse because more waste has occurred and more time has passed by without our planning for the future. And it will get worse every day until we act.

The oil and natural gas that we rely on for 75 percent of our energy are simply running out. In spite of increased effort, domestic production has been dropping steadily at about 6 percent a year. Imports have doubled in the last 5 years. Our Nation's economic and political independence is becoming increasingly vulnerable. Unless profound changes are made to lower oil consumption, we now believe that early in the 1980's the world will be demanding more oil than it can produce.

The world now uses about 60 million barrels of oil a day, and demand increases each year about 5 percent. This means that just to stay even we need the production of a new Texas every year, an Alaskan North Slope every 9 months, or a new Saudi Arabia every 3 years. Obviously, this cannot continue.

We must look back into history to understand our energy problem. Twice in the last several hundred years, there has been a transition in the way people use energy.

The first was about 200 years ago, when we changed away from wood—which had provided about 90 percent of all fuel—to coal, which was much more efficient. This change became the basis of the Industrial Revolution.

The second change took place in this century, with the growing use of oil and natural gas. They were more convenient and cheaper than coal, and the supply seemed to be almost without limit. They made possible the age of automobile and airplane travel. Nearly everyone who is alive today grew up during this period, and we have never known anything different.

Because we are now running out of gas and oil, we must prepare quickly for a third change—to strict conservation and to the renewed use of coal and to permanent renewable energy sources like solar power.

The world has not prepared for the future. During the 1950's, people used twice as much oil as during the 1940's. During the 1960's, we used twice as much as during the 1950's. And in each of those decades, more oil was consumed than in all of man's previous history combined.

World consumption of oil is still going up. If it were possible to keep it rising during the 1970's and 1980's by 5 percent a year as it has in the past, we could use up all the proven reserves of oil in the entire world by the end of the next decade.

I know that many of you have suspected that some supplies of oil and gas are being withheld from the market. You may be right, but suspicions about the oil companies cannot change the fact that we are running out of petroleum.

All of us have heard about the large oil fields on Alaska's North Slope. In a few years, when the North Slope is producing fully, its total output will be just about equal to 2 years' increase in our own Nation's energy demand.

Each new inventory of world oil reserves has been more disturbing than the last. World oil production can probably keep going up for another 6 or 8 years. But sometime in the 1980's, it can't go up any more. Demand will overtake production. We have no choice about that.

But we do have a choice about how we will spend the next few years. Each American uses the energy equivalent of 60 barrels of oil per person each year. Ours is the most wasteful nation on earth. We waste more energy than we import. With about the same standard of living, we use twice as much energy per person as do other countries like Germany, Japan, and Sweden.

One choice, of course, is to continue doing what we've been doing before. We can drift along for a few more years.

Our consumption of oil would keep going up every year. Our cars would continue to be too large and inefficient. Three-quarters of them would carry only one person—the driver—while our public transportation system continues to decline. We can delay insulating our homes, and they will continue to lose about 50 percent of their heat in waste. We can continue using scarce oil and natural gas to generate electricity and continue wasting two-thirds of their fuel value in the process.

If we do not act, then by 1985 we will be using 33 percent more energy than we use today.

We can't substantially increase our domestic production, so we would need to import twice as much oil as we do now. Supplies will be uncertain. The cost will keep going up. Six years ago, we paid $3.7 billion for imported oil. Last year we spent $36 billion for imported oil—nearly 10 times as much—and this year we may spend $45 billion.

Unless we act, we will spend more than $550 billion for imported oil by 1985—more than $2,500 for every man, woman, and child in America. Along with the money that we transport overseas, we will continue losing American jobs and become increasingly vulnerable to supply interruptions.

Now we have a choice. But if we wait, we will constantly live in fear of embargoes. We could endanger our freedom as a sovereign nation to act in foreign affairs. Within 10 years, we would not be able to import enough oil from any country, at any acceptable price.

If we wait and do not act, then our factories will not be able to keep our people on the job with reduced supplies of fuel.

Too few of our utility companies will have switched to coal, which is our most abundant energy source. We will not be ready to keep our transportation system running with smaller and more efficient cars and a better network of buses, trains, and public transportation.

We will feel mounting pressure to plunder the environment. We will have to have a crash program to build more nuclear plants, strip mine and burn more coal, and drill more offshore wells than if we begin to conserve right now.

Inflation will soar; production will go down; people will lose their jobs. Intense competition for oil will build up among nations and also among the different regions within our own country. This has already started.

If we fail to act soon, we will face an economic, social, and political crisis that will threaten our free institutions. But we still have another choice. We can begin to prepare right now. We can decide to act while there is still time. That is the concept of the energy policy that we will present on Wednesday.

Our national energy plan is based on 10 fundamental principles. The first principle is that we can have an effective and comprehensive energy policy only if the Government takes responsibility for it and if the people understand the seriousness of the challenge and are willing to make sacrifices.

The second principle is that healthy economic growth must continue. Only by saving energy can we maintain our standard of living and keep our people at work. An effective conservation program will create hundreds of thousands of new jobs.

The third principle is that we must protect the environment. Our energy problems have the same cause as our environmental problems—wasteful use of resources. Conservation helps us solve both problems at once.

The fourth principle is that we must reduce our vulnerability to potentially devastating embargoes. We can protect ourselves from uncertain supplies by reducing our demand for oil, by making the most of our abundant resources such as coal, and by developing a strategic petroleum reserve.

The fifth principle is that we must be fair. Our solutions must ask equal sacrifices from every region, every class of people, and every interest group. Industry will have to do its part to conserve just as consumers will. The energy producers deserve fair treatment, but we will not let the oil companies profiteer.

The sixth principle, and the cornerstone of our policy, is to reduce demand through conservation. Our emphasis on conservation is a clear difference between this plan and others which merely encouraged crash production efforts. Conservation is the quickest, cheapest, most practical source of energy. Conservation is the only way that we can buy a barrel of oil for about $2. It costs about $13 to waste it.

The seventh principle is that prices should generally reflect the true replacement cost of energy. We are only cheating ourselves if we make energy artificially cheap and use more than we can really afford.

The eighth principle is that Government policies must be predictable and certain. Both consumers and producers need policies they can count on so they can plan ahead. This is one reason that I'm working with the Congress to create a new Department of Energy to replace more than 50 different agencies that now have some control over energy.

The ninth principle is that we must conserve the fuels that are scarcest and make the most of those that are plentiful. We can't continue to use oil and gas for 75 percent of our consumption, as we do now, when they only make up 7 percent of our domestic reserves. We need to shift to plentiful coal, while taking care to protect the environment, and to apply stricter safety standards to nuclear energy.

The tenth and last principle is that we must start now to develop the new, unconventional sources of energy that we will rely on in the next century.

Now, these 10 principles have guided the development of the policy that I will describe to you and the Congress on Wednesday night.

Our energy plan will also include a number of specific goals to measure our progress toward a stable energy system. These are the goals that we set for 1985:

—to reduce the annual growth rate in our energy demand to less than 2 percent;

—to reduce gasoline consumption by 10 percent below its current level;

—to cut in half the portion of U.S. oil which is imported—from a potential level of 16 million barrels to 6 million barrels a day;

—to establish a strategic petroleum reserve of one billion barrels, more than a 6-month supply;

—to increase our coal production by about two-thirds to more than one billion tons a year;

—to insulate 90 percent of American homes and all new buildings;

—to use solar energy in more than 2½ million houses.

We will monitor our progress toward these goals year-by-year. Our plan will call for strict conservation measures if we fall behind. I can't tell you that these measures will be easy, nor will they be popular. But I think most of you realize that a policy which does not ask for changes or sacrifices would not be an effective policy at this late date.

This plan is essential to protect our jobs, our environment, our standard of living, and our future. Whether this plan truly makes a difference will not be decided now here in Washington but in every town and every factory, in every home and on every highway and every farm.

I believe that this can be a positive challenge. There is something especially American in the kinds of changes that we have to make. We've always been proud, through our history, of being efficient people. We've always been proud of our ingenuity, our skill at answering questions. Now we need efficiency and ingenuity more than ever.

We've always been proud of our leadership in the world. And now we have a chance again to give the world a positive example.

We've always been proud of our vision of the future. We've always wanted to give our children and our grandchildren a world richer in possibilities than we have had ourselves. They are the ones that we must provide for now. They are the ones who will suffer most if we don't act.

I've given you some of the principles of the plan. I'm sure that each of you will find something you don't like about the specifics of our proposal. It will demand that we make sacrifices and changes in every life. To some degree, the sacrifices will be painful—but so is any meaningful sacrifice. It will lead to some higher costs and to some greater inconvenience for everyone. But the sacrifices can be gradual, realistic, and they are necessary. Above all, they will be fair. No one will gain an unfair advantage through this plan. No one will be asked to bear an unfair burden.

We will monitor the accuracy of data from the oil and natural gas companies for the first time, so that we will always know their true production, supplies, reserves, and profits. Those citizens who insist on driving large, unnecessarily powerful cars must expect to pay more for that luxury.

We can be sure that all the special interest groups in the country will attack the part of this plan that affects them directly. They will say that sacrifice is fine as long as other people do it, but that their sacrifice is unreasonable or unfair or harmful to the country. If they succeed with this approach, then the burden on the ordinary citizen, who is not organized into an interest group, would be crushing.

There should be only one test for this program—whether it will help our country. Other generations of Americans have faced and mastered great challenges. I have faith that meeting this challenge will make our own lives even richer. If you will join me so that we can work together with patriotism and courage, we will again prove that our great Nation can lead the world into an age of peace, independence, and freedom.

Thank you very much, and good night.

Toward a New Foreign Policy

Commencement Address at the University of Notre Dame
South Bend, Indiana
May 22, 1977

President Carter took the occasion of commencement exercises at Notre Dame to outline 5 goals he would strive to achieve in his foreign policy. As he had during the campaign and again in his letter to Sakharov, Carter made human rights the center-piece for this new foreign policy. In many ways the speech reminds one of Kennedy's speech at American University in 1963. Yet, Carter's address is curiously unaffecting. Perhaps, that is due not so much to content as style. Unlike the Kennedy speech, Carter's contains simple, rather than felicitous, phrasing. It is bland rather than inspiring. Nonetheless, it is clear that these were to be the goals of the Carter administration, and that he expected to be judged by his achievements in these areas.

Thank you for that welcome. I'm very glad to be with you. You may have started a new graduation trend which I don't deplore; that is, throwing peanuts on graduation day. The more that are used or consumed, the higher the price goes.

I really did appreciate the great honor bestowed upon me this afternoon. My other degree is blue and gold from the Navy, and I want to let you know that I do feel a kinship with those who are assembled here this afternoon. I was a little taken aback by the comment that I had brought a new accent to the White House. In the minds of many people in our country, for the first time in almost 150 years, there is no accent.

I tried to think of a story that would illustrate two points simultaneously and also be brief, which is kind of a difficult assignment. I was sitting on the Truman Balcony the other night with my good friend, Charles Kirbo, who told me about a man who was arrested and taken in to court for being drunk and for setting a bed on fire. When the judge asked him how he plead, he said, "not guilty." He said, "I was drunk but the bed was on fire when I got in it."

I think most of the graduates can draw the parallel between that statement and what you are approaching after this graduation exercise. But there are two points to that, and I'll come to the other one in just a few minutes.

In his 25 years as president of Notre Dame, Father Hesburgh has spoken more consistently and more effectively in the support of the rights of human beings than any other person I know. His interest in the Notre Dame Center for Civil Rights has never wavered. And he played an important role in broadening the scope of the center's work—and I visited there last fall—to see this work include, now, all people in the world, as shown by last month's conference here on human rights and American foreign policy.

And that concern has been demonstrated again today in a vivid fashion by the selection of Bishop Donal Lamont, Paul Cardinal Arns, and Stephen Cardinal Kim, to receive honorary degrees. In their fight for human freedoms in Rhodesia, Brazil, and South Korea, these three religious leaders typify all that is best in their countries and in our church. I'm honored to join you in recognizing their dedication, their personal sacrifice, and their supreme courage.

Quite often, brave men like these are castigated and sometimes punished, sometimes even put to death, because they enter the realm where human rights is a struggle. And sometimes, they are blamed for the very circumstance which they helped to dramatize, but it's been there for a long time. And the flames which they seek to extinguish concern us all and are increasingly visible around the world.

Last week, I spoke in California about the domestic agenda for our Nation: to provide more efficiently for the needs of our people, to demonstrate—against the dark faith of our times—that our Government can be both competent and more humane.

But I want to speak to you today about the strands that connect our actions overseas with our essential character as a nation. I believe we can have a foreign policy that is democratic, that is based on fundamental values, and that uses power and influence, which we have, for humane purposes. We can also have a foreign policy that the American people both support and, for a change, know about and understand.

I have a quiet confidence in our own political system. Because we know that democracy works, we can reject the arguments of those rulers who deny human rights to their people.

We are confident that democracy's example will be compelling, and so we seek to bring that example closer to those from whom in the past few years we have been separated and who are not yet convinced about the advantages of our kind of life.

We are confident that democratic methods are the most effective, and so we are not tempted to employ improper tactics here at home or abroad.

We are confident of our own strength, so we can seek substantial mutual reductions in the nuclear arms race.

And we are confident of the good sense of American people, and so we let them share in the process of making foreign policy decisions. We can thus speak with the voices of 215 million, and not just of an isolated handful.

Democracy's great recent successes—in India, Portugal, Spain, Greece—show that our confidence in this system is not misplaced. Being confident of our own future, we are now free of that inordinate fear of communism which once led us to embrace any dictator who joined us in that fear. I'm glad that that's being changed.

For too many years, we've been willing to adopt the flawed and erroneous principles and tactics of our adversaries, sometimes abandoning our own values for theirs. We've fought fire with fire, never thinking that fire is better quenched with water. This approach failed, with Vietnam the best example of its intellectual and moral poverty. But through failure, we have now found our way back to our own principles and values, and we have regained our lost confidence.

By the measure of history, our Nation's 200 years are very brief, and our rise to world eminence is briefer still. It dates from 1945 when Europe and the old international order lay in ruins. Before then America was largely on the periphery of world affairs, but since then we have inescapably been at the center of world affairs.

Our policy during this period was guided by two principles: a belief that Soviet expansion was almost inevitable but that it must be contained, and the corresponding belief in the importance of an almost exclusive alliance among non-Communist nations on both sides of the Atlantic. That system could not last forever unchanged. Historical trends have weakened its foundation. The unifying threat of conflict with the Soviet Union has become less intensive even though the competition has become more extensive.

The Vietnamese war produced a profound moral crisis sapping worldwide faith in our own policy and our system of life, a crisis of confidence made even more grave by the covert pessimism of some of our leaders.

In less than a generation, we've seen the world change dramatically. The daily lives and aspirations of most human beings have been transformed. Colonialism is nearly gone. A new sense of national identity now exists in almost 100 new countries that have been formed in the last generation. Knowledge has become more widespread; aspirations are higher. As more people have been freed from traditional constraints, more have been determined to achieve for the first time in their lives social justice.

The world is still divided by ideological disputes, dominated by regional conflicts, and threatened by danger that we will not resolve the differences of race and wealth without violence or without drawing into combat the major military powers. We can no longer separate the traditional issues of war and peace from the new global questions of justice, equity, and human rights.

It is a new world—but America should not fear it. It is a new world—and we should help to shape it. It is a new world that calls for a new American foreign policy—a policy based on constant decency in its values and on optimism in our historical vision.

We can no longer have a policy solely for the industrial nations as the foundation of global stability, but we must respond to the new reality of a politically awakening world.

We can no longer expect that the other 150 nations will follow the dictates of the powerful, but we must continue—confidently—our efforts to inspire, to persuade, and to lead.

Our policy must reflect our belief that the world can hope for more than simple survival and our belief that dignity and freedom are fundamental spiritual requirements. Our policy must shape an international system that will last longer than secret deals.

We cannot make this kind of policy by manipulation. Our policy must be open; it must be candid; it must be one of constructive global involvement, resting on five cardinal principles.

I've tried to make these premises clear to the American people since last January. Let me review what we have been doing and discuss what we intend to do.

First, we have reaffirmed America's commitment to human rights as a fundamental tenet of our foreign policy. In ancestry, religion, color, place of origin, and cultural background, we Americans are as diverse a nation as the world has even seen. No common mystique of blood or soil unites us. What draws us together, perhaps more than anything else, is a belief in human freedom.

We want the world to know that our Nation stands for more than financial prosperity. This does not mean that we can conduct our foreign policy by rigid moral maxims. We live in a world that is imperfect and which will always be imperfect—a world that is complex and confused and which will always be complex and confused.

I understand fully the limits of moral suasion. We have no illusion that changes will come easily or soon. But I also believe that it is a mistake to undervalue the power of words and of the ideas that words embody. In our own history, that power has ranged from Thomas Paine's "Common Sense" to Martin Luther King, Jr.'s "I have a Dream."

In the life of the human spirit, words are action, much more so than many of us may realize who live in countries where freedom of expression is taken for granted. The leaders of totalitarian nations understand this very well. The proof is that words are precisely the action for which dissidents in those countries are being persecuted.

Nonetheless, we can already see dramatic, worldwide advances in the protection of the individual from the arbitrary power of the state. For us to ignore this trend would be to lose influence and moral authority in the world. To lead it will be to regain the moral stature that we once had.

The great democracies are not free because we are strong and prosperous. I believe we are strong and influential and prosperous because we are free.

Throughout the world today, in free nations and in totalitarian countries as well, there is a preoccupation with the subject of human freedom, human rights. And I believe it is incumbent on us in this country to keep that discussion, that debate, that contention alive. No other country is as well-qualified as we to set an example. We have our own shortcomings and faults, and we should strive constantly and with courage to make sure that we are legitimately proud of what we have.

Second, we've moved deliberately to reinforce the bonds among our democracies. In our recent meetings in London, we agreed to widen our economic cooperation, to promote free trade, to strengthen the world's monetary system, to seek ways of avoiding nuclear proliferation. We prepared constructive proposals for the forthcoming meetings on North-South problems of poverty, development, and global well-being, and we agreed on joint efforts to reinforce and to modernize our common defense.

You may be interested in knowing that at this NATO meeting, for the first time in more than 25 years, all members are democracies. Even more important, all of us reaffirmed our basic optimism in the future of the democratic system. Our spirit of confidence is spreading. Together, our democracies can help to shape the wider architecture of global cooperation.

Third, we've moved to engage the Soviet Union in a joint effort to halt the strategic arms race. This race is not only dangerous, it's morally deplorable. We must put an end to it.

I know it will not be easy to reach agreements. Our goal is to be fair to both sides, to produce reciprocal stability, parity, and security. We desire a freeze on further modernization and production of weapons and a continuing, substantial reduction of strategic nuclear weapons as well. We want a comprehensive ban on all nuclear testing, a prohibition against all chemical warfare, no attack capability against space satellites, and arms limitations in the Indian Ocean.

We hope that we can take joint steps with all nations toward a final agreement eliminating nuclear weapons completely from our arsenals of death. We will persist in this effort.

Now, I believe in détente with the Soviet Union. To me, it means progress toward peace. But the effects of détente should not be limited to our own two countries alone. We hope to persuade the Soviet Union that one country cannot impose its system of society upon another, either through direct military intervention or through the use of a client state's military force, as was the case with Cuban intervention in Angola.

Cooperation also implies obligation. We hope that the Soviet Union will join with us and other nations in playing a larger role in aiding the developing world, for common aid efforts will help us build a bridge of mutual confidence in one another.

Fourth, we are taking deliberate steps to improve the chances of lasting peace in the Middle East. Through wide-ranging consultation with leaders of the countries involved—Israel, Syria, Jordan, and Egypt—we have found some areas of agreement and some movement toward consensus. The negotiations must continue.

Through my own public comments, I've also tried to suggest a more flexible framework for the discussion of the three key issues which have so far been so intractable: the nature of a comprehensive peace—What is peace? What does it mean to the Israelis? What does it mean to their Arab neighbors? Secondly, the relationship between security and borders—How can the dispute over border delineations be established and settled with a feeling of security on both sides? And the issue of the Palestinian homeland.

The historic friendship that the United States has with Israel is not dependent on domestic politics in either nation; it's derived from our common respect for human freedom and from a common search for permanent peace.

We will continue to promote a settlement which all of us need. Our own policy will not be affected by changes in leadership in any of the countries in the Middle East. Therefore, we expect Israel and her neighbors to continue to be bound by United Nations Resolutions 242 and 338, which they have previously accepted.

This may be the most propitious time for a genuine settlement since the beginning of the Arab-Israeli conflict almost 30 years ago. To let this opportunity pass could mean disaster not only for the Middle East but, perhaps, for the international political and economic order as well.

And fifth, we are attempting, even at the risk of some friction with our friends, to reduce the danger of nuclear proliferation and the world-wide spread of conventional weapons.

At the recent summit, we set in motion an international effort to determine the best ways of harnessing nuclear energy for peaceful use while reducing the risks that its products will be diverted to the making of explosives.

We've already completed a comprehensive review of our own policy on arms transfers. Competition in arms sales is inimical to peace and destructive of the economic development of the poorer countries.

We will, as a matter of national policy now in our country, seek to reduce the annual dollar volume of arms sales, to restrict the transfer of advanced weapons, and to reduce the extent of our coproduction arrangements about weapons with foreign states. And, just as important, we are trying to get other nations, both free and otherwise, to join us in this effort.

But all of this that I've described is just the beginning. It's a beginning aimed towards a clear goal: to create a wider framework of international cooperation suited to the new and rapidly changing historical circumstances.

We will cooperate more closely with the newly influential countries in Latin America, Africa, and Asia. We need their friendship and cooperation in a common effort as the structure of world power changes.

More than 100 years ago, Abraham Lincoln said that our Nation could not exist half slave and half free. We know a peaceful world cannot long exist one-third rich and two-thirds hungry.

Most nations share our faith that in the long run, expanded and equitable trade will best help the developing countries to help themselves. But the immediate problems of hunger, disease, illiteracy, and repression are here now.

The Western democracies, the OPEC nations, and the developed Communist countries can cooperate through existing international institutions in providing more effective aid. This is an excellent alternative to war.

We have a special need for cooperation and consultation with other nations in this hemisphere—to the north and to the south. We do not need another slogan. Although these are our close friends and neighbors, our links with them are the same links of equality that we forge for the rest of the world. We will be dealing with them as part of a new, worldwide mosaic of global, regional, and bilateral relations.

It's important that we make progress toward normalizing relations with the People's Republic of China. We see the American and Chinese relationship as a central element of our global policy, and China as a key force for global peace. We wish to cooperate closely with the creative Chinese people on the problems that confront all mankind, and we hope to find a formula which can bridge some of the difficulties that still separate us.

Finally, let be say that we are committed to a peaceful resolution of the crisis in southern Africa. The time has come for the principle of majority rule to be the basis for political order, recognizing that in a democratic system the rights of the minority must also be protected.

To be peaceful, change must come promptly. The United States is determined to work together with our European allies and with the concerned African States to shape a congenial international framework for the rapid and progressive transformation of southern African society and to help protect it from unwarranted outside interference.

Let me conclude by summarizing: Our policy is based on an historical vision of America's role. Our policy is derived from a larger view of global change. Our policy is rooted in our moral values, which never change. Our policy is reinforced by our material wealth and by our military power. Our policy is designed to serve mankind. And it is a policy that I hope will make you proud to be Americans.

Panama Canal Treaties

Televised Address to the Nation
Washington, D.C.
February 1, 1978

In 1903 President Theodore Roosevelt signed a treaty with the "new" Republic of Panama that gave the United States a ten-mile-wide canal zone "in perpetuity," through which the Panama Canal was built. Though minor revisions in the treaty were made over the years, the presence of an American zone became an increasing source of irritation to Panamanians. On January 9, 1964 rioting broke out in the zone, riots that left more than 20 dead. Panama broke off diplomatic relations with the United States until President Johnson ordered a full review of the 1903 treaty. Subsequently, negotiations began and continued for a more equitable settlement of the dispute between the United States and Panama. These lingered on through the Johnson, Nixon and Ford administrations.

In an address before the Permanent Council of the Organization of American States on April 14, 1977, President Carter pledged to develop a new approach to negotiations with Panama which he hoped would result in a new treaty and a new relationship between the two countries. On September 7, General Torrijos and President Carter signed the Panama Canal Treaty and the Treaty Concerning the Permanent Neutrality and Operation of the Panama Canal. The treaties were then sent to the Senate for ratification. Immediately, the White House dispatched pro-treaty spokesmen around the country to drum up support for ratification. They were followed by anti-treaty spokesman, organized principally by Senator Paul Laxalt and labelled a "truth squad."

On the eve of the Senate debates over ratification, President Carter addressed the American people urging ratification. In his speech from the White House library he reviewed the new treaties and gave special attention to specific objections to its ratification, each of which he sought to refute. His central argument though rested on his belief that America should be a generous and humane country, and thus the ratification of the treaties exemplified those traditions.

By a vote of 68–32, or one vote over the minimum needed, the Senate ratified the treaties. It was a victory for the President but at a considerable cost. He had played many of his political "chips" to sway undecided Senators, and he had angered much of his conservative constituency that had helped elect him President.

Seventy-five years ago, our Nation signed a treaty which gave us rights to build a canal across Panama, to take the historic step of joining the Atlantic and Pacific Oceans. The results of the agreement have been of great benefit to ourselves and to other nations throughout the world who navigate the high seas.

The building of the canal was one of the greatest engineering feats of history. Although massive in concept and construction, it's relatively simple in design and has been reliable and efficient in operation. We Americans are justly and deeply proud of this great achievement.

The canal has also been a source of pride and benefit to the people of Panama—but a cause of some continuing discontent. Because we have controlled a 10-mile-wide strip of land across the heart of their country and because they considered the original terms of the agreement to be unfair, the people of Panama have been dissatisfied with the treaty. It was drafted here in our country and was not signed by any Panamanian. Our own Secretary of State who did sign the original treaty said it was "vastly advantageous to the United States and . . . not so advantageous to Panama."

In 1964, after consulting with former Presidents Truman and Eisenhower, President Johnson committed our Nation to work towards a new treaty with the Republic of Panama. And last summer, after 14 years of negotiation under two Democratic Presidents and two Republican Presidents, we reached and signed an agreement that is fair and beneficial to both countries. The United States Senate will soon be debating whether these treaties should be ratified.

Throughout the negotiations, we were determined that our national security interests would be protected; that the canal would always be open and neutral and available to ships of all nations; that in time of need or emergency our warships would have the right to go to the head of the line for priority passage through the canal; and that our military forces would have the permanent right to defend the canal if it should ever be in danger. The new treaties meet all of these requirements.

Let me outline the terms of the agreement. There are two treaties—one covering the rest of this century, and the other guaranteeing the safety, openness, and neutrality of the canal after the year 1999, when Panama will be in charge of its operation.

For the rest of this century, we will operate the canal through a nine-person board of directors. Five members will be from the United States and four will be from Panama. Within the area of the present Canal Zone, we have the right to select whatever lands and waters our military and civilian forces need to maintain, to operate, and to defend the canal.

About 75 percent of those who now maintain and operate the canal are Panamanians; over the next 22 years, as we manage the canal together, this percentage will increase. The Americans who work on the canal will continue to have their rights of employment, promotion, and retirement carefully protected.

We will share with Panama some of the fees paid by shippers who use the canal. As in the past, the canal should continue to be self-supporting.

This is not a partisan issue. The treaties are strongly backed by President Gerald Ford and by Former Secretaries of State Dean Rusk and Henry Kissinger. They are endorsed by our business and professional leaders, especially those who recognize the benefits of good will and trade with other nations in this hemisphere. And they were endorsed overwhelmingly by the Senate Foreign Relations Committee which, this week, moved closer to ratification by approving the treaties, although with some recommended changes which we do not feel are needed.

And the treaties are supported enthusiastically by every member of the Joint Chiefs of Staff—General George Brown, the Chairman, General Bernard Rogers, Chief of Staff of the Army, Admiral James Holloway, Chief of Naval Operations, General David Jones, Chief of Staff of the Air Force, and General Lewis Wilson, Commandant of the Marine Corps—responsible men whose profession is the defense of this Nation and the preservation of our security.

The treaties also have been overwhelmingly supported throughout Latin America, but predictably, they are opposed abroad by some who are unfriendly to the United States and who would like to see disorder in Panama and a disruption of our political, economic, and military ties with our friends in Central and South America and in the Caribbean.

I know that the treaties also have been opposed by many Americans. Much of that opposition is based on misunderstanding and misinformation. I've found that when the full terms of the agreement are known, most people are convinced that the national interests of our country will be served best by ratifying the treaties.

Tonight, I want you to hear the facts. I want to answer the most serious questions and tell you why I feel the Panama Canal treaties should be approved.

The most important reason—the only reason—to ratify the treaties is that they are in the highest national interest of the United States and will strengthen our position in the world. Our security interests will be stronger. Our trade opportunities will be improved. We will demonstrate that as a large and powerful country, we are able to deal fairly and honorably with a proud but smaller sovereign nation. We will honor our commitment to those engaged in world commerce that the Panama Canal will be open and available for use by their ships—at a reasonable and competitive cost—both now and in the future.

Let me answer specifically the most common questions about the treaties.

Will our Nation have the right to protect and defend the canal against any armed attack or threat to the security of the canal or of ships going through it?

The answer is yes, and is contained in both treaties and also in the statement of understanding between the leaders of our two nations.

The first treaty says, and I quote: "The United States of America and the Republic of Panama commit themselves to protect and defend the Panama Canal. Each Party shall act, in accordance with its constitutional processes, to meet the danger resulting from an armed attack or other actions which threaten the security of the Panama Canal or [of] ships transiting it."

The neutrality treaty says, and I quote again: "The United States of America and the Republic of Panama agree to maintain the regime of neutrality established in this Treaty which shall be maintained in order that the Canal shall remain permanently neutral. . . ."

And to explain exactly what that means, the statement of understanding says, and I quote again: "Under (the Neutrality Treaty), Panama and the United States have the responsibility to assure that the Panama Canal will remain open and secure to ships of all nations. The correct interpretation of this principle is that each of the two countries shall, in accordance with their respective constitutional processes, defend the Canal against any threat to the regime of neutrality, and consequently [shall] have the right to act against the Canal or against the peaceful transit of vessels through the Canal."

It is obvious that we can take whatever military action is necessary to make sure that the canal always remains open and safe.

Of course, this does not give the United States any right to intervene in the internal affairs of Panama, nor would our military action ever be directed against the territorial integrity or the political independence of Panama.

Military experts agree that even with the Panamanian Armed Forces joined with us as brothers against a common enemy, it would take a large number of American troops to ward off a heavy attack. I, as President, would not hesitate to deploy whatever armed forces are necessary to defend the canal, and I have no doubt that even in a sustained combat, that we would be successful. But there is a much better way than sending our sons and grandsons to fight in the jungles of Panama.

We would serve our interests better by implementing the new treaties, an action that will help to avoid any attack on the Panama Canal.

What we want is the permanent right to use the canal—and we can defend this right through the treaties—through real cooperation with Panama. The citizens of Panama and their government have already shown their support of the new partnership, and a protocol to the neutrality treaty will be signed by many other nations, thereby showing their strong approval.

The new treaties will naturally change Panama from a passive and sometimes deeply resentful bystander into an active and interested partner, whose vital interests will be served by a well-operated canal. This agreement leads to cooperation and not confrontation between our country and Panama.

Another question is: Why should we give away the Panama Canal Zone? As many people say, "We bought it; we paid for it; it's ours."

I must repeat a very important point: We do not own the Panama Canal Zone. We have never had sovereignty over it. We have only had the right to use it.

The Canal Zone cannot be compared with United States territory. We bought Alaska from the Russians, and no one has ever doubted that we own it. We bought the Louisiana Purchases—Territories from France, and that's an integral part of the United States.

From the beginning, we have made an annual payment to Panama to use their land. You do not pay rent on your own land. The Panama Canal Zone has always been Panamanian territory. The U.S. Supreme Court and previous American Presidents have repeatedly acknowledged the sovereignty of Panama over the Canal Zone.

We've never needed to own the Panama Canal Zone, any more than we need to own a 10-mile-wide strip of land all the way through Canada from Alaska when we build an international gas pipeline.

The new treaties give us what we do need—not ownership of the canal but the right to use it and to protect it. As the Chairman of the Joint Chiefs of Staff has said, "The strategic value of the canal lies in its use."

There's another question: Can our naval ships, our warships, in time of need or emergency, get through the canal immediately instead of waiting in line?

The treaties answer that clearly by guaranteeing that our ships will always have expeditious transit through the canal. To make sure that there could be no possible disagreement about what these words mean, the joint statement says that expeditious transit, and I quote, "is intended . . . to assure the transit of such vessels through the Canal as quickly as possible, without any impediment, with expedited treatment, and in case of need or emergency, to go to the head of the line of vessels in order to transit the Canal rapidly."

Will the treaties affect our standing in Latin America? Will they create a so-called power vacuum, which our enemies might move in to fill? They will do just the opposite. The treaties will increase our Nation's influence in this hemisphere, will help to reduce any mistrust and disagreement, and they will remove a major source of anti-American feeling.

The new agreement has already provided vivid proof to the people of this hemisphere that a new era of friendship and cooperation is beginning and that what they regard as the last remnant of alleged American colonialism is being removed.

Last fall, I met individually with the leaders of 18 countries in this hemisphere. Between the United States and Latin America there is already a new sense of equality, a new sense of trust and mutual respect that exists because of the Panama Canal treaties. This opens up a fine opportunity for us in good will, trade, jobs, exports, and political cooperation.

If the treaties should be rejected, this would all be lost, and disappointment and despair among our good neighbors and traditional friends would be severe.

In the peaceful struggle against alien ideologies like communism, these treaties are a step in the right direction. Nothing could strengthen our competitors and adversaries in this hemisphere more than for us to reject this agreement.

What if a new sea-level canal should be needed in the future? This question has been studied over and over throughout this century, from before the time the canal was built up through the last few years. Every study has reached the same conclusion—that the best place to build a sea-level canal is in Panama.

The treaties say that if we want to build such a canal, we will build it in Panama, and if any canal is to be built in Panama, that we, the United States, will have the right to participate in the project.

This is a clear benefit to us, for it ensures that, say, 10 or 20 years from now, no unfriendly but wealthy power will be able to purchase the right to build a sea-level canal, to bypass the existing canal, perhaps leaving that other nation in control of the only usable waterway across the isthmus.

Are we paying Panama to take the canal? We are not. Under the new treaty, any payments to Panama will come from tolls paid by ships which use the canal.

What about the present and the future stability and the capability of the Panamanian Government? Do the people of Panama themselves support the agreement?

Well, as you know, Panama and her people have been our historical allies and friends. The present leader of Panama has been in office for more than 9 years, and he heads a stable government which has encouraged the development of free enterprise in Panama. Democratic elections will be held this August to choose the members of the Panamanian Assembly, who will in turn elect a President and a Vice President by majority vote. In the past, regimes have changed in Panama, but for 75 years, no Panamanian government has ever wanted to close the canal.

Panama wants the canal open and neutral—perhaps even more than we do. The canal's continued operation is very important to us, but it is much more than that to Panama. To Panama, it's crucial. Much of her economy flows directly or indirectly from the canal. Panama would be no more likely to neglect or to close the canal than we would be to close the Interstate Highway System here in the United States.

In an open and free referendum last October, which was monitored very carefully by the United Nations, the people of Panama gave the new treaties their support.

The major threat to the canal comes not from any government of Panama, but from misguided persons who may try to fan the flames of dissatisfaction with the terms of the old treaty.

There's a final question—about the deeper meaning of the treaties themselves, to us and to Panama.

Recently, I discussed the treaties with David McCullough, author of "The Path Between the Seas," the great history of the Panama Canal. He believes that the canal is something that we built and have looked after these many years; it is "ours" in that sense, which is very different from just ownership.

So, when we talk of the canal, whether we are old, young, for or against the treaties, we are talking about very deep and elemental feelings about our own strength.

Still, we Americans want a more humane and stable world. We believe in good will and fairness, as well as strength. This agreement with Panama is something we want because we know it is right. This is not merely the surest way to protect and save the canal; it's a strong, positive act of a people who are still confident, still creative, still great.

This new partnership can become a source of national pride and self-respect in much the same way that building the canal was 75 years ago. It's the spirit in which we act that is so very important.

Theodore Roosevelt, who was President when America built the canal, saw history itself as a force, and the history of our own time and the changes it has brought would not be lost on him. He knew that change was inevitable and necessary. Change is growth. The true conservative, he once remarked, keeps his face to the future.

But if Theodore Roosevelt were to endorse the treaties, as I'm quite sure he would, it would be mainly because he could see the decision as one by which we are demonstrating the kind of great power we wish to be.

"We cannot avoid meeting great issues," Roosevelt said. "All that we can determine for ourselves is whether we shall meet them well or ill."

The Panama Canal is a vast, heroic expression of that age-old desire to bridge the divide and to bring people closer together. This is what the treaties are all about.

We can sense what Roosevelt called "the lift toward nobler things which marks a great and generous people."

In this historic decision, he would join us in our pride for being a great and generous people, with the national strength and wisdom to do what is right for us and what is fair to others.

"A Framework for Peace in the Middle East"

Address Before a Joint Session of Congress
Washington, D.C.
September 18, 1978

In November, 1977 President Anwar Sadat shocked the world by going to Israel on a mission of peace. Through this dramatic act of personal diplomacy, he sought an end to 3 decades of war and hostility that had existed between Israel and Egypt. Prime Minister Menahem Begin reciprocated by visiting Ismailia in December. The hopes for significant steps toward a lessening of tensions in the Middle East accompanied these visits. But by the summer of 1978 these hopes seemed to have been dashed on the rocks of old animosities and mutual suspicions. President Carter, then, took a bold political risk by interjecting his personal prestige as well as that of his office into the impasse. He invited Sadat and Begin to Washington to negotiate their differences. For 13 days they remained sequestered at Camp David with varying reports about their progress or lack thereof. Finally, two major agreements were reached that broke new ground for new initiatives in the Middle East. It was a supreme moment of triumph for Sadat and Begin. And even more so for Carter. Thus, before a joint session of Congress with the Egyptian President and the Israeli Prime Minister in attendance, the President summarized the accomplishments at Camp David.

It's been more than 2,000 years since there was peace between Egypt and a free Jewish nation. If our present expectations are realized, this year we shall see such peace again.

The first thing I would like to do is to give tribute to the two men who made this impossible dream now become a real possibility, the two great leaders with whom I have met for the last 2 weeks at Camp David: first, President Anwar Sadat of Egypt and the other, of course, is Prime Minister Menahem Begin of the nation of Israel.

I know that all of you would agree that these are two men of great personal courage, representing nations of peoples who are deeply grateful to them for the achievement which they have realized. And I am personally grateful to them for what they have done.

At Camp David, we sought a peace that is not only of vital importance to their own two nations but to all the people of the Middle East, to all the people of the United States, and, indeed, to all the world as well.

The world prayed for the success of our efforts, and I am glad to announce to you that these prayers have been answered.

I've come to discuss with you tonight what these two leaders have accomplished and what this means to all of us.

The United States has had no choice but to be deeply concerned about the Middle East and to try to use our influence and our efforts to advance the cause of peace. For the last 30 years, through four wars, the people of this troubled region have paid a terrible price in suffering and division and hatred and bloodshed. No two nations have suffered more than Egypt and Israel. But the dangers and the costs of conflicts in this region for our own Nation have been great as well. We have longstanding friendships among the nations there and the peoples of the region, and we have profound moral commitments which are deeply rooted in our values as a people.

The strategic location of these countries and the resources that they possess mean that events in the Middle East directly affect people everywhere. We and our friends could not be indifferent if a hostile power were to establish domination there. In few areas of the world is there a greater risk that a local conflict could spread among other nations adjacent to them and then, perhaps, erupt into a tragic confrontation between us superpowers, ourselves.

Our people have come to understand that unfamiliar names like Sinai, Aqaba, Sharm el Sheikh, Ras en Naqb, Gaza, the West Bank of Jordan, can have a direct and immediate bearing on our own well-being as a nation and our hope for a peaceful world. That is why we in the United States cannot afford to be idle bystanders and why we have been full partners in the search for peace and why it is so vital to our Nation that these meetings at Camp David have been a success.

Through the long years of conflict, four main issues have divided the parties involved. One is the nature of peace—whether peace will simply mean that the guns are silenced, that the bombs no longer fall, that the tanks cease to roll, or whether it will mean that the nations of the Middle East can deal with each other as neighbors and as equals and as friends, with a full range of diplomatic and cultural and economic and human relations between them. That's been the basic question. The Camp David agreement has defined such relationships, I'm glad to announce to you, between Israel and Egypt.

The second main issue is providing for the security of all parties involved, including, of course, our friends, the Israelis, so that none of them need fear attack or military threats from one another. When implemented, the Camp David agreement, I'm glad to announce to you, will provide for such mutual security.

Third is the question of agreement on secure and recognized boundaries, the end of military occupation, and the granting of self-government or else the return to other nations of territories which have been occupied by Israel since the 1967 conflict. The Camp David agreement, I'm glad to announce to you, provides for the realization of all these goals.

And finally, there is the painful human question of the fate of the Palestinians who live or who have lived in these disputed regions. The Camp David agreement guarantees that the Palestinian people may participate in the resolution of the Palestinian problem in all its aspects, a commitment that Israel has made in writing and which is supported and appreciated, I'm sure, by all the world.

Over the last 18 months, there has been, of course, some progress on these issues. Egypt and Israel came close to agreeing about the first issue, the nature of peace. They then saw that the second and third issues, that is withdrawal and security, were intimately connected, closely entwined. But fundamental divisions still remained in other areas—about the fate of the Palestinians, the future of the West Bank and Gaza, and the future of Israeli settlements in occupied Arab territories.

We all remember the hopes for peace that were inspired by President Sadat's initiative, that great and historic visit to Jerusalem last November that thrilled the world, and by the warm and genuine personal response of Prime Minister Begin and the Israeli people, and by the mutual promise between them, publicly made, that there would be no more war. These hopes were sustained when Prime Minister Begin reciprocated by visiting Ismailia on Christmas Day. That progress continued, but at a slower and slower pace through the early part of the year. And by early summer, the negotiations had come to a standstill once again.

It was this stalemate and the prospect for an even worse future that prompted me to invite both President Sadat and Prime Minister Begin to join me at Camp David. They accepted, as you know, instantly, without delay, without preconditions, without consultation even between them.

It's impossible to overstate the courage of these two men or the foresight they have shown. Only through high ideals, through compromises of words and not principle, and through a willingness to look deep into the human heart and to understand the problems and hopes and dreams of one another can progress in a difficult situation like this ever be made. That's what these men and their wise and diligent advisers who are here with us tonight have done during the last 13 days.

When this conference began, I said that the prospects for success were remote. Enormous barriers of ancient history and nationalism and suspicion would have to be overcome if we were to meet our objectives. But President Sadat and Prime Minister Begin have overcome these barriers, exceeded our fondest expectations, and have signed two agreements that hold out the possibility of resolving issues that history had taught us could not be resolved.

The first of these documents is entitled, "A Framework for Peace in the Middle East Agreed at Camp David." It deals with a comprehensive settlement, comprehensive agreement, between Israel and all her neighbors, as well as the difficult question of the Palestinian people and the future of the West Bank and the Gaza area.

The agreement provides a basis for the resolution of issues involving the West bank and Gaza during the next 5 years. It outlines a process of change which is in keeping with Arab hopes, while also carefully respecting Israel's vital security.

The Israeli military government over these areas will be withdrawn and will be replaced with a self-government of the Palestinians who live there. And Israel has committed that this government will have full autonomy. Prime Minister Begin said to me several times, not partial autonomy, but full autonomy.

Israeli forces will be withdrawn and redeployed into specified locations to protect Israel's security. The Palestinians will further participate in determining their own future through talks in which their own elected representatives, the inhabitants of the West Bank and Gaza, will negotiate with Egypt and Israel and Jordan to determine the final status of the West Bank and Gaza.

Israel has agreed, has committed themselves, that the legitimate rights of the Palestinian people will be recognized. After the signing of this framework last night, and during the negotiations concerning the establishment of the Palestinian self-government, no new Israeli settlements will be established in this area. The future settlements issue will be decided among the negotiating parties.

The final status of the West Bank and Gaza will be decided before the end of the 5-year transitional period during which the Palestinian Arabs will have their own government, as part of a negotiation which will produce a peace treaty between Israel and Jordan specifying borders, withdrawal, all those very crucial issues.

These negotiations will be based on all the provisions and the principles of Security Council Resolution 242, with which you all are so familiar. The agreement on the final status of these areas will then be submitted to a vote by the representatives of the inhabitants of the West Bank and Gaza, and they will have the right for the first time in their history, the Palestinian people, to decide how they will govern themselves permanently.

We also believe, of course, all of us, that there should be a just settlement of the problems of displaced persons and refugees, which takes into account appropriate United Nations resolutions.

Finally, this document also outlines a variety of security arrangements to reinforce peace between Israel and her neighbors. This is, indeed, a comprehensive and fair framework for peace in the Middle East, and I'm glad to report this to you.

The second agreement is entitled, "A Framework for the Conclusion of a Peace Treaty Between Egypt and Israel." It returns to Egypt its full exercise of sovereignty over the Sinai Peninsula and establishes several security zones, recognizing carefully that sovereignty right for the protection of all parties. It also provides that Egypt will extend full diplomatic recognition to Israel at the time the Israelis complete an interim withdrawal from most of the Sinai, which will take place between 3 months and 9 months after the conclusion of the peace treaty. And the peace treaty is to be fully negotiated and signed no later than 3 months from last night.

I think I should also report that Prime Minister Begin and President Sadat have already challenged each other to conclude the treaty even earlier. And I hope they—. This final conclusion of a peace treaty will be completed late in December, and it would be a wonderful Christmas present for the world.

Final and complete withdrawal of all Israeli forces will take place between 2 and 3 years following the conclusion of the peace treaty.

While both parties are in total agreement on all the goals that I have just described to you, there is one issue on which agreement has not yet been reached. Egypt states that agreement to remove the Israeli settlements from Egyptian territory is a prerequisite to a peace treaty. Israel says that the issue of the Israeli settlements should be resolved during the peace negotiations themselves.

Now, within 2 weeks, with each member of the Knesset or the Israeli Parliament acting as individuals, not constrained by party loyalty, the Knesset will decide on the issue of the settlements. Our own Government's position, my own personal position is well known on this issue and has been consistent. It is my strong hope, my prayer, that the question of Israeli settlements of Egyptian territory will not be the final obstacle to peace.

None of us should underestimate the historic importance of what has already been done. This is the first time that an Arab and an Israeli leader have signed a comprehensive framework for peace. It contains the seeds of a time when the Middle East, with all its vast potential, may be a land of human richness and fulfillment, rather than a land of bitterness and continued conflict. No region in the world has greater natural and human resources than this one, and nowhere have they been more heavily weighed down by intense hatred and frequent war. These agreements hold out the real possibility that this burden might finally be lifted.

But we must also not forget the magnitude of the obstacles that still remain. The summit exceeded our highest expectations, but we know that it left many difficult issues which are still to be resolved. These issues will require careful negotiation in the months to come. The Egyptian and Israeli people must recognize the tangible benefits that peace will bring and support the decisions their leaders have made, so that a secure and a peaceful future can be achieved for them. The American public, you and I, must also offer our full support to those who have made decisions that are difficult and those who have very difficult decisions still to make.

What lies ahead for all of us is to recognize the statesmanship that President Sadat and Prime Minister Begin have shown and to invite others in that region to follow their example. I have already, last night, invited the other leaders of the Arab world to help sustain progress toward a comprehensive peace.

We must also join in an effort to bring an end to the conflict and the terrible suffering in Lebanon. This is a subject that President Sadat discussed with me many times while I was in Camp David with him. And the first time that the three of us met together, this was a subject of heated discussion. On the way to Washington last night in the helicopter, we mutually committed ourselves to join with other nations, with the Lebanese people themselves, all factions, with President Sarkis, with Syria and Saudi Arabia, perhaps the European countries like France, to try to move toward a solution of the problem in Lebanon which is so vital to us and to the poor people in Lebanon who have suffered so much.

We will want to consult on this matter and on these documents and their meaning with all of the leaders, particularly the Arab leaders. And I'm pleased to say to you tonight that just a few minutes ago, King Hussein of Jordan and King Khalid of Saudi Arabia, perhaps other leaders later, but these two have already agreed to receive Secretary Vance, who will be leaving tomorrow to explain to them the terms of the Camp David agreement. And we hope to secure their support for the realization of the new hopes and dreams of the people of the Middle East.

This is an important mission, and this responsibility, I can tell you, based on my last 2 weeks with him, could not possibly rest on the shoulders of a more able and dedicated and competent man than Secretary Cyrus Vance.

Finally, let me say that for many years the Middle East has been a textbook for pessimism, a demonstration that diplomatic ingenuity was no match for intractable human conflicts. Today we are privileged to see the chance for one of the sometimes rare, bright moments in human history—a chance that may offer the way to peace. We have a chance for peace because these two brave leaders found within themselves the willingness to work together to seek these lasting prospects for peace, which we all want so badly. And for that, I hope that you will share my prayer of thanks and my hope that the promise of this moment shall be fully realized.

The prayers at Camp David were the same as those of the shepherd King David, who prayed in the 85th Psalm, "Wilt thou not revive us again: that thy people may rejoice in thee? I will hear what God the Lord will speak; for he will speak peace unto his people, and unto his saints: but let them not return again unto folly."

And I would like to say, as a Christian, to these two friends of mine, the words of Jesus, "Blessed are the peacemakers, for they shall be the children of God."

SALT II

Televised Address before a Joint Session of Congress
Washington, D.C.
June 18, 1979

After 3 days of meetings with General Secretary Brezhnev in Vienna, President Carter and Brezhnev initialled a Strategic Arms Limitation Treaty. It was the second Treaty agreed upon between an American President and his Soviet counter-part. Upon his return, Carter appeared before Congress to urge ratification of the Treaty. Immediately, it became a highly controversial issue. The President intended to campaign in 1980 on the need for ratification. Senator Howard Baker, a leader of the Senate opposition, began to make rejection of the Treaty the center-piece of his Presidential aspirations for 1980. But the brutal Soviet invasion of Afghanistan scuttled any thought of debate on ratification or using SALT II as a campaign issue in 1980.

The truth of the nuclear age is that the United States and the Soviet Union must live in peace, or we may not live at all. From the beginning of history, the fortunes of men and nations were made and unmade in unending cycles of war and peace. Combat was often the measure of human courage. Willingness to risk war was the mark of statecraft. My fellow Americans, that pattern of war must now be broken forever.

Between nations armed with thousands of thermonuclear weapons—each one capable of causing unimaginable destruction—there can be no more cycles of both war and peace. There can only be peace.

About 2 hours ago, I returned from 3 days of intensive talks with President Leonid Brezhnev of the Soviet Union. I come here tonight to meet with you in a spirit of patience, of hope, and of reason and responsibility.

Patience—because the way is long and hard, and the obstacles ahead are at least as great as those that have been overcome in the last 30 years of diligent and dedicated work.

Hope—because I'm thankful to be able to report to you tonight that real progress has been made.

Reason and responsibility—because both will be needed in full measure if the promise which has been awakened in Vienna is to be fulfilled and the way is to be opened for the next phase in the struggle for a safe and a sane Earth.

Nothing will more strongly affect the outcome of that struggle than the relationship between the two predominant military powers in the world, the United States of America and the Soviet Union.

The talks in Vienna were important in themselves. But their truest significance was as a part of a process—a process that, as you well know, began long before I became President.

This is the 10th time since the end of World War II when the leader of the United States and the leader of the Soviet Union have met at a summit conference. During these past 3 days, we've moved closer to a goal of stability and security in Soviet-American relationships.

That has been the purpose of American policy ever since the rivalry between the United States and the Soviet Union became a central fact in international relations more than a generation ago at the end of World War II.

With the support of the Congress of the United States and with the support of the people of this Nation, every President throughout this period has sought to reduce the most dangerous elements of the Soviet-American competition.

While the United States still had an absolute nuclear monopoly, President Truman sought to place control of the atomic bomb under international authority. President Eisenhower made the first efforts to control nuclear testing. President Kennedy negotiated with the Soviet Union prohibition against atmospheric testing of nuclear explosives. President Johnson broadened the area of negotiations for the first time to include atomic weapons themselves. President Nixon concluded the first strategic arms limitation agreement, SALT I. President Ford negotiated the Vladivostok accords. You can see that this is a vital and a continuing process.

Later this week I will deliver to the United States Senate the complete and signed text of the second strategic arms limitation agreement, SALT II.

This treaty is the product of 7 long years of tough, painstaking negotiation under the leadership of three different Presidents. When ratified, it will be a truly national achievement—an achievement of the Executive and of the Congress, an achievement of civilians and of our military leaders, of liberals and conservatives, of Democrats and Republicans.

Of course, SALT II will not end the competition between the United States and the Soviet Union. That competition is based on fundamentally different visions of human society and human destiny. As long as that basic difference persists, there will always be some degree of tension in the relationship between our two countries. The United States has no fear of this rivalry. But we want it to be peaceful.

In any age, such rivalry risks degeneration into war. But our age is unique, for the terrible power of nuclear weapons has created an incentive that never existed before for avoiding war. This tendency transcends even the very deep differences of politics and philosophy. In the age of the hydrogen bomb, there is no longer any meaningful distinction between global war and global suicide.

Our shared understanding of these realities has given the world an interval of peace—a kind of a strange peace—marked by tension, marked by danger, marked even sometimes by regional conflict, but a kind of peace nonetheless. In the 27 years before Hiroshima, the leading powers of the world were twice engulfed in total war. In the 34 years since Hiroshima, humanity has by no means been free of armed conflict. Yet, at least we have avoided a world war.

Yet this kind of twilight peace carries the ever-present danger of a catastrophic nuclear war, a war that in horror and destruction and massive death would dwarf all the combined wars of man's long and bloody history.

We must prevent such a war. We absolutely must prevent such a war.

To keep the peace, to prevent the war, we must have strong military forces, we must have strong alliances, we must have a strong national resolve—so strong that no potential adversary would dare be tempted to attack our country. We have that strength. And the strength of the United States is not diminishing; the strength of our great country is growing, and I thank God for it.

Yet, for these same reasons—in order to keep the peace—we must prevent an uncontrolled and pointless nuclear arms race that would damage the security of all countries, including our own, by exposing the world to an ever greater risk of war through instability and through tension and through uncertainty about the future. That's why the new strategic arms limitation treaty is so important.

SALT II will undoubtedly become the most exhaustively discussed and debated treaty of our time, perhaps of all times. The Secretary of State, the Secretary of Defense, the members of the Joint Chiefs of Staff, the Director of the Arms Control and Disarmament Agency, and many others who hammered out this treaty will testify for it before the Senate, in detail and in public. As President of our country, I will explain it throughout our Nation to every American who will listen. This treaty will withstand the most severe scrutiny because it is so clearly in the interest of American security and of world peace.

SALT II is the most detailed, far-reaching, comprehensive treaty in the history of arms control. Its provisions are interwoven by the give-and-take of the long negotiating process. Neither side obtained everything it sought. But the package that did emerge is a carefully balanced whole, and it will make the world a safer place for both sides.

The restrictions on strategic nuclear weapons are complex, because these weapons represent the highest development of the complicated technical skills of two great nations. But the basic realities underlying this treaty and the thrust of the treaty itself are not so complex. When all is said and done, SALT II is a matter of common sense.

The SALT II treaty reduces the danger of nuclear war. For the first time, it places equal ceilings on the strategic arsenals of both sides, ending a previous numerical imbalance in favor of the Soviet Union.

SALT II preserves our options to build the forces we need to maintain that strategic balance. The treaty enhances our own ability to monitor what the Soviet Union is doing. And it leads directly to the next step in more effectively controlling nuclear weapons.

Again, SALT II does not end the arms competition. But it does make that competition safer and more predictable, with clear rules and verifiable limits, where otherwise there would be no rules and there would be no limits.

It's in our interest because it slows down—it even reverses—the momentum of the Soviet arms buildup that has been of such great concern to all of us. Under this new treaty, the Soviet Union will be held to a third fewer strategic missile launchers and bombers by 1985 than they would have simply by continuing to build at their present rate.

With SALT II, the numbers of warheads on missiles, their throw weight, and the qualitative development of new missiles will all be limited. The Soviet Union will have to destroy or dismantle some 250 strategic missile systems—systems such as nuclear submarines armed with relatively new missiles, built in the early 1970's, and aircraft will have to be destroyed by the Soviet Union carrying their largest multimegaton bomb. Once dismantled, under the provisions of SALT II, these systems cannot be replaced.

By contrast, no operational United States forces will have to be reduced.

For one Soviet missile alone—the SS–18—the SALT II limits will mean that some 6,000 fewer Soviet nuclear warheads can be built and aimed at our country. SALT II limits severely for the first time the number of warheads that can be mounted on these very large missiles of the Soviet Union, cutting down their actual potential by 6,000.

With or without SALT II, we must modernize and strengthen our own strategic forces—and we are doing so—but SALT II will make this task easier, surer, and less expensive.

The agreement constrains none of the reasonable programs we've planned to improve our own defenses. Moreover, it helps us to respond more effectively to our most pressing strategic problem—the prospective vulnerability in the 1980's of problems would escalate into serious super power confrontations.

Rejection would also be a damaging blow to the Western Alliance. All of our European and other allies, including especially those who are most directly and courageously facing Soviet power, all of them strongly support SALT II. If the Senate were to reject the treaty, America's leadership of this alliance would be compromised, and the alliance itself would be severely shaken.

In short, SALT II is not a favor we are doing for the Soviet Union. It's a deliberate, calculated move that we are making as a matter of self-interest for the United States—a move that happens to serve the goals of both security and survival, that strengthens both the military position of our own country and the cause of world peace.

And, of course, SALT II is the absolutely indispensable precondition for moving on to much deeper and more significant cuts under SALT III.

Although we will not begin negotiations on SALT III until SALT II goes into effect, I discussed other nuclear control issues with President Brezhnev, such as much deeper mutual reductions in nuclear weapon inventories, stricter limit on the production of nuclear warheads and launchers, enhanced survivability and stability of missile systems that are authorized under existing SALT agreement, prenotification about missile tests and mass use or exercise of strategic bombers, and limits and controls on types of missiles which are not presently covered under any SALT agreement.

Though SALT is the most important single part of the complex relationship between the United States and the Soviet Union, it is only a part. The U.S.–Soviet relationship covers a broad range of issues, some of which bear directly on our joint responsibility to reduce the possibility of war. President Brezhnev and I discussed these issues in Vienna this morning in a long private session with only the interpreters present.

I undertook all these discussions with a firm confidence in the strength of America. Militarily, our power is second to none. I'm determined that it will remain so. We will continue to have military power to deter any possible aggression, to maintain security of our country, and to permit the continuing search for peace and for the control of arms from a position of strength. We must have that strength so that we will never be afraid to negotiate for peace.

Economically, despite serious problems of energy and inflation, we are by far the most productive nation on Earth. Along with our allies, our economic strength is three times greater than that of the Soviet Union and all its allies.

Diplomatically, we've strengthened our friendships with Western Europe and Japan, with China and India, with Israel and Egypt, and with the countries of the Third World. Our alliances are stronger because they are based not on force, but on common interests and often on common values.

Politically, our democratic system is an enormous advantage, not only to each of us as individuals who enjoy freedom but to all of us together because our Nation is stronger. Our support of human rights, backed by the concrete example of the American society, has aligned us with peoples all over the world who yearn for freedom.

These strengths are such that we need fear no other country. This confidence in our Nation helped me in Vienna as we discussed specific areas of potential, either direct or indirect, confrontation around our land-based silo missiles. The MX missile, which has been so highly publicized, is permitted under SALT II. Yet its verifiable mobile development system will enhance stability as it deprives an attacker of the confidence that a successful first strike could be launched against the United States ICBM's, or intercontinental ballistic missiles.

Without the SALT II limits, the Soviet Union could build so many warheads that any land-based system, fixed or mobile, could be jeopardized.

With SALT II, we can concentrate more effort on preserving the balance in our own conventional and NATO forces. Without the SALT II treaty, we would be forced to spend extra billions and billions of dollars each year in a dangerous, destabilizing, unnecessary nuclear arms race.

As I have said many times, SALT II is not based on trust. Compliance will be assured by our own Nation's means of verification, including extremely sophisticated satellites, powerful electronic systems, and a vast intelligence network. Were the Soviet Union to take enormous risk of trying to violate this treaty in any way that might affect the strategic balance, there is no doubt that we would discover it in time to respond fully and effectively.

It's the SALT II agreement itself which forbids concealment measures—many of them for the first time—forbids interference with our monitoring, and forbids the encryption or the encoding of crucial missile-test information. A violation of this part of the agreement—which we would quickly detect—would be just as serious as a violation of the limits on strategic weapons themselves.

Consider these prospects for a moment. Suppose the Soviet leaders build a thousand additional missiles, above and beyond the ones they have now, many new advanced and of a formidable design. This can happen only if the SALT II treaty is defeated.

Suppose the Soviet leaders wanted to double the number of warheads on all their existing missiles; suppose they wanted to triple the annual production rate of the Backfire bomber and greatly improve its characteristics in range and payload. These kinds of things can happen only if the SALT II treaty is defeated.

Suppose the Soviet Union leaders encrypt all data on their missile tests; suppose they conceal their nuclear launcher deployment rate and hide all their existing missile systems. Those things can happen only if the SALT II treaty is defeated.

SALT II is very important. But it's more than a single arms control agreement; it's part of a long, historical process of gradually reducing the danger of nuclear war—a process that we in this room must not undermine.

The SALT II treaty must be judged on its own merits. And on its own merits, it is a substantial gain for national security for us and the people whom we represent, and it's a gain for international stability. But it would be the height of irresponsibility to ignore other possible consequences of a failure to ratify this treaty.

These consequences would include: greatly increased spending for strategic nuclear arms which we do not need; greater uncertainty about the strategic balance between ourselves and the Soviet Union; vastly increased danger of nuclear proliferation among other nations of the world who do not presently have nuclear explosives; increased political tension between the East and the West, with greater likelihood that other inevitable the world, including places like southern Africa or the Middle East.

For instance, I made it clear to President Brezhnev that Cuban military activities in Africa, sponsored by or supported by the Soviet Union, and also the growing Cuban involvement in the problems of Central America and the Caribbean can only have a negative impact on U.S.–Soviet relations.

Our strength, our resolve, our determination, our willingness to protect our own interests, our willingness to discuss these problems with others are the best means by which we can resolve these differences and alleviate these tests successfully for our people.

Despite disagreements, our exchange in Vienna was useful, because it enabled us to clarify our positions directly to each other, face-to-face, and, thus, to reduce the chances of future miscalculations on both sides.

And, finally, I would like to say to you that President Brezhnev and I developed a better sense of each other as leaders and as men. The responsibility for many decisions involving the very future of the world rests on me as the leader of this great country, and it's vital that my judgments be based on as much firsthand knowledge and experience as possible.

In these conversations, I was careful to leave no doubt about either my desire for peace or my determination to defend the interests of the United States and of our allies. I believe that together we laid a foundation on which we can build a more stable relationship between our two countries.

We look to the future—all of us Americans look to the future—with anticipation and with confidence, not only because of the vast material powers of our Nation but because of the power of our Nation's ideas and ideals and principles. The ultimate future of the human race lies not with tyranny, but with freedom; not with war, but with peace.

With that kind of vision to sustain us, we must now complete the work of ratifying this treaty, a major step in the limitation of nuclear weapons and a major step toward world peace. And then we may turn our energies not only to further progress along that path but also more urgently to our own domestic agenda in the knowledge that we have strengthened the security of a nation which we love and also strengthened peace for all the world.

We will seek to broaden the areas of cooperation, and we will compete where and when we must. We know how determined the Soviet leaders are to secure their interests, and we are equally determined to protect and to advance our own.

The Energy Problem: II

Televised Address to the Nation
Washington, D.C.
July 15, 1979

By the summer of 1979, President Carter found himself in deep political trouble. Inflation had climbed into double-digit figures. Gasoline shortages caused long lines at service stations. Prices for gasoline had greatly increased. And his approval rating with the public had dipped to a low of only 26%. Upon his return from the Tokyo Economic Summit Meeting, a memo on his problems awaited him. The memo, written by his chief advisor on domestic affairs, Stuart Eizenstat, called the energy problem the most significant facing the President and recommended that in his forthcoming speech that he shift the blame for inflation and energy problems to OPEC as a means for regaining "our political losses."[1] Carter cancelled his scheduled speech and retreated to Camp David. He summoned a variety of political, academic, business and labor leaders to Camp David to receive their advice about what needed to be done. Then, on July 15 he spoke to the American people.

His address is more sermon than speech. It appears to come out of the Southern Baptist tradition which should not seem remarkable coming from a "born again Christian" President. It is a kind of "testifying" that those who come from the South are quite familiar with. The "testimony" contains three parts: (1) a confession of sins (the opening section in which he criticizes himself); (2) a reaffirmation of his faith (the "crisis of confidence" section); and (3) the determination to prove his faith by doing good works (the sections that deal with the need to pass a comprehensive energy program and the need to conserve).

This is a special night for me. Exactly 3 years ago, on July 15, 1976, I accepted the nomination of my party to run for President of the United States. I promised you a President who is not isolated from the people, who feels your pain, and who shares your dreams and who draws his strength and his wisdom from you.

During the past 3 years I've spoken to you on many occasions about the national concerns, the energy crisis, reorganizing the Government, our Nation's economy, and issues of war and especially peace. But over those years the subjects of the speeches, the talks, and the press conferences have become increasingly narrow, focused more and more on what the isolated world of Washington thinks is important. Gradually, you've heard more and more about what the Government thinks or what the Government should be doing and less and less about our Nation's hopes, our dreams, and our vision of the future.

Ten days ago I had planned to speak to you again about a very important subject—energy. For the fifth time I would have described the urgency of the problem and laid out a series of legislative recommendations to the Congress. But as I was preparing to speak, I began to ask myself the same question that I now know has been troubling many of you. Why have we not been able to get together as a nation to resolve our serious energy problem?

It's clear that the true problems of our Nation are much deeper—deeper than gasoline lines or energy shortages, deeper even than inflation or recession. And I realize more than ever that as President I need your help. So, I decided to reach out and listen to the voices of America.

I invited to Camp David people from almost every segment of our society—business and labor, teachers and preachers, Governors, mayors, and private citizens. And then I left Camp

David to listen to other Americans, men and women like you. It has been an extraordinary 10 days, and I want to share with you what I've heard.

First of all, I got a lot of personal advice. Let me quote a few of the typical comments that I wrote down.

This from a southern Governor: "Mr. President, you are not leading this Nation—you're just managing the Government."

"You don't see the people enough any more."

"Some of your Cabinet members don't seem loyal. There is not enough discipline among your disciples."

"Don't talk to us about politics or the mechanics of government, but about an understanding of our common good."

"Mr. President, we're in trouble. Talk to us about blood and sweat and tears."

"If you lead, Mr. President, we will follow."

Many people talked about themselves and about the condition of our Nation. This from a young woman in Pennsylvania: "I feel so far from government. I feel like ordinary people are excluded from political power."

And this from a young Chicano: "Some of us have suffered from recession all our lives."

"Some people have wasted energy, but others haven't had anything to waste."

And this from a religious leader: "No material shortage can touch the important things like God's love for us or our love for one another."

And I like this one particularly from a black woman who happens to be the mayor of a small Mississippi town: "The big-shots are not the only ones who are important. Remember, you can't sell anything on Wall Street unless someone digs it up somewhere else first."

This kind of summarized a lot of other statements: "Mr. President, we are confronted with a moral and a spiritual crisis."

Several of our discussions were on energy, and I have a notebook full of comments and advice. I'll read just a few.

"We can't go on consuming 40 percent more energy than we produce. When we import oil we are also importing inflation plus unemployment."

"We've got to use what we have. The Middle East has only 5 percent of the world's energy, but the United States has 24 percent."

And this is one of the most vivid statements: "Our neck is stretched over the fence and OPEC has a knife."

"There will be other cartels and other shortages. American wisdom and courage right now can set a path to follow in the future."

This was a good one: "Be bold, Mr. President. We may make mistakes, but we are ready to experiment."

And this one from a labor leader got to the heart of it: "The real issue is freedom. We must deal with the energy problem on a war footing."

And the last that I'll read: "When we enter the moral equivalent of war, Mr. President, don't issue us BB guns."

These 10 days confirmed my belief in the decency and the strength and the wisdom of the American people, but it also bore out some of my longstanding concerns about our Nation's underlying problems.

I know, of course, being President, that government actions and legislation can be very important. That's why I've worked hard to put my campaign promises into law—and I have to admit, with just mixed success. But after listening to the American people I have been reminded again that all the legislation in the world can't fix what's wrong with America. So, I want to speak to you first tonight about a subject even more serious than energy or inflation. I want to talk to you right now about a fundamental threat to American democracy.

I do not mean our political and civil liberties. They will endure. And I do not refer to the outward strength of America, a nation that is at peace tonight everywhere in the world, with unmatched economic power and military might.

The threat is nearly invisible in ordinary ways. It is a crisis of confidence. It is a crisis that strikes at the very heart and soul and spirit of our national will. We can see this crisis in the growing doubt about the meaning of our own lives and in the loss of unity of purpose for our Nation.

The erosion of our confidence in the future is threatening to destroy the social and the political fabric of America.

The confidence that we have always had as a people is not simply some romantic dream or a proverb in a dusty book that we read just on the Fourth of July. It is the idea which founded our Nation and has guided our development as a people. Confidence in the future has supported everything else—public institutions and private enterprise, our own families, and the very Constitution of the United States. Confidence has defined our course and has served as a link between generations. We've always believed in something called progress. We've always had a faith that the days of our children would be better than our own.

Our people are losing that faith, not only in government itself but in the ability as citizens to serve as the ultimate rulers and shapers of our democracy. As a people we know our past and we are proud of it. Our progress has been part of the living history of America, even the world. We always believed that we were part of a great movement of humanity itself called democracy, involved in the search for freedom and that belief has always strengthened us in our purpose. But just as we are losing our confidence in the future, we are also beginning to close the door on our past.

In a nation that was proud of hard work, strong families, close-knit communities, and our faith in God, too many of us now tend to worship self-indulgence and consumption. Human identity is no longer defined by what one does, but by what one owns. But we've discovered that owning things and consuming things does not satisfy our longing for meaning. We've learned that piling up material goods cannot fill the emptiness of lives which have no confidence or purpose.

The symptoms of this crisis of the American spirit are all around us. For the first time in the history of our country a majority of our people believe that the next 5 years will be worse than the past 5 years. Two-thirds of our people do not even vote. The productivity of American workers is actually dropping, and the willingness of Americans to save for the future has fallen below that of all other people in the Western world.

As you know, there is a growing disrespect for government and for churches and for schools, the news media, and other institutions. This is not a message of happiness or reassurance, but it is the truth and it is a warning.

These changes did not happen overnight. They've come upon us gradually over the last generation, years that were filled with shocks and tragedy.

We were sure that ours was a nation of the ballot, not the bullet, until the murders of John Kennedy and Robert Kennedy and Martin Luther King, Jr. We were taught that our armies were always invincible and our causes were always just, only to suffer the agony of Vietnam. We respected the Presidency as a place of honor until the shock of Watergate.

We remember when the phrase "sound as a dollar" was an expression of absolute dependability, until 10 years of inflation began to shrink our dollar and our savings. We believed that our Nation's resources were limitless until 1973 when we had to face a growing dependence on foreign oil.

These wounds are still very deep. They have never been healed.

Looking for a way out of this crisis, our people have turned to the Federal Government and found it isolated from the mainstream of our Nation's life. Washington, D.C., has become an island. The gap between our citizens and our Government has never been so wide. The people are looking for honest answers, not easy answers; clear leadership, not false claims and evasiveness and politics as usual.

What you see too often in Washington and elsewhere around the country is a system of government that seems incapable of action. You see a Congress twisted and pulled in every direction by hundreds of well-financed and powerful special interests.

You see every extreme position defended to the last vote, almost to the last breath by one unyielding group or another. You often see a balanced and a fair approach that demands sacrifice, a little sacrifice from everyone, abandoned like an orphan without support and without friends.

Often you see paralysis and stagnation and drift. You don't like it, and neither do I. What can we do?

First of all, we must face the truth, and then we can change our course. We simply must have faith in each other, faith in our ability to govern ourselves, and faith in the future of this Nation. Restoring that faith and that confidence to America is now the most important task we face. It is a true challenge of this generation of Americans.

One of the visitors to Camp David last week put it this way: "We've got to stop crying and start sweating, stop talking and start walking, stop cursing and start praying. The strength we need will not come from the White House, but from every house in America."

We know the strength of America. We are strong. We can regain our unity. We can regain our confidence. We are the heirs of generations who survived threats much more powerful and awesome than those that challenge us now. Our fathers and mothers were strong men and women who shaped a new society during the Great Depression, who fought world wars, and who carved out a new charter of peace for the world.

We ourselves are the same Americans who just 10 years ago put a man on the Moon. We are the generation that dedicated our society to the pursuit of human rights and equality. And we are the generation that will win the war on the energy problem and in that process rebuild the unity and confidence of America.

We are at a turning point in our history. There are two paths to choose. One is a path I've warned about tonight, the path that leads to fragmentation and self-interest. Down that road lies a mistaken idea of freedom, the right to grasp for ourselves some advantage over others. That path would be one of constant conflict between narrow interests ending in chaos and immobility. It is a certain route to failure.

All the traditions of our past, all the lessons of our heritage, all the promises of our future point to another path, the path of common purpose and the restoration of American values. That path leads to true freedom for our Nation and ourselves. We can take the first steps down that path as we begin to solve our energy problem.

Energy will be the immediate test of our ability to unite this Nation, and it can also be the standard around which we rally. On the battlefield of energy we can win for our Nation a new confidence, and we can seize control again of our common destiny.

In little more than two decades we've gone from a position of energy independence to one in which almost half the oil we use comes from foreign countries, at prices that are going through the roof. Our excessive dependence on OPEC has already taken a tremendous toll on our economy and our people. This is the direct cause of the long lines which have made millions of you spend aggravating hours waiting for gasoline. It's a cause of the increased inflation and employment that we now face. This intolerable dependence on foreign oil threatens our economic independence and the very security of our Nation.

The energy crisis is real. It is world-wide. It is a clear and present danger to our Nation. These are facts and we simply must face them.

What I have to say to you now about energy is simple and vitally important.

Point one: I am tonight setting a clear goal for the energy policy of the United States. Beginning this moment, this Nation will never use more foreign oil than we did in 1977—never. From now on, every new addition to our demand for energy will be met from our own production and our own conservation. The generation-long growth in our dependence on foreign oil will be stopped dead in its tracks right now and then reversed as we move through the 1980's, for I am tonight setting the further goal of cutting our dependence on foreign oil by one-half by the end of the next decade—a saving of over 4½ million barrels of imported oil per day.

Point two: To ensure that we meet these targets, I will use my Presidential authority to set import quotas. I'm announcing tonight that for 1979 and 1980, I will forbid the entry into this country of one drop of foreign oil more than these goals allow. These quotas will ensure a reduction in imports even below the ambitious levels we set at the recent Tokyo summit.

Point three: To give us energy security, I am asking for the most massive peacetime commitment of funds and resources in our Nation's history to develop America's own alternative sources of fuel—from coal, from oil shale, from plant products for gasohol, from unconventional gas, from the Sun.

I propose the creation of an energy security corporation to lead this effort to replace 2½ million barrels of imported oil per day by 1990. The corporation will issue up to $5 billion in energy bonds, and I especially want them to be in small denominations so that average Americans can invest directly in America's energy security.

Just as a similar synthetic rubber corporation helped us win World War II, so will we mobilize American determination and ability to win the energy war. Moreover, I will soon submit legislation to Congress calling for the creation of this Nation's first solar bank which will help us achieve the crucial goal of 20 percent of our energy coming from solar power by the year 2000.

These efforts will cost money, a lot of money, and that is why Congress must enact the windfall profits tax without delay. It will be money well spent. Unlike the billions of dollars that we ship to foreign countries to pay for foreign oil, these funds will be paid by Americans to Americans. These funds will go to fight, not to increase, inflation and unemployment.

Point four: I'm asking Congress to mandate, to require as a matter of law, that our Nation's utility companies cut their massive use of oil by 50 percent within the next decade and switch to other fuels, especially coal, our most abundant energy source.

Point five: To make absolutely certain that nothing stands in the way of achieving these goals, I will urge Congress to create an energy mobilization board which, like the War Production Board in World War II, will have the responsibility and authority to cut through the redtape, the delays, and the endless roadblocks to completing key energy projects.

We will protect our environment. But when this Nation critically needs a refinery or a pipeline, we will build it.

Point six: I'm proposing a bold conservation program to involve every State, county, and city and every average American in our energy battle. This effort will permit you to build conservation into your homes and your lives at a cost you can afford.

I ask Congress to give me authority for mandatory conservation and for standby gasoline rationing. To further conserve energy, I'm proposing tonight an extra $10 billion over the next decade to strengthen our public transportation systems. And I'm asking you for your good and for your Nation's security to take no unnecessary trips, to use carpools or public transportation whenever you can, to park your car one extra day per week, to obey the speed limit, and to set your thermostats to save fuel. Every act of energy conservation like this is more than just common sense—I tell you it is an act of patriotism.

Our Nation must be fair to the poorest among us, so we will increase aid to needy Americans to cope with rising energy prices. We often think of conservation only in terms of sacrifice. In fact, it is the most painless and immediate way of rebuilding our Nation's strength. Every gallon of oil each one of us saves is a new form of production. It gives us more freedom, more confidence, that much more control over our own lives.

So, the solution of our energy crisis can also help us to conquer the crisis of the spirit in our country. It can rekindle our sense of unity, our confidence in the future, and give our Nation and all of us individually a new sense of purpose.

You know we can do it. We have the natural resources. We have more oil in our shale alone than several Saudi Arabias. We have more coal than any nation on Earth. We have the world's highest level of technology. We have the most skilled work force, with innovative genius, and I firmly believe that we have the national will to win this war.

I do not promise you that this struggle for freedom will be easy. I do not promise a quick way out of our Nation's problems, when the truth is that the only way out is an all-out effort. What I do promise you is that I will lead our fight, and I will enforce fairness in our struggle, and I will ensure honesty. And above all, I will act.

We can manage the short-term shortages more effectively and we will, but there are no short-term solutions to our long-range problems. There is simply no way to avoid sacrifice.

Twelve hours from now I will speak again in Kansas City, to expand and to explain further our energy program. Just as the search for solutions to our energy shortages has now led us to a new awareness of our Nation's deeper problems, so our willingness to work for those solutions in energy can strengthen us to attack those deeper problems.

I will continue to travel this country, to hear the people of America. You can help me to develop a national agenda for the 1980's. I will listen and I will act. We will act together. These were the promises I made 3 years ago, and I intend to keep them.

Little by little we can and we must rebuild our confidence. We can spend until we empty our treasuries, and we may summon all the wonders of science. But we can succeed only if we tap our greatest resources—America's people, America's values, and America's confidence.

I have seen the strength of America in the inexhaustible resources of our people. In the days to come, let us renew that strength in the struggle for an energy-secure nation.

In closing, let me say this: I will do my best, but I will not do it alone. Let your voice be heard. Whenever you have a chance, say something good about our country. With God's help and for the sake of our Nation, it is time for us to join hands in America. Let us commit ourselves together to a rebirth of the American spirit. Working together with our common faith we cannot fail.

Notes

1. "Text of Eizenstat's Memorandum on Energy with Recommendations to Carter," *The New York Times* (July 8, 1979), p. 32.

The Carter Doctrine

State of the Union Address
Washington, D.C.
January 23, 1980

From his low point of public approval in the summer of 1979 to the State of the Union in 1980, President Carter's political fortunes rose dramatically. This change, however, was not due to a "born again" grasp of Presidential leadership, but to foreign events over which he had no control, to which he had to react rather than act.

On November 4, 1979 Iranian students captured the American Embassy in Tehran taking some 60 Americans as hostage. They demanded a return of the Shah, Mohammad Reza Pahlavi, for trial as a war criminal. The Shah had entered the United States 12 days before for a cancer operation. President Carter refused to accede to this demand, and the long occupation of the Embassy began. Then, in late December, Soviet armed forces invaded Afghanistan to prop up a faltering pro-Soviet government. Soon, more than a hundred thousand troops occupied much of Afghanistan. Declaring that these "crises" required his full attention as President, Carter suspended all planned campaigning for renomination (including a scheduled debate among himself, Senator Kennedy and Governor Brown in Iowa) and spoke to the public as infrequently as possible.

This State of the Union address is more a State of the World address. Carter devoted most of his time to foreign affairs. (Only 2 sentences were used to mention inflation which had grown to an annual rate of 13.5% in 1979.) The most significant policy statement regarded the Soviet Union: a warning that any attempt to gain control of the Persian Gulf would be repelled by the United States using "any means necessary, including military force." This statement became known as the Carter Doctrine. The speech generally takes a hard-line on foreign policy and stands in illuminating contrast to the President's statements and attitudes during the first 2 years of his administration.

This last few months has not been an easy time for any of us. As we meet tonight, it has never been more clear that the state of our Union depends on the state of the world. And tonight, as throughout our own generation, freedom and peace in the world depend on the state of our Union.

The 1980's have been born in turmoil, strife, and change. This is a time of challenge to our interests and our values and it's a time that tests our wisdom and our skills.

At this time in Iran, 50 Americans are still held captive, innocent victims of terrorism and anarchy. Also at this moment, massive Soviet troops are attempting to subjugate the fiercely independent and deeply religious people of Afghanistan. These two acts—one of international terrorism and one of military aggression—present a serious challenge to the United States of America and indeed to all the nations of the world. Together, we will meet these threats to peace.

I'm determined that the United States will remain the strongest of all nations, but our power will never be used to initiate a threat to the security of any nation or to the rights of any human being. We seek to be and to remain secure—a nation at peace in a stable world. But to be secure we must face the world as it is.

Three basic developments have helped to shape our challenges: the steady growth and increased projection of Soviet military power beyond its own borders; the overwhelming dependence of the Western democracies on oil supplies from the Middle East; and the press of social and religious and economic and political change in the many nations of the developing world, exemplified by the revolution in Iran.

Each of these factors is important in its own right. Each interacts with the others. All must be faced together, squarely and courageously. We will face these challenges, and we will meet them with the best that is in us. And we will not fail.

In response to the abhorrent act in Iran, our Nation has never been aroused and unified so greatly in peacetime. Our position is clear. The United States will not yield to blackmail.

We continue to pursue these specific goals: first, to protect the present and long-range interests of the United States; secondly, to preserve the lives of the American hostages and to secure, as quickly as possible, their safe release, if possible, to avoid bloodshed which might further endanger the lives of our fellow citizens; to enlist the help of other nations in condemning this act of violence, which is shocking and violates the moral and the legal standards of a civilized world; and also to convince and to persuade the Iranian leaders that the real danger to their nation lies in the north, in the Soviet Union and from the Soviet troops now in Afghanistan, and that the unwarranted Iranian quarrel with the United States hampers their response to this far greater danger to them.

If the American hostages are harmed, a severe price will be paid. We will never rest until every one of the American hostages are released.

But now we face a broader and more fundamental challenge in this region because of the recent military action of the Soviet Union.

Now, as during the last 3½ decades, the relationship between our country, the United States of America, and the Soviet Union is the most critical factor in determining whether the world will live at peace or be engulfed in global conflict.

Since the end of the Second World War, America has led other nations in meeting the challenge of mounting Soviet power. This has not been a simple or a static relationship. Between us there has been cooperation, there has been competition, and at times there has been confrontation.

In the 1940's we took the lead in creating the Atlantic Alliance in response to the Soviet Union's suppression and then consolidation of its East European empire and the resulting threat of the Warsaw Pact to Western Europe.

In the 1950's we helped to contain further Soviet challenges in Korea and in the Middle East, and we rearmed to assure the continuation of that containment.

In the 1960's we met the Soviet challenges in Berlin, and we faced the Cuban missile crisis. And we sought to engage the Soviet Union in the important task of moving beyond the cold war and away from confrontation.

And in the 1970's three American Presidents negotiated with the Soviet leaders in attempts to halt the growth of the nuclear arms race. We sought to establish rules of behavior that would reduce the risks of conflict, and we searched for areas of cooperation that could make our relations reciprocal and productive, not only for the sake of our two nations but for the security and peace of the entire world.

In all these actions, we have maintained two commitments: to be ready to meet any challenge by Soviet military power, and to develop ways to resolve disputes and to keep the peace.

Preventing nuclear war is the foremost responsibility of the two superpowers. That's why we've negotiated the strategic arms limitation treaties—SALT I and SALT II. Especially now, in a time of great tension, observing the mutual constraints imposed by the terms of these treaties will be in the best interest of both countries and will help to preserve world peace. I will consult very closely with the Congress on this matter as we strive to control nuclear weapons. That effort to control nuclear weapons will not be abandoned.

We superpowers also have the responsibility to exercise restraint in the use of our great military force. The integrity and the independence of weaker nations must not be threatened. They must know that in our presence they are secure.

But now the Soviet Union has taken a radical and an aggressive new step. It's using its great military power against a relatively defenseless nation. The implications of the Soviet invasion of Afghanistan could pose the most serious threat to the peace since the Second World War.

The vast majority of nations on Earth have condemned this latest Soviet attempt to extend its colonial domination of others and have demanded the immediate withdrawal of Soviet troops. The Moslem world is especially and justifiably outraged by this aggression against an Islamic people. No action of a world power has ever been so quickly and so overwhelmingly condemned. But verbal condemnation is not enough. The Soviet Union must pay a concrete price for their aggression.

While this invasion continues, we and the other nations of the world cannot conduct business as usual with the Soviet Union. That's why the United States has imposed stiff economic penalties on the Soviet Union. I will not issue any permits for Soviet ships to fish in the coastal waters of the United States. I've cut Soviet access to high-technology equipment and to agricultural products. I've limited other commerce with the Soviet Union, and I've asked our allies and friends to join with us in restraining their own trade with the Soviets and not to replace our own embargoed items. And I have notified the Olympic Committee that with Soviet invading forces in Afghanistan, neither the American people nor I will support sending an Olympic team to Moscow.

The Soviet Union is going to have to answer some basic questions: Will it help promote a more stable international environment in which its own legitimate, peaceful concerns can be pursued? Or will it continue to expand its military power far beyond its genuine security needs, and use that power for colonial conquest? The Soviet Union must realize that its decision to use military force in Afghanistan will be costly to every political and economic relationship it values.

The region which is now threatened by Soviet troops in Afghanistan is of great strategic importance: It contains more than two-thirds of the world's exportable oil. The Soviet effort to dominate Afghanistan has brought Soviet military forces to within 300 miles of the Indian Ocean and close to the Straits of Hormuz, a waterway through which most of the world's oil must flow. The Soviet Union is now attempting to consolidate a strategic position, therefore, that poses a grave threat to the free movement of Middle East oil.

This situation demands careful thought, steady nerves, and resolute action, not only for this year but for many years to come. It demands collective efforts to meet this new threat to security in the Persian Gulf and in Southwest Asia. It demands the participation of all those who rely on oil from the Middle East and who are concerned with global peace and stability. And it demands consultation and close cooperation with countries in the area which might be threatened.

Meeting this challenge will take national will, diplomatic and political wisdom, economic sacrifice, and, of course, military capability. We must call on the best that is in us to preserve the security of this crucial region.

Let our position be absolutely clear: An attempt by any outside force to gain control of the Persian Gulf region will be regarded as an assault on the vital interests of the United States of America, and such an assault will be repelled by any means necessary, including military force.

During the past 3 years, you have joined with me to improve our own security and the prospects for peace, not only in the vital oil-producing area of the persian Gulf region but around the world. We've increased annually our real commitment for defense, and we will sustain this increase of effort throughout the Five Year Defense Program. It's imperative that Congress approve this strong defense budget for 1981, encompassing a 5-percent real growth in authorizations, without any reduction.

We are also improving our capability to deploy U.S. military forces rapidly to distant areas. We've helped to strengthen NATO and our other alliances, and recently we and other NATO members have decided to develop and to deploy modernized, intermediate-range nuclear forces to meet an unwarranted and increased threat from the nuclear weapons of the Soviet Union.

We are working with our allies to prevent conflict in the Middle East. The peace treaty between Egypt and Israel is a notable achievement which represents a strategic asset for America and which also enhances prospects for regional and world peace. We are now engaged in further negotiations to provide full autonomy for the people of the West Bank and Gaza, to resolve the Palestinian issue in all its aspects, and to preserve the peace and security of Israel. Let no one doubt our commitment to the security of Israel. In a few days we will observe an historic event when Israel makes another major withdrawal from the Sinai and when Ambassadors will be exchanged between Israel and Egypt.

We've also expanded our own sphere of friendship. Our deep commitment to human rights and to meeting human needs has improved our relationship with much of the Third World. Our decision to normalize relations with the People's Republic of China will help to preserve peace and stability in Asia and in the Western Pacific.

We've increased and strengthened our naval presence in the Indian Ocean, and we are now making arrangements for key naval and air facilities to be used by our forces in the region of northeast Africa and the Persian Gulf.

We've reconfirmed our 1959 agreement to help Pakistan preserve its independence and its integrity. The United States will take action consistent with our own laws to assist Pakistan in resisting any outside aggression. And I'm asking the Congress specifically to reaffirm this agreement. I'm also working, along with the leaders of other nations, to provide additional military and economic aid for Pakistan. That request will come to you in just a few days.

In the weeks ahead, we will further strengthen political and military ties with other nations in the region. We believe that there are no irreconcilable differences between us and any Islamic nation. We respect the faith of Islam, and we are ready to cooperate with all Moslem countries.

Finally, we are prepared to work with other countries in the region to share a cooperative security framework that respects differing values and political beliefs, yet which enhances the independence, security, and prosperity of all.

All these efforts combined emphasize our dedication to defend and preserve the vital interests of the region and of the nation which we represent and those of our allies—in Europe and the Pacific, and also in the parts of the world which have such great strategic importance to us, stretching especially through the Middle East and Southwest Asia. With your help, I will pursue these efforts with vigor and with determination. You and I will act as necessary to protect and to preserve our Nation's security.

The men and women of America's Armed Forces are on duty tonight in many parts of the world. I'm proud of the job they are doing, and I know you share that pride. I believe that our volunteer forces are adequate for current defense needs, and I hope that it will not become necessary to impose a draft. However, we must be prepared for that possibility. For this reason, I have determined that the Selective Service System must now be revitalized. I will send legislation and budget proposals to the Congress next month so that we can begin registration and then meet future mobilization needs rapidly if they arise.

We also need clear and quick passage of a new charter to define the legal authority and accountability of our intelligence agencies. We will guarantee that abuses do not recur, but we must tighten our controls on sensitive intelligence information, and we need to remove unwarranted restraints on America's ability to collect intelligence.

The decade ahead will be a time of rapid change, as nations everywhere seek to deal with new problems and age-old tensions. But America need have no fear. We can thrive in a world of change if we remain true to our values and actively engaged in promoting world peace. We will continue to work as we have for peace in the Middle East and southern Africa. We will continue to build our ties with developing nations, respecting and helping to strengthen their national independence which they have struggled so hard to achieve. And we will continue to support the growth of democracy and the protection of human rights.

In repressive regimes, popular frustrations often have no outlet except through violence. But when peoples and their governments can approach their problems together through open, democratic methods, the basis for stability and peace is far more solid and far more enduring. That is why our support for human rights in other countries is in our own national interest as well as part of our own national character.

Peace—a peace that preserves freedom—remains America's first goal. In the coming years, as a mighty nation we will continue to pursue peace. But to be strong abroad we must be strong at home. And in order to be strong, we must continue to face up to the difficult issues that confront us as a nation today.

The crises in Iran and Afghanistan have dramatized a very important lesson: Our excessive dependence on foreign oil is a clear and present danger to our Nation's security. The need has never been more urgent. At long last, we must have a clear, comprehensive energy policy for the United States.

As you well know, I have been working with the Congress in a concentrated and persistent way over the past 3 years to meet this need. We have made progress together. But Congress must act promptly now to complete final action on this vital energy legislation. Our Nation will then have a major conservation effort, important initiatives to develop solar power, realistic pricing based on the true value of oil, strong incentives for the production of coal and other fossil fuels in the United States, and our Nation's most massive peacetime investment in the development of synthetic fuels.

The American people are making progress in energy conservation. Last year we reduced overall petroleum consumption by 8 percent and gasoline consumption by 5 percent below what it was the year before. Now we must do more.

After consultation with the Governors, we will set gasoline conservation goals for each of the 50 States, and I will make them mandatory if these goals are not met.

I've established an import ceiling for 1980 or 8.2 million barrels a day—well below the level of foreign oil purchases in 1977. I expect our imports to be much lower than this, but the ceiling will be enforced by an oil import fee if necessary. I'm prepared to lower these imports still further if the other oil-consuming countries will join us in a fair and mutual reduction. If we have a serious shortage, I will not hesitate to impose mandatory gasoline rationing immediately.

The single biggest factor in the inflation rate last year, the increase in the inflation rate last year, was from one cause: the skyrocketing prices of OPEC oil. We must take whatever actions are necessary to reduce our dependence of foreign oil—and at the same time reduce inflation.

As individuals and as families, few of us can produce energy by ourselves. But all of us can conserve energy—every one of us, every day of our lives. Tonight I call on you—in fact, all the people of America—to help our Nation. Conserve energy. Eliminate waste. Make 1980 indeed a year of energy conservation.

Of course, we must take other actions to strengthen our Nation's economy.

First, we will continue to reduce the deficit and then to balance the Federal budget.

Second, as we continue to work with business to hold down prices, we'll build also on the historic national accord with organized labor to restrain pay increases in a fair fight against inflation.

Third, we will continue our successful efforts to cut paperwork and to dismantle unnecessary Government regulation.

Fourth, we will continue our progress in providing jobs for America, concentrating on a major new program to provide training and work for our young people, especially minority youth. It has been said that "a mind is a terrible thing to waste." We will give our young people new hope for jobs and a better life in the 1980's.

And fifth, we must use the decade of the 1980's to attack the basic structural weaknesses and problems in our economy through measures to increase productivity, savings, and investment.

With these energy and economic policies, we will make America even stronger at home in this decade—just as our foreign and defense policies will make us stronger and safer throughout the world. We will never abandon our struggle for a just and a decent society here at home. That's the heart of America—and it's the source of our ability to inspire other people to defend their own rights abroad.

Our material resources, great as they are, are limited. Our problems are too complex for simple slogans or for quick solutions. We cannot solve them without effort and sacrifice. Walter Lippmann once reminded us, "You took the good things for granted. Now you must earn them again. For every right that you cherish, you have a duty which you must fulfill. For every good which you wish to preserve, you will have to sacrifice your comfort and your ease. There is nothing for nothing any longer."

Our challenges are formidable. But there's a new spirit of unity and resolve in our country. We move into the 1980's with confidence and hope and a bright vision of the America we want: an America strong and free, an America at peace, an America with equal rights for all citizens— and for women, guaranteed in the United States Constitution—an America with jobs and good health and good education for every citizen, an America with a clean and bountiful life in our cities and on our farms, an America that helps to feed the world, an America secure in filling its own energy needs, an America of justice, tolerance, and compassion. For this vision to come true, we must sacrifice, but this national commitment will be an exciting enterprise that will unify our people.

Together as one people, let us work to build our strength at home, and together as one indivisible union, let us seek peace and security throughout the world.

Together let us make of this time of challenge and danger a decade of national resolve and of brave achievement.

Rescue Operation: Disaster in Iran

Televised Remarks to the American People
Washington, D.C.
April 25, 1980

By April 25 the American hostages had been in captivity in the Embassy in Tehran for 173 days. That night American commandos embarked upon a daring rescue attempt. They got no further than a landing base in the Iranian desert some 200 miles from Tehran. Helicopters, they were flying, malfunctioned. Eight died when a helicopter collided with a cargo airplane. The mission was quickly aborted. It was a failure, complete and final.

The rescue attempt caught the nation and the world by surprise. During the entire period the Carter administration had sought to resolve the problem of the hostages by diplomacy and the use of diplomatic and economic sanctions. Only that week of the 21st, America's allies were meeting to decide whether they would join in such sanctions. Then, without consultations with either Congress or allies, President Carter approved the rescue attempt. At 7 A.M. President Carter announced the failure of the mission.

Late yesterday I canceled a carefully planned operation which was under way in Iran to position our rescue team for a later withdrawal of American hostages who have been held captive there since November 4.

Equipment failure in the rescue helicopter made it necessary to end the mission. As our team was withdrawing after my order to do so, two of our American aircraft collided on the ground following a refueling operation in a remote desert location in Iran.

Other information about this rescue mission will be made available to the American people when it is appropriate to do so.

There was no fighting. There was no combat. But to my deep regret eight of the crewmen of the two aircraft which collided were killed and several other Americans were hurt in the accident.

Our people were immediately airlifted from Iran. Those who were injured have gotten medical treatment and all of them are expected to recover.

No knowledge of this operation by any Iranian officials or authorities was evident to us until several hours after all Americans were withdrawn from Iran.

Our rescue team knew and I knew that the operation was certain to be difficult and it was certain to be dangerous. We were all convinced that if and when the rescue operation had been commenced, that it had an excellent chance of success.

They were all volunteers. They were all highly trained. I met with their leaders before they went on this operation. They knew then what hopes of mine and of all Americans they carried with them.

To the families of those who died and who were wounded, I want to express the admiration I feel for the courage of their loved ones and the sorrow that I feel personally for their sacrifice.

The mission on which they were involved was a humanitarian mission. It was not directed against Iran. It was not directed against the people of Iran. It was not undertaken with any feeling of hostility toward Iran or its people. It has caused no Iranian casualties.

Planning for this rescue effort began shortly after our embassy was seized, but for a number of reasons I waited until now to put those rescue plans into effect.

To be feasible this complex operation had to be the product of intensive planning and intensive training and repeated rehearsal.

However, a resolution of this crisis through negotiations and with voluntary action on the part of Iranian officials was obviously then, has been and will be preferable.

This rescue attempt had to await my judgment that the Iranian authorities could not or would not resolve this crisis on their own initiative.

With the steady unraveling of authority in Iran and the mounting dangers that were posed to the safety of the hostages themselves and the growing realization that their early release was highly unlikely. I made a decision to commence the rescue operations plans.

This attempt became a necessity and a duty. The readiness of our team to undertake the rescue made it completely practical. Accordingly, I made a decision to set our long-developed plans into operation.

I ordered this rescue mission prepared in order to safeguard American lives and protect America's national interests and to reduce the tensions in the world that have been caused among many nations as this crisis has continued.

It was my decision to attempt the rescue operation. It was my decision to cancel it when problems developed in the placement of our rescue team for a future rescue operation. The responsibility is fully my own.

In the aftermath of the attempt, we continue to hold the government of Iran responsible for the safety and for the early release of the American hostages who have been held so long.

The United States remains determined to bring about their safe release at the earliest date possible.

As president I know that our entire nation feels deep gratitude for the brave men who were prepared to rescue their fellow Americans from captivity. And as president I also know that the nation shares not only my disappointment that the rescue effort could not be mounted because of mechanical difficulties, but also my determination to persevere and to bring all of our hostages home to freedom.

We have been disappointed before. We will not give up in our efforts.

Throughout this extraordinarily difficult period, we have pursued and will continue to pursue every possible avenue to secure the release of the hostages.

In these efforts, the support of the American people and of our friends throughout the world has been a most crucial element. That support of other nations is even more important now. We will seek to continue along with other nations and the officials of Iran a prompt resolution of the crisis without any loss of life and through peaceful and diplomatic means.

Farewell Address

Washington, D.C.
January 14, 1981

When President Carter lost the 1980 election to Ronald Reagan, he became only the third elected president in the twentieth-century to fail in a re-election attempt. Six days before he relinquished the presidency to Reagan, he bade farewell to the American people, a traditional address instituted when Washington's farewell appeared in the *American Daily Advertiser* on September 19, 1796.

President Carter's speech is one of his best. It is simple, direct, and a summary of the two major concerns of his administration: preserving peace in a nuclear world and protecting human rights. It is also a melancholy address in which the President comments on the difficulties of governing this nation amid the complexities of contemporary problems and political pressures. Nonetheless, it represents President Carter at his rhetorical best.

In a few days I will lay down my official responsibilities in this office, to take up once more the only title in our democracy superior to that of President, the title of citizen.

Of Vice President Mondale, my Cabinet, and the hundreds of others who have served with me during the last 4 years, I wish to say now publicly what I have said in private: I thank them for the dedication and competence they've brought to the service of our country. But I owe my deepest thanks to you, to the American people, because you gave me this extraordinary opportunity to serve.

We've faced great challenges together, and we know that future problems will also be difficult. But I'm now more convinced than ever that the United States, better than any other country, can meet successfully whatever the future might bring. These last 4 years have made me more certain than ever of the inner strength of our country, the unchanging value of our principles and ideals, the stability of our political system, the ingenuity and the decency of our people.

Tonight I would like first to say a few words about this most special office, the Presidency of the United States. This is at once the most powerful office in the world and among the most severely constrained by law and custom. The President is given a broad responsibility to lead but cannot do so without the support and consent of the people, expressed formally through the Congress and informally in many ways through a whole range of public and private institutions. This is as it should be.

Within our system of government every American has a right and a duty to help shape the future course of the United States. Thoughtful criticism and close scrutiny of all government officials by the press and the public are an important part of our democratic society. Now, as in the past, only the understanding and involvement of the people through full and open debate can help to avoid serious mistakes and assure the continued dignity and safety of the Nation.

Today we are asking our political system to do things of which the Founding Fathers never dreamed. The government they designed for a few hundred thousand people now serves a nation of almost 230 million people. Their small coastal republic now spans beyond a continent, and we also now have the responsibility to help lead much of the world through difficult times to a secure and prosperous future.

Today, as people have become ever more doubtful of the ability of the Government to deal with our problems, we are increasingly drawn to single-issue groups and special interest organizations to ensure that whatever else happens, our own personal views and our own private interests are protected. This is a disturbing factor in American political life. It tends to distort our purposes, because the national interest is not always the sum of all our single or special interests. We are all Americans together, and we must not forget that the common good is our common interest and our individual responsibility.

Because of the fragmented pressures of these special interests, it's very important that the office of the President be a strong one and that its constitutional authority be preserved. The President is the only elected official charged with the primary responsibility of representing all the people. In the moments of decision, after the different and conflicting views have all been aired, it's the President who then must speak to the Nation and for the Nation.

I understand after 4 years in this office, as few others can, how formidable is the task the new President-elect is about to undertake, and to the very limits of conscience and conviction. I pledge to support him in that task. I wish him success, and Godspeed.

I know from experience that Presidents have to face major issues that are controversial, broad in scope, and which do not arouse the natural support of a political majority. For a few minutes now, I want to lay aside my role as leader of one nation, and speak to you as a fellow citizen of the world about three issues, three difficult issues: the threat of nuclear destruction, our stewardship of the physical resources of our planet, and the preeminence of the basic rights of human beings.

It's now been 35 years since the first atomic bomb fell on Hiroshima. The great majority of the world's people cannot remember a time when the nuclear shadow did not hang over the Earth. Our minds have adjusted to it, as after a time our eyes adjust to the dark. Yet the risk of a nuclear conflagration has not lessened. It has not happened yet, thank God, but that can give us little comfort, for it only has to happen once.

The danger is becoming greater. As the arsenals of the superpowers grow in size and sophistication and as other governments, perhaps even in the future dozens of governments, acquire these weapons, it may only be a matter of time before madness, desperation, greed, or miscalculation lets loose this terrible force.

In an all-out nuclear war, more destructive power than in all of World War II would be unleashed every second during the long afternoon it would take for all the missiles and bombs to fall. A World War II every second—more people killed in the first few hours than in all the wars of history put together. The survivors, if any, would live in despair amid the poisoned ruins of a civilization that had committed suicide.

National weakness, real or perceived, can tempt aggression and thus cause war. That's why the United States can never neglect its military strength. We must and we will remain strong. But with equal determination, the United States and all countries must find ways to control and to reduce the horrifying danger that is posed by the enormous world stockpiles of nuclear arms.

This has been a concern of every American President since the moment we first saw what these weapons could do. Our leaders will require our understanding and our support as they grapple with this difficult but crucial challenge. There is no disagreement on the goals or the basic approach to controlling this enormous destructive force. The answer lies not just in the attitudes or the actions of world leaders but in the concern and the demands of all of us as we continue our struggle to preserve the peace.

Nuclear weapons are an expression of one side of our human character. But there's another side. The same rocket technology that delivers nuclear warheads has also taken us peacefully into space. From that perspective, we see our Earth as it really is—a small and fragile and beautiful blue globe, the only home we have. We see no barriers of race or religion or country. We see the essential unity of our species and our planet. And with faith and common sense, that bright vision will ultimately prevail.

Another major challenge, therefore, is to protect the quality of this world within which we live. The shadows that fall across the future are cast not only by the kinds of weapons we've built, but by the kind of world we will either nourish or neglect. There are real and growing dangers to our simple and our most precious possessions: the air we breathe, the water we drink, and the land which sustains us. The rapid depletion of irreplaceable minerals, the erosion of topsoil, the destruction of beauty, the blight of pollution, the demands of increasing billions of people, all combine to create problems which are easy to observe and predict, but difficult to resolve. If we do not act, the world of the year 2000 will be much less able to sustain life than it is now.

But there is no reason for despair. Acknowledging the physical realities of our planet does not mean a dismal future of endless sacrifice. In fact, acknowledging these realities is the first step in dealing with them. We can meet the resource problems of the world—water, food, minerals, farmlands, forests, overpopulation, pollution—if we tackle them with courage and foresight.

I've just been talking about forces of potential destruction that mankind has developed, and how we might control them. It's equally important that we remember the beneficial forces that we have evolved over the ages and how to hold fast to them. One of those constructive forces is the enhancement of individual human freedoms throughout the strengthening of democracy and the fight against deprivation, torture, terrorism, and the persecution of people through the world. The struggle for human rights overrides all differences of color or nation or language. Those who hunger for freedom, who thirst for human dignity, and who suffer for the sake of justice, they are the patriots of this cause.

I believe with all my heart that America must always stand for these basic human rights at home and abroad. That is both our history and our destiny.

America did not invent human rights. In a very real sense, it's the other way around. Human rights invented America. Ours was the first nation in the history of the world to be founded explicitly on such an idea. Our social and political progress has been based on one fundamental principle: the value and importance of the individual. The fundamental force that unites us is not kinship or place of origin or religious preference. The love of liberty is the common blood that flows in our American veins.

The battle for human rights, at home and abroad, is far from over. We should never be surprised nor discouraged, because the impact of our efforts has had and will always have varied results. Rather, we should take pride that the ideals which gave birth to our Nation still inspire the hopes of oppressed people around the world. We have no cause for self-righteousness or complacency, but we have every reason to persevere, both within our own country and beyond our borders.

If we are to serve as a beacon for human rights, we must continue to perfect here at home the rights and the values which we espouse around the world: a decent education for our children, adequate medical care for all Americans, an end to discrimination against minorities and women, a job for all those able to work, and freedom from injustice and religious intolerance.

We live in a time of transition, an uneasy era which is likely to endure for the rest of this century. It will be a period of tensions, both within nations and between nations, of competition for scarce resources, of social, political, and economic stresses and strains. During this period we may be tempted to abandon some of the time-honored principles and commitments which have been proven during the difficult times of past generations. We must never yield to this temptation. Our American values are not luxuries, but necessities—not the salt in our bread, but the bread itself. Our common vision of a free and just society is our greatest source of cohesion at home and strength abroad greater even than the bounty of our material blessings.

Remember these words: "We hold these truths to be self-evident, that all men are created equal, that they are endowed by their Creator with certain inalienable Rights, that among these are Life, Liberty and the pursuit of Happiness."

This vision still grips the imagination of the world. But we know that democracy is always an unfinished creation. Each generation must renew its foundations. Each generation must rediscover the meaning of this hallowed vision in the light of its own modern challenges. For this generation, ours, life is nuclear survival; liberty is human rights; the pursuit of happiness is a planet whose resources are devoted to the physical and spiritual nourishment of its inhabitants.

During the next few days I will work hard to make sure that the transition from myself to the next President is a good one, that the American people are served well. And I will continue, as I have the last 14 months, to work hard and to pray for the lives and the well-being of the American hostages held in Iran. I can't predict yet what will happen, but I hope you will join me in my constant prayer for their freedom.

As I return home to the South, where I was born and raised, I look forward to the opportunity to reflect and further to assess, I hope with accuracy, the circumstances of our times. I intend to give our new President my support, and I intend to work as a citizen, as I've worked here in this office as President, for the values this Nation was founded to secure.

Again, from the bottom of my heart, I want to express to you the gratitude I feel. Thank you, fellow citizens, and farewell.

Ronald Wilson Reagan
(1981-   )

In one of his first speeches as President, Ronald Reagan stated: "The taxing power of government must be used to provide revenues for legitimate government purposes. It must not be used to regulate the economy or bring about social changes. We've tried that, and surely we must be able to see it doesn't work. Spending by government must be limited to those functions which are the proper province of government."[1] This announcement set the theme for his administration. For President Reagan, the legitimate purposes of the federal government are to provide for the national defense and to help the "truly needy." The federal government's attempts to regulate the economy or bring about social changes had, according to the President, created the major problems faced by his administration.

Reagan's basic conservative beliefs had been spelled out in "A Time for Choosing," the speech that originally brought him to prominence during the Goldwater campaign in 1964 and had sustained him as he stalked the Presidency for the next sixteen years.[2] By 1980, the time was propitious for this one-time film actor-turned-national politician. In the presidential campaign Reagan drew votes from a fervent band of conservative true believers, regular Republicans, and anti-Carter Democrats and Independents in sufficient numbers to be elected fortieth President of the United States.

President Reagan sought to establish conservative policies for the ills that beset America, especially the economic ills. To do so required changing the course of American government and marshalling public support to convince Congress that these changes were popular. Thus, the President embarked upon a massive rhetorical campaign to gain that support from the public. He was so effective during his first year that journalists dubbed him the "great communicator." What the President and his advisors actually did was grasp the potentialities inherent in the new rhetorical presidency and exploit them as fully as possible.[3] In this sense, the Reagan presidency is truly the first modern electronic presidency, and it has established techniques and methods that will be studied and copied by subsequent Presidents.

The rhetoric of the Reagan administration can be divided into three periods. During the first year, President Reagan concentrated almost exclusively on economic problems. In his major speeches he urged passage of the largest tax cut in American history, major reductions in domestic spending for social programs, and reform of regulatory agencies. He avoided major statements on foreign affairs and on the "social issues" such as abortion and school prayers.[4]

During the second year of his administration, President Reagan announced in his State of the Union Address his New Federalism, the second stage of his economic renewal program. He proposed transferring major federal programs to state and local control. However, these proposals did not fare as well as his tax and budget cuts of the previous year. State and local officials were not as receptive to assuming responsibilities for certain programs as Reagan had imagined. In addition, the economy did not respond as quickly as he had predicted to his policies of tax and budget cuts. And finally, nineteen eighty-two was an election year. By September, Reagan began spending much of his rhetorical energies defending his conservative policies as he campaigned for Republicans in the mid-term election.[5] When the Republican lost 26 seats in Congress, the election was interpreted as considerably less than an endorsement of the President and his policies.

Shortly after the mid-term elections, Reagan dramatically switched rhetorical strategy. For two years, he had placed foreign affairs in the background. But in November, 1982 he gave a major speech on the MX missile and continued into 1983 devoting major rhetorical energies to foreign affairs. The strategic change was obvious. President Reagan had achieved major successes in domestic legislation, albeit not everything he wanted, during his first two years. Now it was time to concern himself *publicly* with foreign affairs and the defense budget, two areas that are the traditional prerogatives of the President. Such a change in rhetorical emphasis would help the President regain the initiative in directing American policy and would theoretically give him advantages over his opponents.

Richard Beal, one of President Reagan's advisors stated: "The whole issue of running the Presidency in the modern age is control of the agenda."[6] During the first three years of his administration, President Reagan was more effective than not in controlling the agenda. The question facing the American people as they prepare for the 1984 election is whether the substance of that agenda is in the best interests of the country.

Notes

1. Ronald Reagan, "Program for Economic Recovery. Address Before a Joint Session of Congress. February 18, 1981," *Weekly Compilation of Presidential Documents* (February 23, 1981), p. 137.
2. "A Time for Choosing" was delivered by Reagan so many times with only slight changes that it became known as *The Speech*. See Kurt W. Ritter, "Ronald Reagan and 'The Speech': The Rhetoric of Public Relations Politics," *Western Journal of Speech Communication* XXXVII (Winter, 1968), pp. 50–58.
2. See James W. Ceaser, *et. al.*, "The Rise of the Rhetorical Presidency," reprinted in *Essays in Presidential Rhetoric*, ed. by Theodore Windt with Beth Ingold (Dubuque, Iowa: Kendall/Hunt, 1983), pp. 3–22.
4. For an analysis of the rhetoric of this first period, see Theodore Windt with Kathleen Farrell, "Presidential Rhetoric and Presidential Power: The Reagan Initiatives," in *Essays in Presidential Rhetoric*, pp. 310–322.
5. For an analysis of the rhetoric used by President Reagan during the mid-term election, see Beth A. J. Ingold and Theodore Otto Windt, Jr., "Trying to 'Stay the Course': President Reagan's Rhetoric During the 1982 Election," a paper delivered at the Speech Communication Association's national convention in Louisville, November, 1982.
6. Quoted in Sidney Blumenthal, "Marketing the President," *New York Times Magazine* (September 13, 1981), p. 110.

Inaugural Address

Washington, D.C.
January 20, 1981

President Ronald Reagan symbolically broke precedent by having his Inaugural ceremony conducted from the West Front of the Capitol instead of the East Front. But he intended more than symbolism. In his address, President Reagan signaled his intent to change the course American government had followed over the previous fifty years. To embark upon that change would require all the fortitude and abilities of a mythical western hero, and heroism became the theme of his Inaugural Address.

To a few of us here today this is a solemn and most momentous occasion, and yet in the history of our nation it is a commonplace occurrence. The orderly transfer of authority as called for in the Constitution routinely takes place, as it has for almost two centuries, and few of us stop to think how unique we really are. In the eyes of many in the world, this every-4-year ceremony we accept as normal is nothing less than a miracle.

Mr. President, I want our fellow citizens to know how much you did to carry on this tradition. By your gracious cooperation in the transition process, you have shown a watching world that we are a united people pledged to maintaining a political system which guarantees individual liberty to a greater degree than any other, and I thank you and your people for all your help in maintaining the continuity which is the bulwark of our Republic.

The business of our nation goes forward. These United States are confronted with an economic affliction of great proportions. We suffer from the longest and one of the worst sustained inflations in our national history. It distorts our economic decisions, penalizes thrift, and crushes the struggling young and the fixed-income elderly alike. It threatens to shatter the lives of millions of our people.

Idle industries have cast workers into unemployment, human misery, and personal indignity. Those who do work are denied a fair return for their labor by a tax system which penalizes successful achievement and keeps us from maintaining full productivity.

But great as our tax burden is, it has not kept pace with public spending. For decades we have piled deficit upon deficit, mortgaging our future and our children's future for the temporary convenience of the present. To continue this long trend is to guarantee tremendous social, cultural, political, and economic upheavals.

You and I, as individuals, can, by borrowing, live beyond our means, but for only a limited period of time. Why, then, should we think that collectively, as a nation, we're not bound by that same limitation? We must act today in order to preserve tomorrow. And let there be no misunderstanding: We are going to begin to act, beginning today.

The economic ills we suffer have come upon us over several decades. They will not go away in days, weeks, or months, but they will go away. They will go away because we as Americans have the capacity now, as we've had in the past, to do whatever needs to be done to preserve this last and greatest bastion of freedom.

In this present crisis, government is not the solution to our problem; government is the problem. From time to time we've been tempted to believe that society has become too complex to be managed by self-rule, that government by an elite group is superior to government for, by, and of the people. Well, if no one among us is capable of governing himself, then who among us has the capacity to govern someone else? All of us together, in and out of government, must bear the burden. The solutions we seek must be equitable, with no one group singled out to pay a higher price.

We hear much of special interest groups. Well, our concern must be for a special interest group that has been too long neglected. It knows no sectional boundaries or ethnic and racial divisions, and it crosses political party lines. It is made up of men and women who raise our food, patrol our streets, man our mines and factories, teach our children, keep our homes, and heal us when we're sick—professionals, industrialists, shopkeepers, clerks, cabbies, and truck-drivers. They are, in short, "We the people," this breed called Americans.

Well, this administration's objective will be a healthy, vigorous, growing economy that provides equal opportunities for all Americans, with no barriers born of bigotry or discrimination. Putting America back to work means putting all Americans back to work. Ending inflation means freeing all Americans from the terror of runaway living costs. All must share in the productive work of this "new beginning," and all must share in the bounty of a revived economy. With the idealism and fair play which are the core of our system and our strength, we can have a strong and prosperous America, at peace with itself and the world.

So, as we begin, let us take inventory. We are a nation that has a government—not the other way around. And this makes us special among the nations of the Earth. Our government has no power except that granted it by the people. It is time to check and reverse the growth of government, which shows signs of having grown beyond the consent of the governed.

It is my intention to curb the size and influence of the Federal establishment and to demand recognition of the distinction between the powers granted to the Federal Government and those reserved to the States or to the people. All of us need to be reminded that the Federal Government did not create the States; the States created the Federal Government.

Now, so there will be no misunderstanding, it's not my intention to do away with government. It is rather to make it work—work with us, not over us; to stand by our side, not ride on our back. Government can and must provide opportunity, not smother it; foster productivity, not stifle it.

If we look to the answer as to why for so many years we achieved so much, prospered as no other people on Earth, it was because here in this land we unleashed the energy and individual genius of man to a greater extent than has ever been done before. Freedom and the dignity of the individual have been more available and assured here than in any other place on Earth. The price for this freedom at times has been high, but we have never been unwilling to pay that price.

It is no coincidence that our present troubles parallel and are proportionate to the intervention and intrusion in our lives that result from unnecessary and excessive growth of government. It is time for us to realize that we're too great a nation to limit ourselves to small dreams. We're not, as some would have us believe, doomed to an inevitable decline. I do not believe in a fate that will fall on us no matter what we do. I do believe in a fate that will fall on us if we do nothing. So, with all the creative energy at our command, let us begin an era of national renewal. Let us renew our determination, our courage, and our strength. And let us renew our faith and our hope.

We have every right to dream heroic dreams. Those who say that we're in a time when there are not heroes, they just don't know where to look. You can see heroes every day going in and out of factory gates. Others, a handful in number, produce enough food to feed all of us and then the world beyond. You meet heroes across a counter, and they're on both sides of that counter. There are entrepreneurs with faith in themselves and faith in an idea who create new jobs, new wealth and opportunity. They're individuals and families whose taxes support the government and whose voluntary gifts support church, charity, culture, art, and education. Their patriotism is quiet, but deep. Their values sustain our national life.

Now, I have used the words "they" and "their" in speaking of these heroes. I could say "you" and "your," because I'm addressing the heroes of whom I speak—you, the citizens of this blessed land. Your dreams, your hopes, your goals are going to be the dreams, the hopes, and the goals of this administration, so help me God.

We shall reflect the compassion that is so much a part of your makeup. How can we love our country and not love our countrymen; and loving them, reach out a hand when they fall, heal them when they're sick, and provide opportunity to make them self-sufficient so they will be equal in fact and not just in theory?

Can we solve the problems confronting us? Well, the answer is an unequivocal and emphatic "yes." To paraphrase Winston Churchill, I did not take the oath I've just taken with the intention of presiding over the dissolution of the world's strongest economy.

In the days ahead I will propose removing the roadblocks that have slowed our economy and reduced productivity. Steps will be taken aimed at restoring the balance between the various levels of government. Progress may be slow, measured in inches and feet, not miles, but we will progress. It is time to reawaken this industrial giant, to get government back within its means, and to lighten our punitive tax burden. And these will be our first priorities, and on these principles there will be no compromise.

On the eve of our struggle for independence a man who might have been one of the greatest among the Founding Fathers, Dr. Joseph Warren, president of the Massachusetts Congress, said to his fellow Americans, "Our country is in danger, but not to be despaired of. . . . On you depend the fortunes of America. You are to decide the important questions upon which rests the happiness and the liberty of millions yet unborn. Act worthy of yourselves."

Well, I believe we, the Americans of today, are ready to act worthy of ourselves, ready to do what must be done to ensure happiness and liberty for ourselves, our children, and our children's children. And as we renew ourselves here in our own land, we will be seen as having greater strength throughout the world. We will again be the exemplar of freedom and a beacon of hope for those who do not now have freedom.

To those neighbors and allies who share our freedom, we will strengthen our historic ties and assure them of our support and firm commitment. We will match loyalty with loyalty. We will strive for mutually beneficial relations. We will not use our friendship to impose on their sovereignty, for our own sovereignty is not for sale.

As for the enemies of freedom, those who are potential adversaries, they will be reminded that peace is the highest aspiration of the American people. We will negotiate for it, sacrifice for it; we will not surrender for it, now or ever.

Our forbearance should never be misunderstood. Our reluctance for conflict should not be misjudged as a failure of will. When action is required to preserve our national security, we will act. We will maintain sufficient strength to prevail if need be, knowing that if we do so we have the best chance of never having to use that strength.

Above all, we must realize that no arsenal or no weapon in the arsenals of the world is so formidable as the will and moral courage of free men and women. It is a weapon our adversaries in today's world do not have. It is a weapon that we as Americans do have. Let that be understood by those who practice terrorism and prey upon their neighbors.

I'm told that tens of thousands of prayer meetings are being held on this day, and for that I'm deeply grateful. We are a nation under God, and I believe God intended for us to be free. It would be fitting and good, I think, if on each Inaugural Day in future years it should be declared a day of prayer.

This is the first time in our history that this ceremony has been held, as you've been told, on this West Front of the Capitol. Standing here, one faces a magnificent vista, opening up on this city's special beauty and history. At the end of this open mall are those shrines to the giants on whose shoulders we stand.

Directly in front of me, the monument to a monumental man, George Washington, father of our country. A man of humility who came to greatness reluctantly. He led America out of revolutionary victory into infant nationhood. Off to one side, the stately memorial to Thomas Jefferson. The Declaration of Independence flames with his eloquence. And then, beyond the Reflecting Pool, the dignified columns of the Lincoln Memorial. Whoever would understand in his heart the meaning of America will find it in the life of Abraham Lincoln.

Beyond those monuments to heroism is the Potomac River, and on the far shore the sloping hills of Arlington National Cemetery, with its row upon row of simple white markers bearing crosses or Stars of David. They add up to only a tiny fraction of the price that has been paid for our freedom.

Each one of those markers is a monument to the kind of hero I spoke of earlier. Their lives ended in places called Belleau Wood, The Argonne, Omaha Beach, Salerno, and halfway around the world on Guadalcanal, Tarawa, Pork Chop Hill, the Chosin Reservoir, and in a hundred rice paddies and jungles of a place called Vietnam.

Under one such marker lies a young man, Martin Treptow, who left his job in a small town barbershop in 1917 to go to France with the famed Rainbow Division. There, on the western front, he was killed trying to carry a message between battalions under heavy artillery fire.

We're told that on his body was found a diary. On the flyleaf under the heading, "My Pledge," he had written these words: "America must win this war. Therefore I will work, I will save, I will sacrifice, I will endure, I will fight cheerfully and do my utmost, as if the issue of the whole struggle depended on me alone."

The crisis we are facing today does not require of us the kind of sacrifice that Martin Treptow and so many thousands of others were called upon to make. It does require, however, our best effort and our willingness to believe in ourselves and to believe in our capacity to perform great deeds, to believe that together with God's help we can and will resolve the problems which now confront us.

And after all, why shouldn't we believe that? We are Americans.

God bless you, and thank you.

Reaganomics

Washington, D.C.
February 5, 1981

Upon entering the Presidency Reagan confronted the major domestic problem facing the country: the economy. On his first day in office he kept a campaign promise by ordering a federal hiring freeze. Soon thereafter in a rhetorical and media blitz, the President put forward a new set of goals and programs, soon dubbed "Reaganomics," to put the country on the road to recovery. In this first speech to the American people, Reagan declared that we were "in the worst economic mess since the Depression." It is a classic problem-causes speech. He followed it with an address to Congress on February 18 in which he presented his programmatic solutions. His rhetorical efforts were so effective that an *ABC-Washington Post* poll taken on February 19–20 showed better than 2–1 support for his policies. By the end of summer most of his proposals had been passed by Congress and Reaganomics was underway.

I'm speaking to you tonight to give you a report on the state of our Nation's economy. I regret to say that we're in the worst economic mess since the Great Depression.

A few days ago I was presented with a report I'd asked for, a comprehensive audit, if you will, of our economic condition. You won't like it. I didn't like it. But we have to face the truth and then go to work to turn things around. And make no mistake about it, we can turn them around.

I'm not going to subject you to the jumble of charts, figures, and economic jargon of that audit, but rather will try to explain where we are, how we got there, and how we can get back. First, however, let me just give a few "attention getters" from the audit.

The Federal budget is out of control, and we face runaway deficits of almost $80 billion for this budget year that ends September 30th. That deficit is larger than the entire Federal budget in 1957, and so is the almost $80 billion we will pay in interest this year on the national debt.

Twenty years ago, in 1960, our Federal Government payroll was less than $13 billion. Today it is 75 billion. During these 20 years our population has only increased by 23.3 percent. The Federal budget has gone up 528 percent.

Now, we've just had 2 years of back-to-back double-digit inflation—13.3 percent in 1979, 12.4 percent last year. The last time this happened was in World War I.

In 1960 mortgage interest rates averaged about 6 percent. They're 2½ times as high now, 15.4 percent.

The percentage of your earnings the Federal Government took in taxes in 1960 has almost doubled.

And finally there are 7 million Americans caught up in the personal indignity and human tragedy of unemployment. If they stood in a line, allowing 3 feet for each person, the line would reach from the coast of Maine to California.

Well, so much for the audit itself. Let me try to put this in personal terms. Here is a dollar such as you earned, spent, or saved in 1960. And here is a quarter, a dime, and a penny—36 cents. That's what this 1960 dollar is worth today. And if the present world inflation rate should continue 3 more years, that dollar of 1960 will be worth a quarter. What initiative is there to save? And if we don't save we're short of the investment capital needed for business and industry expansion.

Workers in Japan and West Germany save several times the percentage of their income than Americans do.

What's happened to that American dream of owning a home? Only 10 years ago a family could buy a home, and the monthly payment averaged little more than a quarter—27 cents out of each dollar earned. Today, it takes 42 cents out of every dollar of income. So, fewer than 1 out of 11 families can afford to buy their first new home.

Regulations adopted by government with the best of intentions have added $666 to the cost of an automobile. It is estimated that altogether regulations of every kind, on shopkeepers, farmers, and major industries, add $100 billion or more to the cost of the goods and services we buy. And then another 20 billion is spent by government handling the paperwork created by those regulations.

I'm sure you're getting the idea that the audit presented to me found government policies of the last few decades responsible for our economic troubles. We forgot or just overlooked the fact that government—any government—has a built-in tendency to grow. Now, we all had a hand in looking to government for benefits as if government had some source of revenue other than our earnings. Many if not most of the things we thought of or that government offered to us seemed attractive.

In the years following the Second World War it was easy, for a while at least, to overlook the price tag. Our income more than doubled in the 25 years after the war. We increased our take-home pay in those 25 years by more than we had amassed in all the preceding 150 years put together. Yes, there was some inflation, 1 or 1½ percent a year. That didn't bother us. But if we look back at those golden years, we recall that even then voices had been raised, warning that inflation, like radioactivity, was cumulative and that once started it could get out of control.

Some government programs seemed so worthwhile that borrowing to fund them didn't bother us. By 1960 our national debt stood at $284 billion. Congress in 1971 decided to put a ceiling of 400 billion on our ability to borrow. Today the debt is 934 billion. So-called temporary increases or extensions in the debt ceiling have been allowed 21 times in these 10 years, and now I've been forced to ask for another increase in the debt ceiling or the government will be unable to function past the middle of February—and I've only been here 16 days. Before we reach the day when we can reduce the debt ceiling, we may in spite of our best efforts see a national debt in excess of a trillion dollars. Now, this is a figure that's literally beyond our comprehension.

We know now that inflation results from all that deficit spending. Government has only two ways of getting money other than raising taxes. It can go into the money market and borrow, competing with its own citizens and driving up interest rates, which it has done, or it can print money, and it's done that. Both methods are inflationary.

We're victims of language. The very word "inflation" leads us to think of it as just high prices. Then, of course, we resent the person who puts on the price tags, forgetting that he or she is also a victim of inflation. Inflation is not just high prices; it's a reduction in the value of our money. When the money supply is increased but the goods and services available for buying are not, we have too much money chasing too few goods. Wars are usually accompanied by inflation. Everyone is working or fighting, but production is of weapons and munitions, not things we can buy and use.

Now, one way out would be to raise taxes so that government need not borrow or print money. But in all these years of government growth, we've reached, indeed surpassed, the limit of our people's tolerance or ability to bear an increase in the tax burden. Prior to World War II, taxes were such that on the average we only had to work just a little over 1 month each year to pay our total Federal State, and local tax bill. Today we have to work 4 months to pay that bill.

Some say shift the tax burden to business and industry, but business doesn't pay taxes. Oh, don't get the wrong idea. Business is being taxed, so much so that we're being priced out of the world market. But business must pass its costs of operations—and that includes taxes—on to the customer in the price of the product. Only people pay taxes, all the taxes. Government just uses business in a kind of sneaky way to help collect the taxes. They're hidden in the price; we aren't aware of how much tax we actually pay.

Today this once great industrial giant of ours has the lowest rate of gain in productivity of virtually all the industrial nations with whom we must compete in the world market. We can't even hold our own market here in America against foreign automobiles, steel, and a number of other products. Japanese production of automobiles is almost twice as great per worker as it is in America. Japanese steelworkers outproduce their American counterparts by about 25 percent.

Now, this isn't because they're better workers. I'll match the American working man or woman against anyone in the world. But we have to give them the tools and equipment that workers in the other industrial nations have.

We invented the assembly line and mass production, but punitive tax policies and excessive and unnecessary regulations plus government borrowing have stifled our ability to update plant and equipment. When capital investment is made, it's too often for some unproductive alterations demanded by government to meet various of its regulations. Excessive taxation of individuals has robbed us of incentive and made overtime unprofitable.

We once produced about 40 percent of the world's steel. We now produce 19 percent. We were once the greatest producer of automobiles, producing more than all the rest of the world combined. That is no longer true, and in addition, the "Big Three," the major auto companies in our land, have sustained tremendous losses in the past year and have been forced to lay off thousands of workers.

All of you who are working know that even with cost-of-living pay raises, you can't keep up with inflation. In our progressive tax system, as you increase the number of dollars you earn, you find yourself moved up into higher tax brackets, paying a higher tax rate just for trying to hold your own. The result? Your standard of living is going down.

Over the past decades we've talked of curtailing government spending so that we can then lower the tax burden. Sometimes we've even taken a run at doing that. But there were always those who told us that taxes couldn't be cut until spending was reduced. Well, you know, we can lecture our children about extravagance until we run out of voice and breath. Or we can cure their extravagance by simply reducing their allowance.

It's time to recognize that we've come to a turning point. We're threatened with an economic calamity of tremendous proportions, and the old business-as-usual treatment can't save us. Together, we must chart a different course.

We must increase productivity. That means making it possible for industry to modernize and make use of the technology which we ourselves invented. That means putting Americans back to work. And that means above all bringing government spending back within government revenues, which is the only way, together with increased productivity, that we can reduce and, yes, eliminate inflation.

In the past we've tried to fight inflation one year and then, with unemployment increased, turn the next year to fighting unemployment with more deficit spending as a pump primer. So, again, up goes inflation. It hasn't worked. We don't have to choose between inflation and unemployment—they go hand in hand. It's time to try something different, and that's what we're going to do.

I've already placed a freeze on hiring replacements for those who retire or leave government service. I've ordered a cut in government travel, the number of consultants to the government, and the buying of office equipment and other items. I've put a freeze on pending regulations and set up a task force under Vice President Bush to review regulations with an eye toward getting rid of as many as possible. I have decontrolled oil, which should result in more domestic production and less dependence on foreign oil. And I'm eliminating that ineffective Council on Wage and Price Stability.

But it will take more, much more. And we must realize there is no quick fix. At the same time, however, we cannot delay in implementing an economic program aimed at both reducing tax rates to stimulate productivity and reducing the growth in government spending to reduce unemployment and inflation.

On February 18th, I will present in detail an economic program to Congress embodying the features I've just stated. It will propose budget cuts in virtually every department of government. It is my belief that these actual budget cuts will only be part of the savings. As our Cabinet Secretaries take charge of their departments, they will search out areas of waste, extravagance, and costly overhead which could yield additional and substantial reductions.

Now, at the same time we're doing this, we must go forward with a tax relief package. I shall ask for a 10-percent reduction across the board in personal income tax rates for each of the next 3 years. Proposals will also be submitted for accelerated depreciation allowances for business to provide necessary capital so as to create jobs.

Now, here again, in saying this, I know that language, as I said earlier, can get in the way of a clear understanding of what our program is intended to do. Budget cuts can sound as if we're going to reduce total government spending to a lower level than was spent the year before. Well, this is not the case. The budgets will increase as our population increases, and each year we'll see spending increases to match that growth. Government revenues will increase as the economy grows, but the burden will be lighter for each individual, because the economic base will have been expanded by reason of the reduced rates.

Now, let me show you a chart that I've had drawn to illustrate how this can be.

Here you see two trend lines. The bottom line shows the increase in tax revenues. The red line on top is the increase in government spending. Both lines turn upward, reflecting the giant tax increase already built into the system for this year 1981, and the increases in spending built into the '81 and '82 budgets and on into the future. As you can see, the spending line rises at a steeper slant than the revenue line. And that gap between those lines illustrates the increasing deficits we've been running, including this year's $80 billion deficit.

Now, in the second chart, the lines represent the positive effects when Congress accepts our economic program. Both lines continue to rise, allowing for necessary growth, but the gap narrows as spending cuts continue over the next few years until finally the two lines come together, meaning a balanced budget.

I am confident that my administration can achieve that. At that point tax revenues, in spite of rate reductions, will be increasing faster than spending, which means we can look forward to further reductions in the tax rates.

Now, in all of this we will, of course, work closely with the Federal Reserve System toward the objective of a stable monetary policy.

Our spending cuts will not be at the expense of the truly needy. We will, however, seek to eliminate benefits to those who are not really qualified by reason of need.

As I've said before, on February 18th I will present this economic package of budget reductions and tax reform to a joint session of Congress and to you in full detail.

Our basic system is sound. We can, with compassion, continue to meet our responsibility to those who, through no fault of their own, need our help. We can meet fully the other legitimate responsibilities of government. We cannot continue any longer our wasteful ways at the expense of the workers of this land or of our children.

Since 1960 our government has spent $5.1 trillion. Our debt has grown by 648 billion. Prices have exploded by 178 percent. How much better off are we for all that? Well, we all know we're very much worse off. When we measure how harshly these years of inflation, lower productivity, and uncontrolled government growth have affected our lives, we know we must act and act now. We must not be timid. We will restore the freedom of all men and women to excel and to create. We will unleash the energy and genius of the American people, traits which have never failed us.

To the Congress of the United States, I extend my hand in cooperation, and I believe we can go forward in a bipartisan manner. I've found a real willingness to cooperate on the part of Democrats and members of my own party.

To my colleagues in the executive branch of government and to all Federal employees, I ask that we work in the spirit of service.

I urge those great institutions in America, business and labor, to be guided by the national interest, and I'm confident they will. The only special interest that we will serve is the interest of all the people.

We can create the incentives which take advantage of the genius of our economic system— a system, as Walter Lippmann observed more than 40 years ago, which for the first time in history gave men "a way of producing wealth in which the good fortune of others multiplied their own."

Our aim is to increase our national wealth so all will have more, not just redistribute what we already have which is just a sharing of scarcity. We can begin to reward hard work and risk-taking, by forcing this Government to live within its means.

Over the years we've let negative economic forces run out of control. We stalled the judgment day, but we no longer have that luxury. We're out of time.

And to you, my fellow citizens, let us join in a new determination to rebuild the foundation of our society, to work together, to act responsibly. Let us do so with the most profound respect for that which must be preserved as well as with sensitive understanding and compassion for those who must be protected.

We can leave our children with an unrepayable massive debt and a shattered economy, or we can leave them liberty in a land where every individual has the opportunity to be whatever God intended us to be. All it takes is a little common sense and recognition of our own ability. Together we can forge a new beginning for America.

Thank you, and good night.

"START"

Washington, D.C.
November 18, 1981

During the first year of his administration, President Reagan sought to keep foreign affairs in the background of the public agenda as he concentrated attention on passing his new economic programs. However, by November he could no longer avoid a major statement on Soviet-American relations, arms control, and nuclear weapons. In Europe, the "nuclear freeze" movement had attracted much support. The Soviets had attempted to exploit the issue by aligning themselves, at least in part, with the movement. Furthermore, many Europeans had doubts about the President's commitment to arms control, given his belligerent statements about the perfidy of the Soviets. At home, Democrats and liberals attacked the President for reducing money for social programs while dramatically increasing the defense budget. Therefore, on the eve of Chairman Brezhnev's trip to West Germany, President Reagan spoke at the National Press Club and presented his proposals for negotiating control over the deployment of nuclear weapons in Europe and for negotiating a reduction of strategic nuclear weapons at Geneva. The speech, given at 10 a.m. to achieve maximum attention in Europe, was directed primarily at his European audiences and soon became the administration's "zero option" position for arms control.

Officers, ladies and gentlemen of the National Press Club and, as of a very short time ago, fellow members:

Back in April while in the hospital I had, as you can readily understand, a lot of time for reflection. And one day I decided to send a personal, handwritten letter to Soviet President Leonid Brezhnev reminding him that we had met about 10 years ago in San Clemente, California, as he and President Nixon were concluding a series of meetings that had brought hope to all the world. Never had peace and good will seemed closer at hand.

I'd like to read you a few paragraphs from that letter. "Mr. President: When we met, I asked if you were aware that the hopes and aspirations of millions of people throughout the world were dependent on the decisions that would be reached in those meetings. You took my hand in both of yours and assured me that you were aware of that and that you were dedicated with all your heart and soul and mind to fulfilling those hopes and dreams."

I went on in my letter to say: "The people of the world still share that hope. Indeed, the peoples of the world, despite differences in racial and ethnic origin, have very much in common. They want the dignity of having some control over their individual lives, their destiny. They want to work at the craft or trade of their own choosing and to be fairly rewarded. They want to raise their families in peace without harming anyone or suffering harm themselves. Government exists for their convenience, not the other way around.

"If they are incapable, as some would have us believe, of self-government, then where among them do we find any who are capable of governing others?

"Is it possible that we have permitted ideology, political and economic philosophies, and governmental policies to keep us from considering the very real, everyday problems of our peoples? Will the average Soviet family be better off or even aware that the Soviet Union has imposed a government of its own choice on the people of Afghanistan? Is life better for the people of Cuba because the Cuban military dictate who shall govern the people of Angola?

"It is often implied that such things have been made necessary because of territorial ambitions of the United States; that we have imperialistic designs, and thus constitute a threat to your own security and that of the newly emerging nations. Not only is there no evidence to support such a charge, there is solid evidence that the United States, when it could have dominated the world with no risk to itself, made no effort whatsoever to do so.

"When World War II ended, the United States had the only undamaged industrial power in the world. Our military might was at its peak, and we alone had the ultimate weapon, the nuclear weapon, with the unquestioned ability to deliver it anywhere in the world. If we had sought world domination then, who could have opposed us?

"But the United States followed a different course, one unique in all the history of mankind. We used our power and wealth to rebuild the war-ravished economies of the world, including those of the nations who had been our enemies. May I say, there is absolutely no substance to charges that the United States is guilty of imperialism or attempts to impose its will on other countries, by use of force."

I continued my letter by saying—or concluded my letter, I should say—by saying, "Mr. President, should we not be concerned with eliminating the obstacles which prevent our people, those you and I represent, from achieving their most cherished goals?"

Well, it's in the same spirit that I want to speak today to this audience and the people of the world about America's program for peace and the coming negotiations which begin November 30th in Geneva, Switzerland. Specifically, I want to present our program for preserving peace in Europe and our wider program for arms control.

Twice in my lifetime, I have seen the peoples of Europe plunged into the tragedy of war. Twice in my lifetime, Europe has suffered destruction and military occupation in wars that statesmen proved powerless to prevent, soldiers unable to contain, and ordinary citizens unable to escape. And twice in my lifetime, young Americans have bled their lives into the soil of those battlefields not to enrich or enlarge our domain, but to restore the peace and independence of our friends and Allies.

All of us who lived through those troubled times share a common resolve that they must never come again. And most of us share a common appreciation of the Atlantic Alliance that has made a peaceful, free, and prosperous Western Europe in the post-war era possible.

But today, a new generation is emerging on both sides of the Atlantic. Its members were not present at the creation of the North Atlantic Alliance. Many of them don't fully understand its roots in defending freedom and rebuilding a war-torn continent. Some young people question why we need weapons, particularly nuclear weapons, to deter war and to assure peaceful development. They fear that the accumulation of weapons itself may lead to conflagration. Some even propose unilateral disarmament.

I understand their concerns. Their questions deserve to be answered. But we have an obligation to answer their questions on the basis of judgment and reason and experience. Our policies have resulted in the longest European peace in this century. Wouldn't a rash departure from these policies, as some now suggest, endanger that peace?

From its founding, the Atlantic Alliance has preserved the peace through unity, deterrence, and dialog. First, we and our Allies have stood united by the firm commitment that an attack upon any one of us would be considered an attack upon us all. Second, we and our Allies have deterred aggression by maintaining forces strong enough to ensure that any aggressor would lose more from an attack than he could possibly gain. And third, we and our Allies have engaged the Soviets in a dialog about mutual restraint and arms limitations, hoping to reduce the risk of war and the burden of armaments and to lower the barriers that divide East from West.

These three elements of our policy have preserved the peace in Europe for more than a third of a century. They can preserve it for generations to come, so long as we pursue them with sufficient will and vigor.

Today, I wish to reaffirm America's commitment to the Atlantic Alliance and our resolve to sustain the peace. And from my conversations with allied leaders, I know that they also remain true to this tried and proven course.

NATO's policy of peace is based on restraint and balance. No NATO weapons, conventional or nuclear, will ever be used in Europe except in response to attack. NATO's defense plans have been responsible and restrained. The Allies remain strong, united, and resolute. But the momentum of the continuing Soviet military buildup threatens both the conventional and the nuclear balance.

Consider the facts. Over the past decade, the United States reduced the size of its Armed Forces and decreased its military spending. The Soviets steadily increased the number of men under arms. They now number more than double those of the United States. Over the same period, the Soviets expanded their real military spending by about one-third. The Soviet Union increased its inventory of tanks to some 50,000, compared to our 11,000. Historically a land power, they transformed their navy from a coastal defense force to an open ocean fleet, while the United States, a sea power with transoceanic alliances, cut its fleet in half.

During a period when NATO deployed no new intermediate-range nuclear missiles and actually withdrew 1,000 nuclear warheads, the Soviet Union deployed more than 750 nuclear warheads on the new SS-20 missiles alone.

Our response to this relentless buildup of Soviet military power has been restrained but firm. We have made decisions to strengthen all three legs of the strategic triad: sea-, land-, and air-based. We have proposed a defense program in the United States for the next 5 years which will remedy the neglect of the past decade and restore the eroding balance on which our security depends.

I would like to discuss more specifically the growing threat to Western Europe which is posed by the continuing deployment of certain Soviet intermediate-range nuclear missiles. The Soviet Union has three different type such missile systems: the SS-20, the SS-4, and the SS-5, all with the range capable of reaching virtually all of Western Europe. There are other Soviet weapon systems which also represent a major threat.

Now, the only answer to these systems is a comparable threat to Soviet threats, to Soviet targets; in other words, a deterrent preventing the use of these Soviet weapons by the counterthreat of a like response against their own territory. At present, however, there is no equivalent deterrent to these Soviet intermediate missiles. And the Soviets continue to add one new SS-20 a week.

To counter this, the Allies agreed in 1979, as part of a two-track decision, to deploy as a deterrent land-based cruise missiles and Pershing II missiles capable of reaching targets in the Soviet Union. These missiles are to be deployed in several countries of Western Europe. This relatively limited force in no way serves as a substitute for the much larger strategic umbrella spread over our NATO Allies. Rather, it provides a vital link between conventional shorter-range nuclear forces in Europe and intercontinental forces in the United States.

Deployment of these systems will demonstrate to the Soviet Union that this link cannot be broken. Deterring war depends on the perceived ability of our forces to perform effectively. The more effective our forces are, the less likely it is that we'll have to use them. So, we and our allies are proceeding to modernize NATO's nuclear forces of intermediate range to meet increased Soviet deployments of nuclear systems threatening Western Europe.

Let me turn now to our hopes for arms control negotiations. There's a tendency to make this entire subject overly complex. I want to be clear and concise. I told you of the letter I wrote to President Brezhnev last April. Well, I've just sent another message to the Soviet leadership. It's a simple, straightforward, yet, historic message. The United States proposes the mutual reduction of conventional intermediate-range nuclear and strategic forces. Specifically, I have proposed a four-point agenda to achieve this objective in my letter to President Brezhnev.

The first and most important point concerns the Geneva negotiations. As part of the 1979 two-track decision, NATO made a commitment to seek arms control negotiations with the Soviet Union on intermediate range nuclear forces. The United States has been preparing for these negotiations through close consultation with our NATO partners.

We're now ready to set forth our proposal. I have informed President Brezhnev that when our delegation travels to the negotiations on intermediate range, land-based nuclear missiles in Geneva on the 30th of this month, my representatives will present the following proposal: The United States is prepared to cancel its deployment of Pershing II and ground-launch cruise missiles if the Soviets will dismantle their SS-20, SS-4, and SS-5 missiles. This would be an historic step. With Soviet agreement, we could together substantially reduce the dread threat of nuclear war which hangs over the people of Europe. This, like the first footstep on the Moon, would be a giant step for mankind.

Now, we intend to negotiate in good faith and go to Geneva willing to listen to and consider the proposals of our Soviet counterparts, but let me call to your attention the background against which our proposal is made.

During the past 6 years while the United States deployed no new intermediate-range missiles and withdrew 1,000 nuclear warheads from Europe, the Soviet Union deployed 750 warheads on mobile, accurate ballistic missiles. They now have 1,100 warheads on the SS-20s, SS-4s and 5s. And the United States has no comparable missiles. Indeed, the United States dismantled the last such missile in Europe over 15 years ago.

As we look to the future of the negotiations, it's also important to address certain Soviet claims, which left unrefuted could become critical barriers to real progress in arms control.

The Soviets assert that a balance of intermediate range nuclear forces already exists. That assertion is wrong. By any objective measure, as this chart indicates, the Soviet Union has developed an increasingly overwhelming advantage. They now enjoy a superiority on the order of six to one. The red is the Soviet buildup; the blue is our own. That is 1975, and that is 1981.

Now, Soviet spokesmen have suggested that moving their SS-20s behind the Ural Mountains will remove the threat to Europe. Well, as this map demonstrates, the SS-20s, even if deployed behind the Urals, will have a range that puts almost all of Western Europe—the great cities— Rome, Athens, Paris, London, Brussels, Amsterdam, Berlin, and so many more—all of Scandinavia, all of the Middle East, all of northern Africa, all within range of these missiles which, incidentally, are mobile and can be moved on shorter notice. These little images mark the present location which would give them a range clear out into the Atlantic.

The second proposal that I've made to President Brezhnev concerns strategic weapons. The United States proposes to open negotiations on strategic arms as soon as possible next year.

I have instructed Secretary Haig to discuss the timing of such meetings with Soviet representatives. Substance, however, is far more important than timing. As our proposal for the Geneva talks this month illustrates, we can make proposals for genuinely serious reductions, but only if we take the time to prepare carefully.

The United States has been preparing carefully for resumption of strategic arms negotiations because we don't want a repetition of past disappointments. We don't want an arms control process that sends hopes soaring only to end in dashed expectations.

Now, I have informed President Brezhnev that we will seek to negotiate substantial reductions in nuclear arms which would result in levels that are equal and verifiable. Our approach to verification will be to emphasize openness and creativity, rather than the secrecy and suspicion which have undermined confidence in arms control in the past.

While we can hope to benefit from work done over the past decade in strategic arms negotiations, let us agree to do more than simply begin where these previous efforts left off. We can and should attempt major qualitative and quantitative progress. Only such progress can fulfill the hopes of our own people and the rest of the world. And let us see how far we can go in achieving truly substantial reductions in our strategic arsenals.

To symbolize this fundamental change in direction, we will call these negotiations START— Strategic Arms Reduction Talks.

The third proposal I've made to the Soviet Union is that we act to achieve equality at lower levels of conventional forces in Europe. The defense needs of the Soviet Union hardly call for maintaining more combat divisions in East Germany today than were in the whole Allied invasion force that landed in Normandy on D-Day. The Soviet Union could make no more convincing contribution to peace in Europe, and in the world, than by agreeing to reduce its conventional forces significantly and constrain the potential for sudden aggression.

Finally, I have pointed out to President Brezhnev that to maintain peace we must reduce the risks of surprise attack and the chance of war arising out of uncertainty or miscalculation.

I am renewing our proposal for a conference to develop effective measures that would reduce these dangers. At the current Madrid meeting of the Conference on Security and Cooperation in Europe, we're laying the foundation for a Western-proposed conference on disarmament in Europe. This conference would discuss new measures to enhance stability and security in Europe. Agreement in this conference is within reach. I urge the Soviet Union to join us and many other nations who are ready to launch this important enterprise.

All of these proposals are based on the same fair-minded principles—substantial, militarily significant reduction in forces, equal ceilings for similar types of forces, and adequate provisions for verification.

My administration, our country, and I are committed to achieving arms reductions agreements based on these principles. Today I have outlined the kinds of bold, equitable proposals which the world expects of us. But we cannot reduce arms unilaterally. Success can only come if the Soviet Union will share our commitment, if it will demonstrate that its often-repeated professions of concern for peace will be matched by positive action.

Preservation of peace in Europe and the pursuit of arms reduction talks are of fundamental importance. But we must also help to bring peace and security to regions now torn by conflict, external intervention, and war.

The American concept of peace goes well beyond the absence of war. We foresee a flowering of economic growth and individual liberty in a world at peace.

At the economic summit conference in Cancún, I met with the leaders of 21 nations and sketched out our approach to global economic growth. We want to eliminate the barriers to trade and investment which hinder these critical incentives to growth, and we're working to develop new programs to help the poorest nations achieve self-sustaining growth.

And terms like "peace" and "security", we have to say, have little meaning for the oppressed and the destitute. They also mean little to the individual whose state has stripped him of human freedom and dignity. Wherever there is oppression, we must strive for the peace and security of individuals as well as states. We must recognize that progress and the pursuit of liberty is a necessary complement to military security. Nowhere has this fundamental truth been more boldly and clearly stated than in the Helsinki Accords of 1975. These accords have not yet been translated into living reality.

Today I've announced an agenda that can help to achieve peace, security, and freedom across the globe. In particular, I have made an important offer to forego entirely deployment of new American missiles in Europe if the Soviet Union is prepared to respond on an equal footing.

There is no reason why people in any part of the world should have to live in permanent fear of war or its spectre. I believe the time has come for all nations to act in a responsible spirit that doesn't threaten other states. I believe the time is right to move forward on arms control and the resolution of critical regional disputes at the conference table. Nothing will have a higher priority for me and for the American people over the coming months and years.

Addressing the United Nations 20 years ago, another American President described the goal that we still pursue today. He said, "If we all can persevere, if we can look beyond our shores and ambitions, then surely the age will dawn in which the strong are just and the weak secure and the peace preserved."

He didn't live to see that goal achieved. I invite all nations to join with America today in the quest for such a world.

Thank you.

Sounds like a 2nd ... Sov U Address. Refers back to Reagonomics like speech which was a lot S of U

State of the Union:
The New Federalism

Washington, D.C.
January 26, 1982

In his first State of the Union address (Reagan did not present one his first year in office), the President concentrated on the traditional topics for such an address. He recounted his successes from the previous year, gave an optimistic forecast for the future if his policies were continued, and attempted to set the legislative priorities for the coming year. During the first year President Reagan had gotten passed his controversial tax and budget cuts intended to relieve immediate economic ills. In his second year he proposed a New Federalism in which some major federal responsibilities would be returned to state and local governments. This speech represented the opening rhetorical thrust for this second part of his new economic program.

Today marks my first State of the Union address to you, a constitutional duty as old as our Republic itself.

President Washington began this tradition in 1790 after reminding the Nation that the destiny of self-government and the "preservation of the sacred fire of liberty" is "finally staked on the experiment entrusted to the hands of the American people." For our friends in the press, who place a high premium on accuracy, let me say: I did not actually hear George Washington say that. But it is a matter of historic record.

But from this podium, Winston Churchill asked the free world to stand together against the onslaught of aggression. Franklin Delano Roosevelt spoke of a day of infamy and summoned a nation to arms. Douglas MacArthur made an unforgettable farewell to a country he loved and served so well. Dwight Eisenhower reminded us that peace was purchased only at the price of strength. And John F. Kennedy spoke of the burden and glory that is freedom.

When I visited this chamber last year as a newcomer to Washington, critical of past policies which I believed had failed, I proposed a new spirit of partnership between this Congress and this administration and between Washington and our State and local governments. In forging this new partnership for America, we could achieve the oldest hopes of our Republic—prosperity for our nation, peace for the world, and the blessings of individual liberty for our children and, someday, for all of humanity.

It's my duty to report to you tonight on the progress that we have made in our relations with other nations, on the foundation we've carefully laid for our economic recovery, and finally, on a bold and spirited initiative that I believe can change the face of American government and make it again the servant of the people.

Seldom have the stakes been higher for America. What we do and say here will make all the difference to autoworkers in Detroit, lumberjacks in the Northwest, steelworkers in Steubenville who are in the unemployment lines; to black teenagers in Newark and Chicago; to hard-pressed farmers and small businessmen; and to millions of everyday Americans who harbor the simple wish of a safe and financially secure future for their children. To understand the state of the Union, we must look not only at where we are and where we're going but where we've been. The situation at this time last year was truly ominous.

The last decade has seen a series of recessions. There was a recession in 1970, in 1974, and again in the spring of 1980. Each time, unemployment increased and inflation soon turned up again. We coined the word "stagflation" to describe this.

Government's response to these recessions was to pump up the money supply and increase spending. In the last 6 months of 1980, as an example, the money supply increased at the fastest rate in postwar history—13 percent. Inflation remained in double digits, and government spending increased at an annual rate of 17 percent. Interest rates reached a staggering 21½ percent. There were 8 million unemployed.

Late in 1981 we sank into the present recession, largely because continued high interest rates hurt the auto industry and construction. And there was a drop in productivity, and the already high unemployment increased.

This time, however, things are different. We have an economic program in place, completely different from the artificial quick-fixes of the past. It calls for a reduction of the rate of increase in government spending, and already that rate has been cut nearly in half. But reduced spending alone isn't enough. We've just implemented the first and smallest phase of a 3-year tax-rate reduction designed to stimulate the economy and create jobs. Already interest rates are down to 15¾ percent, but they must still go lower. Inflation is down from 12.4 percent to 8.9, and for the month of December it was running at an annualized rate of 5.2 percent. If we had not acted as we did, things would be far worse for all Americans than they are today. Inflation, taxes, and interest rates would all be higher.

A year ago, Americans' faith in their governmental process was steadily declining. Six out of 10 Americans were saying they were pessimistic about their future. A new kind of defeatism was heard. Some said our domestic problems were uncontrollable, that we had to learn to live with this seemingly endless cycle of high inflation and high unemployment.

There were also pessimistic predictions about the relationship between our administration and this Congress. It was said we could never work together. Well, those predictions were wrong. The record is clear, and I believe that history will remember this as an era of American renewal, remember this administration as an administration of change, and remember this Congress as a Congress of destiny.

Together, we not only cut the increase in government spending nearly in half, we brought about the largest tax reductions and the most sweeping changes in our tax structure since the beginning of this century. And because we indexed future taxes to the rate of inflation, we took away government's built-in profit on inflation and its hidden incentive to grow larger at the expense of American workers.

Together, after 50 years of taking power away from the hands of the people in their States and local communities, we have started returning power and resources to them.

Together, we have cut the growth of new Federal regulations nearly in half. In 1981 there were 23,000 fewer pages in the *Federal Register* which lists new regulations, than there were in 1980. By deregulating oil we've come closer to achieving energy independence and helped bring down the cost of gasoline and heating fuel.

Together, we have created an effective Federal strike force to combat waste and fraud in government. In just 6 months it has saved the taxpayers more than $2 billion, and it's only getting started.

Together we've begun to mobilize the private sector, not to duplicate wasteful and discredited government programs, but to bring thousands of Americans into a volunteer effort to help solve many of America's social problems.

Together we've begun to restore that margin of military safety that ensures peace. Our country's uniform is being worn once again with pride.

Together we have made a New Beginning, but we have only begun.

No one pretends that the way ahead will be easy. In my Inaugural Address last year, I warned that the "ills we suffer have come upon us over several decades. They will not go away in days, weeks, or months, but they will go away . . . because we as Americans have the capacity now, as we've had it in the past, to do whatever needs to be done to preserve this last and greatest bastion of freedom."

The economy will face difficult moments in the months ahead. But the program for economic recovery that is in place will pull the economy out of its slump and put us on the road to prosperity and stable growth by the latter half of this year. And that is why I can report to you tonight that in the near future the state of the Union and the economy will be better—much better—if we summon the strength to continue on the course that we've charted.

And so, the question: If the fundamentals are in place, what now? Well, two things. First, we must understand what's happening at the moment to the economy. Our current problems are not the product of the recovery program that's only just now getting underway, as some would have you believe; they are the inheritance of decades of tax and tax and spend and spend.

Second, because our economic problems are deeply rooted and will not respond to quick political fixes, we must stick to our carefully integrated plan for recovery. That plan is based on four commonsense fundamentals: continued reduction of the growth in Federal spending; preserving the individual and business tax reductions that will stimulate saving and investment; removing unnecessary Federal regulations to spark productivity; and maintaining a healthy dollar and a stable monetary policy, the latter a responsibility of the Federal Reserve System.

The only alternative being offered to this economic program is a return to the policies that gave us a trillion-dollar debt, runaway inflation, runaway interest rates and unemployment. The doubters would have us turn back the clock with tax increases that would offset the personal tax-rate reductions already passed by this Congress. Raise present taxes to cut future deficits, they tell us. Well, I don't believe we should buy that argument.

There are too many imponderables for anyone to predict deficits or surpluses several years ahead with any degree of accuracy. The budget in place, when I took office, had been projected as balanced. It turned out to have one of the biggest deficits in history. Another example of the imponderables that can make deficit projections highly questionable—a change of only one percentage point in unemployment can alter a deficit up or down by some $25 billion.

As it now stands, our forecast, which we're required by law to make, will show major deficits starting at less than a hundred billion dollars and declining, but still too high. More important, we're making progress with the three keys to reducing deficits: economic growth, lower interest rates, and spending control. The policies we have in place will reduce the deficit steadily, surely, and in time, completely.

Higher taxes would not mean lower deficits. If they did, how would we explain that tax revenues more than doubled just since 1976; yet in that same 6-year period we ran the largest series of deficits in our history. In 1980 tax revenues increased by $54 billion and in 1980 we had one of our alltime biggest deficits. Raising taxes won't balance the budget; it will encourage more government spending and less private investment. Raising taxes will slow economic growth, reduce production, and destroy future jobs, making it more difficult for those without jobs to find them and more likely that those who now have jobs could lose them. So, I will not ask you to try to balance the budget on the backs of the American taxpayers.

I will seek no tax increases this year, and I have no intention of retreating from our basic program of tax relief. I promise to bring the American people—to bring their tax rates down and to keep them down, to provide them incentives to rebuild our economy, to save, to invest in America's future. I will stand by my word. Tonight I'm urging the American people: Seize these new opportunities to produce, to save, to invest, and together we'll make this economy a mighty engine of freedom, hope, and prosperity again.

Now, the budget deficit this year will exceed our earlier expectations. The recession did that. It lowered revenues and increased costs. To some extent, we're also victims of our own success. We've brought inflation down faster than we thought we could, and in doing this, we've deprived government of those hidden revenues that occur when inflation pushes people into higher income tax brackets. And the continued high interest rates last year cost the government about $5 billion more than anticipated.

We must cut out more nonessential government spending and root out more waste, and we will continue our efforts to reduce the number of employees in the Federal work force by 75,000.

The budget plan I submit to you on February 8th will realize major savings by dismantling the Departments of Energy and Education and by eliminating ineffective subsidies for business. We'll continue to redirect our resources to our two highest budget priorities—a strong national defense to keep America free and at peace and a reliable safety net of social programs for those who have contributed and those who are in need.

Contrary to some of the wild charges you may have heard, this administration has not and will not turn its back on America's elderly or America's poor. Under the new budget, funding for social insurance programs will be more than double the amount spent only 6 years ago. But it would be foolish to pretend that these or any programs cannot be made more efficient and economical.

The entitlement programs that make up our safety net for the truly needy have worthy goals and many deserving recipients. We will protect them. But there's only one way to see to it that these programs really help those whom they were designed to help. And that is to bring their spiraling costs under control.

Today we face the absurd situation of a Federal budget with three-quarters of its expenditures routinely referred to as "uncontrollable." And a large part of this goes to entitlement programs.

Committee after committee of this Congress has heard witness after witness describe many of these programs as poorly administered and rife with waste and fraud. Virtually every American who shops in a local supermarket is aware of the daily abuses that take place in the food stamp program, which has grown by 16,000 percent in the last 15 years. Another example is Medicare and Medicaid—programs with worthy goals but whose costs have increased from 11.2 billion to almost 60 billion, more than 5 times as much, in just 10 years.

Waste and fraud are serious problems. Back in 1980, Federal investigators testified before one of your committees that "corruption has permeated virtually every area of the Medicare and Medicaid health care industry." One official said many of the people who are cheating the system were "very confident that nothing was going to happen to them." Well, something is going to happen. Not only the taxpayers are defrauded; the people with real dependency on these programs are deprived of what they need, because available resources are going not to the needy, but to the greedy.

The time has come to control the uncontrollable. In August, we made a start. I signed a bill to reduce the growth of these programs by $44 billion over the next 3 years while at the same time preserving essential services for the truly needy. Shortly you will receive from me a message on further reforms we intend to install—some new, but others long recommended by your own congressional committees. I ask you to help make these savings for the American taxpayer.

The savings we propose in entitlement programs will total some $63 billion over 4 years and will, without affecting social security, go a long way toward bringing Federal spending under control.

But don't be fooled by those who proclaim that spending cuts will deprive the elderly, the needy, and the helpless. The Federal Government will still subsidize 95 million meals every day. That's one out of seven of all the meals served in America. Head Start, senior nutrition programs, and child welfare programs will not be cut from the levels we proposed last year. More than one-half billion dollars has been proposed for minority business assistance. And research at the National Institute of Health will be increased by over $100 million. While meeting all these needs, we intend to plug unwarranted tax loopholes and strengthen the law which requires all large corporations to pay a minimum tax.

I am confident the economic program we've put into operation will protect the needy while it triggers a recovery that will benefit all Americans. It will stimulate the economy, result in increased savings and provide capital for expansion, mortgages for homebuilding, and jobs for the unemployed.

Now that the essentials of that program are in place, our next major undertaking must be a program—just as bold, just as innovative—to make government again accountable to the people, to make our system of federalism work again.

Our citizens feel they've lost control of even the most basic decisions made about the essential services of government, such as schools, welfare, roads, and even garbage collection. And they're right. A maze of interlocking jurisdictions and levels of government confronts average citizens in trying to solve even the simplest of problems. They don't know where to turn for answers, who to hold accountable, who to praise, who to blame, who to vote for or against. The main reason for this is the overpowering growth of Federal grants-in-aid programs during the past few decades.

In 1960 the Federal Government had 132 categorical grant programs, costing $7 billion. When I took office, there were approximately 500, costing nearly a hundred billion dollars—13 programs for energy, 36 for pollution control, 66 for social services, 90 for education. And here in the Congress, it takes at least 166 committees just to try to keep track of them.

You know and I know that neither the President nor the Congress can properly oversee this jungle of grants-in-aid; indeed, the growth of these grants has led to the distortion in the vital functions of government. As one Democratic Governor put it recently: The National Government should be worrying about "arms control, not potholes."

The growth in these Federal programs has—in the words of one intergovernmental commission—made the Federal Government "more pervasive, more intrusive, more unmanageable, more ineffective and costly, and above all, more [un]accountable." Let's solve this problem with a single, bold stroke: the return of some $47 billion in Federal programs to State and local government, together with the means to finance them and a transition period of nearly 10 years to avoid unnecessary disruption.

I will shortly send this Congress a message describing this program. I want to emphasize, however, that its full details will have been worked out only after close consultation with congressional, State, and local officials.

Starting in fiscal 1984, the Federal Government will assume full responsibility for the cost of the rapidly growing Medicaid program to go along with its existing responsibility for Medicare. As part of a financially equal swap, the States will simultaneously take full responsibility for Aid to Families with Dependent Children and food stamps. This will make welfare less costly and more responsive to genuine need, because it'll be designed and administered closer to the grass-roots and the people it serves.

In 1984 the Federal Government will apply the full proceeds from certain excise taxes to a grassroots trust fund that will belong in fair shares to the 50 States. The total amount flowing into this fund will be $28 billion a year. Over the next 4 years the States can use this money in either of two ways. If they want to continue receiving Federal grants in such areas as transportation, education, and social services, they can use their trust fund money to pay for the grants. Or to the extent they choose to forgo the Federal grant programs, they can use their trust fund money on their own for those or other purposes. There will be a mandatory pass-through of part of these funds to local governments.

By 1988 the States will be in complete control of over 40 Federal grant programs. The trust fund will start to phase out, eventually to disappear, and the excise taxes will be turned over to the States. They can then preserve, lower, or raise taxes on their own and fund and manage these programs as they see fit.

In a single stroke we will be accomplishing a realignment that will end cumbersome administration and spiraling costs at the Federal level while we ensure these programs will be more responsive to both the people they're meant to help and the people who pay for them.

Hand in hand with this program to strengthen the discretion and flexibility of State and local governments, we're proposing legislation for an experimental effort to improve and develop our depressed urban areas in the 1980's and '90's. This legislation will permit States and localities to apply to the Federal Government for designation as urban enterprise zones. A broad range of special economic incentives in the zones will help attract new business, new jobs, new opportunity to America's inner cities and rural towns. Some will say our mission is to save free enterprise. Well, I say we must free enterprise so that together we can save America.

Some will also say our States and local communities are not up to the challenge of a new and creative partnership. Well, that might have been true 20 years ago before reforms like reapportionment and the Voting Rights Act, the 10-year extension of which I strongly support. It's no longer true today. This administration has faith in State and local governments and the constitutional balance envisioned by the Founding Fathers. We also believe in the integrity, decency, and sound, good sense of grassroots Americans.

Our faith in the American people is reflected in another major endeavor. Our Private Sector Initiatives Task Force is seeking out successful community models of school, church, business, union, foundation, and civic programs that help community needs. Such groups are almost invariably far more efficient than government in running social programs.

We're not asking them to replace discarded and often discredited government programs dollar for dollar, service for service. We just want to help them perform the good works they choose and help others to profit by their example. Three hundred and eighty-five thousand corporations and private organizations are already working on social programs ranging from drug rehabilitation to job training, and thousands more Americans have written us asking how they can help. The volunteer spirit is still alive and well in America.

Our nation's long journey towards civil rights for all our citizens—once a source of discord, now a source of pride—must continue with no backsliding or slowing down. We must and shall see that those basic laws that guarantee equal rights are preserved and, when necessary, strengthened.

Our concern for equal rights for women is firm and unshakable. We launched a new Task Force on Legal Equity for Women and a Fifty-States Project that will examine State laws for discriminatory language. And for the first time in our history, a woman sits on the highest court in the land.

So, too, the problem of crime—one as real and deadly serious as any in America today. It demands that we seek transformation of our legal system, which overly protects the rights of criminals while it leaves society and the innocent victims of crime without justice.

We look forward to the enactment of a responsible Clean Air Act to increase jobs while continuing to improve the quality of our air. We're encouraged by the bipartisan initiative of the House and are hopeful of further progress as the Senate continues its deliberations.

So far, I've concentrated largely, now, on domestic matters. To view the state of the Union in perspective, we must not ignore the rest of the world. There isn't time tonight for a lengthy treatment of social—or foreign policy, I should say, a subject I intend to address in detail in the near future. A few words, however, are in order on the progress we've made over the past year, reestablishing respect for our nation around the globe and some of the challenges and goals that we will approach in the year ahead.

At Ottawa and Cancún, I met with leaders of the major industrial powers and developing nations. Now, some of those I met with were a little surprised that I didn't apologize for America's wealth. Instead, I spoke of the strength of the free marketplace system and how that system could help them realize their aspirations for economic development and political freedom. I believe lasting friendships were made, and the foundation was laid for future cooperation.

In the vital region of the Caribbean Basin, we're developing a program of aid, trade, and investment incentives to promote self-sustaining growth and a better, more secure life for our neighbors to the south. Toward those who would export terrorism and subversion in the Caribbean and elsewhere, especially Cuba and Libya, we will act with firmness.

Our foreign policy is a policy of strength, fairness, and balance. By restoring America's military credibility, by pursuing peace at the negotiating table wherever both sides are willing to sit down in good faith, and by regaining the respect of America's allies and adversaries alike, we have strengthened our country's position as a force for peace and progress in the world.

When action is called for, we're taking it. Our sanctions against the military dictatorship that has attempted to crush human rights in Poland—and against the Soviet regime behind that military dictatorship—clearly demonstrated to the world that America will not conduct "business as usual" with the forces of oppression. If the events in Poland continue to deteriorate, further measures will follow.

Now, let me also note that private American groups have taken the lead in making January 30th a day of solidarity with the people of Poland. So, too, the European Parliament has called for March 21st to be an international day of support for Afghanistan. Well, I urge all peace-loving peoples to join together on those days, to raise their voices, to speak and pray for freedom.

Meanwhile, we're working for reduction of arms and military activities, as I announced in my address to the nation last November 18th. We have proposed to the Soviet Union a far-reaching agenda for mutual reduction of military forces and have already initiated negotiations with them in Geneva on intermediate-range nuclear forces. In those talks it is essential that we negotiate from a position of strength. There must be a real incentive for the Soviets to take these talks seriously. This requires that we rebuild our defenses.

In the last decade, while we sought the moderation of Soviet power through a process of restraint and accommodation, the Soviets engaged in an unrelenting buildup of their military forces. The protection of our national security has required that we undertake a substantial program to enhance our military forces.

We have not neglected to strengthen our traditional alliances in Europe and Asia, or to develop key relationships with our partners in the Middle East and other countries. Building a more peaceful world requires a sound strategy and the national resolve to back it up. When radical forces threaten our friends, when economic misfortune creates conditions of instability, when strategically vital parts of the world fall under the shadow of Soviet power, our response can make the difference between peaceful change or disorder and violence. That's why we've laid such stress not only on our own defense but on our vital foreign assistance program. Your recent passage of the Foreign Assistance Act sent a signal to the world that America will not shrink from making the investments necessary for both peace and security. Our foreign policy must be rooted in realism, not naivete or self-delusion.

A recognition of what the Soviet empire is about is the starting point. Winston Churchill, in negotiating with the Soviets, observed that they respect only strength and resolve in their dealings with other nations. That's why we've moved to reconstruct our national defenses. We intend to keep the peace. We will also keep our freedom.

We have made pledges of a new frankness in our public statements and worldwide broadcasts. In the face of a climate of falsehood and misinformation, we've promised the world a season of truth—the truth of our great civilized ideas: individual liberty, representative government, the rule of law under God. We've never needed walls or minefields or barbed wire to keep our people in. Nor do we declare martial law to keep our people from voting for the kind of government they want.

Yes, we have our problems; yes, we're in a time of recession. And it's true, there's no quick fix, as I said, to instantly end the tragic pain of unemployment. But we will end it. The process has already begun, and we'll see its effect as the year goes on.

We speak with pride and admiration of that little band of Americans who overcame insuperable odds to set this Nation on course 200 years ago. But our glory didn't end with them. Americans ever since have emulated their deeds.

We don't have to turn to our history books for heroes. They're all around us. One who sits among you here tonight epitomized that heroism at the end of the longest imprisonment ever inflicted on men of our Armed Forces. Who will ever forget that night when we waited for television to bring us the scene of that first plane landing at Clark Field in the Philippines, bringing our POW's home? The plane door opened and Jeremiah Denton came slowly down the ramp. He caught sight of our flag, saluted it, said, "God bless America," and then thanked us for bringing him home.

Just 2 weeks ago, in the midst of a terrible tragedy on the Potomac, we saw again the spirit of American heroism at its finest—the heroism of dedicated rescue workers saving crash victims from icy waters. And we saw the heroism of one of our young government employees, Lenny Skutnik, who, when he saw a woman lose her grip on the helicopter line, dived into the water and dragged her to safety.

And then there are countless, quiet, everyday heroes of American life—parents who sacrifice long and hard so their children will know a better life than they've known; church and civic volunteers who help to feed, clothe, nurse, and teach the needy; millions who've made our nation and our nation's destiny so very special—unsung heroes who may not have realized their own dreams themselves but then who reinvest those dreams in their children. Don't let anyone tell you that America's best days are behind her, that the American spirit has been vanquished. We've seen it triumph too often in our lives to stop believing in it now.

A hundred and twenty years ago, the greatest of all our Presidents delivered his second State of the Union message in this chamber. "We cannot escape history," Abraham Lincoln warned, "We of this Congress and this administration will be remembered in spite of ourselves." The "trial through which we pass will light us down, in honor or dishonor, to the latest generation."

Well, that President and that Congress did not fail the American people. Together they weathered the storm and preserved the Union. Let it be said of us that we, too, did not fail; that we, too, worked together to bring America through difficult times. Let us so conduct ourselves that two centuries from now, another Congress and another President, meeting in this chamber as we are meeting, will speak of us with pride, saying that we met the test and preserved for them in their day the sacred flame of liberty—this last, best hope of man on Earth.

The Conservative Cause

Address at the Conservative Political Action Conference
Washington, D.C.
February 26, 1982

Each year the President attended the dinner sponsored by the Conservative Political Action Conference. His speeches at these events differed considerably from his major television addresses. And he seemed more relaxed speaking before an audience of true believers to whom he did not have to adjust his ideas to suit a broad spectrum of opinion. The President used these occasions to remind his audience he truly was one of them, but also to point out that changing the course of American government to the right direction would take time and patience.

Well, Nancy and I, Mr. Toastmaster, [Representative] Mickey Edwards, thank you very much for those very generous words—reverend clergy, ladies and gentlemen, we're delighted to be here at the ninth annual Conservative Political Action Conference.

Anyone looking at the exciting program you've scheduled over these 4 days, and the size of this gathering here tonight, can't help but be impressed with the energy and vitality of the conservative movement in America. We owe a special debt of gratitude to the staffs of the American Conservative Union, Young Americans for Freedom, Human Events, National Review, for making this year's conference the most successful in the brief but impressive history of this event.

Now, you may remember that when I spoke to you last year, I said the election victory we enjoyed in November of 1980 was not a victory of politics so much as it was a victory of ideas; not a victory for any one man or party, but a victory for a set of principles, principles that had been protected and nourished during years of grim and heartbreaking defeats by a few dedicated Americans. Well, you are those Americans, and I salute you.

I've also come here tonight to remind you of how much remains to be done, and to ask your help in turning into reality even more of our hopes for America and the world. The agenda for this conference is victory, victory in this year's crucial congressional, State, and local elections.

The media coverage that you've received this week, the attention paid to you by so many distinguished Americans in and out of government—conservative and not so conservative—are testimony to the seachange that you've already brought about in American politics. But, despite the glitter of nights like this and the excitement we all still feel at the thought of enacting reforms we were only able to talk about a few years ago, we should always remember that our strength still lies in our faith in the good sense of the American people. And that the climate in Washington is still opposed to those enduring values, those "permanent things" that we've always believed in.

But Washington's fascination with passing trends and one-day headlines can sometimes cause serious problems over in the West Wing of the White House—they cause them. There's the problem of leaks. Before we even announced the give-away of surplus cheese, the warehouse mice had hired a lobbyist. *[Laughter]*

And then a few weeks ago, those stories broke about the Kennedy tapes. And that caused something of a stir. Al Haig came in to brief me on his trip to Europe. I uncapped my pen, and he stopped talking. *[Laughter]* Up on the Hill, I understand they were saying, "You need eloquence in the State Dining Room, wit in the East Room, and sign language in the Oval Office." *[Laughter]* It got so bad that I found myself telling every visitor there were absolutely no tape recordings being made. And if they wanted a transcript of that remark, just mention it to the potted plant on their way out. *[Laughter]*

But Washington is a place of fads and one-week stories. It's also a company town, and the company's name is government, big government. Now, I have a sneaking suspicion that a few of you just might have agreed when we decided not to ask Congress for higher taxes. And I hope you realize it's going to take more than 402 days to completely change what's been going on for 40 years.

I realized that the other day when I read a story about a private citizen in Louisiana who asked the government for help in developing his property. And he got back a letter that said, "We have observed that you have not traced the title prior to 1803. Before final approval, it will be necessary that the title be traced previous to that year. Well, the citizen's answer was eloquent.

"Gentlemen," he wrote, "I am unaware that any educated man failed to know that Louisiana was purchased from France in 1803. The title of the land was acquired by France by right of conquest from Spain. The land came into the possession of Spain in 1492 by right of discovery by an Italian sailor, Christopher Columbus. The good Queen Isabella took the precaution of receiving the blessing of the Pope. . . . The Pope is emissary of the Son of God, who made the world. Therefore, I believe that it is safe to assume that He also made that part of the United States called Louisiana. And I hope to hell you're satisfied." *[Laughter]*

Now, changing the habits of four decades is, as I say, going to take more than 402 days. But change will come if we conservatives are in this for the long haul, if we owe our first loyalty to the ideas and principles we discussed, debated, developed, and popularized over the years. Last year I pointed to these principles as the real source of our strength as a political movement, and mentioned some of the intellectual giants who fostered and developed them—men like Frank Meyer, who reminded us that the robust individualism of America was part of deeper currents in Western civilization, currents that dictated respect for the law and the careful preservation of our political traditions.

Only a short time ago, conservatives filled this very room for a testimonial dinner to a great conservative intellect and scholar, author of the "The Conservative Mind," Russell Kirk. In a recent speech, Dr. Kirk has offered some political advice for the upcoming elections. He said now, more than ever, we must seek out the "gift of audacity." We must not become too comfortable with our new-found status in Washington. "When the walls of order are breached, the vigorous conservative must exclaim: Arm me, audacity, from head to foot." It was Napoleon, master of the huge battalions, who once said, "It is imagination that rules the human race." And Disraeli who mentioned that "success is the child of audacity."

We must approach the upcoming elections with a forthright and direct message for the American people. We must remind them of the economic catastrophe that we faced on January 20th, 1981: millions out of work, inflation in double digits for 2 years in a row, interest rates hovering at 21½ percent, productivity and the rate of growth in the gross national product down for the third year in a row, the money supply increasing by 12 percent—and all this due to one overriding cause: Government was too big and had spent too much money.

Federal spending, in the last decade, went up more than 300 percent. In 1980 alone, it increased by 17 percent. Almost three-quarters of the Federal budget was routinely referred to as "uncontrollable," largely due to increases in programs like food stamps, which in 15 years had increased by 16,000 percent, or Medicare and Medicaid—up by more than 500 percent in just 10 years. Our national debt was approaching $1 trillion, and we were paying nearly $100 billion a year in interest on that debt—more than enough money to run the entire Federal Government only 20 years ago.

In an effort to keep pace, taxes had increased by 220 percent in just 10 years, and we were looking at a tax increase from 1980 to 1984, already passed before we got here, of more than $300 billion. Unless we stop the spending juggernaut and reverse the trend toward even higher taxes, government by 1984 would be taking nearly one-quarter of the gross national product. Inflation and interest rates, according to several studies, would be heading toward 25 percent—levels that would stifle enterprise and initiative and plunge the Nation into even deeper economic crisis.

Well, we had to address this economic problem first. History tells us of great nations brought to their knees by unchecked inflation and wild government spending. Brooks Adams once put it this way: "Nature has cast the United States into the vortex of the fiercest struggle which the world has ever known. She has become the heart of the economic system of the age, and she must maintain her supremacy by wit and force or share the fate of the discarded."

At this point last year, much of the smart money in Washington was betting, as it is today, on the failure of our proposals for restoring the economy, that we could never assemble the votes we needed to get our program for economic recovery through the Congress. But assemble the votes we did. For the first time in nearly 25 years, we slowed the spending juggernaut and got the taxpayers out from under the Federal steamroller. We cut the rate of growth in Federal spending almost in half. We lowered inflation to a single-digit rate, and it's still going down. It was 8.9 percent for all of 1981, but our January figure at an annualized rate is only 3½ percent.

When they talk of what should be done for the poor, well, one thing alone, by reducing inflation, we increase the purchasing power of poor families by more than $250. We cut taxes for business and individuals and index taxes to inflation. This last step ended once and for all that hidden profit on inflation that had made the Federal bureaucracy America's largest growth industry.

We've moved against waste and fraud with a task force including our Inspectors General, who have already found thousands of people who've been dead for as long as 7 years still receiving benefit checks from the government. We've concentrated on criminal prosecutions, and we've cut back in other areas like the multitude of films, pamphlets, and public relations experts, or, as we sometimes call them, the Federal flood of flicks, flacks, and foldouts. *[Laughter]*

We're cutting the size of the Federal payroll by 75,000 over the next few years and are fighting to dismantle the Department of Energy and the Department of Education, agencies whose policies have frequently been exactly the opposite of what we need for real energy growth and sound education for our children.

Even now, less than 5 months after our program took full effect, we've seen the first signs of recovery. In January, leading economic indicators like housing permits showed an upturn. By 1983 we will begin bringing down the percentage of the gross national product consumed by both the Federal deficit and by Federal spending and taxes.

Our situation now is in some ways similar to that which confronted the United States and other Western nations shortly after World War II. Many economists then were predicting a return to depression once the stimulus of wartime spending was ended. But people were weary of wartime government controls, and here and in other nations like West Germany, those controls were eliminated against the advice of some experts. At first, there was a period of hardship—higher unemployment and declining growth. In fact, in 1946, our gross national product dropped 15 percent, but by 1947, the next year, it was holding steady and in 1948 increased by 4 percent. Unemployment began a steady decline. And in 1949 consumer prices were decreasing. A lot of the experts underestimated the economic growth that occurs once government stops meddling and the people take over. Well, they were wrong then, and they're wrong now.

The job of this administration and of the Congress is to move forward with additional cuts in the growth of Federal spending and thereby ensure America's economic recovery. We have proposed budget cuts for 1983, and our proposals have met with cries of anguish. And those who utter the cries are equally anguished because there will be a budget deficit. They're a little like a dog sitting on a sharp rock howling with pain, when all he has to do is get up and move. *[Laughter]*

On the spending cuts now before the Congress and those tax reductions we've already passed for the American people, let me state we're standing by our program. We will not turn back or sound retreat.

You know, if I could just interject here, some of those people who say we must change direction when we've only been on this new direction for 5 months—and it's only the first limited phase of the whole program—it was described pretty well by Mickey Edwards, sitting right here, while we were having dinner. He said, "If you were sliding downhill on a snowy hill, and you know there's a cliff down there ahead of you at the bottom and suddenly there's a road that turns off·

to the right," he said, "you don't know where that road to the right goes, but," he says, "you take it." *[Laughter]* We know where that other one goes. *[Laughter]*

In the discussion of Federal spending, the time has come to put to rest the sob-sister attempts to portray our desire to get government spending under control as a hard-hearted attack on the poor people of America. In the first place, even with the economies that we've proposed, spending for entitlements—benefits paid directly to individuals—will actually increase by one-third over the next 5 years. And in 1983 nondefense items will amount to more than 70 percent of total spending.

As Dave Stockman pointed out the other day, we're still subsidizing 95 million meals a day, providing $70 billion in health care to the elderly and poor, some 47 million people. Some 10 million or more are living in subsidized housing. And we're still providing scholarships for a million and a half students. Only here in this city of Oz would a budget this big and this generous be characterized as a miserly attack on the poor. *[Laughter]*

Now, where do some of these attacks originate? They're coming from the very people whose past policies, all done in the name of compassion, brought us the current recession. Their policies, drove up inflation and interest rates, and their policies stifled incentive, creativity, and halted the movement of the poor up the economic ladder. Some of their criticism is perfectly sincere. But let's also understand that some of their criticisms comes from those who have a vested interest in a permanent welfare constituency and in government programs that reinforce the dependency of our people.

Well, I would suggest that no one should have a vested interest in poverty or dependency, that these tragedies must never be looked at as a source of votes for politicians or paychecks for bureaucrats. They are blights on our society that we must work to eliminate, not institutionalize.

Now, there are those who will always require help from the rest of us on a permanent basis, and we'll provide that help. To those with temporary need, we should have programs that are aimed at making them self-sufficient as soon as possible. How can limited government and fiscal restraint be equated with lack of compassion for the poor? How can a tax break that puts a little more money in the weekly paychecks of working people be seen as an attack on the needy?

Since when do we in America believe that our society is made up of two diametrically opposed classes—one rich, one poor—both in a permanent state of conflict and neither able to get ahead except at the expense of the other? Since when do we in America accept this alien and discredited theory of social and class warfare? Since when do we in America endorse the politics of envy and division?

When we reformed the welfare system in California and got the cheaters and the undeserving off the welfare rolls, instead of hurting the poor, we were able to increase their benefits by more than 40 percent. By reducing the cost of government, we can continue bringing down inflation, the cruelest of all economic exploitations of the poor and the elderly. And by getting the economy moving again, we can create a vastly expanded job market that will offer the poor a way out of permanent dependency.

So, let's tell the American people the truth tonight and next fall about our economic recovery program. It isn't for one class or group. It's for all Americans—working people, the truly needy, the rich and the poor.

One man who held this office, a President vastly underrated by history, Calvin Coolidge, pointed out that a nation that is united in its belief in the work ethic and its desire for commercial success and economic progress is usually a healthy nation, a nation where it is easier to pursue the higher things in life like the development of science, the cultivation of the arts, the exploration of the great truths of religion and higher learning.

In arguing for economy in government, President Coolidge spoke of the burden of excessive government. He said, "I favor a policy of economy, not because I wish to save money, but because I wish to save people. The men and women of this country who toil are the ones who bear the cost of the government. Every dollar that we carelessly waste means that their life will be so much [the] more meager. Every dollar that we save means that their life will be so much the more abundant. Economy is idealism in its most practical form." And this is the message we conservatives can bring to the American people about our economic program. Higher productivity, a larger gross national product, a healthy Dow Jones average—they are our goals and are worthy ones.

But our real concerns are not statistical goals or material gain. We want to expand personal freedom, to renew the American dream for every American. We seek to restore opportunity and reward, to value again personal achievement and individual excellence. We seek to rely on the ingenuity and energy of the American people to better their own lives and those of millions of others around the world.

We can be proud of the fact that a conservative administration has pursued these goals by confronting the Nation's economic problems head-on. At the same time, we dealt with one other less publicized but equally grave problem: the serious state of disrepair in our national defenses.

The last Democratic administration had increased real defense spending at a rate of 3.3 percent a year. You know how much inflation was, so they were actually losing ground. By 1980 we had fighter planes that couldn't fly, Navy ships that couldn't leave port, a Rapid Deployment Force that was neither rapid nor deployable and not much of a force.

The protection of this Nation's security is the most solemn duty of any President, and that's why I've asked for substantial increases in our defense budget—substantial, but not excessive.

In 1962 President Kennedy's defense budget amounted to 44 percent of the entire budget. Ours is only 29 percent. In 1962 President Kennedy's request for military spending was 8.6 percent of the gross national product. Ours is only 6.3 percent. The Soviet Union outspends us on defense by 50 percent, an amount equal to 15 percent of their gross national product. During the campaign I was asked any number of times: If I were faced with a choice of balancing the budget or restoring our national defenses, what would I do? Every time I said, "Restore our defenses." And every time I was applauded.

So, let me be very clear. We will press for further cuts in Federal spending. We will protect the tax reductions already passed. We will spend on defense what is necessary for our national security. I have no intention of leading the Republican Party into next fall's election on a platform of higher taxes and cut-rate defense. If our opponents want to go to the American people next fall and say, "We're the party that refused to cut spending, we're the party that tried to take away your tax cuts, we're the party that wanted a bargain-basement military and held a fire sale on national security," let's give them all the running room they want. *[Laughter]*

There are other matters on the political agenda for this coming year, matters I know that you've been discussing during the course of this conference. I hope one of them will be our attempt to give government back to the people. One hundred and thirty-two Federal grants-in-aid in 1960 have grown to over 500 in 1981. Our federalism proposal, as Mickey Edwards told you, would return the bulk of these programs to State and local governments, where they can be made more responsive to the people.

We're deeply committed to this program, because it has its roots in deep conservative principles. We've talked a long time about revitalizing our system of federalism. Now, with a single, bold stroke, we can restore the vigor and health of our State and local governments. This proposal lies at the heart of our legislative agenda for the next year, and we'll need your active support in getting it passed.

There are other issues before us. This administration is unalterably opposed to the forced busing of schoolchildren, just as we also support constitutional protection for the right of prayer in our schools. And there is the matter of abortion. We must with calmness and resolve help the vast majority of our fellow Americans understand that the more than 1½ million abortions performed in America in 1980 amount to a great moral evil, an assault on the sacredness of human life.

And, finally, there's the problem of crime, a problem whose gravity cannot be underestimated. This administration has moved in its appointments to the Federal bench and in its legislative proposals for bail and parole reform to assist in the battle against the lawless. But we must always remember that our legal system does not need reform so much as it needs transformation. And this cannot occur at just the Federal level. It can really occur only when society is a whole acknowledges principles that lie at the heart of modern conservatism. Right and wrong matters, individuals are responsible for their actions. Society has a right to be protected from those who prey on the innocent.

This then is the political agenda before us. Perhaps more than any group, your grassroots leadership, your candidate recruitment and training programs, your long years of hard work and dedication have brought us to this point and made this agenda possible.

We live today in a time of climactic struggle for the human spirit, a time that will tell whether the great civilized ideas of individual liberty, representative government, and the rule of law under God will perish or endure.

Whittaker Chambers, who sought idealism in communism and found only disillusionment, wrote very movingly of his moment of awakening. It was at breakfast, and he was looking at the delicate ear of his tiny baby daughter, and he said that, suddenly, looking at that, he knew that couldn't just be an accident of nature. He said, while he didn't realize it at the time, he knows now that in that moment God had touched his forehead with his finger.

And later he wrote, "For in this century, within the next decades, will be decided for generations whether all mankind is to become Communist, whether the whole world is to become free, or whether in the struggle civilization as we know it is to be completely destroyed or completely changed. It is our fate to live upon that turning point in history."

We've already come a long way together. Thank you for all that you've done for me, for the common values we cherish. Join me in a new effort, a new crusade.

Nostalgia has its time and place. Coming here tonight has been a sentimental journey for me, as I'm sure it has been for many of you. But nostalgia isn't enough. The challenge is now. It's time we stopped looking backward at how we got here. We must ask ourselves tonight how we can forge and wield a popular majority from one end of this country to the other, a majority united on basic, positive goals with a platform broad enough and deep enough to endure long into the future, far beyond the lifespan of any single issue or personality.

We must reach out and appeal to the patriotic and fundamental ideals of average Americans who do not consider themselves "movement" people, but who respond to the same American ideals that we do. I'm not talking about some vague notion of an abstract, amorphous American main-stream. I'm talking about Main Street Americans in their millions. They come in all sizes, shapes and colors—blue-collar workers, blacks, Hispanics, shopkeepers, scholars, service-people, house-wives, and professional men and women. They are the backbone of America, and we can't move America without moving their hearts and minds as well.

Fellow Americans, our duty is before us tonight. Let us go forward, determined to serve self-lessly a vision of man with God, government for people, and humanity at peace. For it is now our task to tend and preserve, through the darkest and coldest nights, that "sacred fire of liberty" that President Washington spoke of two centuries ago, a fire that tonight remains a beacon to all the oppressed of the world, shining forth from this kindly, pleasant, greening land we call America.

"To Stay the Course"
Washington, D.C.
October 13, 1982

President Reagan hoped that his new economic recovery program would begin to work by the time of the mid-term elections so that the elections could then serve as a referrendum on his first two years in office. However, recovery was not as rapid as he had hoped. The federal deficit doubled what he had predicted, business bankruptcies increased at a rate not seen since the Depression, and by October un-employment rose to more than 10 per cent. Even though Reagan campaigned extensively for Repub-licans, by October Republican prospects did not appear bright. Thus, the President decided to present his case to the American people in a "non-partisan" speech on the economy, for which two of the three major networks gave him prime television time.

In recent days all of us have been swamped by a sea of economic statistics—some good, some bad, and some just plain confusing. There are times when I think that the paper traffic that crosses my desk in a week could fill a big-city phone book, and then some.

The value of the dollar is up around the world. Interest rates are down by 40 percent. The stock and bond markets surge upward. Inflation is down 59 percent. Buying power is going up. Some economic indicators are down; others are up. But the dark cloud of unemployment hangs over the lives of 11 million of our friends, neighbors, and family.

At times, the sheer weight of all these facts and figures make them hard for anyone to un-derstand. What do they really mean, and what can we do to make them better?

Well, the first step is to understand what they mean in human terms—how they're affecting the everyday lives of our people, because behind every one of those numbers are millions of in-dividual lives—young couples struggling to make ends meet, teenagers looking for work, older Americans threatened by inflation, small businessmen fighting for survival, and parents working for a better future for their children.

All of them have one thing in common. They're Americans who love this country of ours and want to make it a better place. They're brave, hard-working people who know that America today faces serious problems that were long years in the making. And they're desperately trying to make sense out of all the statistics, slogans, and political jargon filling the airwaves in this election year. Above all, they're concerned citizens who are looking for guideposts on the road to recovery—for ways to help see our country through to better times.

I know because I hear from hundreds of them every day—in meetings here at the White House; on visits to schools, meeting halls, factories, and fairgrounds across the country; and in thousands of phone calls and letters. I only wish I could share with you tonight all that they have to say—their hopes, their fears, their concerns, and most of all, their quiet, patient courage. But let me just give you one example that speaks for so many of you, a letter from a wife and mother named Judith, who lives in Selma, Alabama.

"Dear Mr. President," she writes, "It's 3:45 a.m., and for over an hour I've been unable to sleep . . . this morning I need very much to believe in something . . . I'm not writing so much as an individual, but as a representative of so many. We need to talk with you—to believe that you hear us. . . .

"After years of training and experience, we can't find jobs. National unemployment figures sound almost healthy next to the almost 19 percent we're enduring in Selma.

"The costs for basic survival are nearly beyond belief . . . there may never be a house—home of our own—that dream we've worked for so many years. . . . We have said 'no' to so many things . . . we're afraid and confused. We've worked hard—we conserved—we planned—we were frugal—careful. We feel so out of control. We don't want a handout—we just want to help make the system well again.

"We must know that in the tons of bureaucracy . . . we've not been lost . . . we want to help. We want a better life, and we're willing to work for it. We believe. We must—it's all we have."

Well, Judith, I hear you. And millions of other men and women like you stand for the values of hard work, thrift, commitment to family, and love of God that made this country so great and will make us great again. And you deserve to know what we're doing in these very difficult times to bring your dream, the American dream, back to life again, after so many years of mistakes and neglect.

Tonight, in homes across this country, unemployment is the problem uppermost on many people's minds. Getting Americans back to work is an urgent priority for all of us and especially for this administration. But remember, you can't solve unemployment without solving the things that caused it, the out-of-control government spending, the skyrocketing inflation and interest rates that led to unemployment in the first place. Unless you get at the root causes of the problem—which is exactly what our economic program is doing—you may be able to temporarily relieve the symptoms, but you'll never cure the disease. You may even make it worse.

I have a special reason for wanting to solve this problem in a lasting way. I was 21 and looking for work in 1932, one of the worst years of the Great Depression. And I can remember one bleak night in the thirties when my father learned on Christmas Eve that he'd lost his job. To be young in my generation was to feel that your future had been mortgaged out from under you, and that's a tragic mistake we must never allow our leaders to make again. Today's young people must never be held hostage to the mistakes of the past. The only way to avoid making those mistakes again is to learn from them.

The pounding economic hangover America's suffering from didn't come about overnight. And there's no single instant cure. In recent weeks, a lot of people have been playing what I call the "blame game." The accusing finger has been pointed in every direction of the compass, and a lot of time and hot air have been spent looking for scapegoats. Well, there's plenty of blame to go around.

The problems we face are bigger than any one party or group of people. They're the result not of weeks or months, but of years, even decades of past mistakes. The problem isn't who to blame; it's what to blame. So, tonight, let's forget about party politics and take a look at how our country got into this fix and what we can do to get her out of it.

When I said this problem was years in the making, I wasn't just using a figure of speech. This chart shows you what I mean. You see that red line? It represents the rate of unemployment from 1968 through the present, and it tells us two important things. First of all, it's a jagged line, representing rises and dips in unemployment as our economy passed through boom periods and bust periods over the past decade. This reminds us that the current recession is part of a long series—a series that hasn't stopped, because in the past, when the crunch came, too many in government sorted to quick fixes instead of getting to the root cause.

Each time they applied the quick fixes, unemployment dipped for a while, only to take off again. In that sense, you could say that we've been on a decade-long roller coaster ride. The only difference is that on a roller coaster you end up on solid ground once the ride is over. As you can see from the chart, while unemployment zigzagged from year to year, its long-term direction kept notching upward. Notice that each so-called recovery left unemployment higher than before the recession.

In 1968 unemployment stood at 3.6 percent. In 1971 it shot up to 5.9 percent. Then it started coming down again, but instead of going all the way back to 3.6 percent, it bottomed out at 4.9 percent. In 1974 it started shooting up again, and the same thing happened. It bottomed out at a higher level than before. In other words, for all its short-term ups and downs, the unemployment roller coaster was really an escalator, edging its way up the charts throughout the last decade. Unless we reverse that trend, it can only get worse, not just for us but for our children and grandchildren.

Now let's look at what's behind this bad trend in unemployment. What's been causing it for over a decade? A second chart tells much of the story. But before we look at it, I'll bet many of you have already come up with the answer. It's a phenomenon that, last year, a majority of Americans correctly identified as our single most pressing long-term problem: inflation.

Inflation and the high interest rates it leads to are the real culprits. They create the economic climate that leads to unemployment.

This blue line represents inflation. Like unemployment, inflation has zig-zagged over the last decade, but you can see that, up to now, the long-term trend has been upwards. Again, as with unemployment, the old quick fixes simply did not work. Each time they were applied, they gave a little temporary relief to the patient, but left him weaker than he was before.

It's a consistent pattern. Each time inflation has shot up since 1969 there has been a deadly, delayed reaction of rising unemployment. Inflation is like a virus in the economic bloodstream, sometimes dormant and sometimes active, but leaving the patient weaker after every new attack.

My fellow Americans, we've got to stop these trendlines to disaster.

To do that, we have to understand what causes them. Well, for starters, our Federal Government has been living beyond its means for more than a generation. One of the wisest of our Founding Fathers, Thomas Jefferson, warned that the public debt is "the greatest of dangers to be feared." He believed that it was wrong for one generation to forever burden the generations yet to come, and for the first 150 years of our history, our leaders heeded Jefferson's warning.

But not lately. In our lifetimes we've seen government spending rage out of control. We've only had one balanced budget in the last 22 years. So, now we're staggering under a trillion-dollar debt. This year, before government can spend one dime to feed the hungry, care for the sick, or protect our freedom, it must plan to spend $110 billion just to pay interest on that debt. And still the big spenders wonder why the American people want what a stubborn minority in the House of Representatives denied them just 12 days ago: a constitutional amendment to balance the budget.

All of this government spending and red ink can only spawn higher taxes and whopping deficits which for nearly two decades led to inflationary increases in the money supply. Inflation and massive government borrowing drive up interest rates. That makes it difficult or impossible for families to get the credit they need to buy homes, cars, and appliances or for businesses to invest in greater productivity. And ultimately inflation leads to recession and unemployment.

We've had eight recessions since World War II. At the bottom of it all is inflation, government-caused inflation. Over the years our leaders adopted something called the new economics based on a belief that a little inflation each year created prosperity. But each time the economic disruption caused by inflation triggered another round of recession and high unemployment. The government reacted not like your family would, by putting its own house in order, but by spending, borrowing, and printing more money.

Unemployment would dip for a time, but the same quick fix that temporarily eased unemployment was sending inflation back through the ceiling. It was a vicious cycle. Too many people played politics with the economy for too long, and those twin disaster lines kept inching ominously upward, bringing our society closer and closer to catastrophe.

In a way I guess I can understand why so many of our political leaders fell into this trap. I'm sure they did it with the best of intentions. It's easy to lose touch with reality when it is other people's money that you're spending. And there are so many things you want to do for those or this or that special-interest group—so many programs, many of them quite attractive and well-meaning, that can only be subsidized by more government taxing, spending, and borrowing. I can understand how it happened. Indeed, like many others, for a time I accepted government's claim that it was sound economics. But there came a day when I and millions of other Americans began to realize the terrible consequences of all those years of playing politics as usual while the economic disaster lines crept higher and higher.

Well, at my age I didn't come to Washington to play politics as usual. I didn't come here to reward pressure groups by spending other people's money. And most of all, I didn't come here to further mortgage the future of the American people just to buy a little short-term political popularity. I came to Washington to try to solve problems, not to sweep them under the rug and leave them for those who will come later.

A President's greatest responsibility is to protect all our people from enemies, foreign and domestic. Here at home the worst enemy we face is economic—the creeping erosion of the American way of life and the American dream that has resulted in today's tragedy of economic stagnation and unemployment.

Now, I don't pretend for a moment that, in 21 months, we've been able to undo all the damage to our economy that has built up over more than 20 years. The first part of our program has been in the books only 1 year and 13 days. Much of the legislation we need has still not been enacted. We've still got a long way to go before we restore our prosperity. But what I can report to you tonight, my fellow Americans, is that at long last your government has a program in place that faces our problems and has already started solving them.

Twenty-one months ago, we faced five critical problems: high taxes, runaway government spending, inflation, high interest rates, and unemployment. Getting to the roots of unemployment meant fighting inflation and high interest rates caused by runaway government spending and taxing, because we know that when inflation shoots up, it triggers a delayed-action rise in unemployment. Now inflation is being driven back down, and lower unemployment will follow.

So, we started by winning the first real tax cut for the American people in nearly two decades. Our program brings down income tax rates 25 percent. At the same time, we've been cutting costly wasteful government regulations and the rate of increase in government spending. We've reduced the rate of government spending growth by nearly two-thirds. Inflation, which registered 12.4 percent in 1980, is down to just 5.1 percent so far this year.

Interest rates, which had climbed as high as 21½ percent before we took office, have this week fallen to 12 percent—not low enough, but certainly heading in the right direction. Unemployment, always a lagging indicator in times of recession, has not yet stopped its upward drift.

But in 21 months, we've already brought tax rates down by a quarter, with the third installment coming next July, and brought down the rate of increase in government spending by nearly two-thirds. That's helped us to bring down the rate of inflation by more than half, and that's helped us to bring down interest rates by 40 percent.

So, on four out of five problems that faced us in 1980, we've made important progress. We haven't solved them all, but we're making headway.

Just last week, the Federal Reserve Bank decided to lower its discount rate to 9.5 percent—the first time this key interest rate has gone below two digits since 1979, and the fifth reduction in just 4 months. This demonstrates the Fed's confidence that inflation and market rates will continue coming down and its confidence that we can work together for a healthy, noninflationary recovery. All of this lays the groundwork for a recovery that will mean more jobs and more opportunity for all our people. But it's a delayed reaction.

Remember the trendlines. Just as surely as skyrocketing inflation created a negative reaction that drove up unemployment, bringing down inflation and interest rates is creating a positive reaction that will boost employment. I wish there were a quicker, easier way—some magic shortcut—but unemployment is always one of the last things to turn around as an economy heads into recovery. And make no mistake, America is recovery bound. And the world knows it.

The American dollar, beaten down and distrusted in the late 1970's, is showing new strength. Recently, we've been seeing a surge of investment in our stock and bond markets. This is no flash in the pan. Markets will go up and they will come down, but the trend in the United States is up. What's more, this investment is coming from all over, from home, from abroad, from small investors on Main Street to those who manage billions of dollars, including our workers' pension funds.

Why aren't these people heeding the drumbeat of doom and gloom coming from Washington? Because they've been watching this country's inflation and interest rates dropping for months. They realize this administration means business in the battle against inflation. Their decision to put cash on the line is a strong vote of confidence in the foundation being laid for America's recovery—healthy, stable growth that will bring new jobs and opportunity for our people without returning us to runaway inflation and interest rates. That's the one big difference between the recovery America is headed for today and the shaky, temporary recoveries of the recent past. This one is built to last

With your support, we can show the world that we've learned our lesson and that this time we're going to get the job done and get it done right. This time, we're going to keep inflation, interest rates and government spending, taxing and borrowing down, and get Americans back on the job.

Much of the work that remains to be done requires congressional cooperation. As you know, Congress adjourned October 2d for the election campaign. But it left behind a lot of unfinished business. For this reason, I urge the Congress to reconvene after the elections so that it can do its part as quickly as possible to continue the work of recovery. We simply can't afford to wait until next year when something as vital as the economic health of America is at stake.

The Congress will return on November 29th. It will face five top economic priorities, priorities that must be addressed.

First, the Congress must do its part to control government spending. Before adjourning, it sent me only two appropriation bills. Eleven more remain to be passed. And I will use the veto, if necessary, to keep them within the budget. When the Congress passed the tax package this summar, it pledged to save $3 in outlays for every $1 in new revenues. I intend to hold the Congress to its word.

Second, I urge the Congress to reconsider the constitutional amendment to balance the budget. This crucial measure was passed by the Senate and supported by a clear majority in the House of Representatives. It was only defeated because of the hard core opposition of a minority of Representatives who prefer continued big spending.

Third, the Congress should act on regulatory reform to help make government more economical and efficient and the private sector more productive. Regulatory reform legislation was passed unanimously by the Senate but was bottled up in committee in the House.

Fourth, the time has come for passage of the enterprise zones initiative to revive declining inner city and rural communities by providing new incentives to develop business and jobs. This program was approved by the Senate Finance Committee, but still awaits action on the Senate floor and in the House.

And, fifth, we need to pass the clean air bill which, while protecting the environment, will make it possible for industry to rebuild its productive base and create more jobs.

But it's not an easy job, this challenge to rebuild America and renew the American dream. And I know it can be tempting, listening to some who would go back to the old ways and the quick fix. But consider the choice. A return to the big spending and big taxing that left us with 21½-percent interest rates is no real alternative. A return to double-digit inflation is no alternative. A return to taxing and taxing the American people—that's no alternative. That's what destroyed millions of American jobs.

Together we've chosen a new road for America. It's a far better road. We need only the courage to see it through. I know we can. Throughout our history, we Americans have proven again and again that no challenge is too big for a free, united people. Together, we can do it again. We can do it by slowly but surely working our way back to prosperity that will mean jobs for all who are willing to work, and fulfillment for all who still cherish the American dream.

We can do it, my fellow Americans, by staying the course.

Thank you, good night, and God bless you.

State of the Union

Washington, D.C.
January 25, 1983

President Reagan's second State of the Union Address was much less optimistic than his first. He recognized that the economy had not responded as quickly to his policies as he had expected, and he predicted only modest gains for the coming year. This speech marks a considerable rhetorical change in the President's public approach to domestic problems. In the past, he had stated that problems could not be solved overnight, but emphasized the optimism that he had about his own programs. In this speech, the emphasis was on perseverence and lowered expectations.

The address, however, contains essentially the same domestic message of his previous speeches. After the mid-term elections, there had been considerable speculation in the press that the President might interpret the loss of 26 Republican seats in the House of Representatives as a call for a change in his policies. Journalists reported a "battle for the mind of Reagan" among his advisors and reported a disarray in the White House. Reagan sought in his Address to reassert his conservative positions and his control over his administration.

This solemn occasion marks the 196th time that a President of the United States has reported on the State of the Union since George Washington first did so in 1790. That's a lot of reports, but there's no shortage of new things to say about the State of the Union. The very key to our success has been our ability, foremost among nations, to preserve our lasting values by making change work for us rather than against us.

I would like to talk with you this evening about what we can do together—not as Republicans and Democrats, but as Americans—to make tomorrow's America happy and prosperous at home, strong and respected abroad, and at peace in the world.

As we gather here tonight, the state of our Union is strong, but our economy is troubled. For too many of our fellow citizens—farmers, steel and auto workers, lumbermen, black teenagers, working mothers—this is a painful period. We must all do everything in our power to bring their ordeal to an end. It has fallen to us, in our time, to undo damage that was a long time in the making, and to begin the hard but necessary task of building a better future for ourselves and our children.

We have a long way to go, but thanks to the courage, patience, and strength of our people, America is on the mend.

But let me give you just one important reason why I believe this—it involves many members of this body.

Just 10 days ago, after months of debate and deadlock, the bipartisan Commission on Social Security accomplished the seemingly impossible. Social security, as some of us had warned for so long, faced disaster. I, myself, have been talking about this problem for almost 30 years. As 1983 began, the system stood on the brink of bankruptcy, a double victim of our economic ills. First, a decade of rampant inflation drained its reserves as we tried to protect beneficiaries from the spiraling cost of living. Then the recession and the sudden end of inflation withered the expanding wage base and increasing revenues the system needs to support the 36 million Americans who depend on it.

When the Speaker of the House, the Senate majority leader, and I performed the bipartisan—or formed the bipartisan Commission on Social Security, pundits and experts predicted that party divisions and conflicting interests would prevent the Commission from agreeing on a plan to save social security. Well, sometimes, even here in Washington, the cynics are wrong. Through compromise and cooperation, the members of the Commission overcame their differences and achieved a fair, workable plan. They proved that, when it comes to the national welfare, Americans can still pull together for the common good.

Tonight, I'm especially pleased to join with the Speaker and the Senate majority leader in urging the Congress to enact this plan by Easter.

There are elements in it, of course, that none of us prefers, but taken together it performs a package that all of us can support. It asks for some sacrifice by all—the self-employed, beneficiaries, workers, government employees, and the better-off among the retired—but it imposes an undue burden on none. And, in supporting it, we keep an important pledge to the American people: The integrity of the social security system will be preserved, and no one's payments will be reduced.

The Commission's plan will do the job; indeed, it must do the job. We owe it to today's older Americans and today's younger workers. So, before we go any further, I ask you to join with me in saluting the members of the Commission who are here tonight and Senate Majority Leader Howard Baker and Speaker Tip O'Neill for a job well done. I hope and pray the bipartisan spirit that guided you in this endeavor will inspire all of us as we face the challenges of the year ahead.

Nearly half a century ago, in this Chamber, another American President, Franklin Delano Roosevelt, in his second State of the Union message, urged America to look to the future, to meet the challenge of change and the need for leadership that looks forward, not backward.

"Throughout the world," he said, "change is the order of the day. In every nation economic problems long in the making have brought crisis to [of] many kinds for which the masters of old practice and theory were unprepared." He also reminded us that "the future lies with those wise political leaders who realize that the great public is interested more in Government than in politics."

So, let us, in these next 2 years—men and women of both parties, every political shade—concentrate on the long-range, bipartisan responsibilities of government, not the short-range or short-term temptations of partisan politics.

The problems we inherited were far worse than most inside and out of government had expected; the recession was deeper than most inside and out of government had predicted. Curing those problems has taken more time and a higher toll than any of us wanted. Unemployment is far too high. Projected Federal spending—if government refuses to tighten its own belt—will also be far too high and could weaken and shorten the economic recovery now underway.

This recovery will bring with it a revival of economic confidence and spending for consumer items and capital goods—the stimulus we need to restart our stalled economic engines. The American people have already stepped up their rate of saving, assuring that the funds needed to modernize our factories and improve our technology will once again flow to business and industry.

The inflationary expectations that led to a 21½-percent interest prime rate and soaring mortgage rates 2 years ago are now reduced by almost half. Leaders have started to realize that double-digit inflation is no longer a way of life.

I misspoke there, I should have said "lenders."

So, interest rates have tumbled, paving the way for recovery in vital industries like housing and autos.

The early evidence of that recovery has started coming in. Housing starts for the fouth quarter of 1982 were up 45 percent from a year ago, and housing permits, a sure indicator of future growth, were up a whopping 60 percent.

We're witnessing an upsurge of productivity and impressive evidence that American industry will once again become competitive in markets at home and abroad, ensuring more jobs and better incomes for the Nation's work force. But our confidence must also be tempered by realism and patience. Quick fixes and artificial stimulants repeatedly applied over decades are what brought us the inflationary disorders that we've now paid such a heavy price to cure.

The permanent recovery in employment, production, and investment we seek won't come in a sharp, short spurt. It'll build carefully and steadily in the months and years ahead. In the meantime, the challenge of government is to identify the things that we can do now to ease the massive economic transition for the American people.

The Federal budget is both a symptom and a cause of our economic problems. Unless we reduce the dangerous growth rate in government spending, we could face the prospect of sluggish economic growth into the indefinite future. Failure to cope with this problem now could mean as much as a trillion dollars more in national debt in the next 4 years alone. That would average $4,300 in additional debt for every man, woman, child, and baby in our nation.

To assure a sustained recovery, we must continue getting runaway spending under control to bring those deficits down. If we don't, the recovery will be too short, unemployment will remain too high, and we will leave an unconscionable burden of national debt for our children. That we must not do.

Let's be clear about where the deficit problem comes from. Contrary to the drumbeat we've been hearing for the last few months, the deficits we face are not rooted in defense spending. Taken as a percentage of the gross national product, our defense spending happens to be only about four-fifths of what it was in 1970. Nor is the deficit, as some would have it, rooted in tax cuts. Even with our tax cuts, taxes as a fraction of gross national product remain about the same as they were in 1970. The fact is, our deficits come from the uncontrolled growth of the budget for domestic spending.

During the 1970's the share of our national income devoted to this domestic spending increased by more than 60 percent, from 10 cents out of every dollar produced by the American people to 16 cents. In spite of all our economies and efficiencies, and without adding any new programs, basic, necessary domestic spending provided for in this year's budget will grow to almost a trillion dollars over the next 5 years.

The deficit problem is a clear and present danger to the basic health of our Republic. We need a plan to overcome this danger—a plan based on these principles. It must be bipartisan. Conquering the deficits and putting the Government's house in order will require the best effort of all of us. It must be fair. Just as all will share in the benefits that will come from recovery, all would share fairly in the burden of transition. It must be prudent. The strength of our national defense must be restored so that we can pursue prosperity and peace and freedom while maintaining our commitment to the truly needy. And finally, it must be realistic. We can't rely on hope alone.

With these guiding principles in mind, let me outline a four-part plan to increase economic growth and reduce deficits.

First, in my budget message, I will recommend a Federal spending freeze. I know this is strong medicine, but so far, we have only cut the rate of increase in Federal spending. The Government has continued to spend more money each year, though not as much more as it did in the past. Taken as a whole, the budget I'm proposing for the fiscal year will increase no more than the rate of inflation. In other words, the Federal Government will hold the line on real spending. Now, that's far less than many American families have had to do in these difficult times.

I will request that the proposed 6-month freeze in cost-of-living adjustments recommended by the bipartisan Social Security Commission be applied to other government-related retirement programs. I will, also, propose a 1-year freeze on a broad range of domestic spending programs, and for Federal civilian and military pay and pension programs. And let me say right here, I'm sorry, with regard to the military, in asking that of them, because for so many years they have been so far behind and so low in reward for what the men and women in uniform are doing. But I'm sure they will understand that this must be across the board and fair.

Second, I will ask the Congress to adopt specific measures to control the growth of the so-called uncontrollable spending programs. These are the automatic spending programs, such as food stamps, that cannot be simply frozen and that have grown by over 400 percent since 1970. They are the largest single cause of the built-in or structural deficit problem. Our standard here will be fairness, ensuring that the taxpayers' hard-earned dollars go only to the truly needy; that none of them are turned away, but that fraud and waste are stamped out. And I'm sorry to say, there's a lot of it out there. In the food stamp program alone, last year, we identified almost [$]1.1 billion in overpayments. The taxpayers aren't the only victims of this kind of abuse. The truly needy suffer as funds intended for them are taken not by the needy, but by the greedy. For everyone's sake, we must put an end to such waste and corruption.

Third, I will adjust our program to restore America's defenses by proposing $55 billion in defense savings over the next 5 years. These are savings recommended to me by the Secretary of Defense, who has assured me they can be safely achieved and will not diminish our ability to negotiate arms reductions or endanger America's security. We will not gamble with our national survival.

And fourth, because we must ensure reduction and eventual elimination of deficits over the next several years, I will propose a standby tax, limited to no more than 1 percent of the gross national product, to start in fiscal 1986. It would last no more than 3 years, and it would start only if the Congress has first approved our spending freeze and budget control program. And there are several other conditions also that must be met, all of them in order for this program to be triggered.

Now, you could say that this is an insurance policy for the future, a remedy that will be at hand if needed but only resorted to if absolutely necessary. In the meantime, we'll continue to study ways to simplify the tax code and make it more fair for all Americans. This is a goal that every American who's ever struggled with a tax form can understand.

At the same time, however, I will oppose any efforts to undo the basic tax reforms that we've already enacted, including the 10-percent tax break coming to taxpayers this July and the tax indexing which will protect all Americans from inflationary bracket creep in the years ahead.

Now, I realize that this four-part plan is easier to describe than it will be to enact. But the looming deficits that hang over us and over America's future must be reduced. The path I've outlined is fair, balanced, and realistic. If enacted, it will ensure a steady decline in deficits, aiming toward a balanced budget by the end of the decade. It's the only path that will lead to a strong, sustained recovery. Let us follow that path together.

No domestic challenge is more crucial than providing stable, permanent jobs for all Americans who want to work. The recovery program will provide jobs for most, but others will need special help and training for new skills. Shortly, I will submit to the Congress the Employment Act of 1983, designed to get at the special problems of the long-term unemployed, as well as young people trying to enter the job market. I'll propose extending unemployment benefits, including special incentives to employers who hire the long-term unemployed, providing programs for displaced workers, and helping federally funded State-administered unemployment insurance programs provide workers with training and relocation assistance. Finally, our proposal will include new incentives for summer youth employment to help young people get a start in the job market.

We must offer both short-term help and long-term hope for our unemployed. I hope we can work together on this. I hope we can work together as we did last year in enacting the landmark Job Training Partnership Act. Regulatory reform legislation, a responsible clean air act, and passage of enterprise zone legislation will also create new incentives for jobs and opportunity.

One of out of every five jobs in our country depends on trade. So, I will propose a broader strategy in the field of international trade—one that increases the openness of our trading system and is fairer to America's farmers and workers in the world marketplace. We must have adequate export financing to sell American products overseas. I will ask for new negotiating authority to remove barriers and to get more of our products into foreign markets. We must strengthen the organization of our trade agencies and make changes in our domestic laws and international trade policy to promote free trade and the increased flow of American goods, services, and investments.

Our trade position can also be improved by making our port system more efficient. Better, more active harbors translate into stable jobs in our coalfields, railroads, trucking industry, and ports. After 2 years of debate, it's time for us to get together and enact a port modernization bill.

Education, training, and retraining are fundamental to our success as are research and development and productivity. Labor, management, and government at all levels can and must participate in improving these tools of growth. Tax policy, regulatory practices, and government programs all need constant reevaluation in terms of our competitiveness. Every American has a role and a stake in international trade.

We Americans are still the technological leaders in most fields. We must keep that edge, and to do so we need to begin renewing the basics—starting with our educational system. While we grew complacent, others have acted. Japan, with a population only about half the size of ours, graduates from its universities more engineers than we do. If a child doesn't receive adequate math and science teaching by the age of 16, he or she has lost the chance to be a scientist or an engineer. We must join together—parents, teachers, grassroots groups, organized labor, and the business community—to revitalize American education by setting a standard of excellence.

In 1983 we seek four major education goals: a quality education initiative to encourage a substantial upgrading of math and science instruction through block grants to the States; establishment of education savings accounts that will give middle- and lower-income families an incentive to save for their children's college education and, at the same time, encourage a real increase in savings for economic growth; passage of tuition tax credits for parents who want to send their children to private or religiously affiliated schools; a constitutional amendment to permit voluntary school prayer. God should never have been expelled from America's classrooms in the first place.

Our commitment to fairness means that we must assure legal and economic equity for women, and eliminate, once and for all, all traces of unjust discrimination against women from the United States Code. We will not tolerate wage discrimination based on sex, and we intend to strengthen enforcement of child support laws to ensure that single parents, most of whom are women, do not suffer unfair financial hardship. We will also take action to remedy inequities in pensions. These initiatives will be joined by others to continue our efforts to promote equity for women.

Also in the area of fairness and equity, we will ask for extension of the Civil Rights Commission, which is due to expire this year. The Commission is an important part of the ongoing struggle for justice in America, and we strongly support its reauthorization. Effective enforcement of our nation's fair housing laws is also essential to ensuring equal opportunity. In the year ahead, we'll work to strengthen enforcement of fair housing laws for all Americans.

The time has also come for major reform of our criminal justice statutes and acceleration of the drive against organized crime and drug trafficking. It's high time that we make our cities safe again. This administration hereby declares an all-out war on bigtime organized crime and the drug racketeers who are poisoning our young people. We will also implement recommendations of our Task Force on Victims of Crime, which will report to me this week.

American agriculture, the envy of the world, has become the victim of its own successes. With one farmer now producing enough food to feed himself and 77 other people, America is confronted with record surplus crops and commodity prices below the cost of production. We must strive, through innovations like the payment-in-kind crop swap approach and an aggressive export policy, to restore health and vitality to rural America. Meanwhile, I have instructed the Department of Agriculture to work individually with farmers with debt problems to help them through these tough times.

Over the past year, our Task Force on Private Sector Initiatives has successfully forged a working partnership involving leaders of business, labor, education, and government to address the training needs of American workers. Thanks to the Task Force, private sector initiatives are now underway in all 50 States of the Union, and thousands of working people have been helped in making the shift from dead-end jobs and low-demand skills to the growth areas of high technology and the service economy. Additionally, a major effort will be focused on encouraging the expansion of private community child care. The new advisory council on private sector initiatives will carry on and extend this vital work of encouraging private initiative in 1983.

In the coming year, we will also act to improve the quality of life for Americans by curbing the skyrocketing cost of health care that is becoming an unbearable financial burden for so many. And we will submit legislation to provide catastrophic illness insurance coverage for older Americans.

I will also shortly submit a comprehensive federalism proposal that will continue our efforts to restore to States and local governments their roles as dynamic laboratories of change in a creative society.

During the next several weeks, I will send to the Congress a series of detailed proposals on these and other topics and look forward to working with you on the development of these initiatives.

So far, now, I've concentrated mainly on the problems posed by the future. But in almost every home and workplace in American, we're already witnessing reason for great hope—the first flowering of the man-made miracles of high technology, a field pioneered and still led by our country.

To many of us now, computers, silicon chips, data processing, cybernetics, and all the other innovations of the dawning high technology age are as mystifying as the workings of the combustion engine must have been when that first Model T rattled down Main Street, U.S.A. But as surely as America's pioneer spirit made us the industrial giant of the 20th century, the same pioneer spirit today is opening up on another vast front of opportunity, the frontier of high technology.

In conquering the frontier we cannot write off our traditional industries, but we must develop the skills and industries that will make us a pioneer of tomorrow. This administration is committed to keeping America the technological leader of the world now and into the 21st century.

But let us turn briefly to the international arena. America's leadership in the world came to use because of our own strength and because of the values which guide us as a society: free elections, a free press, freedom of religious choice, free trade unions, and above all, freedom for the individual and rejection of the arbitrary power of the state. These values are the bedrock of our strength. They unite us in a stewardship of peace and freedom with our allies and friends in NATO, in Asia, in Latin America, and elsewhere. They are also the values which in the recent past some among us had begun to doubt and view with a cynical eye.

Fortunately, we and our allies have rediscovered the strength of our common democratic values, and we're applying them as a cornerstone of a comprehensive strategy for peace with freedom. In London last year, I announced the commitment of the United States to developing the intrastructure of democracy throughout the world. We intend to pursue this democratic initiative vigorously. The future belongs not to governments and ideologies which oppress their peoples, but to democratic systems of self-government which encourage individual initiative and guarantee personal freedom.

But our strategy for peace with freedom must also be based on strength—economic strength and military strength. A strong American economy is essential to the well-being and security of our friends and allies. The restoration of a strong, healthy American economy has been and remains one of the central pillars of our foreign policy. The progress I've been able to report to you tonight will, I know, be as warmly welcomed by the rest of the world as it is by the American people.

We must also recognize that our own economic well-being is inextricably linked to the world economy. We export over 20 percent of our industrial production, and 40 percent of our farmland produces for export. We will continue to work closely with the industrialized democracies of Europe and Japan and with the International Monetary Fund to ensure it has adequate resources to help bring the world economy back to strong, noninflationary growth.

As the leader of the West and as a country that has become great and rich because of economic freedom, America must be an unrelenting advocate of free trade. As some nations are tempted to turn to protectionism, our strategy cannot be to follow them, but to lead the way toward freer trade. To this end, in May of this year America will host an economic summit meeting in Williamsburg, Virginia.

As we begin our third year, we have put in place a defense program that redeems the neglect of the past decade. We have developed a realistic military strategy to deter threats to peace and to protect freedom if deterrence fails. Our Armed Forces are finally properly paid; after years of neglect are well trained and becoming better equipped and supplied. And the American uniform is once again worn with pride. Most of the major systems needed for modernizing our defenses are already underway, and we will be addressing one key system, the MX missile, in consultation with the Congress in a few months.

America's foreign policy is once again based on bipartisanship, on realism, strength, full partnership, in consultation with our allies, and constructive negotiation with potential adversaries. From the Middle East to southern Africa to Geneva, American diplomats are taking the initiative to make peace and lower arms levels. We should be proud of our role as peacemakers.

In the Middle East last year, the United States played the major role in ending the tragic fighting in Lebanon and negotiated the withdrawal of the PLO from Beirut.

Last September, I outlined principles to carry on the peace process begun so promisingly at Camp David. All the people of the Middle East should know that in the year ahead we will not flag in our efforts to build on that foundation to bring them the blessings of peace.

In Central America and the Caribbean Basin, we are likewise engaged in a partnership for peace, prosperity, and democracy. Final passage of the remaining portions of our Caribbean Basin Initiative, which passed the House last year, is one of this administration's top legislative priorities for 1983.

The security and economic assistance policies of this administration in Latin America and elsewhere are based on realism and represent a critical investment in the future of the human race. This undertaking is a joint responsibility of the executive and legislative branches, and I'm counting on the cooperation and statesmanship of the Congress to help us meet this essential foreign policy goal.

At the heart of our strategy for peace is our relationship with the Soviet Union. The past year saw a change in Soviet leadership. We're prepared for a positive change in Soviet-American relations. But the Soviet Union must show by deeds as well as words a sincere commitment to respect the rights and sovereignty of the family of nations. Responsible members of the world community do not threaten or invade their neighbors. And they restrain their allies from aggression.

For our part, we're vigorously pursuing arms reduction negotiations with the Soviet Union. Supported by our allies, we've put forward draft agreements proposing significant weapon reductions to equal and verifiable lower levels. We insist on an equal balance of forces. And given the overwhelming evidence of Soviet violations of international treaties concerning chemical and biological weapons, we also insist that any agreement we sign can and will be verifiable.

In the case of intermediate-range nuclear forces, we have proposed the complete elimination of the entire class of land-based missiles. We're also prepared to carefully explore serious Soviet proposals. At the same time, let me emphasize that allied steadfastness remains a key to achieving arms reductions.

With firmness and dedication, we'll continue to negotiate. Deep down, the Soviets must know it's in their best interest as well as ours to prevent wasteful arms race. And once they recognize our unshakable resolve to maintain adequate deterrence, they will have every reason to join us in the search for greater security and major arms reductions. When that moment comes—and I'm confident that it will—we will have taken an important step toward a more peaceful future for all the world's people.

A very wise man, Bernard Baruch, once said that America has never forgotten the nobler things that brought her into being and that light her path. Our country is a special place, because we Americans have always been sustained, through good times and bad, by a noble vision—a vision not only of what the world around us is today but what we as a free people can make it be tomorrow.

We're realists; we solve our problems instead of ignoring them, no matter how loud the chorus of despair around us. But we're also idealists, for it was an ideal that brought our ancestors to these shores from every corner of the world.

Right now we need both realism and idealism. Millions of our neighbors are without work. It is up to us to see they aren't without hope. This is a task for all of us. And may I say, Americans have rallied to this cause, proving once again that we are the most generous people on Earth.

We who are in government must take the lead in restoring the economy. *[Applause]* And here all that time, I thought you were reading the paper. *[Laughter]*

The single thing—the single thing that can start the wheels of industry turning again is further reduction of interest rates. Just another 1 or 2 points can mean tens of thousands of jobs.

Right now, with inflation as low as it is, 3.9 percent, there is room for interest rates to come down. Only fear prevents their reduction. A lender, as we know, must charge an interest rate that recovers the depreciated value of the dollars loaned. And that depreciation is, of course, the amount of inflation. Today, interest rates are based on fear—fear that government will resort to measures, as it has in the past, that will send inflation zooming again.

We who serve here in this Capital must erase that fear by making it absolutely clear that we will not stop fighting inflation; that, together, we will do only those things that will lead to lasting economic growth.

Yes, the problems confronting us are large and forbidding. And, certainly, no one can or should minimize the plight of millions of our friends and neighbors who are living in the bleak emptiness of unemployment. But we must and can give them good reason to be hopeful.

Back over the years, citizens like ourselves have gathered within these walls when our nation was threatened; sometimes when its very existence was at stake. Always with courage and common sense, they met the crises of their time and lived to see a stronger, better, and more prosperous country. The present situation is no worse and, in fact, is not as bad as some of those they faced. Time and again, they proved that there is nothing we Americans cannot achieve as free men and women.

Yes, we still have problems—plenty of them. But it's just plain wrong—unjust to our country and unjust to our people—to let those problems stand in the way of the most important truth of all: America is on the mend.

We owe it to the unfortunate to be aware of their plight and to help them in every way we can. No one can quarrel with that. We must and do have compassion for all the victims of this economic crisis. But the big story about America today is the way that millions of confident, caring people—those extraordinary "ordinary" Americans who never make the headlines and will never be interviewed—are laying the foundation, not just for recovery from our present problems but for a better tomorrow for all our people.

From coast to coast, on the job and in classrooms and laboratories, at new construction sites and in churches and community groups, neighbors are helping neighbors. And they've already begun the building, the research, the work, and the giving that will make our country great again.

I believe this, because I believe in them—in the strength of their hearts and minds, in the commitment that each one of them brings to their daily lives, be they high or humble. The challenge for us in government is to be worthy of them—to make government a help, not a hindrance to our people in the challenging but promising days ahead.

If we do that, if we care what our children and our children's children will say of us, if we want them one day to be thankful for what we did here in these temples of freedom, we will work together to make America better for our having been here—not just in this year or this decade but in the next century and beyond.

"Star Wars"
Washington, D.C.
March 23, 1983

Soon after the mid-term elections, President Reagan radically changed the direction of his rhetoric from domestic issues to national security. On November 22, 1982 he presented a major television address seeking to gain support for the MX missile. Subsequent speeches continued to stress either defense spending or foreign affairs. However, these speeches were not as successful with the public or Congress as his speeches on the economy had been during the first two years of his administration. By March, his newly proposed budget was under attack by Democrats and Republicans, and his priorities in federal spending and international relations were being seriously questioned.

In this speech the President sought to recapture the initiative in the debate over spending priorities by stressing the threat the Soviets posed to the United States and by justifying his proposed defense budget as only adequate to meet this threat. However, what caught the public's attention was the President's call for scientific development of defensive weapons in outer space to intercept Soviet missiles were they to attack the United States. Immediately, journalists dubbed the speech Reagan's "Star Wars" proposal.

My fellow Americans, thank you for sharing your time with me tonight.

The subject I want to discuss with you, peace and national security, is both timely and important. Timely, because I've reached a decision which offers a new hope for our children in the 21st century, a decision I'll tell you about in a few minutes. And important because there's a very big decision that you must make for yourselves. This subject involves the most basic duty that any President and any people share, the duty to protect and strengthen the peace.

At the beginning of this year, I submitted to the Congress a defense budget which reflects my best judgment of the best understanding of the experts and specialists who advise me about what we and our allies must do to protect our people in the years ahead. That budget is much more than a long list of numbers, for behind all the numbers lies America's ability to prevent the greatest of human tragedies and preserve our free way of life in a sometimes dangerous world. It is part of a careful, long-term plan to make America strong again after too many years of neglect and mistakes.

Our efforts to rebuild America's defenses and strengthen the peace began 2 years ago when we requested a major increase in the defense program. Since then, the amount of those increases we first proposed has been reduced by half, through improvements in management and procurement and other savings.

The budget request that is now before the Congress has been trimmed to the limits of safety. Further deep cuts cannot be made without seriously endangering the security of the Nation. The choice is up to the men and women you've elected to the Congress, and that means the choice is up to you.

Tonight, I want to explain to you what this defense debate is all about and why I'm convinced that the budget now before the Congress is necessary, responsible, and deserving of your support. And I want to offer hope for the future.

But first, let me say what the defense debate is not about. It is not about spending arithmetic. I know that in the last few weeks you've been bombarded with numbers and percentages. Some say we need only a 5-percent increase in defense spending. The so-called alternate budget backed by liberals in the House of Representatives would lower the figure to 2 to 3 percent, cutting our defense spending by $163 billion over the next 5 years. The trouble with all these numbers is that they tell us little about the kind of defense program America needs or the benefits and security and freedom that our defense effort buys for us.

What seems to have been lost in all this debate is the simple truth of how a defense budget is arrived at. It isn't done by deciding to spend a certain number of dollars. Those loud voices that are occasionally heard charging that the Government is trying to solve a security problem by throwing money at it are nothing more than noise based on ignorance. We start by considering what must be done to maintain peace and review all the possible threats against our security. Then a strategy for strengthening peace and defending against those threats must be agreed upon. And, finally, our defense establishment must be evaluated to see what is necessary to protect against any or all of the potential threats. The cost of achieving these ends is totaled up, and the result is the budget for the national defense.

There is no logical way that you can say, let's spend x billion dollars less. You can only say, which part of our defense measures do we believe we can do without and still have security against all contingencies? Anyone in the Congress who advocates a percentage or a specific dollar cut in defense spending should be made to say what part of our defenses he would eliminate, and he should be candid enough to acknowledge that his cuts mean cutting our commitments to allies or inviting greater risk or both.

The defense policy of the United States is based on a simple premise: The United States does not start fights. We will never be an aggressor. We maintain our strength in order to deter and defend against aggression—to preserve freedom and peace.

Since the dawn of the atomic age, we've sought to reduce the risk of war by maintaining a strong deterrent and by seeking genuine arms control. "Deterrence" means simply this: making sure any adversary who thinks about attacking the United States, or our allies, or our vital interests, concludes that the risks to him outweigh any potential gains. Once he understands that, he won't attack. We maintain the peace through our strength; weakness only invites aggression.

This strategy of deterrence has not changed. It still works. But what it takes to maintain deterrence has changed. It took one kind of military force to deter an attack when we had far more nuclear weapons than any other power; it takes another kind now that the Soviets, for example, have enough accurate and powerful nuclear weapons to destroy virtually all of our missiles on the ground. Now, this is not to say that the Soviet Union is planning to make war on us. Nor do I believe a war is inevitable—quite the contrary. But what must be recognized is that our security is based on being prepared to meet all threats.

There was a time when we depended on coastal forts and artillery batteries, because, with the weaponry of that day, any attack would have had to come by sea. Well, this is a different world, and our defenses must be based on recognition and awareness of the weaponry possessed by other nations in the nuclear age.

We can't afford to believe that we will never be threatened. There have been two world wars in my lifetime. We didn't start them and, indeed, did everything we could to avoid being drawn into them. But we were ill-prepared for both. Had we been better prepared, peace might have been preserved.

For 20 years the Soviet Union has been accumulating enormous military might. They didn't stop when their forces exceeded all requirements of a legitimate defensive capability. And they haven't stopped now. During the past decade and a half, the Soviets have built up a massive arsenal of new strategic nuclear weapons—weapons that can strike directly at the United States.

As an example, the United States introduced its last new intercontinental ballistic missile, the Minute Man III, in 1969, and we're now dismantling our even older Titan missiles. But what has the Soviet Union done in these intervening years? Well, since 1969 the Soviet Union has built five new classes of ICBM's, and upgraded these eight times. As a result, their missiles are much more powerful and accurate than they were several years ago, and they continue to develop more, while ours are increasingly obsolete.

The same thing has happened in other areas. Over the same period, the Soviet Union built 4 new classes of submarine-launched ballistic missiles and over 60 new missile submarines. We built 2 new types of submarine missiles and actually withdrew 10 submarines from strategic missions. The Soviet Union built over 200 new Backfire bombers, and their brand new Blackjack bomber is now under development. We haven't built a new long-range bomber since our B-52's were deployed about a quarter of a century ago, and we've already retired several hundred of those because of old age. Indeed, despite what many people think, our strategic forces only cost about 15 percent of the defense budget.

Another example of what's happened: In 1978 the Soviets had 600 intermediate range nuclear missiles based on land and were beginning to add the SS 20—a new, highly accurate, mobile missile with 3 warheads. We had none. Since then the Soviets have strengthened their lead. By the end of 1979, when Soviet leader Brezhnev declared "a balance now exists," the Soviets had over 800 warheads. We still had none. A year ago this month, Mr. Brezhnev pledged a moratorium, or freeze, on SS-20 deployment. But by last August, their 800 warheads had become more than 1,200. We still had none. Some freeze. At this time Soviet Defense Minister Ustinov announced "approximate parity of forces continues to exist." But the Soviets are still adding an average of 3 new warheads a week, and now have 1,300. These warheads can reach their targets in a matter of a few minutes. We still have none. So far, it seems that the Soviet definition of parity is a box score of 1,300 to nothing, in their favor.

So, together with our NATO allies, we decided in 1979 to deploy new weapons, beginning this year, as a deterrent to their SS–20's and as an incentive to the Soviet Union to meet us in serious arms control negotiations. We will begin that deployment later this year. At the same time, however, we're willing to cancel our program if the Soviets will dismantle theirs. This is what we've called a zero-zero plan. The Soviets are now at the negotiating table—and I think it's fair to say that without our planned deployments, they wouldn't be there.

Now, let's consider conventional forces. Since 1974 the United States has produced 3,050 tactical combat aircraft. By contrast, the Soviet Union has produced twice as many. When we look at attack submarines, the United States has produced 27 while the Soviet Union has produced 61. For armored vehicles, including tanks, we have produced 11,200. The Soviet Union has produced 54,000—nearly 5 to 1 in their favor. Finally, with artillery, we've produced 950 artillery and rocket launchers while the Soviets have produced more than 13,000—a staggering 14–to–1 ratio.

There was a time when we were able to offset superior Soviet numbers with higher quality, but today they are building weapons as sophisticated and modern as our own.

As the Soviets have increased their military power, they've been emboldened to extend that power. They're spreading their military influence in ways that can directly challenge our vital interests and those of our allies.

The following aerial photographs, most of them secret until now, illustrate this point in a crucial area very close to home: Central America and the Caribbean Basin. They're not dramatic photographs. But I think they help give you a better understanding of what I'm talking about.

This Soviet intelligence collection facility, less than a hundred miles from our coast, is the largest of its kind in the world. The acres and acres of antennae fields and intelligence monitors are targeted on key U.S. military installations and sensitive activities. The installation in Lourdes, Cuba, is manned by 1,500 Soviet technicians. And the satellite ground station allows instant communications with Moscow. This 28 square-mile facility has grown by more than 60 percent in size and capability during the past decade.

In western Cuba, we see this military airfield and its complement of modern, Soviet-built MIG-23 aircraft. The Soviet Union uses this Cuban airfield for its own long-range reconnaissance missions. And earlier this month, two modern Soviet antisubmarine warfare aircraft began operating from it. During the past 2 years, the level of Soviet arms exports to Cuba can only be compared to the levels reached during the Cuban missile crisis 20 years ago.

This third photo, which is the only one in this series that has been previously made public, shows Soviet military hardware that has made its way to Central America. This airfield with its MI-8 helicopters, anti-aircraft guns, and protected fighter sites is one of a number of military facilities in Nicaragua which has received Soviet equipment funneled through Cuba, and reflects the massive military buildup going on in that country.

On the small island of Grenada, at the southern end of the Caribbean chain, the Cubans, with Soviet financing and backing, are in the process of building an airfield with a 10,000-foot runway. Grenada doesn't even have an air force. Who is it intended for? The Caribbean is a very important passageway for our international commerce and military lines of communication. More than half of all American oil imports now pass through the Caribbean. The rapid buildup of Grenada's military potential is unrelated to any conceivable threat to this island country of under 110,000 people and totally at odds with the pattern of other eastern Caribbean States, most of which are unarmed.

The Soviet-Cuban militarization of Grenada, in short, can only be seen as power projection into the region. And it is in this important economic and strategic area that we're trying to help the Governments of El Salvador, Costa Rica, Honduras, and others in their struggles for democracy against guerrillas supported through Cuba and Nicaragua.

These pictures only tell a small part of the story. I wish I could show you more without compromising our most sensitive intelligence sources and methods. But the Soviet Union is also supporting Cuban military forces in Angola and Ethiopia. They have bases in Ethiopia and South Yemen, near the Persian Gulf of oil fields. They've taken over the port that we built at Cam Ranh Bay in Vietnam. And now for the first time in history, the Soviet Navy is a force to be reckoned with in the South Pacific.

Some people may still ask: Would the Soviets ever use their formidable military power? Well, again, can we afford to believe they won't? There is Afghanistan. And in Poland, the Soviets denied the will of the people and in so doing demonstrated to the world how their military power could also be used to intimidate.

The final fact is that the Soviet Union is acquiring what can only be considered an offensive military force. They have continued to build far more intercontinental ballistic missiles than they could possibly need simply to deter an attack. Their conventional forces are trained and equipped not so much to defend against an attack as they are to permit sudden, surprise offensives of their own.

Our NATO allies have assumed a great defense burden, including the military draft in most countries. We're working with them and our other friends around the world to do more. Our defensive strategy means we need military forces that can move very quickly, forces that are trained and ready to respond to any emergency.

Every item in our defense program—our ships, our tanks, our planes, our funds for training and spare parts—is intended for one all-important purpose: to keep the peace. Unfortunately, a decade of neglecting our military forces had called into question our ability to do that.

When I took office in January 1981, I was appalled by what I found: American planes that couldn't fly and American ships that couldn't sail for lack of spare parts and trained personnel and insufficient fuel and ammunition for essential training. The inevitable result of all this was poor morale in our Armed Forces, difficulty in recruiting the brightest young Americans to wear the uniform, and difficulty in convincing our most experienced military personnel to stay on.

There was a real question then about how well we could meet a crisis. And it was obvious that we had to begin a major modernization program to preserve the peace in the years ahead.

We had to move immediately to improve the basic readiness and staying power of our conventional forces, so they could meet—and therefore help deter—a crisis. We had to make up for lost years of investment by moving forward with a long-term plan to prepare our forces to counter the military capabilities our adversaries were developing for the future.

I know that all of you want peace, and so do I. I know too that many of you seriously believe that a nuclear freeze would further the cause of peace. But a freeze now would make us less, not more, secure and would raise, not reduce, the risks of war. It would be largely unverifiable and would seriously undercut our negotiations on arms reduction. It would reward the Soviets for their massive military buildup while preventing us from modernizing our aging and increasingly vulnerable forces. With their present margin of superiority, why should they agree to arms reductions knowing that we were prohibited from catching up?

Believe me, it wasn't pleasant for someone who had come to Washington determined to reduce government spending, but we had to move forward with the task of repairing our defenses or we would lose our ability to deter conflict now and in the future. We had to demonstrate to any adversary that aggression could not succeed, and that the only real solution was substantial, equitable, and effectively verifiable arms reduction—the kind we're working for right now in Geneva.

Thanks to your strong support, and bipartisan support from the Congress, we began to turn things around. Already, we're seeing some very encouraging results. Quality recruitment and retention are up dramatically—more high school graduates are choosing military careers, and more experienced career personnel are choosing to stay. Our men and women in uniform at last are getting the tools and training they need to do their jobs.

Ask around today, especially among our young people, and I think you will find a whole new attitude toward serving their country. This reflects more than just better pay, equipment, and leadership. You the American people have sent a signal to these young people that it is once again an honor to wear the uniform. That's not something you measure in a budget, but it's a very real part of our nation's strength.

It'll take us longer to build the kind of equipment we need to keep peace in the future, but we've made a good start.

We haven't built a new long-range bomber for 21 years. Now we're building the B-1. We hadn't launched one new strategic submarine for 17 years. Now we're building one Trident submarine a year. Our land-based missiles are increasingly threatened by the many huge, new Soviet ICBM's. We're determining how to solve that problem. At the same time, we're working in the START and INF negotiations with the goal of achieving deep reductions in the strategic and intermediate nuclear arsenals of both sides.

We have also begun the long-needed modernization of our conventional forces. The Army is getting its first new tank in 20 years. The Air Force is modernizing. We're rebuilding our Navy, which shrank from about a thousand ships in the late 1960's to 453 during the 1970's. Our nation needs a superior navy to support our military forces and vital interests overseas. We're now on the road to achieving a 600-ship navy and increasing the amphibious capabilities of our marines, who are now serving the cause of peace in Lebanon. And we're building a real capability to assist our friends in the vitally important Indian Ocean and Persian Gulf region.

This adds up to a major effort, and it isn't cheap. It comes at a time when there are many other pressures on our budget and when the American people have already had to make major sacrifices during the recession. But we must not be misled by those who would make defense once again the scapegoat of the Federal budget.

The fact is that in the past few decades we have seen a dramatic shift in how we spend the taxpayer's dollar. Back in 1955, payments to individuals took up only about 20 percent of the Federal budget. For nearly three decades, these payments steadily increased and, this year, will account for 49 percent of the budget. By contrast, in 1955 defense took up more than half of the Federal budget. By 1980 this spending had fallen to a low of 23 percent. Even with the increase that I am requesting this year, defense will still amount to only 28 percent of the budget.

The calls for cutting back the defense budget come in nice, simple arithmetic. They're the same kind of talk that led the democracies to neglect their defenses in the 1930's and invited the tragedy of World War II. We must not let that grim chapter of history repeat itself through apathy or neglect.

This is why I'm speaking to you tonight—to urge you to tell your Senators and Congressmen that you know we must continue to restore our military strength. If we stop in midstream, we will send a signal of decline, of lessened will, to friends and adversaries alike. Free people must voluntarily, through open debate and democratic means, meet the challenge that totalitarians pose by compulsion. It's up to us, in our time, to choose and choose wisely between the hard but necessary task of preserving peace and freedom and the temptation to ignore our duty and blindly hope for the best while the enemies of freedom grow stronger day by day.

The solution is well within our grasp. But to reach it, there is simply no alternative but to continue this year, in this budget, to provide the resources we need to preserve the peace and guarantee our freedom.

Now, thus far tonight I've shared with you my thoughts on the problems of national security we must face together. My predecessors in the Oval Office have appeared before you on other occasions to describe the threat posed by Soviet power and have proposed steps to address that threat. But since the advent of nuclear weapons, those steps have been increasingly directed toward deterrence of aggression through the promise of retaliation.

This approach to stability through offensive threat has worked. We and our allies have succeeded in preventing nuclear war for more than three decades. In recent months, however, my advisers, including in particular the Joint Chiefs of Staff, have underscored the necessity to break out of a future that relies solely on offensive retaliation for our security.

Over the course of these discussions, I've become more and more deeply convinced that the human spirit must be capable of rising above dealing with other nations and human beings by threatening their existence. Feeling this way, I believe we must thoroughly examine every opportunity for reducing tensions and for introducing greater stability into the strategic calculus on both sides.

One of the most important contributions we can make is, of course, to lower the level of all arms, and particularly nuclear arms. We're engaged right now in several negotiations with the Soviet Union to bring about a mutual reduction of weapons. I will report to you a week from tomorrow my thoughts on that score. But let me just say, I'm totally committed to this course.

If the Soviet Union will join with us in our effort to achieve major arms reduction, we will have succeeded in stabilizing the nuclear balance. Nevertheless, it will still be necessary to rely on the specter of retaliation, on mutual threat. And that's a sad commentary on the human condition. Wouldn't it be better to save lives than to avenge them? Are we not capable of demonstrating our peaceful intentions by applying all our abilities and our ingenuity to achieving a truly lasting stability? I think we are. Indeed, we must.

After careful consultation with my advisers, including the Joint Chiefs of Staff, I believe there is a way. Let me share with you a vision of the future which offers hope. It is that we embark on a program to counter the awesome Soviet missile threat with measures that are defensive. Let us turn to the very strengths in technology that spawned our great industrial base and that have given us the quality of life we enjoy today.

What if free people could live secure in the knowledge that their security did not rest upon the threat of instant U.S. retaliation to deter a Soviet attack, that we could intercept and destroy strategic ballistic missiles before they reached our own soil or that of our allies?

I know this is a formidable, technical task, one that may not be accomplished before the end of this century. Yet, current technology has attained a level of sophistication where it's reasonable for us to begin this effort. It will take years, probably decades of effort on many fronts. There will be failures and setbacks, just as there will be successes and breakthroughs. And as we proceed, we must remain constant in preserving the nuclear deterrent and maintaining a solid capability for flexible response. But isn't it worth every investment necessary to free the world from the threat of nuclear war? We know it is.

In the meantime, we will continue to pursue real reductions in nuclear arms, negotiating from a position of strength that can be ensured only by modernizing our strategic forces. At the same time, we must take steps to reduce the risk of a conventional military conflict escalating to nuclear war by improving our non-nuclear capabilities.

America does possess—now—the technologies to attain very significant improvements in the effectiveness of our conventional, non-nuclear forces. Proceeding boldly with these new technologies, we can significantly reduce any incentive that the Soviet Union may have to threaten attack against the United States or its allies.

As we pursue our goal of defensive technologies, we recognize that our allies rely upon our strategic offensive power to deter attacks against them. Their vital interests and ours are inextricably linked. Their safety and ours are one. And no change in technology can or will alter that reality. We must and shall continue to honor our commitments.

I clearly recognize that defensive systems have limitations and raise certain problems and ambiguities. If paired with offensive systems, they can be viewed as fostering an aggressive policy, and no one wants that. But with these considerations firmly in mind, I call upon the scientific community in our country, those who gave us nuclear weapons, to turn their great talents now to the cause of mankind and world peace, to give us the means of rendering these nuclear weapons impotent and obsolete.

Tonight, consistent with our obligations of the ABM treaty and recognizing the need for closer consultation with our allies, I'm taking an important first step. I am directing a comprehensive and intensive effort to define a long-term research and development program to begin to achieve our ultimate goal of eliminating the threat posed by strategic nuclear missiles. This could pave the way for arms control measures to eliminate the weapons themselves. We seek neither military superiority nor political advantage. Our only purpose—one that all people share—is to search for ways to reduce the danger of nuclear war.

My fellow Americans, tonight we're launching an effort which holds the promise of changing the course of human history. There will be risks, and results take time. But I believe we can do it. As we cross this threshold, I ask for your prayers and your support.

'Crisis' in Central America

Washington, D.C.
April 27, 1983

From the beginning of his administration, President Reagan had concentrated his major attention on what he believed to be communist infiltration and subversion in Central America. For the most part, he was able to avoid making a major "crisis" speech on the issue during his first two years in office. However, by early 1983, President Reagan found himself on the defensive in foreign affairs, especially his insistence on supporting the government of El Salvador in its civil war with rebel guerrillas. Therefore, the President called a special joint session of Congress—only nine times before in the twentieth-century had such sessions been called for a Presidential speech—to attempt to persuade Congress and the American people to support his policies in Central America. The President revived the harsh anti-communist rhetoric of the nineteen-forties, but the speech was notably unsuccessful. Congress did not vote to provide the economic and military aid the President requested nor did it approve his uses of covert operations.

A number of times in past years, Members of Congress and a President have come together in meetings like this to resolve a crisis. I have asked for this meeting in the hope that we can prevent one.

It would be hard to find many Americans who aren't aware of our stake in the Middle East, the Persian Gulf, or the NATO line dividing the free world from the Communist bloc. And the same could be said for Asia.

But in spite of, or maybe because of, a flurry of stories about places like Nicaragua and El Salvador and, yes, some concerted propaganda, many of us find it hard to believe we have a stake in problems involving those countries. Too many have thought of Central America as just that place way down below Mexico that can't possibly constitute a threat to our well-being. And that's why I've asked for this session. Central America's problems do directly affect the security and the well-being of our own people. And Central America is much closer to the United States than many of the world trouble spots that concern us. So, we work to restore our own economy; we cannot afford to lose sight of our neighbors to the south.

El Salvador is nearer to Texas than Texas is to Massachusetts. Nicaragua is just as close to Miami, San Antonio, San Diego, and Tucson as those cities are to Washington, where we're gathered tonight.

But nearness on the map doesn't even begin to tell the strategic importance of Central America, bordering as it does on the Caribbean—our lifeline to the outside world. Two-thirds of all our foreign trade and petroleum pass through the Panama Canal and the Caribbean. In a European crisis, at least half of our supplies for NATO would go through these areas by sea. It's well to remember that in early 1942, a handful of Hitler's submarines sank more tonnage there than in all of the Atlantic Ocean. And they did this without a single naval base anywhere in the area. And today, the situation is different. Cuba is host to a Soviet combat brigade, a submarine base capable of servicing Soviet submarines, and military air bases visited regularly by Soviet military aircraft.

Because of its importance, the Caribbean Basin is a magnet for adventurism. We're all aware of the Libyan cargo planes refueling in Brazil a few days ago on their way to deliver "medical supplies" to Nicaragua. Brazilian authorities discovered the so-called medical supplies were actually munitions and prevented their delivery.

You may remember that last month, speaking on national television, I showed an aerial photo of an airfield being built on the island of Grenada. Well, if that airfield had been completed, those planes could have refueled there and completed their journey.

If the Nazis during World War II and the Soviets today could recognize the Caribbean and Central America as vital to our interests, shouldn't we, also? For several years now, under two administrations, the United States has been increasing its defense of freedom in the Caribbean Basin. And I can tell you tonight, democracy is beginning to take root in El Salvador which, until a short time ago, knew only dictatorship.

The new Government is now delivering on its promises of democracy, reforms, and free elections. It wasn't easy, and there was resistance to many of the attempted reforms, with assassinations of some of the reformers. Guerrilla bands and urban terrorists were portrayed in a worldwide propaganda campaign as freedom fighters, representative of the people. Ten days before I came into office, the guerrillas launched what they called "a final offensive" to overthrow the government. And their radio boasted that our new administration would be too late to prevent their victory.

Well, they learned that democracy cannot be so easily defeated. President Carter did not hesitate. He authorized arms and munitions to El Salvador. The guerrilla offensive failed, but not America's will. Every President since this country assumed global responsibilities has known that those responsibilities could only be met if we pursued a bipartisan foreign policy.

As I said a moment ago, the Government of El Salvador has been keeping its promises, like the land reform program which is making thousands of farm tenants, farm owners. In a little over 3 years, 20 percent of the arable land in El Salvador has been redistributed to more than 450,000 people. That's one in ten Salvadorans who have benefited directly from this program.

El Salvador has continued to strive toward an orderly and democratic society. The government promised free elections. On March 28th, a little more than a year ago, after months of campaigning by a variety of candidates, the suffering people of El Salvador were offered a chance to vote, to choose the kind of government they wanted. And suddenly, the so-called freedom fighters in the hills were exposed for what they really are—a small minority who want power for themselves and their backers, not democracy for the people. The guerrillas threatened death to anyone who voted. They destroyed hundreds of buses and trucks to keep people from getting to the polling places. Their slogan was brutal: "Vote today, die tonight." But on election day, an unprecedented 80 percent of the electorate braved ambush and gunfire and trudged for miles, many of them, to vote for freedom. Now, that's truly fighting for freedom. We can never turn our backs on that.

Members of this Congress who went there as observers told me of a woman who was wounded by rifle fire on the way to the polls, who refused to leave the line to have her wound treated until after she had voted. Another woman had been told by the guerrillas that she would be killed when she returned from the polls, and she told the guerrillas, "You can kill me, you can kill my family, you can kill my neighbors. You can't kill us all." The real freedom fighters of El Salvador turned out to be the people of that country—the young, the old, the in-between—more than a million of them out of a population of less than 5 million. The world should respect this courage and not allow it to be belittled or forgotten. And again I say, in good conscience, we can never turn our backs on that.

The democratic political parties and factions in El Salvador are coming together around the common goal of seeking a political solution to their country's problems. New national elections will be held this year, and they will be open to all political parties. The government has invited the guerrillas to participate in the election and is preparing an amnesty law. The people of El Salvador are earning their freedom, and they deserve our moral and material support to protect it.

Yes, there are still major problems regarding human rights, the criminal justice system, and violence against non-combatants. And, like the rest of Central America, El Salvador also faces severe economic problems. But in addition to recession-depressed prices for major agricultural exports, El Salvador's economy is being deliberately sabotaged.

Tonight in El Salvador—because of ruthless guerrilla attacks—much of the fertile land cannot be cultivated; less than half the rolling stock of the railways remains operational; bridges, water facilities, telephone and electric systems have been destroyed and damaged. In one 22–month period, there were 5,000 interruptions of electrical power. One region was without electricity for a third of the year.

I think Secretary of State Shultz put it very well the other day: "Unable to win the free loyalty of El Salvador's people, the guerrillas," he said, "are deliberately and systematically depriving them of food, water, transportation, light, sanitation, and jobs. And these are the people who claim they want to help the common people." They don't want elections because they know they'd be defeated. But, as the previous election showed, the Salvadoran people's desire for democracy will not be defeated.

The guerrillas are not embattled peasants, armed with muskets. They're professionals, sometimes with better training and weaponry than the government's soldiers. The Salvadoran battalions that have received U.S. training have been conducting themselves well on the battlefield and with the civilian population. But so far, we've only provided enough money to train one Salvadoran soldier out of ten, fewer than the number of guerrillas that are trained by Nicaragua and Cuba.

And let me set the record straight on Nicaragua, a country next to El Salvador. In 1979 when the new government took over in Nicaragua, after a revolution which overthrew the authoritarian rule of Somoza, everyone hoped for the growth of democracy. We in the United States did, too. By January of 1981, our emergency relief and recovery aid to Nicaragua totalled $118 million— more than provided by any other developed country. In fact, in the first 2 years of Sandinista rule, the United States directly or indirectly sent five times more aid to Nicaragua than it had in the 2 years prior to the revolution. Can anyone doubt the generosity and the good faith of the American people?

These were hardly the actions of a nation implacably hostile to Nicaragua. Yet, the Government of Nicaragua has treated us as an enemy. It has rejected our repeated peace efforts. It has broken its promises to us, to the Organization of American States and, most important of all, to the people of Nicaragua.

No sooner was victory achieved than a small clique ousted others who had been part of the revolution from having any voice in the government. Humberto Ortega, the Minister of Defense, declared Marxism-Leninism would be their guide, and so it is.

The Government of Nicaragua has imposed a new dictatorship. It has refused to hold the elections it promised. It has seized control of most media and subjects all media to heavy prior censorship. It denied the bishops and priests of the Roman Catholic Church the right to say Mass on radio during Holy Week. It insulted and mocked the Pope. It has driven the Miskito Indians from their homelands, burning their villages, destroying their crops, and forcing them into involuntary internment camps far from home. It has moved against the private sector and free labor unions. It condoned mob action against Nicaragua's independent human rights commission and drove the director of that commission into exile.

In short, after all these acts of repression by the government, is it any wonder that opposition has formed? Contrary to propaganda, the opponents of the Sandinistas are not diehard supporters of the previous Somoza regime. In fact, many are anti-Somoza heroes and fought beside the Sandinistas to bring down the Somoza government. Now they've been denied any part in the new government because they truly wanted democracy for Nicaragua and they still do. Others are Miskito Indians fighting for their homes, their lands, and their lives.

The Sandinista revolution in Nicaragua turned out to be just an exchange of one set of autocratic rulers for another, and the people still have no freedom, no democratic rights, and more poverty. Even worse than its predecessor, it is helping Cuba and the Soviets to destabilize our hemisphere.

Meanwhile, the Government of El Salvador, making every effort to guarantee democracy, free labor unions, freedom of religion, and a free press, is under attack by guerrillas dedicated to the same philosophy that prevails in Nicaragua, Cuba, and, yes, the Soviet Union. Violence has been Nicaragua's most important export to the world. It is the ultimate in hypocrisy for the unelected Nicaraguan Government to charge that we seek their overthrow, when they're doing everything they can to bring down the elected Government of El Salvador. *[Applause]* Thank You. The guerrilla attacks are directed from a headquarters in Managua, the capital of Nicaragua.

But let us be clear as to the American attitude toward the Government of Nicaragua. We do not seek its overthrow. Our interest is to ensure that it does not infect its neighbors through the export of subversion and violence. Our purpose, in conformity with American and international law, is to prevent the flow of arms to El Salvador, Honduras, Guatemala, and Costa Rica. We have attempted to have a dialog with the Government of Nicaragua, but it persists in its efforts to spread violence.

We should not, and we will not, protect the Nicaraguan Government from the anger of its own people. But we should, through diplomacy, offer an alternative. And as Nicaragua ponders its options, we can and will—with all the resources of diplomacy—protect each country of Central America from the danger of war.

Even Costa Rica, Central America's oldest and strongest democracy—a government so peaceful it doesn't even have an army—is the object of bullying and threats from Nicaragua dictators.

Nicaragua's neighbors know that Sandinista promises of peace, nonalliance, and nonintervention have not been kept. Some 36 new military bases have been built. There were only 13 during the Somoza years. Nicaragua's new army numbers 25,000 men, supported by a militia of 50,000. It is the largest army in Central America, supplemented by 2,000 Cuban military and security advisers. It is equipped with the most modern weapons—dozens of Soviet-made tanks, 800 Soviet-bloc trucks, Soviet 152-millimeter howitzers, 100 anti-aircraft guns, plus planes and helicopters.

There are additional thousands of civilian advisers from Cuba, the Soviet Union, East Germany, Libya, and the PLO. And we're attacked because we have 55 military trainers in El Salvador.

The goal of the professional guerrilla movements in Central America is as simple as it is sinister: to destabilize the entire region from the Panama Canal to Mexico. And if you doubt beyond this point, just consider what Cayetano Càrpio, the now-deceased Salvadoran guerrilla leader, said earlier this month. Càrpio said that after El Salvador falls, El Salvador and Nicaragua would be "arm-in-arm and struggling for the total liberation of Central America."

Nicaragua's dictatorial junta, who themselves made war and won power operating from bases in Honduras and Costa Rica, like to pretend that they are today being attacked by forces based in Honduras. The fact is, it is Nicaragua's government that threatens Honduras, not the reverse. It is Nicaragua who has moved heavy tanks close to the border, and Nicaragua who speaks of war. It was Nicaraguan radio that announced on April 8th the creation of a new, unified, revolutionary coordinating board to push forward the Marxist struggle in Honduras.

Nicaragua, supported by weapons and military resources provided by the Communist bloc, represses its own people, refuses to make peace, and sponsors a guerrilla war against El Salvador.

President Truman's words are as apt today as they were in 1947 when he, too, spoke before a joint session of the Congress:

"At the present moment in world history, nearly every nation must choose between alternate ways of life. The choice is not too often a free one. One way of life is based upon the will of the majority and is distinguished by free institutions, representative government, free elections, guarantees of individual liberty, freedom of speech and religion, and freedom from political oppression. The second way of life is based upon the will of a minority forcibly imposed upon the majority. It relies upon terror and oppression, a controlled press and radio, fixed elections, and the suppressions of personal freedoms.

"I believe that it must be the policy of the United States to support free peoples who are resisting attempted subjugation by armed minorities or by outside pressures. I believe that we must assist free peoples to work out their own destinies in their own way. I believe that our help should be primarily through economic and financial aid which is essential to economic stability and orderly political processes.

"Collapse of free institutions and loss of independence would be disastrous not only for them but for the world. Discouragement and possibly failure would quickly be the lot of neighboring peoples striving to maintain their freedom and independence."

The countries of Central America are smaller than the nations that prompted President Truman's message. But the political and strategic stakes are the same. Will our response—economic, social, military—be as appropriate and successful as Mr. Truman's bold solutions to the problems of postwar Europe?

Some people have forgotten the successes of those years and the decades of peace, prosperity, and freedom they secured. Some people talk as though the United States were incapable of acting effectively in international affairs without risking war or damaging those we seek to help.

Are democracies required to remain passive while threats to their security and prosperity accumulate? Must we just accept the destabilization of an entire region from the Panama Canal to Mexico on our southern border? Must we sit by while independent nations of this hemisphere are integrated into the most aggressive empire the modern world has seen? Must we wait while Central Americans are driven from their homes like the more than a million who've sought refuge out of Afghanistan, or the 1½ million who have fled Indochina, or the more than a million Cubans who have fled Castro's Caribbean utopia? Must we, by default, leave the people of El Salvador no choice but to flee their homes, creating another tragic human exodus?

I don't believe there's a majority in the Congress or the country that counsels passivity, resignation, defeatism, in the face of this challenge to freedom and security in our own hemisphere. *[Applause]* Thank you. Thank you.

I do not believe that a majority of the Congress or the country is prepared to stand by passively while the people of Central America are delivered to totalitarianism and we ourselves are left vulnerable to new dangers.

Only last week, an official of the Soviet Union reiterated Brezhnev's threat to station nuclear missiles in this hemisphere, 5 minutes from the United States. Like an echo, Nicaragua's Commandante Daniel Ortega confirmed that, if asked, his country world consider accepting those missiles. I understand that today they may be having second thoughts.

Now, before I go any further, let me say to those who invoke the memory of Vietnam, there is no thought of sending American combat troops to Central America. They are not needed—*[applause]*

Thank you. And, as I say, they are not needed and, indeed, they have not been requested there. All our neighbors ask of us is assistance in training and arms to protect themselves while they build a better, freer life.

We must continue to encourage peace among the nations of Central America. We must support the regional efforts now underway to promote solutions to regional problems.

We cannot be certain that the Marxist-Leninist bands who believe war is an instrument of politics will be readily discouraged. It's crucial that we not become discouraged before they do. Otherwise, the region's freedom will be lost and our security damaged in ways that can hardly be calculated.

If Central America were to fall, what would the consequences be for our position in Asia, Europe, and for alliances such as NATO? If the United States cannot respond to a threat near our own borders, why should Europeans or Asians believe that we're seriously concerned about threats to them? If the Soviets can assume that nothing short of an actual attack on the United States will provoke an American response, which ally, which friend will trust us then?

The Congress shares both the power and the responsibility for our foreign policy. Tonight, I ask you, the Congress, to join me in a bold, generous approach to the problems of peace and poverty, democracy and dictatorship in the region. Join me in a program that prevents Communist victory in the short run, but goes beyond, to produce for the deprived people of the area the reality of present progress and the promise of more to come.

Let us lay the foundation for a bipartisan approach to sustain the independence and freedom of the countries of Central America. We in the administration reach out to you in this spirit.

We will pursue four basic goals in Central America:

First, in response to decades of inequity and indifference, we will support democracy, reform, and human freedom. This means using our assistance, our powers of persuasion, and our legitimate leverage to bolster humane democratic systems where they already exist and to help countries on their way to that goal complete the process as quickly as human institutions can be changed. Elections in El Salvador and also in Nicaragua must be open to all, fair and safe. The international community must help. We will work at human rights problems, not walk away from them.

Second, in response to the challenge of world recession and, in the case of El Salvador, to the unrelenting campaign of economic sabotage by the guerrillas, we will support economic development. And by a margin of 2 to 1 our aid is economic now, not military. Seventy-seven cents out of every dollar we will spend in the area this year goes for food, fertilizers, and other essentials for economic growth and development. And our economic program goes beyond traditional aid. The Caribbean Initiative introduced in the House earlier today will provide powerful trade and investment incentives to help these countries achieve self-sustaining economic growth without exporting U.S. jobs. Our goal must be to focus our immense and growing technology to enhance health care, agriculture, industry, and to ensure that we who inhabit this interdependent region come to know and understand each other better, retaining our diverse identities, respecting our diverse traditions and institutions.

And, *third,* in response to the military challenge from Cuba and Nicaragua—to their deliberate use of force to spread tyranny—we will support the security of the region's threatened nations. We do not view security assistance as an end in itself, but as a shield for democratization, economic development, and diplomacy. No amount of reform will bring peace so long as guerrillas believe they will win by force. No amount of economic help will suffice if guerrilla units can destroy roads and bridges and power stations and crops, again and again, with impunity. But with better training and material help, our neighbors can hold off the guerrillas and give democratic reform time to take root.

And, *fourth,* we will support dialog and negotiations both among the countries of the region and within each country. The terms and conditions of participation in elections are negotiable. Costa Rica is a shining example of democracy. Honduras has made the move from military rule to democratic government. Guatemala is pledged to the same course. The United States will work toward a political solution in Central America which will serve the interests of the democratic process.

To support these diplomatic goals, I offer these assurances: The United States will support any agreement among Central American countries for the withdrawal, under fully verifiable and reciprocal conditions, of all foreign military and security advisers and troops. We want to help opposition groups join the political process in all countries and compete by ballots instead of bullets. We will support any verifiable, reciprocal agreement among Central American countries on the renunciation of support for insurgencies on neighbors' territory. And, finally, we desire to help Central America end its costly arms race and will support any verifiable, reciprocal agreements on the nonimportation of offensive weapons.

To move us toward these goals more rapidly, I am tonight announcing my intention to name an Ambassador at Large as my special envoy to Central America. He or she will report to me through the Secretary of State. The Ambassador's responsibilities will be to lend U.S. support to the efforts of regional governments to bring peace to this troubled area and to work closely with the Congress to assure the fullest possible, bipartisan coordination of our policies toward the region.

What I'm asking for is prompt congressional approval for the full reprogramming of funds for key current economic and security programs so that the people of Central America can hold the line against externally supported aggression. In addition, I am asking for prompt action on the supplemental request in these same areas to carry us through the current fiscal year and for early and favorable congressional action on my requests for fiscal year 1984.

And finally, I am asking that the bipartisan consensus, which last year acted on the trade and tax provisions of the Caribbean Basin Initiative in the House, again take the lead to move this vital proposal to the floor of both Chambers. And, as I said before, the greatest share of these requests is targeted toward economic and humanitarian aid, not military.

What the administration is asking for on behalf of freedom in Central America is so small, so minimal, considering what is at stake. The total amount requested for aid to all of Central America in 1984 is about $600 million. That's less than one-tenth of what Americans will spend this year on coin-operated video games.

In summation, I say to you that tonight there can be no question: The national security of all the Americas is at stake in Central America. If we cannot defend ourselves there, we cannot expect to prevail elsewhere. Our credibility would collapse, our alliances would crumble, and the safety of our homeland would be put in jeopardy.

We have a vital interest, a moral duty, and a solemn responsibility. This is not a partisan issue. It is a question of our meeting our moral responsibility to ourselves, our friends, and our posterity. It is a duty that falls on all of us—the President, the Congress, and the people. We must perform it together. Who among us would wish to bear responsibility for failing to meet our shared obligation?

Selected Bibliography

Writings on the modern Presidency and the six Presidents considered here are so extensive that a selective bibliography becomes a necessity rather than a luxury. For works on the Presidency I have chosen books that chronicle, analyze or influence the recent conception of that office. For each of the Presidents I have chosen biographies that give us some sense of the man, books on each's administration as well as studies that deal specifically with major crisis during these years. Those interested in a more extensive, annotated bibliography should consult a recent publication by Fred I. Greenstein, Larry Berman, Alvin S. Felzenberg with Doris Lidtke, *Evolution of the Modern Presidency. A Bibliographical Survey* (Washington, D.C.: American Enterprise Institute for Public Policy Research, 1977). Those interested in the complete speeches of one of these six Presidents should consult the appropriate volumes of *The Public Papers of the Presidents*.

The Presidency

Bailey, T. A., *Presidential Greatness: The Image and the Man from George Washington to the Present* (New York: Appleton-Century, 1966).

Barber, J. D., *The Presidential Character: Predicting Performance in the White House* (Englewood Cliffs, N.J.: Prentice-Hall, 1972).

Burns, J. M., *Presidential Government: The Crucible of Leadership* (Boston: Houghton Mifflin, 1966).

———, *The Deadlock of Democracy: Four-party Politics in America* (Englewood Cliffs N.J.: Prentice-Hall, 1963; rev. 1965).

Chester, E. W., *Radio, Television and American Politics* (New York: Sheed and Ward, 1969).

Commanger, H. S., *The Defeat of America: Presidential Power and the National Character* (New York: Simon and Schuster, 1975).

Cornwell, E. E., *Presidential Leadership of Public Opinion* (Bloomington: Indiana University Press, 1965).

Corwin, E. S., *Presidential Power and the Constitution* (Ithaca: Cornell University Press, 1976).

———, *The President, Office and Powers, 1787–1957* (New York: New York University Press, 1957).

Cronin, T. E., *The State of the Presidency* (Boston: Little, Brown, 1975).

Edwards III, G. C., *The Public Presidency. The Pursuit of Popular Support* (New York: St. Martin's Press, 1983).

Filler, L., *The President Speaks: From McKinley to Lyndon Johnson* (New York: Capricorn Books, 1965).

Grossman, M. B. and Kumar, M. J., *Portraying the President: The White House and the Media* (Baltimore: Johns Hopkins University Press, 1981).

Hargrove, E. C., *The Power of the Modern Presidency* (Philadelphia: Temple University Press, 1974).

Hodgson, G., *All Things to All Men: The False Promise of the Presidency* (New York: Simon and Schuster, 1980).

Hughes, E. J., *The Living Presidency* (New York: Coward, McCann, and Geoghegan, 1973).

Minow, N. N., Martin, J. B., and Mitchell, L. M., *Presidential Television* (New York: Basic Books, 1973).

Neustadt, R. E., *Presidential Power: The Politics of Leadership with Reflections on Johnson and Nixon* (New York: Wiley, 1976).

Pollard, J. E., *The Presidents and the Press: Truman to Johnson* (Washington, D.C.: Public Affairs Press, 1964).

Reedy, G., *The Twilight of the Presidency* (New York: World, 1970).

Rossiter, C. L., *The American Presidency* (New York: Harcourt, Brace, 1960).

Rubin, B., *Political Television* (Belmont, Cal.: Wadsworth, 1967).

Schlesinger, A. M., Jr., *The Imperial Presidency* (Boston: Houghton, Mifflin, 1973).

Strum, P., *Presidential Power and American Democracy* (Pacific Palisades: Goodyear, 1972).

Tugwell, R. G. and Cronin, T. E. (eds.), *The Presidency Reappraised* (New York: Praeger, 1974).

Watson, R. A. and Thomas, N. C., *The Politics of the Presidency* (New York: John Wiley & Sons, 1983).

Wildavsky, A., (ed.), *Perspectives on the Presidency* (Boston: Little, Brown, 1975).

——— (ed.), *The Presidency* (Boston: Little, Brown, 1969).

Windt, T. with Ingold, B. (eds.), *Essays in Presidential Rhetoric* (Dubuque, Iowa: Kendall/Hunt, 1983).

John F. Kennedy

Abel, E., *The Missile Crisis* (Philadelphia: Lippincott, 1966).

Allison, G. T., *Essence of Decision: Explaining the Cuban Missile Crisis* (Boston: Little, Brown, 1971).

Blair, J. and Blair, C., Jr., *The Search for J. F. K.* (New York: Berkley, 1976).

Burns, J. M., *John Kennedy: A Political Profile* (New York: Harcourt, Brace and World, 1961).

Dinerstein, H. S., *The Making of a Missile Crisis: October 1962* (New York: Quadrangle, 1971).

Fairlie, H., *The Kennedy Promise: The Politics of Expectation* (Garden City: Doubleday, 1973).

Halberstam, D., *The Best and the Brightest* (New York: Random House, 1972).

Heath, J. F., *John F. Kennedy and the Business Community* (Chicago: University of Chicago Press, 1969).

Hilsman, R., *To Move a Nation: The Politics of Foreign Policy in the Kennedy Administration* (Garden City: Doubleday, 1967).

Kennedy, R. F., *Thirteen Days: A Memoir of the Cuban Missile Crisis* (New York: W.W. Norton, 1969).

Lasky, V., *J.F.K.: The Man and the Myth* (New York: Macmillian, 1963).

Latham, E. (ed.), *J.F. Kennedy and Presidential Power* (Lexington, Mass.: Heath, 1972).

Lepper, M. M., *Foreign Policy Formulation: A Case Study of the Nuclear Test Ban Treaty of 1963* (Columbus, Ohio: Charles E. Merrill, 1971).

McConnell, G., *Steel and the Presidency, 1962* (New York: W.W. Norton, 1963).

Meyer, K. D. and Szulc, T. (eds.), *The Cuban Invasion: The Chronicle of a Disaster* (New York: Praeger, 1962).

Navasky, V. S., *Kennedy Justice* (New York: Atheneum, 1971).

O'Brien, L., *No Final Victories: A Life in Politics from John F. Kennedy to Watergate* (New York: Doubleday, 1974).

O'Donnell, K. and Powers, D., *Johnny, We Hardly Knew Ye* (Boston: Little, Brown, 1972).

Paper, L. J., *The Promise and the Performance: The Leadership of John F. Kennedy* (New York: Crown, 1975).

Salinger, P., *With Kennedy* (Garden City: Doubleday, 1966).

Schlesinger, A. M., Jr., *A Thousand Days: John F. Kennedy in the White House* (Boston: Houghton Mifflin, 1965).

———, *Kennedy or Nixon: Does It Make Any Difference?* (New York: Macmillan, 1960).

Sidey, H., *John F. Kennedy, President* (New York: Atheneum, 1964).

Slusser, R. M., *The Berlin Crisis of 1961: Soviet-American Relations and the Struggle for Power in the Kremlin, June–November, 1961* (Baltimore: Johns Hopkins University Press, 1973).

Sorensen, T. C., *Decision-making in the White House. The Olive Branch or the Arrows* (New York: Columbia University Press, 1963).
————, *Kennedy* (New York: Harper and Row, 1965).
————, *The Kennedy Legacy* (New York: Macmillan, 1969).
Thompson, R. E. and Myers, H., *Robert F. Kennedy: The Brother Within* (New York: Macmillan, 1962).
Trewhitt, H. L., *McNamara: His Ordeal in the Pentagon* (New York: Harper Row, 1971).
Walton, R., *Cold War and Counterrevolution: The Foreign Policy of John F. Kennedy* (Baltimore: Pelican, 1973).
White, T. H., *The Making of the President 1960* (New York: Atheneum, 1961).
Wicker, T., *Kennedy Without Tears* (New York: Morrow, 1964).
————, *JFK and LBJ: The Influence of Personality on Politics* (New York: Morrow, 1968).

Lyndon B. Johnson

Austin, A., *The President's War: The Story of the Tonkin Gulf Resolution and How the Nation Was Trapped in Vietnam* (New York: Lippincott, 1971).
Baker, L., *The Johnson Eclipse: A President's Vice Presidency* (New York: Macmillan, 1966).
Bell, J., *The Johnson Treatment: How Lyndon B. Johnson Took Over the Presidency and Made It His Own* (New York: Harper and Row, 1965).
Burns, J. M. (ed.), *To Heal and to Build: The Programs of President Lyndon B. Johnson* (New York: McGraw-Hill, 1968).
Christian, G., *The President Steps Down: A Personal Memoir of the Transfer of Power* (New York: MacMillan, 1970).
Cooper, C., *The Lost Crusade: America in Vietnam* (New York: Dodd, Mead 1970).
Evans, R. and Novak, R., *Lyndon B. Johnson: The Exercise of Power* (New York: New American Library, 1966).
Galloway, J., *The Gulf of Tonkin Resolution* (Rutherford, N.J.: Fairleigh Dickinson University Press, 1970).
Gettleman, M. E. and Mermelstein, D. (eds.), *The Great Society Reader: The Failure of American Liberalism* (New York: Random House, 1967).
Geyelin, P. L., *Lyndon B. Johnson and the World* (New York: Praeger, 1966).
Goldman, E. F., *The Tragedy of Lyndon Johnson* (New York: Alfred A. Knopf, 1969).
Goulden, J., *Truth Is the First Casualty* (Chicago: Rand McNally, 1969).
Goulding, P. G., *Confirm or Deny: Informing the People on National Security* (New York: Harper and Row, 1970).
Graff, H. F., *The Tuesday Cabinet: Deliberation and Decision on Peace and War Under Lyndon B. Johnson* (Englewood Cliffs, N.J.: Prentice-Hall, 1970).
Haley, J. E., *A Texan Looks at Lyndon: A Study in Illegitimate Power* (Canyon, Texas: Palo Duro Press, 1964).
Harvey, J. C., *Black Civil Rights During the Johnson Administration* (Jackson, Miss.: University of Mississippi Press, 1973).
Hoopes, T., *The Limits of Intervention: An Inside Account of How the Johnson Policy of Intervention Was Reversed* (New York: David McKay, 1969).
Johnson, L. B., *The Vantage Point: Perspectives of the Presidency, 1963–1969* (New York: Holt, Rinehart and Winston, 1971).
Kearns, D., *Lyndon Johnson and the American Dream* (New York: Harper and Row, 1976).
Lowenthal, A. F., *The Dominican Intervention* (Cambridge, Mass.: Harvard University Press, 1972).
Roche, J. P., *Sentenced to Life* (New York: Macmillan, 1974).
Rostow, W. W., *The Diffusion of Power: An Essay in Recent History* (New York: Macmillan, 1972).
Sheehan, N. and et al., *The Pentagon Papers as Published by the New York Times* (New York: Quadrangle, 1971).
Sherrill, R., *The Accidental President* (New York: Grossman, 1967).
Sidey, H., *A Very Personal Presidency: Lyndon Johnson in the White House* (New York: Atheneum, 1968).

Steinberg, A., *Sam Johnson's Boy: A Close-up of the President from Texas* (New York: Macmillan, 1968).

The Pentagon Papers: The Defense Department History of United States Decision Making in Vietnam, The Senator Gravel Edition, 5 vols. (Boston: Beacon, 1971).

Valenti, J., *A Very Human President* (New York: W.W. Norton, 1975).

White, T. H., *The Making of the President 1964* (New York: Atheneum, 1965).

White, W. S., *The Professional: Lyndon B. Johnson* (Boston: Houghton Mifflin, 1964).

Richard M. Nixon

Costello, W., *The Facts about Nixon: The Unauthorized Biography of Richard M. Nixon, The Formative Years: 1913–1959* (New York: Viking, 1960).

Coyne, J. R., Jr., *The Impudent Snobs: Agnew vs. the Intellectual Establishment* (New Rochelle, N.Y.: Arlington, 1972).

Dean, J. W., III, *Blind Ambition: The White House Years* (New York: Simon and Schuster, 1976).

Evans, R. and Novak, R., *Nixon in the White House: The Frustration of Power* (New York: Random House, 1971).

Harris, R., *Decision* (New York: E.P. Dutton, 1971).

———, *Justice: The Crisis of Law, Order and Freedom in America* (New York: E.P. Dutton, 1970).

Jaworski, L., *The Right and the Power: The Prosecution of Watergate* (New York: Reader's Digest Press, 1976).

Keogh, J., *President Nixon and the Press* (New York: Funk and Wagnells, 1972).

Kissinger, H., *White House Years* (Boston: Little, Brown and Co., 1979).

———, *Years of Upheaval* (Boston: Little, Brown and Company, 1982).

Kurnitzer, B., *The Real Nixon: An Intimate Biography* (New York: Rand McNally, 1960).

Lasky, V., *It Didn't Start with Watergate* (New York: Dial, 1977).

Lukas, J. A., *Nightmare: The Underside of the Nixon Years* (New York: Viking, 1976).

Magruder, J. S., *An American Life: One Man's Road to Watergate* (New York: Atheneum, 1974).

Mankiewicz, F., *Perfectly Clear: Nixon from Whittier to Watergate* (New York: Quadrangle, 1973).

———, *U.S. v. Richard M. Nixon: The Final Crisis* (New York: Quadrangle, 1975).

Mazlish, B., *In Search of Nixon: A Psychohistorical Inquiry* (Scranton, Pa.: Basic Books, 1972).

Mazo, E. and Hess, S., *Nixon: A Political Portrait* (New York: Harper and Row, 1968).

McCord, J. W., Jr., *A Piece of Tape. The Watergate Story: Fact and Fiction* (Rockville, Maryland: Washington Media Services, 1974).

McGinniss, J., *The Selling of the President, 1968* (New York: Trident, 1969).

Mollenhoff, C. F., *Game Plan for Disaster. An Ombudsman's Report on the Nixon Years* (New York: W.W. Norton, 1976).

Nathan, R., *The Plot That Failed: Nixon and the Administrative Presidency* (New York: Wiley, 1975).

New York Times, The Staff of, *The End of a Presidency* (New York: Bantam, 1973).

———, *The Watergate Hearings* (New York: Bantam, 1973).

———, *The White House Transcripts* (New York: Bantam, 1974).

Nixon, R. M. *Six Crises* (New York: Pyramid, 1968).

———, *The Memoirs of Richard Nixon* (New York: Grosset and Dunlap, 1978).

Osborne, J., *The Nixon Watch* (New York: Liveright, 1970).

———, *The Second Year of the Nixon Watch* (New York: Liveright, 1971).

———, *The Third Year of the Nixon Watch* (New York: Liveright, 1972).

———, *The Fourth Year of the Nixon Watch* (New York: Liveright, 1973).

———, *The Last Nixon Watch* (Washington, D.C.: New Republic, 1975).

Panetta, L. E., *Bring Us Together: The Nixon Team and the Civil Rights Retreat* (Philadelphia: Lippincott, 1971).

Porter, W. E., *Assault on the Media: The Nixon Years* (Ann Arbor: University of Michigan Press, 1975).

Safire, W., *Before the Fall: An Inside View of the Pre-Watergate White House* (New York: Doubleday, 1975).

Schell, J., *Time of Illusion* (New York: Alfred A. Knopf, 1976).
Shawcross, W., *Sideshow: Nixon, Kissinger and the Destruction of Cambodia* (New York: Simon and Schuster, 1979).
Szulc, T., *The Illusion of Peace* (New York: Viking, 1978).
Whalen, R. J., *Catch the Falling Flag: A Republican's Challenge to His Party* (Boston: Houghton Mifflin, 1972).
White, T. H., *Breach of Faith: The Fall of Richard Nixon* (New York: Atheneum, 1975).
———, *The Making of the President 1968* (New York: Atheneum, 1969).
———, *The Making of the President 1972* (New York: Atheneum, 1973).
Wills, G., *Nixon Agonistes: The Crisis of Self-made Man* (Boston: Houghton Mifflin, 1970).
Witcover, J., *The Resurrection of Richard Nixon* (New York: G.P. Putnam's Sons, 1970).
Woodward, B. and Bernstein, C., *All the President's Men* (New York: Simon and Schuster, 1974).
———, *The Final Days* (New York: Simon and Schuster, 1976).

Gerald R. Ford

Casserly, J. J., *The Ford White House* (Boulder, Colo.: Colorado Associated University Press, 1977).
Ford, G.R., *A Time to Heal* (New York: Harper and Row, 1979).
Mollenhoff, C. R., *The Man Who Pardoned Nixon* (New York: St. Martin's, 1976).
Reeves, R., *A Ford, Not a Lincoln* (New York: Harcourt, Brace, Jovanovich, 1975).
Rowan, R., *The Four Days of Mayaguez* (New York: Norton, 1975).
Sidey, H., *Portrait of a President* (New York: Harper and Row, 1975).
Sobel, L. A. (ed.) *Presidential Succession: Ford, Rockefeller and the 25th Amendment* (New York: Facts on File, 1975).
Ter Horst, J., *Gerald Ford and the Future of the Presidency* (New York: Third Press, 1974).
Vestal, B., *Jerry Ford, Up Close* (New York: Coward, McCann and Geoghegan, 1974).
Witcover, J., *Marathon* (New York: Viking, 1977).

Jimmy Carter

Adams, B., *Promise and Performance: Carter Builds a New Administration* (Lexington, Mass.: Lexington Books, 1979).
Brown, H., *Thinking About National Security: Defense and Foreign Policy in a Dangerous World* (Westview: 1983).
Brzezinski, Z., *Power and Principle* (New York: Farrar, Straus, Giroux, 1983).
Califano, Jr., J., *Governing America* (New York: Simon and Schuster, 1981).
Carter, J., *A Government as Good as Its People* (New York: Simon and Schuster, 1977).
Carter, J., *Keeping Faith* (New York: Bantam, 1982).
Johnson, H., *In the Absence of Power* (New York: Viking, 1980).
Jordon, H., *Crisis* (New York: G.P. Putnam's Sons, 1982).
Kucharsky, D., *The Man From Plains* (New York: Harper and Row, 1976).
Lasky, V., *Jimmy Carter: The Man and the Myth* (New York: R. Marek, 1979).
Miller, W. L., *Yankee from Georgia: The Emergence of Jimmy Carter* (New York: Time Books, 1978).
Mollenhoff, C. R., *The President Who Failed* (New York: Macmillan, 1980).
The Presidential Campaign 1976, Volume One, Parts One and Two (Washington: Government Printing Office, 1979).
Schram, M., *Running for President 1976* (New York: Stein and Day, 1977).
Shogan, R., *Promises to Keep* (New York: Thomas Y. Crowell, 1977).
Shoup, L. H., *The Carter Presidency and Beyond* (Palo Alto, Calif.: Ramparts, 1980).
Stroud, K., *How Jimmy Won: The Victory Campaign from Plains to the White House* (New York: Morrow, 1977).

Ronald W. Reagan

Cannon, L., *Reagan* (New York: G.P. Putnam's Sons, 1982).

Evans, R. and Novak, R., *The Reagan Revolution* (New York: E. P. Dutton, 1982).

Germond, J. W. and Witcover, J., *Blue Smoke and Mirrors* (New York: Viking, 1981).

Greider, W., *The Education of David Stockman and Other Americans* (New York: E.P. Dutton, 1981).

Heritage Foundation, *A Mandate for Leadership Report: The First Year* ed. by R. N. Holwill (Washington, D.C.: 1982).

Palmer, J. L. and Sawhill, I. U., *The Reagan Experiment* (Washington, D.C.: Urban Institute, 1982).

Reagan, R., *Where's the Rest of Me?* (New York: Duell, Sloan, Pearce, 1965).

White House, Office of Public Affairs, *The Reagan Presidency: A Review of the First Year* (Washington, D.C., 1982).